MISSIONARY LINGUISTICS VI

STUDIES IN THE HISTORY OF THE LANGUAGE SCIENCES

AMSTERDAM STUDIES IN THE THEORY AND HISTORY
OF LINGUISTIC SCIENCE – Series III

ISSN 0304-0720

General Editor

E.F.K. KOERNER

Leibniz-Zentrum Allgemeine Sprachwissenschaft, Berlin
efk.koerner@rz.hu-berlin.de

As a companion to the journal *Historiographia Linguistica* "Studies in the History of the Language Sciences" (SiHoLS) is a series of book-length scholarly works in the history of linguistic thought. Although its emphasis is on the Western tradition from antiquity to the modern day, it also includes, and welcomes, studies devoted to non-Western traditions. It comprises monographs, selective, thematically unified volumes, and research bibliographies.

A complete list of titles in this series can be found on
benjamins.com/catalog/sihols

Volume 130

Otto Zwartjes and Paolo De Troia (eds.)

Missionary Linguistics VI. Missionary Linguistics in Asia. Selected papers from the Tenth International Conference on Missionary Linguistics, Rome, 21–24 March 2018

MISSIONARY LINGUISTICS VI

MISSIONARY LINGUISTICS IN ASIA

SELECTED PAPERS FROM
THE TENTH INTERNATIONAL CONFERENCE ON
MISSIONARY LINGUISTICS, ROME, 21–24 MARCH 2018

Edited by

OTTO ZWARTJES

Université de Paris, UMR 7597 HTL

PAOLO DE TROIA

Sapienza Università di Roma

JOHN BENJAMINS PUBLISHING COMPANY
AMSTERDAM/PHILADELPHIA

DOI 10.1075/sihols.130

Cataloging-in-Publication Data available from Library of Congress:
LCCN 2021041992

ISBN 978 90 272 1004 3 (HB)
ISBN 978 90 272 5843 4 (E-BOOK)

John Benjamins Publishing Company · https://benjamins.com

Table of contents

Part III. Vietnam

Part IV. India

Foreword and acknowledgements

The Missionary Linguistics conference series, initiated by the OsProMil project (Oslo Project on Missionary Linguistics, supported by the Norwegian Research Council/ Norges Forskningsråd) from 2003 onwards, aimed at bringing together scholars devoted to the historiography of missionary linguistics worldwide. The conferences have been organized in three continents, Europe, America and Asia, with venues in Oslo, São Paulo, Hong Kong/ Macau, Valladolid, Mérida (Yucatán), Tokyo, Bremen, Lima, Manila, and Rome. Ten volumes have been published with papers derived from these conferences; five in the series "Studies in the History of the Languages Sciences" (Zwartjes & Hovdhaugen, eds. 2004; Zwartjes & Altman, eds. 2005; Zwartjes, James & Ridruejo, eds. 2007; Zwartjes, Arzápalo Marín & Smith-Stark, eds. 2009; Zwartjes, Zimmermann & Schrader-Kniffki, eds. 2014) (SiHoLS vols. 106, 109, 111, 114 and 122), one in the series Koloniale und Postkoloniale Linguistik (vol. 5) (Zimmermann & Kellermeier-Rehbein, eds. 2015), one volume in Spanish appeared in Peru (Cerrón-Palomino, Ezcurra Rivero & Zwartjes, eds. 2019) and several journals published special issues, such as *Historiographia Linguistica, Revista Internacional de Lingüística Iberoamericana* and the *Revista Argentina de Historiografía Lingüística*. (Zwartjes & Koerner, eds. 2009; Zwartjes, ed. 2020; and Zwartjes & Regúnaga 2020).

The selected papers of the Tenth International Conference, co-organized by Paolo De Troia and Otto Zwartjes (21st–24th March, 2018) at the Sapienza Università di Roma and the Pontificia Università Urbaniana in Rome, are published in two volumes. The present volume offers selected papers in English focusing on Asia. The second volume in Spanish is devoted to Latin America with contributions on Purépecha, Nahuatl, Tzeldal, Cumanagoto, Muysca, Mochica, and Quechua and some papers not focusing on one specific language, but providing a broader perspective of Amerindian languages (Zwartjes, ed. 2020). The latter includes some papers which were not derived from this conference. Both selections of papers cannot pretend to cover a whole area, but they can at least be seen as representative for certain traditions in missionary linguistics.

The Tenth International Conference on Missionary Linguistics (Rome, March 21–24, 2018) focuses on Asia, but as stated above, papers in Spanish related to Latin America are published separately. As in the previous conferences, older texts, colonial, postcolonial, mainly from missionaries, are studied with the objective of

https://doi.org/10.1075/sihols.130.fow

contributing to the following domains: the history of linguistics, linguistic documentation, translation studies and sociocultural analysis. The cognitive appropriation of foreign languages and cultures motivated Westerners to reflect upon transcultural processes such as transference and translation, based on intercultural encounters and interactions between European missionaries and speakers of the various indigenous languages and cultures in Asia. In the field of the history of applied linguistics, the perspective of language study, documentation, and teaching was radically changing during the age of great discoveries. In Europe, grammars and dictionaries of vernacular languages appeared, and in the Americas the colonization and evangelization of the indigenous tribes went hand in hand with linguistic studies, which often antedate the documentation of many European "national" languages. These pioneering works contain many innovative aspects on all levels of analysis: phonology, morphology, syntax, semantics and pragmatics and even beyond (translation theory and practices, rhetoric, stylistics, cultural studies, anthropology), since the languages they encountered often did not share the features Westerners were familiar with.

From the perspective of the History of Linguistics, the languages encountered in Asia were a great challenge for missionaries who mainly based their work on the Graeco-Latin model, which was developed for the description of Greek and Latin and which puts particular emphasis on inflectional and derivational morphology. The tonal systems in several varieties of Chinese, Vietnamese, the agglutinative patterns of Dravidian languages or Japanese, are just a few examples that can be studied from the perspective of the history of linguistics. In the rich lexicographical production of missionaries, a great deal of information can be studied about "cultural encounters".

As most of the previous volumes, the papers are arranged according to region or language. Most papers concentrate on languages spoken in Maritime Asia (Chinese, Japanese, Vietnamese and Tamil). The book opens with a paper with a general character, followed by sections on China, Japan, Vietnam and India. Contributions to the OsProMil conferences have tended to address the period up until about 1850. The metalanguages used in the linguistic works studied in this book are Latin, Italian, Portuguese and French. Several papers focus on Jesuit sources, but in this volume the linguistic works of other religious congregations and institutions, such as the *Sacra Congregatio de Propaganda Fide* and the *Société des Missions Étrangères de Paris*, as well as of other religious orders are analysed, such as the Order of the Franciscans and the Order of the Discalced Carmelites. Thematically, this book includes papers on the history of the romanization systems of the Asian languages, phonology (with particular attention to the description of tones in Chinese and Vietnamese), lexicography, translation, pragmatics (politeness and the use of honorifics in Japanese) and the adaptation of the Graeco-Latin framework (parts of speech and verbal morphology in Tamil, in particular mood and modality). Some papers do not directly analyze the languages in question, but provide insights for the study of Asian languages in Europe (Humboldt, Golius, Reland, Bayer, etc.).

The book opens with a paper written by Zwartjes and Paolo De Troia, which analyzes André Palmeiro's *Epistola* (1632) written in Portuguese to the Superior General in Rome, the "minutes" in Latin of a linguistic investigation, coordinated and edited by Alexandre de Rhodes (SJ; 1593–1660), discussing some important features of the Asian languages Chinese, Japanese and Vietnamese, followed by a quadrilingual *Oratio Dominica Pater Noster* in these languages. The linguistic ideas are analyzed, the three romanization systems are discussed, and an English translation of the text is attached as appendix. Finally, the diffusion of the letter in early-modern Europe is described.

The section on Chinese contains three papers. Erica Cecchetti's contribution deals with the "Nuovo metodo per scrivere la lingua volgare cinese" of the Italian Franciscan Eligio Cosi (OFM, 1818–1885). His new alphabet contains 33 symbols and was spread through the Catholic communities of Shandong and Henan until the first half of the 20th century. Cosi's method also influenced Celestino Ibáñez's (OFM, 1873–1951) romanization of Chinese in 1921. The aim of "Cosi's script" was twofold: firstly, the need to teach spoken Chinese to foreign missionaries. Secondly, he wanted to help Chinese peasants to teach and easily understand the Gospel in romanized script. In Noël Golvers's paper the role of the Jesuits in West-East and East-West communication is discussed, through an analysis of their activities as translators. Golvers demonstrates that the Jesuits had in fact a systematic program of translation starting in the early 17th century and the various imperatives and aims behind it are impressive and merit investigation. Golvers describes the complex linguistic situation in China, in which they worked; the methods of working and the instruments they used, from European wordlists to native Chinese dictionaries and the different 'strategies' they followed to transpose Chinese realities to Western textual contexts, from simple romanizations to morphological adaptation and full translation. Miriam Castorina's paper investigates the linguistic works of Joseph Maximilian Pruggmayr (OCD; 1713–1791), with a special focus on the Italian-Chinese dictionary he compiled during his years in Beijing. His work is in fact unique both for the richness of the lexicon and for the features it presents and could be useful to reconstruct the linguistic situation in 18th century Northern China.

The third section contains two papers that concentrate on Japanese, although Japanese sources are also dealt with in the general introduction, and in the section on Vietnamese. Olivia Yumi Nakaema selected the Portuguese concepts of "honra" (honour), "humildade/ abatimento" (humility) and the metalinguistic terms related to honorificity, such as "particulas de honra", "verbos honrados", partículas humiliativas", in João Rodrigues's (1561–1634) two grammars of Japanese viz. his

Arte da Lingoa de Iapam (Nagasaki, 1604–1608) and *Arte Breve da Lingoa Iapoa* (Macau, 1620), Rodrigues developed an innovative model of describing politeness in Japanese. Atsuko Kawaguchi studies the so-called *Kirishitan* texts, focusing on the romanization system of Japanese, the alphabet (*Rōmaji*) developed by Jesuits, which is mainly based on Portuguese orthography and later also adapted by the Spanish Dominicans. In this paper some "irregularities" in Jesuit manuscripts, different from printed Jesuit works (such as the alternative spellings of the closed syllable <-t>, <-tç>, <-tçu>, <-tu> and <-zu>) are explained and compared with Spanish sources like Bernardino Ávila Girón's *Relación del Reino de Nippon*, Diego de Chinchón's *Relación cierta y verdadera de los ocho Mártires de Arima* and Diego Collado's *Vocabulario de la lengua Japona*.

Section 4 on Vietnamese gathers three articles. Emi Kishimoto's paper contains an analysis of Alexandre de Rhodes references to the Japanese languages in his published work on Vietnamese, *Dictionarium Annamiticum Lusitanicum, et Latinum*, a Vietnamese-Portuguese-Latin dictionary, and a short grammatical description of the Vietnamese language, entitled *Linguae Annamiticae seu Tunchinensis Brevis Declaratio*. It is shown that de Rhodes not only included quite a few Japanese loanwords in his trilingual dictionary, but it is also likely that de Rhodes in his *Brevis Declaratio* appears to have used at least one of the two Japanese grammars composed by João Rodrigues, the *Arte da lingoa de Iapam* (1604–1608) and/or the *Arte breve da lingoa Iapoa* (1620). The aim of Raf Van Rooy is to discuss the "Greek" part of the concept of "Graeco-Latin". Van Rooy took as case study, de Rhodes's grammar of Vietnamese, which explains why his paper is placed in this section. The model on which most missionary grammarians depended in describing foreign languages was principally that of Latin grammar or its vernacular adaptations. Due to the fact that Latin grammar was itself an adaptation (at the same time a reduction and an expansion) of Ancient Greek grammar, this model has often been dubbed "Graeco-Latin" in current historiography. Yet how Greek was this so-called Graeco-Latin model? In his paper, Van Rooy addresses this question by investigating how Greek grammar served as an additional model in Alexandre de Rhodes's (1593–1660) early description of the Vietnamese tone system (1651), possibly inspired by Jacob Gretser's (1562–1625) Greek grammar, the standard manual in Jesuit schools. His study, though based on a limited body of sources, allows us to formulate some metahistoriographical afterthoughts of wider relevance. The third paper in this section by Ly Pham focuses mainly on the grammars written by the French fathers of the Missions Étrangères de Paris (MEP) and the grammar by Trương, – considered to have been the first Vietnamese person to compose a grammar of the native language. Trương was trained at the General College of the MEP in Penang (Malaysia), with the aim of revealing the 'inspired sources' of these linguistic descriptions by missionaries in relation to the description of the Vietnamese language and the evolution of the ways in which parts of speech in Vietnamese were conceived. A comparison of the grammars written in Latin by Taberd (1838) and Theurel (1877) and the translation of Taberd's grammar by Aubaret (1861) reveals the role of the Latin grammatical tradition in the description of the Vietnamese language and the adaptation of some of the characteristics of French grammar in the two grammars and in the translated version.

Section 5 deals with the Indian subcontinent. Cristina Muru underscores the importance of two Portuguese grammars of Tamil, the first composed by the Jesuit Balthasar da Costa (ca. 1610–1673) and a second *Arte* composed by Gaspar de Aguilar (1548–?) bound together with texts from Philippus Baldaeus (1632–1671). Muru focuses on mood and modality, as described in the two grammars, mainly the *imperative* and *subjunctive* moods. The paper points out how these missionaries incorporated Tamil equivalents which did not have the same morphological properties as Latin into the Latin categories of subjunctive and imperative, resulting in interesting extensions of the model of reference, both in terminology and conceptualization. Finally, Swiggers, Thomas and Van Hal investigate an extensive letter of Wilhelm von Humboldt published in 1828 by the Royal Asiatic Society of Great Britain and Ireland in its *Transactions*. The reason why this paper is included in the section on India is that the paper focuses on the topic of "ascertaining the affinities between the languages of India and Ceylon". In his letter Humboldt warns against the use of lexical comparison as the absolute proof for linguistic relationship, and he expounds his own criterion of analogy in grammatical form. Humboldt's text is analysed here from the point of view of its methodological relevance, as well as for its historiographical interest, linking it to the tradition of missionary and colonial linguistics, and for the information it sheds on the complex network of scholarly exchanges concerning languages spoken outside Europe.

This volume thus presents intriguing analyses of pre-modern documents as viewed from various angles. We gratefully acknowledge the assistance and support of the Istituto Confucio in Rome, the Dipartimento Istituto Italiano di Studi Orientali of the Sapienza Università di Roma, the Centre for Chinese Studies of the Pontificia Università Urbaniana in Rome and the Beijing Foreign Studies University. We would also like to thank the general editor of the series in which this volume appears and the professional assistance of the editorial staff at John Benjamins, in particular Anke de Looper and Patricia Leplae.

Rome, Paris 2021
The Editors

References

Cerrón-Palomino, Rodolfo, Álvaro Ezcurra Rivero & Otto Zwartjes, eds. 2019. *Lingüística misionera. Aspectos lingüísticos discursivos, filológicos y pedagógicos*. Lima: Pontificia Universidad Católica del Perú/ Fondo Editorial.

Zimmermann, Klaus & Birte Kellermeier-Rehbein, eds. 2015. *Colonialism and Missionary Linguistics*. Berlin: De Gruyter. https://doi.org/10.1515/9783110403169

Zwartjes, Otto, ed. 2020. *Nuevos enfoques y desafíos metodológicos para el estudio de la lingüística misionera latinoamericana (siglos XVI–XVIII). Sección temática: Revista Internacional de Lingüística Iberoamericana (RILI)*, vol. 18. 2 (32).

Zwartjes, Otto & Cristina Altman, eds. 2005. *Missionary Linguistics II/ Lingüística misionera II: Orthography and Phonology. Selected Papers from the Second International Conference on Missionary Linguistics, São Paulo, 10–13 March, 2004*. Amsterdam & Philadelphia: John Benjamins. https://doi.org/10.1075/sihols.109

Zwartjes, Otto, Ramón Arzápalo Marín & Thomas C. Smith-Stark, eds. 2009. *Missionary Linguistics IV/ Lingüística misionera IV. Lexicography. Selected papers from the Fifth International Conference on Missionary Linguistics, Mérida, Yucatán, 14–17 March 2007*. Amsterdam & Philadelphia: John Benjamins. https://doi.org/10.1075/sihols.114

Zwartjes, Otto & Even Hovdhaugen, eds. 2004. *Missionary Linguistics/ Lingüística misionera [I]. Selected Papers from the First International Conference on Missionary Linguistics, Oslo, March, 13th–16th, 2003*. Amsterdam & Phildadelphia: John Benjamins. https://doi.org/10.1075/sihols.106

Zwartjes, Otto, Gregory James & Emilio Ridruejo, eds. 2007. *Missionary Linguistics III/ Lingüística misionera III. Morphology and Syntax. Selected papers from the Third and Fourth International Conferences on Missionary Linguistics, Hong Kong/Macau, 12–15 March 2005, Valladolid, 8–11 March 2006*. Amsterdam & Philadelphia: John Benjamins. https://doi.org/10.1075/sihols.111

Zwartjes, Otto & Konrad Koerner, eds. 2009. *Quot homines tot artes. New Studies on Missionary Linguistics. Special issue: Historiographia Linguistica* 36(2/3).

Zwartjes, Otto & María Alejandra Regúnaga, eds. 2020. *Continuidades y rupturas en la lingüística misionera del siglo XIX. Special issue: Revista Argentina de Historiografía Lingüística* 12(1).

Zwartjes, Otto, Klaus Zimmermann & Martina Schrader-Kniffki, eds. 2014. *Missionary Linguistics V /Lingüística misionera V. Translation Theories and Practices. Selected papers from the Seventh International Conference on Missionary Linguistics, Bremen, 28 February–2 March 2012*. Amsterdam & Philadelphia: John Benjamins. https://doi.org/10.1075/sihols.122

André Palmeiro's *Epistola* (Macau 8/V 1632) *cum paradigmate Orationis Dominicae Pater Noster in lingua Sinica, Japonica, Annamitica*

A linguistic analysis

Otto Zwartjes and Paolo De Troia

Université de Paris / Sapienza Università di Roma

1. Introduction

André Palmeiro (spelled "Palmeyro" in this letter) (1569–1635) was born in Lisbon, where he started his classical studies at the Colégio de Santo Antão in the late 1570s or early 1580s. On January 14, 1584 he entered the Society of Jesus at the Colégio de Jesus in Coimbra, an important institution in Portugal at that time. After having been a talented student, Palmeiro became a teacher there: in 1598 he began his career as professor of Philosophy in Coimbra. He taught Humanities, Philosophy and Theology at the University of Coimbra and was rector in Braga, he took part in the canonization process of Queen Elisabeth (Isabel) of Portugal (c. 1271–1336), an important event for the Portuguese clergy of that time. The queen, popularly known as a Rainha Santa (The Holy Queen) was canonized in 1625 by Pope Urban VIII.

During the first decades of the 17th century, Palmeiro's life was interwoven with that of his institution: he was an academic, and he was probably chosen as Visitor because he was a reliable, keen and dedicated man for missionary purposes. Thus he was sent to the East as Visitor, with the aim of checking the activities and the apostolic work of his confreres and to directly report to the Superior General of the Society of Jesus. In 1617 he went to India. He was Visitor of the Province of Malabar first, then in the Province of Goa and the Province of Malabar and later, in the Province of Japan and the Vice-Province of China.[1] He was one of the main figures in the so-called Terms Controversy, in the Jesuits' attempts to find the best equivalent for key concepts in Christian doctrine, such as *Tianzhu* 天主

---

1. For his role in the Catholic missions in Asia and his theological and political achievements and practices as "visitor", see Bartoli (1663) and Brockey (2007: 85–88) and Brockey (2014).

https://doi.org/10.1075/sihols.130.01zwa

['Lord of Heaven'], *Tianshen* 天神 ['angels'] and *Linghun* 靈魂 ['soul']. Palmeiro accepted the dress code of Chinese literati and several Chinese rituals as Matteo Ricci (1552–1610) had done before some decades earlier (Phan 1998: 59, citing Pfister 1932: 30; 195–196 and Bartoli 1663: 119–121).[2]

Since the linguistic situation in East Asia was complex and relatively unknown in Europe, the Superior General of the Society of Jesus Muzio Vitelleschi (1563–1645) asked André Palmeiro to consider using one language for all the Asian missions, as occured in many other regions of the Americas (Brockey 2014: 356–357).[3] If a similar situation could be created for Asia, Chinese was considered the best option, since Chinese characters were also used outside China. Different from what happened in the Americas,[4] the script played a crucial role among missionaries, voyagers, historians and scholars, who were aware that these "universal" characters could be understood in territories outside China, where Chinese was not spoken. For Westerners, it was a great discovery that this script, – often compared in this period with Egyptian hieroglyphs –, was intelligible to native speakers of other languages, such as Vietnamese or Japanese and it was astonishing to see that when Chinese characters were read aloud, the same characters were pronounced differently, as they were written in Vietnamese or Japanese, where they have not only a different reading but also sometimes differences in meaning.[5] Sometimes, these

---

2. Bartoli (1663: 121).

3. In American earlier pre-Columbian "imperial" indigenous languages, such as Quechua and Nahuatl served as *linguae francae*, which also were used as vehicular languages by native speakers of other indigenous languages in the Inca and Aztec empires, and even beyond. In Brazil, we see a similar linguistic policy; Tupi(nambá), the most commonly spoken language of the coast, was given the status of *língua geral* for the Jesuit missions. Missionaries almost always tried to concentrate on the language, or the variety of a certain language, which had the highest degree of intelligibility among the people, or which had the highest esteem. From a world-wide perspective, the strategies and linguistic policies vary considerably and often priests created their own varieties (often supra-dialectal or inter-dialectal, as a koine variety, such as "Pastoral Quechua", etc.). In the region corresponding with the current Mexican state Oaxaca, Náhuatl was used as *lingua franca* but a great number of languages belonging to different linguistic families were studied and taught. In this geographically small region, languages vary. Seen from a typological perspective, Mixe, Mixtec and Nahuatl vary, as Chinese and Japanese or Vietnamese. When Nahuatl was not understood, the local languages had to be studied and the same applies to Asia.

4. See for the history of the study of the reception of the so-called Chinese *characteristica universalis* and other scripts (Indian, Mayan) in pre-Modern Europe Demonet & Uetani (2008).

5. This was also widely diffused in Academic circles, as the following citation from Adrianus Reland demonstrates: "Sic per universum imperium Annamiticum …& in regno Siam, Camboiae, uti & in Insula Japon, iidem characteres Sinici leguntur & intelliguntur, sed alios sonos illis atttribuit [sic] incola regni Annamitici, alios Japonici. Sic ut nec Annamita Japonensem, nec Japonensis Annamitam, Sinensis neutrum, loquentem intelligat, licet iisdem literis, vel signis aut characteribus in scribendo, utantur" (Reland 1708, Diss. XI: 108). ['Thus, throughout the Empire

characters were compared with the "universal" applicability of the Arabic numbers, since the symbols 1, 2, 3, 4, etc. represent the same numerals, independently from how they are pronounced in every single language, such as Latin, English, French, Basque. According to Vitelleschi's view, it would be recommendable and easier to use Chinese alone as *língua geral* for all East Asian missions, not only for practical reasons – in any didactic program, the use of only one language is always easier to organize –, but also for cultural reasons. One of the reasons why the Jesuits in China focused on learning and teaching of Chinese was because they wanted to be able to understand the Chinese Classics, which were seen as a key to comprehend the local culture and to create an effective missionary strategy. In these teaching programs, there was also space for the teaching and acquisition of informal conversational adequacy, but the main focus in the Jesuit educational program was to acquire the right skills in order to read and translate Classical Chinese.

The study of non-standard varieties or any other language than Chinese was less important, unlike the linguistic studies produced in the Americas, where so many other languages than *lenguas generales* were described,[6] documented, taught and studied in the Catholic missions. Since Mandarin was positioned by the Chinese as the most prestigious medium for culture, order and power (Luca 2016: 93), Vitelleschi – either him or whomever pressured him, perhaps one of the cardinals of the newly founded Propaganda Fide – believed that it would be recommendable to use Mandarin[7] in the process of evangelization throughout China, or even beyond. He was not the first Jesuit who considered the possibility of using Mandarin only in the missions. It is likely, although this cannot be confirmed by evidence, that he was informed by the writings of the Jesuit visitor to the missions of the Indies, Alessandro Valignano (1539–1606):[8]

---

of Annam and in the Kingdom of Siam, Combodia and in the Island of Japan, the same Chinese characters are read and understood, but an inhabitant of the Kingdom of Annam assigns other sounds to these, and the Japanese [assign] yet other sounds [to the same characters]. And since a Vietnamese does not understand a Japanese when he speaks, nor a Japanese understands a Vietnamese [when he speaks], and a Chinese does not understand neither of the two, it is allowed to use the same letters, signs, or characters in their writings]. A similar description is also found in Bartoli (1663: 53).

6.   For more detailed information concerning the Hispanic 'lenguas generales' and the 'língua geral', see Zwartjes (2011b: 146, n. 6).

7.   The term "Mandarin" is confusing. In this paper Mandarin refers generally to *guānhuà*, the written administrative language of the officials (or mandarins) (see for more details Norman 1988: 157–158), called "mandarim" in Portuguese, "lengua mandarina" in Spanish, "lingua mandarina/ mandarinica" in Latin.

8.   Valignano was likely responding to this knowledge from Japan, not from experience of China which he did not have.

Tienen los chinas en diversas provincias diferentes lenguas, tanto que no se entienden unos a otros, aunque por escrito sí, porque escriben los mesmos caracteres y letras, las quales, como son figuras de cosas, y como las cosas tienen en todas partes una mesma figura, de todos son entendidas, aunque en diversas lenguas tienen diversos vocablos, y de aqui viene entenderse por escripto, y no por lengua; y lo mesmo acontesce con los japones, con los quales se comunican y entienden por escripto y no se entienden de palabra, porque tienen la mesma manera de escrebir los japones, aunque también tienen otra, que es propria suya y que no entienden los chinas.

Tienen también los chinas otro lenguaje, que es casi universal y común, y este es el proprio lenguaje de los mandarines y de la corte, y es entre ellos como entre nosotros el latín; y como aquella lengua sea propria de los mandarines, en los quales está todo el poder y mando, como diximos, todos procuran de aprender a hablar o bien o mal esta lengua, para poderse negociar con los mandarines.[9] *De donde paresce, que si nuestro Señor fuere servido de abrir la puerta a su Evangelio entre esta gente, paresce que con ellos se haría mucho mayor fructo que con todas las demás naciones del Oriente.*   (Valignano 1584, ed. Wicki 1944: 254–255 [f. 135])

[The Chinese have different languages in different provinces, to such an extent that they cannot understand each other, although they can in writing, because they write the same characters and letters; these, since they are figures of things and since things have the same figure everywhere, are understood by all, even if they have different words in different languages; this is why (the Chinese) understand one another in writing and not through speech. And the same happens to them with the Japanese: they communicate with them and they understand one another in writing and not through speech, because the Japanese have the same way of writing. The Japanese also have another way, which is their own and which the Chinese do not understand. The Chinese have yet another language which is, as it were, universal and common. And this is the language used by the Mandarins and the court, and to them it is like Latin to us. And since that language is the Mandarin's own language, who have all the power and rule, everyone tries to learn and speak this language, be it well or badly, in order to be able to negociate with the Mandarins. We can deduce from this that if our Lord would served to open the gate to his Gospel among these people, it seems that with them [using Mandarin] would yield a greater success than using any other language of the other Nations of the East (a part from this translation is cited from Luca 2016: 90 and 92), emphasis is ours.]

In Jiangxi 江西, Palmeiro presided over a team of eleven Jesuits and three literati discussing the word *Tian* 天 ['Heaven'] and *Shangdi* 上帝 ['the August Emperor'], as in Phan, ['Sovereign on High'] as in Brockey (2007: 85; 2014: 356) to refer to God (Pfister 1932: 196; Phan 1998: 59), and he made an investigation among those

---

9. Here he seems to be talking about inside China, not outside of it.

specialists competent in the various languages of the nations[10] in Macau with the purpose of sending a report to Rome regarding the linguistic situation in Asia. When these specialists were heard, Palmeiro came to the conclusion that he should discourage any attempt to impose Chinese as the only language of instruction and spreading the Faith in these regions;[11] the languages were too diverse. After inquiry and meetings with several specialists, he decided to write a letter, the *Epistola* to be discussed here, including *specimina* in these three languages, in order to demonstrate how different Chinese in fact was from Japanese and Vietnamese. In spite of the obvious differences between these languages, Palmeiro understood that Chinese indeed was used in Japan, Korea, Tonkin and Cochinchina, which all belonged to a certain degree to a "Chinese cultural zone", but seen from a linguistic perspective, these regions were too diverse. Palmeiro's aim was clearly to demonstrate that any attempt to impose or prescribe a universal language in Asia would not bear fruit.

Only the first folio of the *Epistola P. Andr. Palmeiro, Macao 8/V 1632 cum paradigmate Orationis Dominicae Pater Noster in lingua Sinica, Japonica, Annamitica* – sent to Vitelleschi in Rome via the Philippines and Goa –, is written in Portuguese and signed by "Andre Palmeyro", in answer to Vitelleschi's request.[12]

---

10. As Palmeiro writes in his letter: "pessoas intelligentes nas varias lingoas das Naçois que nas Prou[inci]as deste meu districto ha" (Palmeiro first folio). [persons who understand the various languages of the Nations of the Provinces of my district] and another time in the same letter "pessoas ... que tinhaõ mui boa noticia destas lingoas" [persons who have a thorough knowledge of these languages]. See for the complete text the appendix.

11. Similar discussions occurred also in the Americas. Should the religious conversion and instruction take place in the *lingua franca* or in another local language? It was an advantage for missionaries to concentrate on one "general" language and often there were not enough missionaries available to learn each language, since too many languages were spoken. According to Nicolás de Barreda's (fl. 1708–1730), no one has ever written anything in Chinantec, an Oto-Manguean language. The language is, according to the author, 'rural' and so difficult that it was even considered "impenetrable". He informs his readers that in other parish churches they even attempted "to extinguish" the language, shifting to religious instruction in Nahuatl, the *lingua franca* in these territories. According to Barreda (1730: prologue, no numbered pages), the decision to impose Nahuatl did not lead to any advantage in the spread of the faith, on the contrary, it even caused more confusion among the Chinantecs. For that reason, he decided to develop a teaching program in Chinantec.

12. As Brockey observes (p.c.) it was a separate written order ("hum papel"), likely not made by the general himself, but by someone who gave him this order ("a pessoa que isto pedio") which was then included in the letter Palmeiro received. Indeed, it is clear that someone outside the order asked for this and likely someone high up at the papal curia, but it could be some royal official, too, if a patron of the Society of Jesus, or a Cardinal of the Propaganda Fide, which was still working with the Jesuits in the early 1630s.

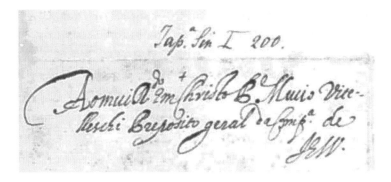

Figure 1. The recipient of the *Epistola* Muzio Vitelleschi[13]

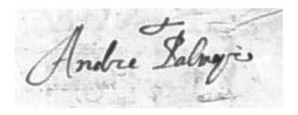

Figure 2. The signature of André Palmeiro on the bottom of the first folio

All the remaining folios are written in Latin by a different scribe. These *specimina* of the three Asian languages start with the *Oratio Dominica* (The Lord's Prayer), followed by a basic vocabulary, starting with the so-called *tetragrammaton*, followed by a list of kinship terms, inanimate objects, body parts, and numbers. This wordlist is quadrilingual arranged in five columns, from left to right starting with Latin first, followed by Japanese equivalents in romanization (Japonicé), Chinese characters, Chinese romanization (Sinicé) and finally Vietnamese[14] (Annam). The total number of Latin words is 49 from the Latin *Oratio Dominica* and a vocabulary with 68 other items, followed by the numerals 1–13, 20, 21, 30, 40–100, 200. 1,000 and 10,000. Generally, there is one equivalent for each single Latin word, but in some cases, one entry has more translations, as the word "tentationem", which has three different Chinese characters, with three romanizations of each of them in Chinese and also three in Vietnamese. The *Oratio Dominica* is not a word-for-word list,

---

13. According to Jacques (2004: 192), the letter was addressed to Francesco Ingoli (1578–1649), secretary of the Congregation of the Propaganda Fide (Pham 2018: 221) and one of the main figures in the foundation of the Propaganda Fides' multilingual printing press.

14. In this paper, the anachronistic term "Vietnamese" will be used, the national languages of Vietnam (*Việt Nam*), instead of the terms Annamese or Annamite. This region was divided in two "Kingdoms", Tonkin (North) and Cochinchina (South) where two varieties were spoken.

Figure 3. *Tentationem* and its equivalents in Japanese, Chinese characters, Chinese romanization and Vietnamese

which would have lead to distorted syntax. Japanese *nacare* does not correspond with Latin *tentationem* in the same grid; *nakare* from *nak[u] áre* means 'let there not be', used in negative commands and corresponds in fact with Latin "ne", wheras we find right from Latin "ne" in the expression "Et ne nos inducas in tentationem" the loanword 'tentationi' in the Japanese translation.

The use of the Lord's Prayer (*Oratio Dominica*) as a sample for language comparison in the *Epistola* of Palmeiro is not an isolated case. Conrad Gessner (1516–1565) collected 22 versions of the *Oratio Dominica* in his work *Mithridates* (1555). The idea was taken up by Hieronymus Megiser (c.1554–1618/1619) in 1593, Thomas Lüdeken (1630?–1694) in 1680, John Chamberlayne (c.1668–1723) in 1715 and Johann Christoph Adelung (1732–1806) and Johann Severin Vater (1771–1826) in 1809.

The text in Palmeiro's letter contains other interesting aspects. It starts with a linguistic introduction, highlighting some of the most important typological features of the three Asian languages, and no less importantly, some interlinguistic comparisons are given as well. Finally, the word list also contains some glosses written in the margins by the same hand, most of them related to Vietnamese (only one Chinese entry is accompanied by such a gloss, and no glosses refer to Japanese). The Latin section included in Palmeiro's letter does not have any signature, so it appears that the author or the scribe had the intent to present it as the "minutes" of a collective project.

Why should this *Epistola* be re-studied?

1. Firstly, the question of its authorship merits being treated again. Jacques (2004, cited in Pham 2018) argues that the word list with these *specimina* is a product of a collective enterprise, and that Alexander de Rhodes (1593–1660) was the scribe who strictly copied the text, and not the primary author. Recently, Pham (ibid.) identified the names of some of the specialists who participated in this linguistic inquiry, and corroborates Jacques' view that Alexandre de Rhodes was indeed the scribe;

2. we shall cast new light on the diffusion of this text among scholars in pre-Modern Europe. We will demonstrate that the *epistola* was not just a letter used for internal communication within the Society of Jesus. According to Pham (2018: 221)

"ce document, (désormais *le texte de Macao*), a été découvert par Roland Jacques qui l'a présenté lors d'un congrès en 1998, puis traduit en français". It is less commonly known that the *epistola* was already printed and studied in pre-modern times among European scholars, and that another copy circulated in Europe. As we shall demonstrate, the text appeared in print as early as 1708;

3. we shall provide a detailed analysis of the linguistic data themselves, the introductory remarks on linguistic typologies of Asian languages, the romanization systems used, (the year 1632 falls in a crucial period of the evolution and establishment of the romanization systems of these languages), and finally, the linguistic remarks written in the margins;

4. In the appendix, the original text will be reproduced accompanied by an English translation.[15]

2. Its authorship and the informants

As explained in the preceding section, André Palmeiro was the author of the first page in Portuguese, the rest was written by another person. Palmeiro called together several specialists on the three Asian languages in order to achieve the right information about these languages. Jacques (2004: 190) concludes that Alexandre de Rhodes[16] not only co-operated in this project as specialist who was asked to provide Palmeiro with information on Vietnamese, but that he was indeed also the person who wrote the text, (as the scribe or the minute-taker of the meeting) and that he was not considered as the "author":

> Les parties écrites en caractères latins sont indiscutablement de la main d'Alexandre de Rhodes, qui a donc servi de secrétaire au groupe. Il est important de comprendre que l'on a là, non pas l'œuvre d'une personne isolée, mais la résultante d'un travail collectif de longue haleine.   (Jacques 2004: 190, cited in Pham 2018: 222)

---

15. For a French translation see Jacques (2004), and Pham (2018: 566–567).

16. Alexandre de Rhodes (1593–1660) was a Jesuit and born in Avignon (Papal states, now in France), but his family came from Spain as converts from Jewish origin (the name of the family was earlier Rueda, or Rode). He arrived in 1624 in Cochinchina. He spent many years in Vietnam, from where he was also expelled several times. He taught Theology in Macau from 1630–1640. At the end of his life, he was sent to Persia (Isfahan) where he died in 1660. His main linguistic works include a trilingual dictionary Vietnamese-Latin-Portuguese (1651a), a grammar of Vietnamese, written in Latin (1651b) and a Catechism written in Vietnamese (1651c), all published in Rome by the Sacra Congregatio de Propaganda Fide Press. Some of his historical writings reached Europe and were translated into French and published in the same year (*Histoire du Royaume de Tunquin*) (de Rhodes 1651d). Another important work is his bibliography entitled *Divers voyages*, published in 1653.

Thanks to the kindness of Thị Kiều Ly Phạm, who provided us digital copies of other autograph writings of Alexandre de Rhodes, we have been able to compare the handwriting of the text accompanying Palmeiro's letter with other texts written by him. Indeed, the handwriting is the same:

Figure 4. The handwriting of the text appended to Palmeiro's letter

Figure 5. Jap-Sin. 83/fl. 062 written in 1632 later published in his work on the history of the Kingdom Tonkin (de Rhodes 1653)

The Latin text and the word lists arranged in separate columns are written by the same person, Alexandre de Rhodes, but it is not likely that Alexandre de Rhodes also copied the Chinese characters. Indeed, it is likely that de Rhodes produced a text which is the result of a collective enterprise, gathering input from several language specialists in Chinese and Japanese. It is likely that he wrote the Vietnamese sections himself, but it is also possible that these are also the result of a collective undertaking by specialists on Vietnamese (see for more details, the section below).

It is unknown who assisted him for this purpose. We do not have the names of all the specialists involved in this project, but according to Jacques (2004: 236–238), Alexandre de Rhodes's contribution to the Vietnamese translations was probably limited, due to his "limited linguistic competences" (Pham 2018: 222), but his point of view has been criticized by Pham (2018: 224–225), who sustains that Alexandre de Rhodes's contribution in this project was significant. As Pham observes, in February 1631, de Rhodes left Macau with Gaspar do Amaral (1594–1646), Antonio de Fontes (1569–1648) and Francisco Cardim (1569–1659) for Tonkin.

Two Portuguese Jesuits, who were specialists in Vietnamese, Gaspar do Amaral and António Barbosa (1594–1647), compiled manuscript dictionaries of Vietnamese, but left their manuscripts unfinished when they died. These two Portuguese Jesuits were the direct sources for de Rhodes's *Dictionarium* (Zwartjes 2011b: 291), as he himself acknowledges in his prologue.[17] They were not resident in Macau during the years 1630–1632, when this project was ongoing.[18] António de Fontes was in Macau, where he arrived in August 1630, after his mission in Cochinchina from 1624 until 1630. He travelled to Tonkin in February 1631, where he stayed until 1648 (Pham 2018: 220). As Pham (2018: 221) argues, "António de Fontes ouvre un nouveau chapitre dans l'histoire de la romanization du vietnamien et, en outre, que les travaux de ce jésuite représentent un tournant important dans l'histoire de la nouvelle écriture". Pham (2018: 226) provides the following names with corresponding dates of their presence in Macau in summary:

Table 1. Jesuit experts in the Vietnamese languages in Macau (Pham 2018: 226, Table 3.25)

Name of the missionary	Residence in Annam	Arrival in Macau	Departure from Macau
Alexandre de Rhodes	18 months in Cochinchina Jan. 1625 => July 1626	May 1630	Febr. 1640: departure to Cochinchina
Gaspar do Amaral	7 months in Tonkin Oct. 1629 => May 1630	May 1630	18 Febr. 1631: departure to Tonkin
Francesco Buzomi	13 years in Cochinchina Jan. 1615 => 1629 (one return to Macau in 1617)	August 1630	24 Jan. 1631: departure to Cambodia
Girolamo Majorica	5 years in Cochinchina Dec. 1624 => 1629	August 1630	19 Oct. 1631: departure to Tonkin
António de Fontes	5 years in Cochinchina Jan. 1625 => August	August 1630	18 Feb. 1631: departure to Tonkin

---

17. "Aliorum etiam ejusdem Societatis Patrum laboribus sum usus praecipue P. Gasparis de Amaral, & P. Antonij Barbosae, qui ambo suum composuere Dictionarium ille lingua Annamitica incipiens, hic á Lusitana, sed inmatura iterque morte nobis erectus: utriusque ergo laboribus sum usus" (de Rhodes 1651a: prologue). [I have also used the works of other priests belonging in the same Brotherhood, in particular those of Father Gaspar do Amaral and Father Antonio Barbosa, each of whom composed a dictionary, the former starting from the Vietnamese, the latter from the Portuguese language. However, because of their untimely death, I was the one to gather it up: therefore, I have used both of their works.]

18. Gaspar do Amaral was in Macau from 1638 until 1645 and António Barbosa arrived in May 1642 and stayed there until 1647 (Pham 2018: 119).

Regarding possible names of persons involved with the Japanese translations, it is hard to find concrete names. João Rodrigues "Tçuzzu" (or Tsuji, "the interpeter") (1562–1633) – the author of the two famous Japanese grammars, the first, *Arte grande* (Rodrigues 1604–1608), printed in Japan, and the second, *Arte breve* (Rodrigues 1620), printed in Macau may seem a possible candidate, as proposed by Jacques (2004: 212), but there were many other Jesuits formerly delegated to Japan present in Macau in 1630 who could have done this work too.[19] João Rodrigues was not in Macau during the period of 1630–1632. After the expulsion of the Christians from Japan, starting in 1614, Rodrigues, after having lived over 30 years in Japan, went on a tour of China (Macau, Canton, Nanjing and Beijing). In 1629, when he was 68 years old, he participated with two other interpreters (Simão Coelho and a Chinese 'jurubaça' with the name Horatio Nerete) in an expedition under Gonçalo Teixeira-Corrêa (c. 1583–1632) to Beijing (Pfister 1932: 214; Blue 2001: 44). In February 1632, Captain Teixeira and 11 other Portuguese were killed in a battle in Dengzhou, and Rodrigues escaped by jumping from the high city wall into a bed of snow (Cooper 2001: xx) and continued his journey to Beijing. Rodrigues returned to Macau in 1633 where he died the same year, a year after Palmeiro signed his letter. On March 20th 1633 he was buried in front of the altar of St. Michael in the Jesuit church in Macau (Zwartjes 2011b: 95). This means that he could not have participated in this specific team of linguistic specialists convoked by Palmeiro, but it is not unlikely that his notebooks reached others among his colleagues.[20] Studying Japanese was still seen as relevant, since missionaries never gave up the hope to return to Japan, but we do not know the names of any assistants involved in the Japanese translations in Palmeiro's linguistic inquiry. As we will discuss below, it appears that the informant who assisted in the composition of the Japanese component was an Italian, since the Portuguese romanization which was developed for Japanese is

---

19. "[Rodrigues] était d'ailleurs personellement présent au collège de Macao à cette époque et a vraisamblablement pris part à la redaction du manuscrit" (Jacques 2004: 212). Rodrigues also started learning Japanese himself when he arrived in Macau, since his original destination was not Cochinchina but the mission in Japan. (See de Rhodes 1653: 57 and Kishimoto, in this volume, p. 190).

20. Rodrigues also played a prominent role in the so-called Terms Controversy. As Brockey observes (2007: 85–86) "The crux of Rodrigues's objections to the way that Ricci and his successors had promoted Christianity in the Ming empire rested on their use of dubious doctrinal terminology. […] Rodrigues further argued that the terms for "soul" and "angel" were "pernicious and wicked", and that all the books that had been printed by the missionaries up to that point should be emended or destroyed". Palmeiro disagreed with the views regarding the use of doctrinal terms with Rodrigues. As Brockey summarizes: "João Rodrigues went so far as to upbraid Rodrigo de Figueiredo for his "most ardent" defense of *Shangdi* – an outburst that drove Palmeiro to impose a period of fasting on the interpreter from Japan" (Brockey 2007: 87; Pina 2003).

not followed strictly; we see some apparent Italian features. It is also possible that the Italian-like features of the Japanese romanization were the result of de Rhodes's work as 'secretary' of the group.

Regarding the Chinese sections, of course, Chinese specialists were easily available in Macau. We can exclude the possibility that Nicolas Trigault (1577–1628) was invited to participate in this meeting. As Brockey (2007: 260–261) summarizes, the Jesuit novices acquired a familiarity of spoken *guānhuà* over the initial six months as they began learning to read and write characters, using Nicolas Trigault's *Xiru ermuzi* ['Aid to the Eyes and Ears of Western Literati'] for building their vocabularies.[21] Trigault refined the romanization systems of his predecessors Matteo Ricci, Michele Ruggieri (1543–1607) and Lazzaro Cattaneo (1560–1640). *Xiru ermuzi* was completed six years before the *Epistola* was written and it is obvious that the informants who gave their linguistic input for the linguistic inquiry based their reports on a pre-Trigault romanization system, as will be demonstrated below. Trigault worked mainly in Hangzhou, and it has been reported that he wrote *Xiru ermuzi* in a remote Shanxi province and it is likely that Trigault's work had not reached Macau yet. Maybe Palmeiro's informants decided not to follow Trigault's system, or maybe they did, but Alexandre de Rhodes, as the scribe and editor, could have simplified it, as occurs with the romanization of Japanese.[22]

We may find other possible candidates in the list of the interpreters operating in Macau, or more generally in China at that time. The following are individuals associated with the Jesuits who could have performed this function:

- Pascoal Mendes (1584–1640). He was engaged in the controversy of the Christian terms and the author of a text on this question, adressed to Visitor Palmeiro;

---

21. *Xiru ermuzi* 西儒耳目資 (Trigault 1626). is one of the most important and influential works made by Jesuit missionaries about the Chinese language. Published in 1626, it is composed by three volumes: the first volume, entitled "Yi yin shou pu 譯引首譜", explaining the theory of romanization system; the second volume, entitled "Lie yinyun pu 列音韻譜", listing characters according to the pronunciation; the third volume, "Lie bianzheng pu 列邊正譜", through which was possible to look for the pronunciation of characters starting from his writing. The book had an important diffusion and certain impact among Chinese culture: it was included in the imperial collection *Siku quanshu* 四庫全書 and was listed by *Kangxi zidian* 康熙字典, one of the most important dictionaries of Chinese history, as one of its reference books. *Xiru ermuzi* was also studied and taken as a reference for phonological research in modern time by Chinese linguists. See: Luo Changpei (2004).

22. It is obvious that Andre Palmeiro knew who Nicolas Trigault was, since he was aware of his suicide comitted November 14th, 1628 and Palmeiro was the only person who has documented his "shameful" death, a mortal sin in the Catholic church. As Brockey describes (2003: 161), "he wrote a coded message that was deciphered by its contemporary recipient : « Father Trigault hanged himself »".

–   Domingos Mendes (1579/1581–1652),[23] who in Jesuit sources is described as an excellent interpreter, fluent in both Chinese and Portuguese. Domingos Mendes is described as an "ottima lingua" and seemed to have taught Chinese to João Rodrigues. He was born in Zhèjiāng, 浙江 and later he became novice again in Shaozhou 韶州. He was sent to Cochinchina (1621–1626) and in 1632 he was sent to Hainan 海南 in order to spread the Faith on that island (Pfister 1932: 124);

–   Other persons mentioned in this context are Francisco de Lágea (arrived in Macau in 1610, died c.1645?),[24] teacher of Álvaro Semedo (1586–1658) and Pedro Ribeiro (1570–1640), Francisco Ferreira (1605–1652), teacher of Chinese of Giovanni Francesco de Ferraris (1609–1671) and Martino Martini,[25] or the Chinese – Javanese Manuel Gomes (1608–1648/1649), who helped Francesco Brancati (1607–1671) reading Confucian classics. All of them, in terms of time and place, could be indicated as possible candidates for the Chinese script of Palmeiro's letter, not to mention the missionaries themselves, of course.[26]

It seems possible that Domingos Mendes was the informant who gave input on Chinese. One of these Chinese manuscripts possessed by Golius (see below) was, according to Lundbæk (1986: 98–99) "a notebook in which Martini and his *famulus* Dominicus had written some words in Chinese, Japanese and Vietnamese, among other things the Lord's Prayer". It is plausible that this *Dominicus* was in fact Domingos Mendes, since his Latinate name is explicitly mentioned as author of the Lord's Prayer. He is mentioned as possible translator/ co-author author of the Chinese catechism entitled the "Explanation of the [Hanging] Image of the Lord of Heaven" (*Tianzhu shengxiang lueshuo* 天主聖像略說) completed between 1616 and 1623 (Lopes 2020: 88).[27] Since Domingos died in 1652, he could have been perfectly one of the informants for Chinese who was asked to contribute with his Chinese part of the *Epistola*, although we do not have hard evidence for such an assumption.[28]

---

23. According to Pfister he could have died in 1632? (1932: ii).

24. Pfister (1932: ii).

25. According to Pina (2012: 129), "Ferreira taught Martini Chinese with whom he lived in Shanghai and Hangzhou between 1643 and 1648".

26. As for the reconstruction of the world of interpreters and translators in Macau during the 17th century, see: Pina (2012: 128–129) and Pina (2013: 37–38).

27. According to Lopes, "this text is traditionally attributed to Xu Guanqi and an anonymous Jesuit, eventually João da Rocha (1565–1623), Pedro Ribeiro, and Domingos Mendes, mentioned in 1619 editions" (Lopes 2020: 110, note 17).

28. Information based on Pina (2013: 38–40).

3.   The reception of this text among scholars in pre-Modern Europe

As we have already indicated in the introduction, another copy of the text of this linguistic inquiry circulated. Jacob Golius (1596–1667), a Professor of Arabic and Mathematics at the university of Leiden, possessed a considerable number of Chinese manuscripts. Some of them were given to him by the Jesuit Martino Martini (1614–1661), when he was in the Low Countries, although Golius already possessed other Chinese manscripts before he met Martini.[29]

Theophilus (Gottlieb) Siegfried Bayer (1694–1738), a Professor of Greek and Roman Antiquities at St. Petersburg Academy of Sciences, also refers to Chinese texts which belonged to Golius's collection in his *Museum Sinicum*. After the death of Golius, the University of Leiden had taken over the entire legacy of oriental manuscripts, against a reasonable indemnity to his heirs (Duyvendak 1936: 314), but the necessary funds could not be found and thirty years after his death the collection was publicly sold at the auction of Johannes du Vivie. The complete list of Chinese manuscripts and printed works is included in his auction catalogue entitled *Catalogus insignium in omni facultate, Arabica, Persica, Turcica, Chinensi &c. librorum*, published in 1696. In this catalogue we find two sections, the first is entitled "Libri Chinenses, & C. M. S." including 17 titles, although not all refer to Chinese works.[30] The second section includes printed works "Libri chinensi impressi" (*Catalogus insignium* 1696: 26–27).[31] As will be demonstrated in Zwartjes (forthcoming), this section comprises an anonymous Chinese-Spanish dictionary attributed to Francisco Díaz, whereas Duyvendak demonstrates that another Chinese dictionary[32] can be attributed to the Dutch doctor of medicine Justus Heurnius (1587–1651/2), together with other texts, such as the Chinese Creed, the Ten Commandments and the Lord's Prayer. Heurnius went to Batavia in 1624

---

29. See for more details Zwartjes (2011a). For a complete list of Golius's collection (16 manuscripts and 19 printed works), see Duyvendak (1936: 314–316).

30. For instance, the collection includes also the Spanish version of Diego Collado's grammar of Japanese ("Arte de lengua japona per las ocho partes de la Oracion"), and others include Icelandic, Slavic languages and languages from India.

31. The Chinese works from this *Catalogus insignium* are also included in Duyvendak (1936: 314–316).

32. The dictionary appears in the catalogue of de Jong (1862: 274–275, no. 226) Notice that the page reference and manuscript numbers in Duyvendak (1936: 317, note 3) are not correct. The work has the title *Lexicon Belgico-Sinicum*. A comment has been added by a librarian that the author and translator of the Chinese characters of this work was a Dutch, whose name is unknown: "…waarin bij elk der Chinesche teekenen, de uitspraak en vertaling door een Hollander, wiens naam niet gemeld wordt, is bijgevoegd" (de Jong 1862: 275).

where he tried to establish a seminary of local boys who would train for missionary work among the Malay, Malabarese and Chinese, a project that was not met with success (Kuiper 2005: 111). In 1628 he compiled these texts with the aid of a Chinese assistant who understands Latin and who was educated in Macau. Duyvendak discovered that in the *Catalogue of Chinese printed books* (Douglas 1877: 331) a dictionary is mentioned with exactly the same title as Heurnius's dictionary. As Kuiper (2005: 115) demonstrates, Heurnius's romanization system is partly based on Trigault's system, and partly adapted to Dutch spelling, which seems to prove that the Chinese assistant educated in Macau was already familiar with Trigault's system at this time. We also find the Jesuit translation for God *Tianzhu*. Heurnius's Chinese dictionary was sent to Holland in November 1629, soon after it was finished (Kuiper 2005: 121).

The second title of Golius's legacy mentioned in the *Catalogus insignium* is Heurnius's *Compendium Doctrinae Christianae*. Kuiper (2005: 121–138) describes three copies of this text and in the London copy we find materials added by Philippe Masson (married in 1699, no other dates are known), all bound together as one volume, together with the dictionary. At the end of this volume, we find "various sinological notes" (Kuiper 2005: 129) and the first of these notes is entitled:

> Miscellanea quaedam Sinica, partim a P. Martinio ejusque famulo Sinensi Dominico accepta, partim ex eorundem ore per me excerpta. Item quasita varia, imprimis, circa computum Sinarum astronomicum.   (Duyvendak (1936: 322)
>
> [Some Chinese miscellaneous works, partly received from Father Martinius and his Chinese attendant Dominicus, partly collected by me from the same persons. Besides, various issues, mostly regarding the Chinese astronomical calculation.]

The same title *Miscellanea quaedam* appears also in the *Catalogue Raisonné* of van Voorst & van Voorst's collection (*Catalogue* 1859: 7, no. 60) where we read that Golius wrote this title on the manuscript and unfortunately in this catalogue we do not find the titles of the different works bound together in this bundle.[33] In Douglas's *Catalogue* (1877: 336) the same title *Miscellanea quaedam* is written, where it is attributed to Phillipe Masson. As Kuiper (2005: 130) demonstrates, Douglas was misled by the fact that the text was written by Masson and that "me" in the expression "per me excerpta" was referring to Phillipe Masson, whose name also appears on top of the same page, although it was a text written by Golius.

Furthermore, Bayer explains, referring to the dictionary and many other texts "lexicon et multa alia" which were added to Golius's collection:

---

33. "Ms. de J. Golius (J. Gool) qui a ajouté ce titre. C'est une collection curieuse de glossaires, etc." (*Catalogue raisonnée* 1859: 7, no. 60).

Golius et hoc lexicon et multa alia Martino Martinio acceperat, quae cum vno fasciculo coligasset, ipse manu sua inscripsit, miscellanea haec Sinica partem se a Martinio eius famulo Sinensi Dominico impetrasse, partem ex eorum sermone excepisse. In iis quoque fuerunt oratio Dominica ab ipso Martinio exarata, quam Relandus postea Ioannis Chamberlaynii editioni commodauit.

(Bayer 1730: 127–128)

[Golius had received this lexicon and many other things from Martinus Martinius, which he bound together in one volume, and in which he had written with his own hand, of which he had obtained a part of these Chinese writings on miscellaneous subjects [written by] Martinius and his Chinese servant (*famulus*) Dominicus, and which partly contains notes based on direct communication with them. Among these papers, was also a Lord's Prayer composed by Martini himself, which Reland contributed to John Chamberlayne's edition.]

Some of these texts mentioned in Golius's catalogue were sold to Narcissus Marsh (1638–1713), who passed them later to the Bodleian Library at Oxford, whereas others were acquired by Adriaan Reland, (Hadrianus Relandus, also spelled as Reeland) (1676–1718), Professor of Oriental languages and Ecclesiastical Antiquities in Utrecht.[34]

In Duyvendak (1936: 322) we find a description of a certain glossary, included in a collection possessed by Reland, also entitled *Miscellanea quaedam*, i.e. verbatim the same title as the work mentioned above). As Kuiper (2005: 130) observes, "Duyvendak was misled into believing this collection also contained the bundle of Golius/ Reland's manuscripts".

When we analyse the corresponding section in Reland's *Dissertationum miscellanearum* (Reland 1708: 109 ff.) we read that he has found a manuscript in Golius's collection ("inter plurimas schedas manuscriptas") containing a "Vocabularium" with Latin, Chinese, Japanese and Vietnamese ("in quo voces aliquae Latinae Sinice, Japonice, & Annamitice scriptae continebantur"). Apart from these glossaries, Reland argues that other texts were included, such as the Lord's Prayer (*Oratio Dominica*), the Apostolic Creed (*Symbolus Apostolicus*), the Decalogue (*Decalogus*), and the Thousand characters (*Soei-ngan-chien*).

Reland also informs his readers that there were four Chinese characters for naming "God", numbered from one to four, accompanied by the romanizations in Chinese, Japanese and Vietnamese. To our great surprise, when we checked the

---

34. For his collection see *Catalogus Codicum* (1761). According to Anna Pytlowany (personal communication), – referring to Josephus Serrurier's (1663–1742) funeral oration – Reland befriended the German student Heinrich Sike (Sikius) (1669–1712), who taught him Arabic. In 1696 we find them both in Leiden at the auction of the manuscripts of the deceased professor of mathematics and Arabic, Jacobus Golius (1596–1667) (Serrurier 1718: 18).

text in Reland's *Dissertationum miscellanearum* we found verbatim the same text referring to the tetragrammaton including the references to Matthew and Acts of the Apostles.[35] This was not the only surprise: we found in Reland's dissertation exactly the same word list as the one copied by Alexandre de Rhodes in the *epistola* of Palmeiro under the title *Tabella vocum, cum pronuntiatione earum Japonica, Sinica et Annamitica* and the Lord's Prayer in Chinese, as well as certain other texts.

It is not clear if Golius received this text from Martini, or if he already possessed it in his Chinese collection, before the meeting with Martini took place, since the title *Miscellanea quaedam* is misleading. Both Martini and de Rhodes were imprisoned in Batavia by the Dutch,[36] de Rhodes for a span of eight months in 1646[37] and Martini from May 1652 until February 1653 (Martini 1988 [1651–1653]). It has been documented that Martini left a copy of his Chinese grammar with the Dutch in Batavia, which was later sent to the Prussian physician and botanist Christian Mentzel (Mentzelius, 1622–1701) by the Dutch doctor and botanist Andreas Cleyer (1634–1697/98) in 1689 (Paternicò 2011: 55). According to Pfister, the Chinese grammar, was brought to Golius by Martini himself, and according to him this was the copy used later by Mentzel and Bayer (Pfister 1932: 262). If the *epistola* was indeed a part of the bundle entitled *Miscellanea quaedam*, it is indeed correct that Golius received this text from Martini. On the other hand, it is not impossible that Cleyer received another copy of the quadrilingual *Oratio Dominica* and wordlists from Alexandre de Rhodes when he was in Batavia, and sent it to Holland where it finally settled in Golius's collection, before Martini came to visit him.[38] Unfortunately, no further details are given in his biography (de Rhodes 1653). Palmeiro writes in his letter to Vitelleschi, that he had sent these papers "by way of

---

35. The text "Praterea, cum his tribus linguis …….. ineffabili nomini tetragrammato responde-ant" is identical tot he corresponding section in Palmeiro's epistle.

36. Pfister (1932: 185).

37. De Rhodes devotes several chapters to this episode of his life (see de Rhodes 1653, II, 13–26).

38. As Pham (2018: 201) observes, Jesuits usually wrote three of the same letters and put different dates on them, in order to be guaranteed the reception of the letter by the recipient. This is in fact not true, two copies for two different vias, yes, but the dates were the same for reference. As Pham argues, there was at least another copy circulating in Asia of this text. Majorica should have taken a copy to Tonkin, where other Jesuits, such as António de Fontes and Gaspar do Amaral could benefit from it. Amaral's letter of 1632 exhibits clearly some evolutions in the romanization of Tonkinese (Pham 2018: 230–231). Gaspar do Amaral was sent with André Palmeiro, António de Fontes and António Cardim to Tonkin in 1631. Amaral's report was written in December 1632. Alexandre de Rhodes and Gaspar do Amaral were expelled from Tonkin in May 1630, and the preparation for the *Oratio Dominica* started around 1630, after their arrival in Macau (Pham 2018: 225).

the Philippines", and the following year (1633), these papers will have been sent via Goa as well ("Mando por esta via das Felipinas estes papeis, e polla da India irão o anno que vem"). This practice is far from unusual. When Palmeiro reports (also in 1633) other important news to his superiors, such as the last update regarding the Japan martyrdom, he sent two copies, one via Goa, "fearing that the fleets headed to India might not make it safely to their destination" (Brockey 2014: 396), and another via the Philippines, i.e. the Manila-Acapulco route. Although it is mere speculation, the letter could have reached Europe via Acapulco, but it is also possible that it was intercepted by the Dutch and brought to Batavia, where Cleyer could have sent it to Europe.

Bayer was also aware of the existence of this text, referring to a glossary of Chinese characters, their Latin translation, and their pronunciation in Japanese, Chinese and Vietnamese.[39] In a footnote Bayer says that he does not agree with Golius, – who claims according to him that Martini was the author of these glosses –, but he believes that Alexandre de Rhodes or any other specialist in Vienamese for that matter, could have been the author:

> Auctorem earum autumat esse Martinium, citius crediderim Alexandrum Rhodesum, aut aliquem certe alium, qui in Anamiticis regionibus sit versatus.
>
> (Bayer 1730, vol. 1 'Praefatio': 127)

> [Golius thinks that Martinius was the author of these glosses, but I rather believe that Alexandre de Rhodes was the author, or maybe someone else, who has dwelled in the territories of Annam.]

Here, we reproduce the first part of the *Tabella* as it was published by Reland, compared with the text included in Palmeiro's *Epistola*:

---

39. "Ubi ad litteras Sinicas sermonem flectit, e Iacobi Golii glossis Sinicis Iapanicis Annamiticis (*) quasdam cum characteribus profert, ut ostendat, quem in modum littera una et eadem a diversis gentibus diversis modis pronuncietur" (Bayer 1730: 127). [When the conversation turns to Chinese letters, he submits some with the characters derived from Golius' Chinese, Japanese and Vietnamese glosses, in order to show how the exact same letter is pronounced differently by different peoples.] See also Lundbæk (1986: 99) and Weststeijn (2016: 18).

INSULARUM ORIENTALIUM. 113

Latine.	Japonice.	Sinice.	Annam.
1 Coeli	ten	thien	3 that
2 Terrae	cino	ti	4 chua
3 Verus	macotono	cin	1 bloi
4 Domin.	arugi	chu	2 det
5 Homo	fito	gin	nguei
6 Vir	votocò	nàn	cònblai
7 Mulier	vonna	niu	congai
8 Uxor	tſuma	tſi	boe
9 Maritus	vottò	fu	ciaum
10 Pater	cici	fù	cia
11 Mater	fafa	mu	me
12 Frater	ani vòtoto hium ti		aim em
13 Soror	ymoto ane mui		ci em
14 Filius	co	tſu	con nam
15 Filia	muſume	niu tſu	con nu
16 Avus	vogi	tſu	om
17 Avia	uba	tſu mu	ba
18 Puer, pu-ella	varabe co-muſume	thom nieu	con blai tle
19 Coelum	ten	thien	bloi
20 Ignis	fi	ho	lua
21 Aer	fuki	khî	khi
22 Aqua	mizzu	xui	nuoe
23 Terra	ci	tî	det
24 Sol	fi	ge	mât bloi
25 Luna	tſuki	yue	mât blam
26 Stellae	foxi	ſim	ſau
27 Mons	yama	ſcian	nui
		H	28 Fla-

Figure 6. "Tabella vocum cum pronuntiatione earum Japonica, Sinica et Annamitica" (Reland 1708: 113)

Reland's version has no separate column with Chinese characters, but there is one page where the Chinese characters are reproduced. As Duyvendak (1936: 323) demonstrates, "the errors and confusions of the glossary are too numerous to be here enumerated". The page of Reland with numbered Chinese characters (Figure 8) is a copy, in terms of characters used, of Palmeiro, but numbers are wrong. For instance, 15 must be *Filia*, but the character is given of *Avus* (*zu gong* 祖公). This word, moreover, differs from Palmeiro, where we have only <tsú> (*zu*) and not *zugong*.

Figure 7. The word list starting with the *tetragrammaton* (f. 9r)

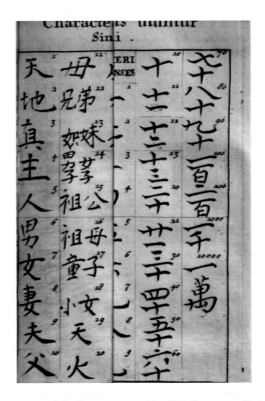

Figure 8. Chinese version of the first section of the *Tabella vocum* (Reland 1708: 112)

The final question to be raised is what happened with the original manuscript which was used by Reland. As Kuiper (2005: 129–130) observes, the manuscript was borrowed by Phillipe Masson. In Bart Jaski's catalogue (Jaski forthcoming, no. 25) the title appears.

> Cat. Van Voorst 1859: 'Miscellanea quaedam Sinica, partim a P. Martinio ejusque famulo Sinensi Dominico accepta, partim ex eorundem ore per me (J. Golium) excerpta; item quaesita varia, imprimis circa computum Sinarum astronomicum. In fol. 76 pag. Rel, en vélin …'. This title is also mentioned in Reland 1708, p. 111 (stating that Golius had written the title on the bundle of papers) and on London, British Library, Sloane 2746, fol. 213r (Cat. Golius [=*Catalogus Insignium*] 1696, p. 26, 2), for which see Duyvendak 1936, p. 321, and Kuiper 2005, p. 129. Sloane 2746 was in the possession of Philippe Mason before 1713, and later acquired by Sir Hans Sloane (1660–1753). The item at A qu 25 was probably a copy of a part of the original documents written by Justus Heurnius (1587–1661/2); several other existed.
> (Jaski 2021: 440–441)

In this section we have demonstrated that Jacques and Pham's research has been corroborated by additional evidence from some centuries ago. Bayer's suspicions were correct: Alexandre de Rhodes was the author, or maybe someone else, who had dwelled in the territories of Annam, and not Martini. Pham's research confirms that the Palmeiro's appended report is indeed written by Alexandre de Rhodes and we have demonstrated that this text reached intellectual circles in Europe long before it was "re-discovered" by others. The section in Reland not only includes an almost identical version of the quadrilingual wordlist, but also refers to the *Oratio Dominica*[40] and the introductory remarks about the linguistic situation in Asia, the "universal" features of the Chinese script, compared with the symbols used in the Arabic numeral system. Since all these elements are mentioned by Reland, and since all of them are indeed documented in Palmeiro's letter, we can conclude that there was at least another copy, or maybe even more copies of this remarkable text circulating in various circles and that these were already diffused and discussed

---

40. "In iis quoque inveni Orationem Dominicam Sinicis notis expressam cum pronuntiatione Sinica & earundem interpretatione Sinica Latina a P. Martinio exarata, una cum Symbolo Apostolico, Decalogo, & brevi Catechismo; ad quorum omnium singulas voces character Sinicus penicillo, ut Sinae solent, appictus, & ejus pronuntiatio & interpretatio est addita" (Reland 1708: 111). [In these papers I have also found the Lord's prayer noted down in Chinese characters with the Chinese pronunciation and their Latin interpretation written/suggested by Father Martinius, together with the Creed, the Decalogue and a short Catechism; the Chinese character corresponding to every single word of all of these was painted up, as is the Chinese custom, with a brush, along with its pronunciation and interpretation.]

in Europe over the second half of the 17th and the first half of the 18th century. It is plausible that whoever asked for the document was the one who circulated it, maybe one of the Propaganda Fide cardinals, but this assumption is based on mere speculation.

We observed that Palmeiro's letter and Reland's printed version are "almost identical". Nevertheless, there are some differences. As we shall demonstrate below, Palmeiro's document has some corrections inside the wordlist. There are two corrections in the Chinese word list <chai> is corrected as <ciāi> and <chi> as <cin>. In the Vietnamese word list of Palmeiro's letter we find the Italian spelling <ciüá>, whereas Reland has the Portuguese <chua>, which demonstrates that Reland has taken his examples from another copy in which this example was not adapted or corrected to Italian orthography. In the Chinese section of Palmeiro's letter, we find the numeral 2 written as <lh˜> (the tilde appears after the <h>), whereas Reland has <ul>, as it is often spelled elsewhere, representing /ɚ/ (Raini 2010: 82). The same occurs systematically in the numerals 12, 20 and 21. The Japanese word <scioguaci> in Palmeiro's letter follows Italian orthography, which appears as <xioguaci> in Reland's text, in agreement with the Portuguese orthography, which also demonstrates that Reland has taken his examples from another copy in which these examples are not adapted or corrected to Italian orthography.

Table 2. Differences in spelling between Palmeiro's letter and Reland

Palmeiro	Reland
Japanese	
<scioguaci> (f.11r)	<xioguaci> (p. 115)
Chinese	
(2) <lh˜>	<ul>
(12) <xē lh˜>	<xe ul>
(20) <lh˜ xē>	<ul xê>
(21) <lh˜ xē yē>	<ul xê ye>
Vietnamese	
<ciüá>	<chua>

4. The linguistic introduction

4.1   Asian languages, glottonyms and linguistic varieties

The Latin section,[41] copied by Alexandre de Rhodes, opens with the three glotto-
nyms, the lingua Sinica, lingua Japonica, and Annam ['Annamese'], consistently abbreviated, as Annam not "Annamitica", throughout the entire text), which is spoken
in the Northern region, Tonkin, and in the South, Cochinchina ['quae Tonkinam
et Cocincinam complectitur'].[42]

Furthermore, a distinction has to be made between "Chinese proper" ['sinicum
proprium'] and "corrupted Chinese ['sinicum corruptum'], which has been omitted
['quod omittimus']. The variety which is chosen for Chinese, is what the Portuguese
call "the language of the Mandarins", which is commonly used in the missions ['eo
quod existimavimus sufficere sinicum proprium quo Sinae in sua curia utantur, et
mandarinicum vocant Lusitani']. Dialectal varieties of each province are infinite,
and differences are not less bigger than those between Italian and Spanish ['non sit
minor inter illos differentia quam inter italicam et hispanicam']. These varieties are
derived all from Mandarin ['harum tamen omnium origo est ista quam mandarini-
cam vocant'], the language which was adopted by the Japanese and the Vietnamese,
together with their characters ['illam Japones et Annam simul cum characteribus
acceperunt'], but rather corrupt and accomodated to their own language. General
Chinese is not intelligible for Japanese and Vietnamese. Neither the Japanese nor
the Vietnamese understand Chinese but only those who are educated, and among
them it has the same status as Latin among us ['Illa tamen in vulgari sermone, nec
illam vulgo intelligunt sive Japones sive Annam, sed solum qui literas didicerunt,
et apud illos se habet sicuti apud nos latina lingua'].

The Japanese and Vietnamese also use their own languages. Their own language, however, which the Japanese or Vietnamese use in general, does not depend
more on the Chinese language than German depends on Latin ['propria tamen
qua vulgó utuntur sive Japones sive Annam, non magis á sinica pendet quam
Germanica a latina'].

---

41. For the complete text and translation, see the appendix.

42. De Rhodes learned "Cochinchinese" in four months, and later he learned "Tonkinese" between 1627 and 1630, the period which immediately precedes his stay in Macau. This explains his
choice (cf. Pham 2018: 225). The Portuguese Jesuits had missions in both regions and described
both varieties. The Province of Japan, headquartered at Macau, included South East Asia as well
as Japan, and after 1658 southern China.

4.2   The Chinese characters (f. 7r)

Chinese characteres ['characteres'][43] are like hieroglyphs ['characteres jerogliphicos'], each one of them means a different concept ['qui singulas dictiones singuli
proferant']. These characters are common for the three languages ['communes
quidem esse tribus his linguis'] and they can refer to the same object, although
they are pronounced differently ['eandemque rem ipsis significare diverso tamen
idiomate proferri'], as occurs in European languages with the symbols 1, 2, 3, ['sicuti et apud Europaeos numerorum characteres 1 2 3 etc.'].The Japanese have also
other characters which are commonly used ['Japones tamen alios etiam habent
characteres quibus vulgo utuntur'].[44] In this text only Chinese characters are given,
not the Japanese ones, since the Chinese are commonly used ['ideo solum sinicos
subjicio qui omnibus sunt communes'].

4.3   Romanization (f. 7r)

4.3.1   *Tone diacritics*
It is hardly possible to represent the genuine pronunciation ['germanam pronuntiationem'] of these languages with our letters ['nostris characteribus'], in particular
Chinese and Vietnamese, because the different meanings of the words depend
heavily on the different tones. It is obvious that the author here was aware that
tones are phonemically important, mainly in these two languages, Chinese and
Vietnamese ['exprimi sinicae praesertim et Annam, eo quod ex tono diverso qui
literis diversis exprimi non potest vocabulorum diversitas maxime pendeat'], and
that this feature is less prominent in Japanese, although he does not exclude the
existence of tones in Japanese explicitly (using the word "praesertim" is important,

---

43. The Latin word 'character' is a loanword from Greek (χαρακτήρ,'brand', 'stamp', 'impress',
'distinctive mark'. which is derived from χαράσσω, 'to brand', 'engrave', 'carve', 'inscribe'). In
Lucian's *Hermotimus* the term is used with the meaning of 'sign', opposed to γράμματα. (Luc,
Herm. 44):
    https://www.loebclassics.com/view/lucian-hermotimus_sects/1959/pb_LCL430.345.xml

44. The Visitor Alessandro Valignano (1539–1606) brought the press to the Jesuit college at
Kazusa in the Nagasaki prefecture in 1590 with carved wooden types, possibly manufactured in
Macau (Moran 1993: 155), starting with printing in *katakana* (one of the two syllabaries); *kanji*
characters have been available since the start of printing. For the printing of the confessionary
Salvator mundi (1598) onwards, metal Japanese types were used. In the same year, the dictionary
called *Rakuyōshū* (see below) was printed in *kana* and in the Chinese/Japanese *kanji* characters
(for more details and references, see Zwartjes 2011b: 93–94).

i.e. "mainly Chinese and Vietnamese").[45] We use the Greek accents, the acute, grave and circumflex, and if the differences [in tones] are not understood and perceived, it is hardly possible to express the genuine differences between them. Furthermore, the tone differences are compared with musical terms. The author uses a loanword from Italian "falsetto", diminutive of "falso" ('false') not existing in Classical Latin, designating the voice register or frequency range higher than the modal voice, and "bassi" is used for the low register. The circumflex is compared with the modulating (lit. "bending", 'inflectere') the intonation as in interrogations ['in modum falseti musici proferat, gravi vero in modum bassi, circunflexo denique vocem inflectendo ad modum interrogantis']. In fact, the author also describes the meaning of a 'zero-marker', (using no diacritic) ['vocabula nullo accentu notata'], to be pronounced without any "modulation".[46] No mention is made of other diacritics, such as the 'jota subscript' and the interrogation mark used later in Alexandre de Rhodes's *Dictionarium.*[47]

4.3.2 *Aspiration. (f. 7r)*

In both Chinese and Vietnamese, aspiration occurs frequently ['Aspirationes in his linguis sinica et Annam esse frequentissimas'] and their equivalents are the graphs *ph, kh, th* as in Greek φ, χ, θ, and pronounced with 'rough breathing', as in German or Dutch, whereas other words are pronounced as in Italian ['ut in *ph, kh, th* aequivalent enim aspiratis φ, χ, θ, cum asperé pronuntiantur ut á Germanis aut Belgis, in reliquis pronuntiatione Italica secuti sumus plerumque'], as we can find in the many Italian-based romanizations in the word list, to be discussed below.

---

45. Most varieties of Japanese have a pitch accent and the existence of tones in Japanese is a matter of debate.

46. In fact, in the Latin text we see two different categories, "low and high", as in register-tone languages which uses tones as level, and "pitch movements", as occurs in interrogations, as occurs in contour-tone languages. The diacritics are used for Vietnamese and Chinese. Mandarin Chinese has contour tones, such as rising, falling. In Vietnamese tones are accompanied by other phonation differences, such as glottalization and the use of creaky or breathy voice. This may explain why romanizations of Chinese and Vietnamese do not use diacritics exclusively for tone differences, but aspiration and vowel qualities are also marked; the first with the *spiritus asper*, the second using a dot ("puntillo") in Varo's terminology, or iota subscript in de Rhodes's romanization of Vietnamese.

47. "Utimur ergo triplici accentu linguae graecae, acuto, gravi & circunflexo, qui quia non sufficiunt, addimus iota subscriptum, & signum interrogationis nostrae" (Rhodes 1651b: 8). [We use the three accent from the Greek language, the acute, grave and the circumflex. Since these are not sufficient, we have added the sign for the iota subscript and our interrogation mark.]

4.4   Comparative syntax: Word order (*collocatio*)(f. 8v)

The author observes that the *Pater noster* is not translated word-for-word, since the word order ['collocatio'] in the three Asian languages is completely different from each other, and also differ from the Latin word order. There are generally not always direct equivalents in these languages horizontally arranged in each column from left to right, as occurs in the glossary. The translations must be read from top to bottom and do not follow the translation strategy of word-for-word ['verbum verbo'] but sentence-to-sentence ['oratio orationi']. The text illustrates what would have happened if we would translate word-for-word the Latin phrase "pater noster qui es in coelis", this would be:

– In Japanese: "coelis in es Pater noster"
– In Chinese: "es coelis noster pater"
– In Vietnamese: "Pater noster es in coelis"

The author is not the first Jesuit in Asia who compares word order in different languages. João Rodrigues reports that Japanese has a 'reverse word order' compared to the European languages.[48]

4.5   The lack of relative pronouns (f. 8v)

When the invited experts in Chinese, Japanese and Vietnamese were asked to translate the sentence "Pater noster qui es in coelis", they concluded that there is no equivalent of the Latin relative pronoun *qui* (the three word-for-word translations of the Latin phrase "pater noster qui es in coelis" clearly demonstrate that "qui" is

---

48. ".. a collocaçam das partes da oração contraria a das nossas lingoas de Europa ..." (1620: 'Ao leitor', no numbered pages). According to Rodrigues, word order in Japanese is twofold, depending on the 'style'. *Coye* is the style which follows the strict 'Chinese' order ("que propriamente he a Sinica, donde vieram as letras, he direita a nosso modo", 1620: 60r), opposed to *Yomi*, which is 'natural' for Japanese ("que he a propria, & natural de Iapam, tem contraria ordem no fallar", *ibid.*). In *Coye* syntax, the particles are placed in initial position, whereas in *Yomi* syntax, the 'suposto do verbo' (the subject of the verb), also often called the 'nominative', is in the initial position, which is considered 'natural' for Japanese. For Vietnamese, not many rules are given by de Rhodes in his grammar; subjects must precede the verb, and he provides an example in order to demonstrate that word order is crucial in distinguishing the syntactic function of the participants, as in the two examples *tôi mến Chúa* ['ego amo Dominum'] versus etc. *Chúa mến tôi* ['Dominus amat me'] (De Rhodes 1651b: 29; Zwartjes 2011b: 295). There are no extant grammars of Mandarin Chinese from this early period. In Martini's grammar, syntax or word order are not described. In later grammars, such as the *Arte de la lengua mandarina* of the Dominican Francisco Varo, syntax and word order is treated in detail (Varo 1703: Chapter XI: "Del modo de formar las oraçiones" [On the Way of Forming Sentences]; ff. 68–71).

left untranslated). The scribe (Alexandre de Rhodes) claims that these languages do not have them, but they are "understood from different word orders" ['carent autem hae linguae pronomine relativo, ex diversa tamen collocatione id subauditur']. Of course, this information maybe does not represent exactly the "minutes" of these meetings, since it is also possible that Alexandre de Rhodes used other written sources and added some observations from his own. In the first place, the non-existence of the relative pronouns in Japanese has been documented by João Rodrigues. Japanese is a left branching and word final language, which means that the concept of "antecedent" as we know it from Latin is inapplicable. Adjectives and adverbial embedded clauses are placed on the left of the head, preceding the main clause. Rodrigues's describes the relative pronoun ['provocabulo *qui, quae, quod*'] as follows:

> Carece esta lingoa dos provocabulos relatiuos, que respondem a *Qui, quae, quod*, 'o que', 'a que', 'o qual' …, & quando a oraçam he relatiua, suprem o relatiuo tacitamente no modo de fallar & collocaçam do antecedente em respeito do verbo, de que se rege. Geralmente, quando a oraçam he relatiua, o antecede[n]te, ou a cousa referida se pospoem immediatamente ao verbo, pondo no primeiro lugar, a oraçam, onde entra a voz relatiua em nossa lingoa, & depois a oraçam, donde se rege o antecedente.   (Rodrigues 1620: 17v)[49]

> [This language does not have the relative pronouns that correspond with *qui, quae, quod* (or [Portuguese] 'o que', 'a que', 'o cual',…etc.). When the clause is a relative, the relative pronoun is silently surpressed in speech and in the positioning of the antecedent with regard to the verb which governs it. In general, when the clause is a relative, the antecedent, or the thing referred to, is postponed directly after the verb, putting on the first position the [subordinate] clause, where in our language the relative pronoun appears, and it is placed after the clause which is governed by the antecedent.]

Indeed, in Japanese different constructions have to be searched for in order to translate the relative clause, but when Alexandre de Rhodes observes that "ex diversa tamen collocatione id subauditur" he refers apparently to Vietnamese, but we do not exclude the possibility that the expression "subauditur" was inspired by Rodrigues's "suprem tacitamente".[50] Later, in his grammar published in 1651, we find a more detailed description of the non-existence of the relative pronoun, and

---

49. There are also examples in Japanese, illustrating how relative clauses are translated, and the author comes back to the topic in the section on Syntax (f. 63r), where he also refers to his *Arte Grande*, although he admits that the description is there quite "diffuse".

50. See for a possible influence of Rodrigues's work on de Rhodes the paper of Kishimoto in this book.

how they are expressed, or tacitly understood in Vietnamese, using different word orders (*collocationes*):

> Non datur propriè relatiuum qui quae, quod, sed praeponendo nomen & ex oratio passiua faciendo actiuam, ut *mày đặọc sách*, 'tu legis librum', si dicam, *sách, mày đặọc*, idest 'liber à te lectus' sive, 'liber quem tu legis', *nó làm việc*, 'ille facit opus', si dicam *việc nó làm*, 'opus ab illo factum', vel 'opus quid ille facit' & sic de reliquis.
>
> (de Rhodes 1651b: 21)

> [An appropriate relative as *qui quae quod* is not given, but instead, the noun of a passive clause is preposed in the active, as *mày đặọc sách*, "you read a book", as if I would say *sách, mày đặọc*, which means "the book read by you", "the book that you read".]

On the same page of his grammar, de Rhodes gives also a translation of the *Pater Noster*:

> … reliqua de relatiuis vsus docebit, vt, *Cha chúng tôi ở tlên blời*. 'Pater noster qui est in coelis', & *lạy Cha chúng tôi ở tlên blời*. 'Pater noster qui es in coelis'.
>
> (De Rhodes ibid.)[51]

> [Other matters concerning the relatives will be learned in practice, as in *Cha chúng tôi ở tlên blời*. 'Pater noster qui est in coelis' ("Our Father who is in Heaven"), & *lạy Cha chúng tôi ở tlên blời*. 'Pater noster qui es in coelis' ("Our Father who art in Heaven")]

In Chinese, it is indeed true that there is usually no relative pronoun in the relative clause, which is a usual property of prenominal relative clauses. Unlike European as English, Dutch and Spanish, *wh*-words in Mandarin can only introduce interrogatives, whereas in most European languages these interrogatives can be also used for relativization (Wen 2020: 51). Relative clauses precede the noun they modify and are marked with the final particle *de* (的), for example, 吃的; *chī de* 'eat (particle)' may mean 'that which is eaten', i.e. 'food', or 'those who eat' (Sun 2006: 187–189). There are no extant grammars of the language called *lengua mandarina* by the Spaniards, or *língua mandarina* in Portuguese[52] antedating Palmeiro's epistle, so

---

51. We can see here how the romanization of Vietnamese has evolved in the 19 years between the *Epistola* and the Propaganda Fide grammar published in 1651. The *Epistola* has *cia ciúm toi ẽ tlen blœi*. The only difference in the two examples in the printed grammar is the word *lại*, which has several meanings. The dictionary gives the meaning 'vir' ('man'), 'iterum' ('again') and "copulam carnale habere siue licitam, sive illicitam" / 'ajuntarse cõ molher', written with the same tone diacritic and obviously not applicable in this context. This also demonstrates that it is indeed true that tone differences were crucial, but even when the tones are pronounced correctly, there are still great risques that homophones can lead to serious misunderstandings.

52. The only complete grammars antedating Palmeiro's epistle are the ones describing Early Manila Hokkien (Southern Mǐn) (cf. Klöter 2011).

we are not able to verify if the Chinese informants gave their input from previous sources, or if they came to the conclusion that Chinese would not have any relative pronouns, having in mind examples like those cited here. On the other hand, it is also true that in Martini's grammar, there is no section on relative pronouns, but in Francisco Varo's (1627–1687) grammar a section is devoted to the relative pronouns (Varo 2000 [1703]: f.40–41).[53]

4.6   The tetragrammaton (f. 9r)

In this section we analyse the fragment regarding the *tetragrammaton*. In Hebrew, the four letters יהוה, (JHWH) is the name for God. For Jews who follow the Talmudic traditions, the tetragrammaton is ineffable, unutterable (i.e. never pronounced) and instead, the *tetragrammaton* is substituted with a different term, such as *hakadosh baruch hu* ['The Holy One, Blessed Be He'], *Adonai* ['My Lord'], or *HaShem* ['The Name']. The Septuagint translates the tetragrammaton as Κύριος (*Kyrios*) ['Lord'] and in the Latin Vulgate *Dominus* ['Lord'] is used, a translation of the Hebrew *Adonai*. It would require much more space to summarize the various translation strategies in missionary dictionaries of the period under study, but in the section of the Latin text appended to Palmeiro's letter, we read that in these three languages (Japanese, Chinese and Vietnamese), there is not one word for God ['Praeterea cum in his tribus linguis nulla sit vox quae unica nomen Dei explicet absque erroris periculo'], but they invented neologisms, according to this letter, based on Matthew 11 and the Acts of the Apostles (*actus* 17: 24) "Father, Lord of Heaven and Earth", for which four Chinese characters are given, in order to render "the ineffable tetra-grammaton".[54] The term tetragrammaton does not refer to the four radical letters <JHWH> in Hebrew, but to the four characters in Chinese that are given for Latin *coelum, terra, verus* and *Dominus*.

---

53. Varo sums up *tiè, chè, t'ā, chī, k'y, fân* and *tán fân* and gives examples for each.

54. In the Vulgata: "In illo tempore respondens Jesus dixit: Confiteor tibi, Pater, Domine caeli et terrae, quia abscondisti haec a sapientibus, et prudentibus, et revelasti ea parvulis" (Matthew 11, 25) [At that time Jesus said, "I praise you, Father, Lord of heaven and earth, because you have hidden these things from the wise and learned, and revealed them to little children.]. Acts of the apostles (actus 17: 24): "Deus, qui fecit mundum et omnia, quae in eo sunt, hic, caeli et terrae cum sit Dominus, non in manufactis templis inhabitat" [The God that made the world and all things therein, he, being Lord of heaven and earth, dwelleth not in temples made with hands.] (quoted from the *Nova vulgata,* online). For more background information of Jesuit theologists regarding the concept of "ineffability" and how the name must be "communicabilis", see for instance the *quaestio XIII* entitled "De Nominibus Dei" in Diego Ruiz de Montoya Hispalensis's (1562–1632) work *Commentaria* (1625) and Antonio Bernaldo de Quirós Tordelagunensis's 1613–1668) *Selectae disputationes* (1654).

In this text, the four Chinese characters correspond with the Latin words and are numbered 1, 2, 3, 4, whereas the Vietnamese version has a translation in a different order: 3, 4, 1, 2. Alexandre de Rhodes wrote in the margin "Hoc ordine proferunt ut faciant sensum" [They pronounce it in this order, so that they make sense]. The history of the translations of the "nomen ineffabilis" as "tertagramma-ton" goes at least back to Valignano's *Catechismus*, written in Japan from 1579 and 1582 and published in 1586 (Valignano 1586), the *Dochirina Kirishitan* ドチリナ・キリシタン) Ruggieri's *The True Record of the Lord of Heaven* (*Tianzhu shilu* 天主實錄, 1585), and Ricci's True meaning of the Lord of Heaven (*Tianzhu shiyi* 天主實義, first published in 1603), imported to Japan in 1605. The Society of Jesus had a central administration in Rome. The most important role of the visitations in the Provinces was "to bring the spirit of the Society's founders from Rome to the provinces. That is, the inspections were intended as pastoral exercises, not inquis-itorial ones. The visitor, as a representative of the superior general, was to act as a peacemaker between factions…" (Brockey 2014: 13). One of the tasks of Palmeiro as Visitor, was to take decisions in establishing the most adequate translation of the word for God in these remote regions, where many proposed translations of-ten had different connotations, in particular when such terms were also used in Buddhism, Confucianism, Taoism, and 'indigenous' beliefs, such as Shintoism in Japan or those in Vietnam.

The Japanese glosses for 天地真主 are given as *ten, cino macotono arugi.* (Kornicki 1993: 517) (i.e. *tenchi no makoto no aruji*). There are no *kana* symbols used, such as の (the particle *no* is used in possessive constructions) in addition to the *kanji*; only the romanization in Japanese is given. As occurs later in China and Vietnam, there was a discussion among the Jesuits how to translate the word for God into Japanese. The earliest attempt was the proposal by Francis Xavier (1506–1552) who used in 1549 mistakenly the word *Dainichi* (大日), the name of one of the Buddhas (Tollini 2018: 95). The alternative was the word *aruji* (主), also used in the *Vocabulário da Lingoa de Iapam* (*Nippō jisho*) and translated as "senhor, ou senhora, ou dono [owner] da cousa" ("gentleman or lady, or owner of something, without any reference to God"; Tollini 96–97). As Tollini (ibid.) demonstrates we find terms composed with *ten* 天 ['sky', 'heaven']. As Phan (1998: 116) demonstrates, Ricci's text has been the source of inspiration for de Rhodes's *Catechismus*, written prob-ably between 1636 and 1645, but printed in Rome in 1651 (Phan 1998: 123). The translation of the word for God was a matter of debate in Japan, China and Vietnam. As Phan demonstrates (1998: 135), "Ricci argued that it would be inappropriate to designate God with words such as "Supreme Ultimate" (*T'ai-chi*) and "Principle" (*li*), as the Neo-Confucianist philosophers appeared to him to have done". Ricci proposed to use the three words for Heaven (*tian*), sovereign on high (*shangdi*) and

Lord of heaven (*tianzhu*, or *tiandi*). The discussions lead to the final official ban of the use of these three concepts which together designate the name of God in 1693. De Rhodes's firstly objected the use of the two Vietnamese words *but* and *phat*, which were used for Buddha. Francesco Buzomi (1576–1639) proposed the use of the Chinese concept (*tianzhu*), in Vietnamese *tianzhu* and in 1626, during a general meeting of Jesuit missionaries in Cochinchina in which de Rhodes and Buzomi participated, it was agreed that the expression *Tianzhu* could be adopted, which are in fact used here as two of the four Vietnamese concepts of the *tetragrammaton* of Palmeiro's epistle. Later, in his *Catechismus* de Rhodes decided not to use the Chinese concepts of *tianzhu* and introduces the four concepts *đức* ['Noble'], *chúa* ['Lord'], *trời* ['Heaven'], *đất* ['earth'] ['= the Noble Lord of Heaven and Earth'] (Phan 1998: 136–137; 164–165). It appears also in his *Dictionarium*: (117) translated as "O S[enh]or do ceo e da terra: Dominus caeli & terrae, nomen quo vocatur apud Tunchinenses Deus".

Palmeiro's epistle has a different translation of the word for God: *blœì-đét-thāt-ciüá*. Apparently, de Rhodes decided to omit the concept of 'True' (Latin 'verus') later in his *Dictionarium* and his *Catechismus*. The Vietnamese equivalent for Latin 'verus' is *thāt* according to the romanization of 1632, which is later rendered as *thật* in his dictionary (in Modern Vietnamese *thật* ('real', 'true'). In the lemma of this word we do not find the expression *Duc Chua Troi Dat*, but it is only translated ('verdade, certo, veritas', etc.) (1651a: 752 and 760). His choice of an equivalent for the name for Heaven is more complex. In his dictionary, we find the entries of the Vietnamese concept of *blời* ['ceo, caelum'] ('heaven') (1651a: 45) (which corresponds with *troi*), and the Chinese term *Thien* (1651a: 762–763) 'coelum' and *Thien Chua* ['coeli Dominus']; *Chúa blời* ('Senhor de ceo, caeli Dominus, melius *thien chúa*'). The addition of 'melius' ('better') reflects the decision made by de Rhodes between 1632, when he wrote the text of Palmeiro's epistle, and the moment he published his dictionary and catechism. Phan observes that de Rhodes "preferred the expression *Chua Troi Dat* instead of *Thien Chua*", but the expression of 'melius' leads to an opposite conclusion.[55]

In the dictionaries of the Dominicans, we find the expression of 'verus' as well, in the Chinese name for God: "el verdadero señor de cielo y tierra".[56]

---

55. In the *Catechismus*, we find many other words for God, corresponding with expressions like "The Noble Supreme Lord", "Supreme Lord above all things", "the supreme Artisan", "the sovereign on high or august emperor" (Phan 1998: 137).

56. In Chinese: *Tiēn^c tý chīn chủ* (Varo 2006 [between 1677–1687]: 213).

The main objective of Palmeiro's letter was to demonstrate that the three Asian languages were different from each other, but probably, a secondary implicit objective could have been to demonstrate that there was a consensus in the translation strategies in light of the longstanding (over a decade) arguments over the terms. The Japanese and Vietnamese translations were all derived from the same source, the four Chinese characters which were on their turn derived from the Latin Vulgate. As Brockey (2014: 18) demonstrates, Palmeiro's role was the assessment of the attitudes and methods of translation. The translations of the name for God in these languages were a clear attempt to show to the Superior General Vitelleschi that in Asia, there was one synchronized translation, although arranged in a different order, all based on the four Chinese characters, as a direct answer to the many debates about the terms proposed by others, such as the pioneering Jesuits Valignano and Ricci and, more importantly, the Jesuits exiled from Japan who were in Macau in the late 1610s and 1620s. Although Palmeiro was not proficient in any of these three languages, he trusted that the language specialists of each language gave him unanimously the best translation for the name of God, as represented by the four Chinese characters of the tetragrammaton. In the context of the Terms Controversy, Palmeiro was against the use of *cobitas*: transliterations from European languages, and when it was decided to avoid terms like *Shangdi*, and *Tian* the Jesuits were expected to return to the Chinese lexicon (Brockey 2014: 312–313). The four Chinese characters were the source text for the translations into Vietnamese and Japanese, but later, in 1651, Alexandre de Rhodes decided to follow his own translation strategy, combining elements from Sino-Vietnamese (Sino-xenic), and "pure" Vietnamese terms (Phan 1998: 136).

4.7   Glosses in the margins

Palmeiro's letter does not contain a theoretical introduction but there are also some glosses written in the margins of the word lists which deserve our attention. There are only glosses relating to Chinese and Vietnamese, no comments are written referring to Japanese. These glosses, grosso modo, are verbatim the same as the ones found in other writings of de Rhodes, such as his historical treatise *Royaume* and his printed Propaganda Fide grammar of 1651.

Table 3. Glosses in the margins

Chinese	
tsāi (f.7r)	*ts* idem atque hebraeis צ *tsadê* [The \<ts\> is pronounced as in Hebrew צ *tsadê*]
ngó (f. 7r)	*ng* idem atque hebraeis ע *ngain* [\<ng\> like in Hebrew ע *ngain*]*
lh' (f. 7v)	pronuntiatur absque uocali lingua palato admota [\<lh\> is pronounced without a vowel, putting the tongue to the palate.]**
ā mēm 亞孟 (f. 8v)	His duabus literis exprimunt Sinę uocem, Amen, non eius significationem [With these two characters, the Chinese represent the word "Amen" and not its meaning.]

Vietnamese	
3, 4, 1, 2 (f. 7r)	Hoc ordine proferunt ut faciant sensum [They pronounce it in this order, so that they make sense.]
æ̃ (f. 9r)	diphtongus *œ* pronuntiatur ut a Gallis in voce *oeil* oculus [The diphtongue *œ* is pronounced as French *oeil* ("eye").]
sam̀ (f. 7v)	litera *s* in hac lingua est aspera ac si esset duplex*** [In this language, the letter \<s\> is sharp, as if it is a double \<ss\>.]
đen (f. 7v)	hoc notatum signo non est parú[m] *d* latinú[m], sed quid mediú[m] inter *d* et *r* huius linguae proprium [the sign *đ* is not like Latin \<d\> but it is an proper sound in this language.]

Japanese: No glosses	

* "Alium habet usum litera, *g*, praeponendo illi, *n*, vt, *ngà*, 'ebur', & habet pronunciationem seu aequiualet *ngain* ע Hebraeo" (De Rhodes 1651b: 4). [The letter **g** has another use: preceding it with an **n**, as in **ngà** (ivory), whereby it is pronounced or is the equivalent of the Hebrew **ngain** ע.] (Translation Gaudio 2019: 85).
** In other romanizations, often spelled as \<ul\>, representing /ə/ (Raini 2010: 82).
*** S, Est solùm in usu in principio dictionis, & cum maiori asperitate, quàm nostrum, quasi esset duplex, & cum minori sibilo: pronunciatur autem cum quadam inflectione linguae ad palatum ut, *sa*, 'cadere': in medio, aut in fine dictionis nunquam reperitur (De Rhodes 1651b: 6). [S is only in use at the beginning of a word and with more aspiration than our s, as if it were doubled and with less hissing. However, it is pronounced with the same curving of the tongue at the palate, as in *sa* (to fall). It is never found in the middle at the end of a word.] (Translation Gaudio 2019: 88).

5. The romanization systems

5.1   Introduction

Alexandre de Rhodes wrote a text based on his linguistic inquiries and the input of the different language specialist. In general, in the romanization systems of the three Asian languages, we can trace influences from the native languages of the authors. Some of them evolved into an orthographical tradition based on

Portuguese whereas others were based on Italian, Spanish or French. Frequently, such spelling discrepancies are discussed by the missionary-linguists themselves.[57] Since the Jesuits working in Macau came from many different nations, and spoke different European languages, it was important to make some decisions. Alexandre de Rhodes obviously operates here as an editor of the minutes, attempting to give one consistent romanization system. He explicitly claims that the Italian spelling conventions will be used ("in reliquis pronuntiatione Italica secuti sumus plerum-que"). It will be difficult to know if the Italianizing tendencies in the spelling of some words are in fact the editing work of Alexandre de Rhodes himself, or that this was the result of the input of Italian-speaking Jesuits, such as the Italian Jesuit Majorica (1591–1656), who was in Macau until October 1631. In a broader context, this editing policy could have been developed in order not to find only one standard romanization system for one of these languages, but for these three languages. It seems that in Macau, it was a desideratum among the Jesuits to synchronize the different romanization systems developed for each single language, in order to create a more "universally applicable" romanization system in which the same symbol, letter or diacritic would represent the same (or approximate) phoneme.

5.2   Japanese

Jesuit missionaries began to produce studies of the Japanese language in c.1552.[58] In 1595 an anonymous trilingual Latin-Portuguese-Japanese dictionary, *Dictionarium Latino Lusitanicum, ac Iaponicum*, was published in Amakusa (Anonymous 1595). Another dictionary composed by some Fathers and Brothers ('alguns Padres e Irmãos') of the Society of Jesus appeared in 1603; the *Vocabulario da Lingoa de Iapam com a declaração em Portugues* published at Nagasaki by the Collegio de Iapam da Companhia de Iesus, with a supplement which appeared in 1604 (Anonymous 1603–1604). Grammars were produced by João Rodrigues (*Arte grande*, published in Japan and *Arte breve*, printed in Macau in 1620. Diego de

---

57. For instance, in Spanish Dominican sources we find remarks on orthographical conventions of the Portuguese Jesuits (Padres de la Compañía), as in Marsh 696 (Anonymous c.1642) and in Varo's Mandarin grammar, and later, Melchor Oyanguren de Santa Inés (1688–1747) also refers to the Portuguese romanization system in his grammar of Tagalog (1743) in which Chinese grammar rules are included. (see for more details Zwartjes 2010).

58. The pioneering Jesuits are Duarte da Silva (1536–1564), João Fernandes (Juan Fernández, 1526–1567) and Luis Frois (1532–1597). In the annual reports of the Jesuits of 1585, the production of dictionaries and grammars in the Colleges of Funai and Arima is documented (see also Zwartjes 2011b: 93–94).

Collado (c. 1587–1638), author of a Latin-language grammar of Japanese (Collado 1632a), also produced a dictionary (Collado 1632b) and a catechism (Collado 1632c).[59] The first was mainly based on the *Dictionarium* of 1603–1604, but the author warns his readers that they should rely on the Spanish, rather than on the Latin explanation of Japanese, since he added the Latin version at the last minute by order of his superiors of the *Propaganda Fide*. For reasons of space, we cannot give here a comprehensive overview of the history of the romanization of Japanese, but we shall select some conspicuous features of the *Oratio dominica* (*Pater noster*) and the word list included in Palmeiro's letter.

In the Japanese data from Palmeiro the 'Japonice' column gives the Japanese vernacular readings of the characters exclusively, except for the concept of 'coelum' for which <ten> is given as romanization, which is the Sino-xenic reading of 天.[60]

As the author observes, word order in Japanese is completely different from Chinese, Vietnamese, or Latin. This means that this word list is arranged in such a manner that the Japanese appear after the Latin words, as if they were direct translations. This is not always the case (in the word-list, we find one to one translations). This means that a person who does not know Japanese could have the impression that *nacare* is a translation of Latin *tentationem*, which might surprise the user, since the loanword 'tentationi' is also found in the same phrase in the Japanese version (*nakare* from *nak[u] áre* 'let there not be' in Japanese is used in negative commands and means 'be not', 'do not', 'must not'. It is a more literary imperative, compared to the particle *na*).

As we can see in the Japanese version, almost no diacritics are used for the distinction of vowel qualities and quantities. In the sources mentioned at the beginning of this paragraph generally use diacritics, as occurs elsewhere in the world. The three Greek accents, acute, grave and circumflex (see below) were available in descriptive linguistics and could be used for vowel qualities (as in French), or suprasegmentals, such as stress (Spanish), tone (Vietnamese, Chinese), or quantity (Nahuatl).

---

59. See for more details Bonnet (2019).

60. The term of Sino-xenic readings refers to Sino-Japanese, Sino-Korean and Sino-Vietnamese readings of Chinese characters, as they occur as loanwords in these three languages (Martin 1953: 4). Missionary linguists of this period were aware of the different readings of these characters, which today in Japanese is referred to with the terms "on-reading" (according to Chinese) and "kun-reading" (according to Japanese phonology). Rodrigues (1620: 1r) distinguishes between three "registers", *Yomi, Coye* and a mixture of these two. The anonymous *Rakuyōshū* (Anonymous 1598), printed in 1598, is a "dictionary of characters" which was in particular developed for these Sino-Japanese readings. Every Sino-Japanese character (*kanji*) and their compounds, pronounced according to both *yomi* and *coye* (modern Japanese, *kundoku* and *ondoku*) and the third part also contains accompanying *kana* symbols.

Japanese romanization efforts achieved their 'perfection' much earlier than Chinese and Vietnamese. The vowel inventory of Japanese was less complex for speakers of Portuguese, but for speakers of other European languages, such as Spanish, for instance, vowel qualities needed some explanation. Tone does not play as prominent a role in Japanese as in the two other Asian language described in this letter, but vowel quantity (length) did not escape the attention of the missionary-linguists. In Japanese-Latin-Portuguese dictionaries and grammars we find a vowel with the 'zero' diacritic <o> (unmarked), the *haček* <ŏ> and the circumflex <ô>. When we limit ourselves to the letter <o>, Japanese distinguishes, long and short vowels and they differ also regarding openness. The /ɔː/ (long low mid back) is spelt <ŏ> in Rodrigues, and /oː/ (long high mid back) is spelt <ô>. Rodrigues compares Japanese with Portuguese ŏ = long ŏ, as if with two o' s, as in *Minha avŏ, capa de dŏ, Enxŏ, Pŏ*, with the mouth and the lips open ('com o boca & beiços abertos'): circumflex ô, as if with the two vowels *o* and *u*, with the mouth somewhat closed and the lips rounded ('com a boca hum pouco fechada ajuntando os beiços em roda'; f. 12r, as in the Portuguese *meu avô, Bôca, Môcho, Côrpo*).[61]

The consonantal repertory of Japanese did not cause serious problems for Westerners, or caused obviously less problems than Chinese, but the main problem for the development of a Romanization system was that the native speakers of different European languages pronounced the same letters differently, as the graphs <ch>, <tç>, <z>, <zz>, <c>, <k> and/ or <qu>, <gh> and even within a specific language, the same graph can be pronounced differently, as the graph <z> for instances, pronounced differently in Old Spanish compared to the Spanish of the 17th century, and even seen from a synchronic perspective, the same graph could be pronounced differently by an Andalusian, compared to a speaker of central Spain. In the Americas there were also many missionaries from different countries, Italians, French, etc., but the sources written in Spanish are almost without an exception strongly hispancized. In Asia, we often see that authors give specific information regarding the pronunciation, seen from the perspective of Portuguese, Italian, French or Spanish spelling conventions.[62]

In Jesuit Japanese sources /ts/ is usually spelled <tç>, /s/ as <s> (sometimes as <ç>). If we compare the Japanese words in Palmeiro's letter with the *Vocabulario* we find the following differences:

---

61. See for more details Moran (1972: 118–119).

62. Or sometimes even Dutch (Heurnius) or German, as in the *Manuductio* which corroborates the hypothesis of Pham that the author was not Francisco de Pina (1618–1625), but the German-speaking Jesuit Philip Sibin (1679–1759).

Table 4. Japanese romanizations compared

Palmeiro/ de Rhodes	Vocabulario
ci 'terra' (f. 9v) (ji 地)	*chi* ("terra") (92)
tsuki 'luna/ mensis' (f.9v) (tsuki, 月)	*tçuqi* ("mes") (496)
uo 'Rex' (no diacritic) (f. 10v) (o, 王)	*vŏ* (548)
camighe 'capilli' (f. 10v) (kami, 髪)	*camigue* ("cabellos de cabeça") (68)
fighe 'barba' (f. 10v) (hige, 髭)	*figue* ("barba") (179)

Although the amount of data is limited, it looks like the informant who assisted with the Japanese part, did not follow strictly the Portuguese romanization which was developed for Japanese, but we see apparently some Italian features, possibly the result, as we argued above –, of de Rhodes's editing work (in the introduction, he explains that the Italian spelling conventions are followed), but it is also possible that he copied the Japanese words from an Italian-speaking Jesuit.

As in the Italian-based romanization of Chinese developed by the Italian Jesuits Ricci and Ruggieri, and also in romanizations of Vietnamese by Italian Jesuits such as Cristoforo Borri (1583–1632)[63] and Girolamo Majorica we find the grapheme <c> representing [tʃ] before <e> and <i>. The digraph <sc> is used representing [ʃ], the <g> before <e> and <i> represents [ʒ]. The digraph <gh> is written when it precedes the vowels <i> and <e> (<g> is used when it precedes the other vowels, as in <gotocu> 'sicut'), representing [g] (as in <fighe> 'barba' versus <gotocu> 'sicut', <uareraga> 'et'). On the other hand, <k> is also used, which is usually represented in other Italian-based romanizations as <c> (before <a>, <o>, and <u>, or as <ch>. This choice is understandable, since the digraph <ch> could cause easily mispronounciations for speakers of Spanish, Portuguese, French, Flemish, German, etc.);[64] for the same reasons, the Greek <k> is also frequently used in other romanizations, such as Chinese (see below). For Japanese, a Portuguese-based romanization was developed earlier, and in Collado's work on Japanese we see also some changes. Collado explicitly informs his readers that "si vero litera, *i*, ponatur immediate post, *g*, absque, *v*, pronunciatur sicut Italicè, 'giorno', v.g. *Xitāgi*", or "Litera, *z*, pronunciatur ea vi, qua in lingua Hispaniæ, 'Zumbar', v.g. *mizu*. Si verò fuerint duo, *zz*, violentiùs feriuntur, v.g. *mizzu*." Notwithstanding, we find also a clear impact of the Portuguese sources of Collado, as the following examples demonstrate:

---

63. Borri's most important work was printed in Europe (Borri 1631) and translated in several European languages. See fort he Italian features in Borri's romanization Pham (2018: 196) and for Majorica's romanization Pham (2018: 200–201).

64. Palmeiro's text shows also some corrections, such as <ichi> ('unum') corrected as <ici> (f. 11r)

Table 5. Palmeiro's romanization of Japanese compared with Collado

	Collado	Palmeiro
Dominus	arùji (39)	arugi[65] (f. 9r)
Homo	fito (57)	fito (f. 9r)
Uir	votòco (1420	uotoco (f. 9r)
Mulier	vonna (83	uonna (f. 9r)
Uxor	tçùma (146	tsuma (f. 9r)
Pater	chichi (97)	cici (f. 9r)
Mater	haua, vel fafa (79)	fafa (f. 9r)
Coelum	ten (16)	ten (f. 9v)
Terra	gi (133)	ci (f. 9v)
Aqua	mizzu (11)	midzu (f. 9v)
Luna	tçùqi (75)	tsuki (f. 9v)
Stella	fòxi (128)	foxi (f. 9v)
Barba	figue (14)	fighe (f. 10v)

According to Jacques, Palmeiro's Japanese version of the *Oratio Dominica* is identical to the one from the anonymous doctrinal text *Nippon no Iesus*:

> Le texte japonais du *Pater* est identique à celui du catéchisme publié à Amacusa (Japon) dès 1592, à l'exception de retouches mineures: abandon du diacritique des syllabes longues, ajout de trois particules, et traduction du mot portugais « vontade », « volonté », qui figurait curieusement en portugais dans l'ancien texte. Par contre, en 1632 on n'a toujours pas trouvé d'équivalent japonais à la « tentation ».
>
> (Jacques 2004: 212)

If we take a closer look at the two texts, we come to the conclusion that the two texts are far from "identical". Word and morpheme boundaries are almost systematically placed in different places, and there are a great number of spelling differences:

Table 6a. Palmeiro's Japanese text compared with *Nippon no Iesus*

Palmeiro	Tenni mascimasu uareraga uonuoya minauo tattomare tamaye
Nippon no Iesus	Ten ni maximasu va eraga von voya mi na uo tattomare tamaye
Palmeiro	Miyo kitari tamaye. Tenni uoite uoboscimesu mamanaru gotocu,
Nippon no Iesus	miyo qitari tamaye. Ten ni voite go Vontade no mama naru gotoqu,
Palmeiro	cini uoitemo arasce tamaye.
Nippon no Iesus	chi ni voi te mo araxe tamaye.
Palmeiro	uareraga nicinicino uonyascinaiuo connicimo ataye tabi tamaye.
Nippon no Iesus	Vareraga nichinichi no von yaxinai uo connichi ataye tabi tamaye.
Palmeiro	varerayori ukeuoytaru fitoni yurusci mosu gotocu
Nippon no Iesus	Varera yori voitaru fito ni yuruxi mŏsu gotoqu:
Palmeiro	uareraga uoi tatematsuru cotouo yurusci tamaye.

---

65. This word has been corrected by the scribe. It is not clear if the letter is corrected from \<g\> to \<j\> or from \<j\> to \<g\>.

Table 6a. (*continued*)

Nippon no Iesus	varera voiratematçuru coto uo yuruxi tamaye.
Palmeiro	uarerauo tentationi fascifanasci tamo coto nacare
Nippon no Iesus	Varera Tentaçã ni fanaxi tamŏ coto nacare:
Palmeiro	varerauo kio acuyori nogasci tamaye.
Nippon no Iesus	Varera uo qeoacu yori nogaxi tamaye. Amen.

We find the following discrepancies in spelling in the two texts:

Table 6b. Palmeiro's Japanese text compared with *Nippon no Iesus*

Palmeiro (1632)	*Nippon no Jesus* (1592: 16–17)
\<sc\>	\<x\>
\<u\>	\<v\>
\<k\>	\<q\>
\<c\>	\<ch\>
\<ts\>	\<tç\>

5.3   Chinese

At the end of 16th century, Portuguese was the *lingua franca* among missionaries in the territories which fell under the Portuguese patronage (*padroado*) and most letters, books and, thus, linguistic material follow the Portuguese orthography. Unlike Jesuit descriptions of Japanese, there are no extant grammars of the language which was called "Mandarin" by the Jesuits prior to 1632, the year when Palmeiro wrote his letter. The earliest printed grammar of Mandarin Chinese is the work composed by the Jesuit Martino Martini, whose *Grammatica Sinica* or *Grammatica linguae sinensis* was written between 1651 and 1653, revised in 1656. The first printed version is included in Melchisédec Thévenot's (1620–1692) *Relations des divers voyages curieux,* which appeared in 1663 and 1672, and with the appended grammar in the second volume published in 1696 (Paternicò 2011: 39). Bayer reworked Martini's material and included it later in 1730 in his *Museum sinicum.*

The earliest published sources related to Chinese are the Manila incunabula, not only for Mandarin studies, but mainly Early Hokkien studies (Southern Mǐn) (Van der Loon 1966 and 1967). The three pioneering Jesuits who developed a romanization system for Mandarin, were Ricci, Ruggieri and Cattaneo. Ricci developed the earliest romanization system when he was in Zhaoqing (1583–1588) and did not distinguish tones or aspiration (also known as Ricci Earlier System; RES).[66] In the so-called Ricci Later System (RLS), the system is further refined and enriched with tone and aspiration diacritics, as it is used in his *Xizi qiji* 西字奇跡 ['The

---

66. For more details see also Masini (2005: 185–189) and in particular the detailed analyses and description of the history in Raini (2010: 58–95).

Wonder of Western Script'] (Beijing, 1605). This so-called RLS has been developed in cooperation with the Chinese convert Zhong Mingren (鈡銘仁 Sebastião Fernandes. ca. 1563–1622) and Lazzaro Cattaneo, Trigault's confessor. Six years before Palmeiro wrote his letter, the Jesuit Nicolas Trigault published his *Xiru ermuzi* completed in 1626 (Coblin 2006: 25). Trigault's romanization as it appears in his *Xiru ermuzi* is a further refinement and expansion of the system developed by Ricci and is also called the Ricci-Trigault System. In this work the romanization of Chinese Trigault's reached its most mature form and determined other missionary works, not only in the Jesuit sources, but also in the works of Dominicans, such as Francisco Díaz (1606–1646) and Francisco Varo.

The question to be raised regards whether Trigault's *Xiru ermuzi* was available at the time Palmeiro wrote his letter. Trigault completed his work with the help of Han Yun and Wang Zheng in Hangzhou (Masini 2005: 187). Brockey (2007: 261) argues that the novices acquired a familiarity of spoken *guānhuà* during the initial six months while they started learning to read and write characters, using Nicolas Trigault's *Xiru ermuzi* for building their vocabularies. Trigault's work was an essential part of the Jesuit language training program, but unfortunately, Brockey does not supply an exact date when Trigault's work reached Macao and when it was decided to use his vocabulary in the language acquisition program. On the other hand, according to Jacques (2004: 204), there was at least one copy available in Macau, when Palmeiro wrote his letter, but he does not give any reference to support such a view.[67] As we shall demonstrate below, Palmeiro's Chinese language specialists and informants were not familiar with Trigault's romanization system, or, maybe, they have seen it but decided not to follow it. It is also possible that the linguistic data supplied by the informants was simplified by de Rhodes, as he did with the Japanese section. If we characterize the romanization system of the Chinese texts and words in Palmeiro's letter, we conclude that the Chinese romanization used in Palmeiro's letter are partially in compliance with the so called Ricci Later System (RLS), it is an hybrid with some peculiarities that we discuss below. As Jacques (2004: 206) argues, the linguistic data of Palmeiro's letter is limited. It contains the romanization of only 22 distinctive initials and around 32 finals. Between the period when the first pioneering works were written and the completion of this letter, romanization systems were Portuguese or Italian based, or in a mixture of both. Palmeiro's letter obviously reflects Italian orthography, which was probably the work of his informants, but we must not exclude the possibility that Italian features were the result of the editing work of Alexandre de Rhodes, as we have observed in the previous section on Japanese.

---

67. "Xi-ru er-mu-zi […] xylogravé à Pékin en 1626 et dont au moins un exemplaire avait dû atteindre Macao en 1632" (Jacques 2004: 204). It seems that Heurnius's informant also made use of Trigault's system as early as 1628.

Table 7 represents the *Pater noster* including Palmeiro's romanization and RES, RLS and EMZ (Trigault's romanization in his work *Xiru ermuzi*, as reconstructed in South Coblin 1997: 294–307). The Latin in the first column reproduces the order of the original document and does not correspond always with each Chinese character.

Table 7. Palmeiro's *Pater Noster*

Latin	Chinese	Modern Mandarin Pinyin	Palmeiro's romanization	Ruggieri/ RES	RLS	EMZ
[f. 7r] Pater*	在	zài	tsãi	zai, zoi	–	çài, çái
noster	天	tiān	thien	tien, tiē	t'iēn	'tiēn
qui	我	wǒ	ngó	ngo	ngò	gò
es	等	děng	tém	ten	tèm	tèm
in	父	fù	fũ			
coelis	者	zhě	cé	cie	chè	chè
sanctificatur	我	wǒ	ngó	ngo	ngò	gò
[f. 7v] nomen	等	děng	tém	ten	tèm	tèm
tuum	願	yuàn	yüēn			
	爾	ěr	lh/			
	名	míng	mim̀			
	成	chéng	cim̀			
	聖	shèng	scim̃			
adveniat	爾	ěr	lh/			
regnum	國	guó	quẽ	cuo	quo	quoě
tuum	臨	lín	lim̀			
	格	gé	kē			
fiat	爾	ěr	lh/			
voluntas	旨	zhǐ	ci/			
tua	承	chéng	ᶜcim̀			
sicut	行	xíng	him̀			
in	於	yú	yù	iu	yû	iȗ
coelo	地	dì	tĩ			
et	如	rú	giù			
in	於	yú	yù	iu	yû	iȗ
terra	天	tiān	thien	tien, tiē	t'iēn	'tiēn
	焉	yān	yen	ien	iên	iēn iên
panem	我	wǒ	ngó	ngo	ngò	gò
nostrum	等	děng	tém	ten	tèm	tèm
[f. 8r] quotidianum	望	wàng	üãm	van		uàm
da	爾	ěr	lh/			
nobis	今	jīn	kin	chin		kīn

(*continued*)

Table 7. (*continued*)

Latin	Chinese	Modern Mandarin Pinyin	Palmeiro's romanization	Ruggieri/ RES	RLS	EMZ
hodie	日	rì	gē	gi	gǐ	jě
	與	yǔ	yú			
	我	wǒ	ngó	ngo	ngò	gò
	我	wǒ	ngó	ngo	ngò	gò
	日	rì	gē	gi	gǐ	jě
	用	yòng	yūm	yum	yúm	iúm
	糧	liáng	leaṁ			
et	而	ér	lh\	gi	lɦ	ûl
dimitte	免	miǎn	mién			
nobis	我	wǒ	ngó	ngo	ngò	gò
debita	債	zhài	~~chai~~ ciāi			
nostra	如	rú	giù			
sicut	我	wǒ	ngó	ngo	ngò	gò
et	亦	yì	yẽ			
nos	赦	shè	scẽ			
dimittimus	負	fù	fú			
debitoribus	我	wǒ	ngó	ngo	ngò	gò
[f. 8v] nostris	債	zhài	ciāi			
	者	zhě	cé	cie	chè	chè
et	又	yòu	yēu			
ne	不	bù	pū	po	pǒ	pǒ
nos	我	wǒ	ngó	ngo	ngò	gò
inducos	許	xǔ	hiú	schiu		hiừ
in	陷**	xiàn	hiẽn			
tentationem	於	yú	yù	iu	yû	iừ
	誘	yòu	yéu			
	感	gǎn	cán	can	càn	kàn
sed	乃	nǎi	nái			
libera	救	jiù	kiēu	chieu		kiéu
nos	我	wǒ	ngó	ngo	ngò	gò
a	於	yú	yù	iu	yû	iừ
malo	凶	xiōng	hium			
	惡	è	uō			
	亞	yà	ā			
	孟	mèng	mēm			

* Translation of the Lord's Prayer: ['Our Father, who art in heaven, hallowed be thy name; thy kingdom come; thy will be done on earth as it is in heaven. Give us this day our daily bread; and forgive us our trespasses as we forgive those who trespass against us; and lead us not into temptation, but deliver us from evil. Amen.']
** Maybe Japanese variant of 陷.

Table 8 is Palmeiro's thematically arranged word list including the characters, Palmeiro's romanization and RES, RLS and EMZ (Trigault's *Xiru ermuzi*). In this list, the author mantains a correspondance between the Latin meaning and the Chinese characters.

Table 8. Palmeiro's word list including RES, RLS and EMZ

Latin	Chinese	Modern Mandarin Pinyin	Palmeiro's romanization	Ruggieri/ RES	RLS	EMZ
[f. 9r] Coeli ['Heaven']	天	tiān	thien	tien, tiē	t'iēn	'tiēn
Terra ['Eath']	地	dì	tī			
Verus ['true']	真	zhēn	cin			
Dominus ['Lord']	主	zhǔ	ciú	ciu	chù	chù
Homo ['man'; 'human being']	人	rén	gìn	gin	gîn	jìn
Vir ['man']	男	nán	nàn			
Mulier ['woman']	女	nǚ	niú	nu, gnu	niù	niǜ
Maritus ['husband']	夫	fū	fu	fu		fū
Uxor ['spouse']	妻	qī	tsi	cie'		çī
Pater ['father']	父	fù	fū			
Mater ['mother']	母	mǔ	mú			
[f. 9v] frater maior, minor ['older/ younger brother']	兄弟	xiōngdì	hium tī	schium --	hiûm --	
soror ma[ior] mi[nor][a] ['older/ younger sister']	姐妹	jiěmèi	mūi	moi		moéi, múi
filius[b] ['son']	男子	nánzǐ	tsé	zi, çi	-- çù	çù
Filia ['daughter']	女子	nǚzǐ	niú tsé	nu, gnu-zi, çi	niù- çù	niǜ- çù
~~Avus~~[c]	~~孫~~	sūn	~~tsú~~			
Avus ['grandfather']	祖	zǔ	tsú			
Avia ['grandmother']	祖母	zǔmǔ	tsú mú			
Puer[d] ['boy']	孩童	háitóng	thóm			
Puella ['girl']	小女	xiǎonǚ	siáu niú	siau nu/ gnu	siào niù	siào niǜ
Coelum ['heaven']	天	tiān	thien	tien, tiē	t'iēn	'tiēn
Ignis ['fire']	火	huǒ	hó	cuo, fo	hùo	hò, hùo
Aër[e] ['air']	風氣	fēngqì	khī	chi		'kí
Aqua ['water']	水	shuǐ	scúi			
Terra ['earth']	地	dì	tī			
Sol ['sun']	日	rì	gē	gi	gǐ	gē
Luna ['moon']	月	yuè	yüē	iuo	iuě	iuě

(continued)

Table 8. (*continued*)

Latin	Chinese	Modern Mandarin Pinyin	Palmeiro's romanization	Ruggieri/RES	RLS	EMZ
Stella ['star']	星	xīng	hìm			
Mons ['mountain']	山	shān	scian	san		xān
Flumen ['river']	川	chuān	^ccioan[f]			
Annus ['year']	年	nián	nièn			
Mensis[g] ['Month']	日	rì	yüē	iuo	iuĕ	iuĕ
Dies ['day']	月	yuè	gē	gi	gĭ	gē
[f. 10r] Nox ['night']	夜	yè	yē	ie	yè	ié
Dominus ['Lord']	主	zhǔ	ciú	ciú	ciu	chù
servus[h] ['servant']	僕	pú	nú			
Urbs[i] ['city']	所在	suǒzài	fú			
Gladius[j] ['sword']	劍	jiàn	kiēn			
Panis ['bread']	餅	bǐng	pím			
Vinum ['wine']	酒	jiǔ	tsiéu	çiu		çièu
Bonus ['good']	善	shàn	scēn	scien	xén	xién, xén, xièn, xèn
Malus ['bad']	惡	è	uō			
Mors ['death']	死	sǐ	sú	ssi	sù	sù
Saccus ['sack']	袋	dài	tāi			
Edere ['to eat']	食	shí	scē	cie'		xē̆[k]
Bibere ['to drink']	飲	yǐn	ín			
loqui[l] ['to speak']	說	shuō	yú			
Niger ['black']	黑	hēi	hē	he'		hĕ
Albus ['white']	白	bái	pē			
Croceus ['saffron']	黃	huáng	hoàm	guam	hôam	hoâm
Ruber[m] ['red']	紅	hóng	^cciē	cum, gum		hûm
Viridis[n] ['green']	青	qīng	lō			
Cęruleus[o] ['blue']	藍	lán	thien tsim			
[f. 10v] Rex ['king']	王	wáng	üàm	guam		vâm, uâm
Fulmen[p] ['lightning']	震	shēn	lùi scē			
Tonitru ['thunder']	雷	léi	lùi			
Coruscatio ['flash']	電	diàn	scen tiēn			
Nubes ['clouds']	雲	yún	yùn	iun, iuon		iûn
Caput ['head']	頭	tóu	thèu	teū		'têu
Brachia ['arms']	腕	wàn	scéu pám			
Manus ['hand']	手	shǒu	sceu	scieu	xèu	xièu, xèu
Pedes ['feet']	足	zú	kiō			
Crura ['legs']	脛	jìng	kiō pám			
Capilli ['hair']	髮	fà	fā			

Table 8. (*continued*)

Latin	Chinese	Modern Mandarin Pinyin	Palmeiro's romanization	Ruggieri/ RES	RLS	EMZ
Os ['mouth']	口	kǒu	khèu	cheu		'kèu
Nasus ['nose']	鼻	bí	pī			
Aures[q] ['ears']	身	shēn	lh´	gi	lh`	ùl
Dentes ['teeth']	齒	chǐ	ci	ci	ch'ì	ch'ì
Barba ['beard']	鬚	xū	siu			
frons ['forehead']	額	é	nghē	nghe		gě

a. The editor of the table inserted only the romanization of the second character, *mei*.
b. Same as indicated above.
c. This item is deleted in the original table, in fact the Chinese character and the pronunciation are wrong: *sūn* 孫 means 'grandson'.
d. In the original table on the manuscript the handwriting of the character *hái* 孩 slightly differs from the standard one.
e. Same as indicated above.
f. In the original manuscript, the spiritus asper appears on top of the initial consonant.
g. Chinese characters for *mensis* ['month'] and *dies* ['day'] are inverted. the character of servus, 僕 *pu*, is different compared to the romanization, which suggests another word, *nu* 奴. Similar mismatches occur with the words for *urbs, ruber, viridis, ceruleus*. 1. Chinese characters do not correspond with romanization but with the meaning of Latin words; 2. two Chinese characters in the list but only one romanization is given; 3. Chinese characters not corresponding with Latin words and romanization, placed erroneously, i.e. not in the right order in the list. These mismatches may be explained by the fact that missionaries usually were preparing this kind of wordlist or glossaries first, then a Chinese assistant helped with writing the characters, not always at the same time and occasion. Sometimes the Chinese assistant was not able to read Latin letters and therefore he could not check the correspondence between the character and the romanization and Latin words.
h. The handwriting of this character slightly differs from the standard form. While the meaning is correct, the romanization is wrong, it must be read *pú*. But maybe the romanization is referring to the word *nú* 奴, 'slave'.
i. Both Chinese character and romanization of this item are not corresponding to the Latin word: *suǒzài* 所在 is a bysillabic compound that means 'place', 'location'. The handwriting of the character *suǒ* 所 slightly differs from the standard one. The romanization may be referred to the word *fǔ* 府 which means "city".
j. In the original manuscript the handwriting of this character slightly differs from the standard form.
k. The dot has to appear under the breve accent
l. The romanization of this character is ambiguous: when it means of 'to speak', in modern *pinyin* it is *shuō*. The romanization may refer to the word *yù* 語, which also means 'to tell'.
m. The romanization 'ciē is not related to the character of this line, but may be linked to *chì* 赤, which also means 'red'.
n. Same as above, the character and its romanization are not matching, but the sound *lō* used by Palmeiro may be linked to the word *lǜ* 綠, which also means 'green'.
o. Same as above, character and romanization are not matching, but the sound *thien tsim* may be linked to the word *tiānqīng* 天青 which means 'cerulean blue'.
p. Character and romanization not matching as occurs with the entries *coruscatio, brachia* and *crura*.
q. Character and romanization are not matching, but the sound *lh´* may be linked to the word *ěr* 耳 which means 'ear'.

As for initials, there is some consistency in applying the Italian orthography, for instance <c> for /tʃ/ and /tʃʰ/ before <e> and <i> (e.g.: 成: <cìm>); <sc> for /ʃ/ before <i> (e.g.: 聖: <scĩm>); <z >for /ts/ (eg.: 在: <tsãi>). This may suggest that this romanization is similar to Ruggeri's, but on the other hand, Palmeiro's text contains some discrepancies, such as the marking of aspiration which Palmeiro's text marks with <h>, absent in RES and indicated with a spiritus asper, or a small superscript ᶜ in RLS: 天: Palmeiro: <thien>, RES: <tien>, <tie>, RLS: <tʼiēn>, EMZ <ʻtiēn>. Another difference is the use of initial <i- / y->, 於: Palmeiro: <yù>, RES: <iu>, RLS: <yû>. On the other hand, aspiration is not always marked consistently with <h>; we find also in some cases a superscript spiritus asper, as in ᶜ*cìm* and ᶜ*cioan.*

Another point of interest is the use of diacritics, which are present in Palmeiro's letter romanization but not in RES. Three diacritics are used, acute, grave and the tilde; the circumflex is not used. This is probably the work of Alexandre de Rhodes, since he co-authored a report with Francisco Buzomi a few years earlier, in 1625,[68] using exactly the same diacritics. According to Pham, these diacritics were copied from Ricci (Pham 2018: 202), whose work was brought to Cochinchina. The acute and grave accents are written on top of the vowels, but generally after final <-m> and after <lh> the diacritics follow the final consonant, and sometimes they are also written on top.

Here follows a sample of syllables with diacritics from Palmeiro's.

Table 9. Palmeiro's diacritics

Chinese	Pinyin	Palmeiro
如	rú	giù
我	wǒ	ngó
格*	gé	kē

These data testify a certain evolution in the romanization system that goes in the direction of RLS, although there are some differences. In fact, the romanization for Chinese in Palmeiro's letter could be labeled as an intermediate step between the two (RES/RLS). According to Raini (2010), there are some documents that prove the existence of an intermediate phase between the two romanization systems, for instance the data contained in *Jiaoyou Lun* 交友論 ['On Friendship'], 1601, by Matteo Ricci. The main innovations of this system are the addition of an <h> after the initial as aspiration mark, and in the tone diacritics. The data discussed above from Palmeiro's letter may be linked with this transition phase. Finally, it is also evident that Palmeiro's letter tends toward the system of Trigault. For instance,

---

68. Jap.Sin 68 f. 028r-29v; discussed in Pham (2018: 201–202).

Table 10. Palmeiro's text compared (RES, RLS, EMZ)

Chinese	Modern Mandarin Pinyin	Palmeiro's romanization	Ruggieri/RES	RLS	EMZ
救	jiù	kiēu	chieu		kiéu
今	jīn	kin	chin		kīn
救	jiù	kiēu	chieu		kiéu
望	wàng	üām	van		uàm

This may suggest, that the Chinese language specialist(s) who gave his/their linguistic samples as input for this letter, would have had access to Trigault's work, but it is also obvious that the latter was not followed strictly.

Another important point that emerges through the analysis of the romanization data of Palmeiro's letter is the possible osmosis between the romanization systems of Chinese and Vietnamese. This could have been also the contribution of Alexandre de Rhodes as editor, who decided to present an Italian-based unified language sample to Vitelleschi. As Raini already pointed out, many missionary texts of the 17th century often present unusual romanization of some syllables. For instance, the Portuguese Jesuit Álvaro Semedo, in his relation of 1640, systematically used the <h> as aspiration mark. In fact, Semedo substituted the apostrophe of aspiration (') used in Ricci and Trigault system with <h>, showing in this way the influence of a different non-Chinese based romanization system. This consideration is based on the fact that the <h> as a marker for aspiration is seldom used in Mandarin romanizations, whereas it is largely adopted when describing Chinese dialects and, most of all, in the romanization of Vietnamese. The use of <h> as a marker of aspiration in Vietnamese transcriptions is testified in Alexandre de Rhodes's *Dictionarium Annamiticum Lusitanum et Latinum* of 1651 (Raini 2010: 245–246). Here below follows a table showing Palmeiro's samples of romanized syllables with <h> as aspiration mark.

Table 11. Syllables with <h> as aspiration mark

Latin	Japanese	Character	Chinese	Vietnamese
Mensis [f. 9v]	tsuki	月	yüē	thám
Aer [f. 9v]	fuki	風氣	khī	khi
Caput [f. 10v]	cascira	頭	thèu	laù

Palmeiro's letter does not contain a completely consistent Italian based orthography, but we find also Portuguese-based spelling conventions, as occurs in the finals, as the following examples demonstrate:

Table 12. Portuguese spellings in the finals

Chinese	pinyin	Palmeiro	Ruggieri/RES	RLS	EMZ
等	děng	Tém	ten	tèm	tèm
望	wàng	Üãm	van		Uàm

Finally, we may highlight that in the transcription of the *Pater Noster* and inside the wordlist there are two corrections, that means that the scribe, Alexandre de Rhodes, had some doubts while writing. How can we explain these corrections? Our hypothesis is that de Rhodes copied from a draft version, and while copying he standardized the romanization in order to be consistent. Below are the two cases of corrections and a strike through:

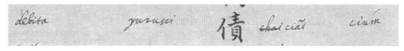

a. Correction a (f. 8r)

b. Correction b (f. 9r)

Figure 9. Two cases of corrections

5.4   Vietnamese

The Vietnamese glosses are discussed earlier in Jacques (2004) and recently in detail by Pham (2018). In this section we shall summarize the most important features of the romanization system of Vietnamese in this letter. As occurs with the romanization systems of Japanese and Chinese, the native tongue of the missionaries often plays a prominent role in the selection of an adequate romanization system. Alexandre de Rhodes wrote different texts in different periods and his romanization system underwent several stages. Jesuits who contributed to the romanization of Vietnamese came from different nations and like in other regions in Asia, we find a Portuguese- and an Italian-based system. On the one hand we have the reports of the Portuguese Jesuits João Rodrigues, Gaspar Luis and António de Fontes, (Pham 2018: 188), whereas we have also reports written by Italians such as Cristoforo Borri, Francisco de Pina, Girolamo Majorica, and Francesco Buzomi.

Alexandre de Rhodes wrote reports in Portuguese, and adapted his romanization system to this language.[69] He copied a report with Francisco Buzomi in Italian as well,[70] so he was familiar with both systems. In his Latin reports, he used the Latin or Italian orthography.[71] His grammar, dictionary and cathechism was published much later and in his grammar he explains how the different systems easily can lead to confusion, as for example his defintion of the graphs <k> and <ʃ>:

> Littera *k*, vel litera *ʃ*; vt infra; vtemur etiam, *c*, cum, *h*, ad exprimendum quod Itali scribunt, *cia*, nos autem dicemus, *cha*, quia apud lusitanos ita est in vsu, & in libris etiam scriptis in lingua Tunchinensi ita vsus inualuit, vt, *cha*, sit idem quod apud Italos *cia*, & *che*, idem quod, *ce*, apud eosdem, & sic de omnibus alijs literis vocalibus cum *ch*, quae pronunciantur more lusitano, non Italico nec Latino, quia sic commodius nobis visum est.

> [The letter <k>, or the letter <ʃ>; as below, we rather use <c> with <h> in order to represent the sound which in Italian is written as <cia>, however, we say <cha>, since this is customary among the Portuguese, and even in the written texts in the Tonkinese language it is used and is prevailed, as <cha>, is the same as Italian <cia> and <che>, and the same applies to Italian <ce> among them as applies to all the other vowels combined with <ch>, that are pronounced in the Portuguese manner, and not according to Italian or Latin pronunciation, since this seems more appropriate to us.]

As Pham (2018: 216) concludes, "la période 1626–1631 montre que les jésuites n'ont pas encore établi une convention homogène pour la transcription du vietnamien et que, comme dans la période précédente, leur langue maternelle joue toujours un rôle important dans le choix des graphèmes." The romanization of Vietnamese was further refined in the years 1631 and 1632. The main protagonists of this second period were Gaspar do Amaral, António Cardim, and António de Fontes. Alexandre de Rhodes wrote his letter precisely in this crucial period in the history of the romanization of Vietnamese, considerably more precise than most of the earlier documents, but still not reaching the orthographical perfection of the texts written two years later, such as the one applied in the report of Gaspar do Amaral.[72] In these reports written in 1634, as Pham (2018: 244–245) demonstrates, "Nous trouvons onze graphies dans son texte: *a, ă, â, e, ê, i, o, ô, ơ, u, ư* qui couvrent parfaitement onze voyelles du vietnamien. Gaspar do Amaral parvint à transcrire

---

69. Jap. Sin 68 f. 13r-v, analysed in Pham (2018: 201).

70. Jap. Sin. 68 f. 28r-29v, see Pham (2018: 201).

71. Jesuítas na Ásia, vol. 49-V-31 f. 24r-27 (Pham 2018: 216).

72. Jesuítas na Ásia, vol. 49-V-31, f. 303r-305r; discussed in Pham (2018: 243).

les rimes vietnamiennes avec un taux d'exactitude remarquable et la pluplart des graphèmes ont été maintenus dans l'orthographe du *quốc ngữ* moderne".

The Vietnamese text in Palmeiro's letter contains five vowels.[73] The vowel <a> is under-differentiated, representing three different phonemes [a], [ă] and [ɤ̆], Latin <o> represents both [ɔ], [o] and <u> is the symbol used for both [u] and [ɯ]. It is remarkable that in Palmeiro's letter the diaeresis is also used, which is not current at all in other texts. <ä>, as in <täi>, <ngäi> represents [aj] and [ăj]; <aim> is again Italian based and represents [ĕŋj]; the digraph <œ> is used representing Vietnamese [ɤ]; initials follow generally the Italian spelling conventions, such as <sc> representing [ɕ] instead of the grapheme <x>; <ci> representing Vietnamese [c] is used, whereas we find also the Portuguese-based spelling <ch>; <gi> representing [ʒ]; the Portuguese digraph [nh] for the Vietnamese velar nasal [ŋ] is not used but no special symbol is used here at all.

6. Conclusions and final remarks

The first question to be raised is the following: *Does this text give a clear answer to Vitelleschi's request?*

Muzio Vitelleschi (1563–1645) was the sixth Superior General of the Society of Jesus from 1615 until 1645. As we can expect from a Jesuit occupying such a high position, Vitelleschi was an erudite scholar. Before he was professor of theology, he taught logic, natural philosophy and metaphysics, as many Jesuits who had professed their fourth vow had done. The questions that follow are why he ordered Palmeiro to scrutinize the linguistic situation in East Asia and who actually was the person who asked him to do this ("a pessoa que isto pedio"). Probably, he was doing a favor to the Propaganda Fide Cardinals. We have demonstrated that at least some of the answers to his questions contain significant details regarding the writing system and the existence of languages like Vietnamese and Japanese which are strikingly different in spoken form, although the educated all use and are able to read the Chinese characters. On the other hand, there was no systematic comparison of the lexicon and some syntactic features available, and Palmeiro's answer based on the paper written by Alexandre de Rhodes provided sufficient proof of the differences between these languages. Such data were not yet available in pre-modern Europe.

It has been demonstrated that several sources, not only in manuscript form, such as letters, but also printed works, such as González de Mendoza (1585), Ricci/Trigault (1615), Rodrigues (c.1620–1622), provide some answers to the questions of

73. This section is based on Pham (2018).

the supposed "universality" of the Chinese script. These works were quickly translated in many European languages. It is not unlikely that these books also circulated in Rome, but we do not know if Vitelleschi was aware of the existence of these sources.

There was an obvious ambiguity: if the Japanese use Chinese characters, and so do the Chinese and Vietnamese – as Jesuit writings all say very clearly – then why can't they understand each other in writing? In China, they averred, the same language was written for different dialects. So why not outside of China, if those others used the same characters? If missionaries had to be educated and trained in the local languages, they would not be using written texts exclusively, since they had to preach, hear confessions and communicate with the newly converts. Therefore the person ordered Vitelleschi to ask to verify the correctness of these descriptions. He probably wanted to know more about this "universality myth". It is also likely that Vitelleschi was not well informed. He was a competent theologian, but not a linguist necessarily. He was a trained administrator and a man of some charisma. Obviously he would have been intelligent, but not necessarily an outstanding linguist or scholar, eager to learn from any new linguistic discovery related to Asian languages.

Since the decision to impose Chinese as a general language for all the missions in these territories would have so many consequences, organizational, practical and ideological, much energy could be saved, if missionaries just could concentrate on one language. It seems that the question was whether or not things might be printed in Chinese and distributed in that language across the region. Therefore, the person who sent orders to Vitelleschi decided to make such an important decision as soon as he had the correct firsthand data provided by language specialists. The original letter of Vitelleschi's order to Palmeiro has been lost, so we do not exactly know the details about what he wanted to learn from these specialists.

We would expect that Palmeiro would have given a clear answer, "yes", or "no". In fact the text gives an answer to Valignano's query; Chinese is an important language, with high prestige among and used by the Mandarins. The language is understood in writings, but Japanese and Vietnamese are obviously different and mutually unintelligible. Even within China, there are mutually unintelligible varieties of Chinese, and even unrelated languages, and the use of Chinese characters facilitates communication for commercial and cultural reasons, but Palmeiro's reply does not give a direct final recommendation to discourage or advise against the use of Chinese in the Asian missions, although he does comment on the implausibility of the project. The three Asian languages share some features, such as the lack of relatives, but not only is the lexicon completely different, except for some Chinese loanwords which were diffused outside of China, but also the word order, as illustrated with the calques in Latin of the *Oratio Dominica* in these three languages.

In this paper, we have demonstrated that Palmeiro's epistle was an important document for several reasons. The letter includes theoretical observations about some important typological features of Asian languages and discrepancies between these and European languages, and in fact we have one of the earliest extant cross-linguistic syntactic comparisons, including Chinese, Japanese and Vietnamese. The lack of relative pronouns deserves further specific attention and some remarks are included regarding corrupted and standard languages and the role of the language of the Mandarins in these regions and the different word orders in these languages. Secondly, we have demonstrated that this text was not only a document that was diffused inside the Society of Jesus or the Propaganda Fide; it was also circulating in academic circles in Europe at a relative early stage and attracted the attention of scholars like Golius, Reland and Bayer; it is less commonly known that the text was printed as early as 1708 by Reland.

An implicit objective of Palmeiro's letter was probably to show that in Asia there was one translation of the name for the tetragrammaton. With the Asian equivalents of what Alexandre de Rhodes calls the "tetragrammaton", the Superior in Rome could see that there was one standard synchronized translation of the four concepts of 'True', 'Lord', 'Heaven' and 'Earth' all based on Chinese characters.

Regarding its authorship, we have repeated what others already observed earlier. Bayer was the first who came into the insight that Alexandre de Rhodes was in fact the author of this text, corroborated again much later by Jacques (2004) and recently by Pham (2018), who compared Alexandre de Rhodes's handwriting of the one used in this text. We have also suggested, as far as possible, some names of assistants who could have contributed to the linguistic data for this letter. Regarding the romanization of these three languages, we conclude that Palmeiro's letter was written during a crucial period for the history of the romanization of Vietnamese and Chinese.

It is evident that Alexandre de Rhodes held the role of "editor"; as he observes in his theoretical section, the romanization should follow "Italian orthography" for the three Asian languages. *Grosso modo*, the romanizations indeed do follow these conventions and this was an important achievement, seen from the point of view of the historiography of linguistics. We have demonstrated that Palmeiro's letter was written in a transition period; for Chinese between Ricci-Ruggieri-Cattaneo and Trigault, for Vietnamese between earlier writings of Alexandre de Rhodes himself, Italian and Portuguese Jesuits, such as Gaspar Luis, António de Fontes, Cristoforo Borri, Francisco de Pina, Girolamo Majorica and Francesco Buzomi. In the reports written in 1634, two years after the completion of Palmeiro's letter, in particular the writings of Gaspar do Amaral, the romanization of Vietnamese reached its highest degree of perfection. The position of the Japanese section in the history of the romanization of Japanese is different, since the highest degree of perfection was achieved much earlier by Portuguese Jesuits in Japan. Compared with other works on Japanese, mainly Collado which by coincidence appeared the same year 1632, the Japanese section of Palmeiro's letter does not contribute any innovation to Japanese romanizations, nor does it reveal any serious adaptation or evolution of Japanese romanizations, nor are there any interesting glosses in the margins related to Japanese, as occurs with Chinese and Vietnamese. Nevertheless, the role of de Rhodes is interesting, as he decided to follow Italian spelling conventions for Japanese, different from Collado, who took his information mainly from the Portuguese sources, such as Rodrigues. Finally, this paper provides the first complete translation into English of the text.

As Brockey demonstrates (2014: 11) "Upon arriving in Asia, André Palmeiro stood at the center of that Jesuit world. For nearly two decades he occupied the office of visitor, also known by its Latin equivalent, visitator. He was not a linguist, but as we have demonstrated, he contributed to the diffusion of knowlegde in Europe, gathered from firsthand language specialists in Asia. He worked closely together with quite a few renowned linguists "avant la lettre", the pioneering scholars such as Roberto Nobili (1577–1656), the author of impressive works on and in Tamil, Nicolas Trigault, one of the main figures for Chinese studies, João Rodrigues, the interpreter who was a pioneering grammarian of Japanese, and finally Alexandre de Rhodes, one of the protagonists of this paper, the specialist on Vietnamese, and the "editor" (or one of the editors) of the minutes of a fascinating linguistic investigation in Macau, where the features of Asian languages were compared and the Chinese script was discussed. Thanks to the impressive organization and infrastructure of Jesuit networks at least two versions of this report reached Europe via Goa and Acapulco, or maybe via Batavia, and arrived in Rome and in Golius's collection. Hopefully the original letter for the second copy will be found somewhere in the future, and unfortunately, the original letter which was written by "a pessoa que isto pedio" has not been located, but maybe it is still somewhere in the Roman Archives of the Society of Jesus in the general's correspondence tomes, or in the Archives of the Propaganda Fide. Hopefully this letter will be located in the future, so that we will know who this "pessoa" in fact was.

Acknowledgements

We want to acknowledge Ly Pham for her kindness to provide copies of writings of Alexandre de Rhodes and other texts, Emanuele Raini for having discussed with the authors some issues related to the romanization system of Chinese used by Palmeiro, Ly Pham for checking the sections on Vietnamese, Maxime Bonnet and Atsuko Kawaguchi for the section on Japanese, Martina Farese and Pierre Winkler for checking the translations from Latin texts. We also want to acknowledge Anna Pytlowany for sharing her knowledge on Adriaan Reland with us. In particular we wish to express our gratitude to Liam Brockey for his detailed and helpful comments on an earlier draft of this paper and Justin Case and Kathryne Rhodes for checking the English of the final version. Regular disclaimers apply. While the paper was written under the authorship and responsibility of both authors, the individual sections were divided as follows: Paolo De Troia is the main author of the Section 1, the section on Chinese of paragraph 2 and 5.3. Otto Zwartjes is the author of Section (except fort he section on Chinese, section 3, 4, and 5 (except 5.3). Both authors are responsible of the general idea, the conclusions and the translation of the original text. We also want to acknowledge ARSI for their authorization of the reproduction of the original letter, which was given April, 14th 2021, no. 485).

References

A.   Primary sources

Adelung, Johann Christoph & Johann Severin Vater. 1809. *Mithridates oder allgemeine Sprachkunde mit dem Vater Unser als Sprachprobe in beynahe fünfhundert Sprachen und Mundarten*. Berlin: In der Vossischen Buchhandlung.

Anonymous. 1592. *Nippon no Iesvs no Companhia no Superior yorî Christan ni sŏtŏ no cotouari uo tagaino mondŏ no gotoqu xidai uo vacachi tamŏ DOCTRINA*. Amakusa: Iesvs no Compania no collegio Amacusa ni voite Superiores no von yuru xi uo cŏmuri, core uo fan to nasu nari. Toqini go xuxxe no NENQI.

Anonymous. 1595. *Dictionarivm latino lvsitanicvm, ac iaponicvm, ex Ambrosii Calepini volumine depromptum…* Amacusa: In Collegio Iaponico Societatis Iesv.

Anonymous. 1598. *Ra cu yo xu sive Dictionarium Japonicum; Characteres habet hinc Sinicus, illinc Iapponicus*. Nagasaki (?): Collegio Iaponico Societatis Iesu.

Anonymous. 1603–1604. *Evolabon nippo jisho (Vocabvlario da Lingoa de IAPAM com adeclaração em Portugués), feito por algvns padres, e irmãos da companhia de IESV. Com licença do ordinario, & superiores*. Nangasaqui: no Collegio de Iapam da Companhia de IESVS.

Anonymous (attributed to Francisco de Pina, according to Jacques, but recently attributed to Philip Sibin, according to Pham 2018 and 2019). 2002 [17th century, or beginning 18th century]. *Manuductio ad linguam tunckinensem*. [Ms. Biblioteca da Ajuda, Lisboa, *Jesuitas na Asia* collection, vol. 49/VI/8, fol. 313r to 323v.]. In: Roland Jacques: *Portuguese Pioneers of Vietnamese Linguistics Prior to 1650*. Appendix 2.146–197. Bangkok: Orchid Press.

Barreda, Nicolás de. 1730. *Doctrina christiana en lengua chinanteca, añadida la explicacion de los principales mysterios de la fee, modo de baptizar en caso de necessidad, y de ayuda a bien morir, y methodo de administracion de Sacramentos*. México: Por los Herederos de la Viuda de Francisco Rodríguez Lupercio.

Bartoli, Daniele. 1663. *Dell'Historia della Compagnia di Giesv. La Cina, Terza Parte, Dell'Asia, descritta dal P. Daniello Bartoli della medesima Compagnia*. Roma: Nella Stamperia del Varese.

Bayer, Theophilus S. 1730. *Mvsevm sinicvm, in quo Sinicae Linguae et Litteraturae ratio explicatur*. Tomvs primvs. Petropoli [St. Petersburg]: Ex Typographia Academiae Imperatoriae.

Borri, Christoforo. 1631. *Relatione della nvova Missione delli PP. della Compagnia di Giesv, al Regno della Cocincina, scritta dal Padre Christoforo Borri Milanese della medesima Compagnia, che fu vno de primi ch'entrarono in detto Regno.* Roma: Francesco Corbeletti. French translation: *Relation de la novvelle Mission des Peres de la Compagnie de Iesvs, au royavme de la Cochinchine.* Lille: Pierre de Rache, 1631. Two years later, in 1633, three other translations appeared (into Latin, German and English).

Catalogue Raisonné. 1859. =*Catalogue Raissonné de la précieuse collection de manuscrits et d'autographes de MM. D.C. Van Voorst, père et J.J. Van Voorst, fils, pasteurs Evangéliques à Amsterdam.* Amsterdam: Frederik Muller.

Catalogus Codicum. 1761. =*Catalogus Codicum Manuscriptorum Arabicorum, Persicorum, Malaicorum, Sinicorum, Japonicorum Aliorumque, In: Naam-Lyst Van een zeer keurige verzameling Latynsche, Fransche doch meest Nederduitsche welgeconditioneerde, zeer zindelyk in Fransche en Hoorne banden gebondene Boeken, Bestaande in de voornaamste Historische, Reizen- Land- En Aardryk-Beschryvende, Natuur- En Dichtkundige, en andere Mengelwerken.* Utrecht: Willem Kroon & Gijsbert Tieme van Paddenburg.

Catalogus Insignium. 1696. =*Catalogus insignium in omni facultate, linguisque, Arabica, Persica, Turcica, Chinensi &c. librorum M.ss. quos Doctissimus Clarissimusque Vir D. Jacobus Golius dum viveret: Mathesios & Arabicae Linguae in Acad. Lugd. Batav. Professor Ordinarius…* Lugduni Batavorum [Leiden]: Apud Joannem du Vivie.

Chamberlayne, John (Joannes Chamberlayn). 1715. *Oratio Dominica in diversas omnium fere gentium linguas versa et propriis cujusque linguae characteribus expressa.* Amstelaedami (Amsterdam): Typis Guilielmi & Davidis Goerei.

Collado, Diego (Didacus Colladus). 1632a. *Ars grammaticae iaponicae lingvae. In gratiam et adivtorivm eorum, qui praedicandi Evangelij causa ad Iaponiae Regnum se volverint conferre.* Romae: Typis et impensis Sacr. Congr. de Propag. Fide.

Collado, Diego (Didacus Colladus). 1632b. *Dictionarivm sive Thesavri linguæ Iaponicæ compendivm.* Romæ: Typis & impensis Sacr. Congr. de Prop. Fide.

Collado, Diego. 1632c. *Niffon no Cotobani yo confesion, vo mosu yodai to mata confesor yori goxensa cu … Modus confitendi et examinandi poenitentem Iaponensem, formula suamet lengua Iaponica.* Romae: Typis & impensis Sac. Congreg. de Prop. Fide.

Douglas, Robert Kennaway. 1877. *Catalogue of Chinese Printed Books, Manuscripts and Drawings in the Library of the British Museum.* London: Longman & B. Quaritch.

Gessner, Conrad. 1555. *Mithridates, de diferentiis lingvarvm tvm vetervm tum quae hodie apud diuersas nationes in toto urbe terraru[m] in usu sunt.* Tigurini (Zurich): C. Froschoverus.

Gonçalez Mendoça, Iuan (Juan González de Mendoza). 1585. *Historia de las cosas mas notables, ritos, y costvmbres del Gran Reyno de la China, sabidas assi por los libros de los mesmos Chinas, como por relacion de Religiosos, y otras personas que an estado en el dicho Reyno.* Roma: Vincentio Accolti.

Jong, P[ieter] de. 1862. *Catalogus codicum orientalium Bibliothecae Academiae Regiae scientiarum.* Lugduni Batavorum [Leiden]: E.J. Brill Academiae Typographus.

Lüdeken, Thomas [= Andreas Müller]. 1680. *Oratio orationum, ss. Orationis Dominicae versiones praeter authenticam ferè centum eaque longé emendatiùs quàm antehàc et è probatissimis Auctoribus potius quàm prioribus collectionibus, Iamque singulae genuinis Linguae suae characteribus adeòque magnam partem ex aere ad editionem à Barnimô Hagiô traditae.* Berolini [Berlin]: Ex Officina Rungiana.

Anonymous (Marsh 696). c.1642. *Arte de la lengua mandarina.* (grammatical appendix bound together with the Chinese-Spanish dictionary, atttributed to Francisco Díaz).

Martini, Martino. 1998 [1651–1653]. "Grammatica Sinica". In *Martino Martini (1614–1661) Opera Omnia* ed. by Franco Demarchi. Vol. II: *Martino Martini S.J. (1614–1661). Opere minori* ed. by Giuliano Bertuccioli, 349–481. Trento: Università degli Studi di Trento.

Megiser, Hieronymus (Megiserus). 1593. *Specimen qvadraginta diversarvm atqve inter se differentium linguarum, & dialectorum videlicet, Oratio Dominica, totidem linguae expressa.* Francoforti [Frankfurt am Main]: Ex Typographeo Ioannis Spiessii.

Oyanguren de Santa Inés, Melchor. 1743. *Tagalysmo elucidado, y reducido (en lo posible) a la Latinidad de Nebrija.* México: La imprenta de Francisco Xavier Sánchez.

Palmeiro, Andre (Andrés, Andrea Palmeyro, Palmiero). May 8, 1632. *Epistola P. Andr. Palmeiro, Macao 8/V 1632 cum paradigmate Orationis Dominicae Pater Noster in lingua Sinica, Japonica, Annamitica* (in earlier catalogues MS Jap. Sin. I, 200, today MS Jap. Sin. 194, 7–11v), Archivum Romanum Societatis Iesu (ARSI), Rome.

Quirós Tordelagunensis, Antonio Bernaldo de. 1654. *Selectae disputationes theologicae de Deo.* Lvgdvni [Lyon]: Phil. Borde. Lavt. Arnavd, & Cl. Rigavd.

Relandus, Hadrianus (Adriaan Reland, Reeland). 1708. "Tabella vocum cum pronunntiatione earum Japonica, Sinica et Annamitica". In: "XI: Dissertatio de linguis insularum quarundam Orientalium". *Dissertationum miscellanearum. Pars Tertia et ultima*, 112–116. Trajecti ad Rhenum [Utrecht]: Ex Officina Gulielmi Broedelet.

Rhodes, Alexandre de. 1651a. *Dictionarium annnamiticum [sic] lvsitanvm, et latinvm op Sacrae Congregationis de Propaganda Fide.* Romae: Typis & sumptibus eiusdem Sacr. Congreg.

Rhodes, Alexandre de. 1651b. "Lingvae annamiticae sev Tvnchinensis Declaratio". Grammatical compendium, appended to the *Dictionarium*. (De Rhodes 1651a).

Rhodes, Alexandre de. 1651c. *Cathechismvs pro ijs, qui volunt suscipere Baptismvm in Octo dies diuisus. Phép giảng tám ngày cho kẻ muãn chiụ phép rứa tọi, ma ßẻáo đạo thánh đức Chúa blỏi.* Romae; Typis Sacrae Congregationis de Propaganda Fide.

Rhodes, Alexandre de. 1651d. *Histoire dv Royavme de Tvnqvin, et des grands progrez qve la predication de l'evangile y a faits en la conuersion des Infidelles. Depuis l' Année 1627, iusques à l'Année 1646. Composée en Latin par le R.P. Alexandre de Rhodes, de la Compagnie de IESVS et tradvite en François par le R.P. Henry Albi, de la mesme Compagnie.* Lyon: Chez Iean Baptiste Devenet.

Rhodes, Alexandre de. 1653. *Divers voyages et missions dv P. Alexandre de Rhodes en la Chine, & autres Royaumes de l'Orient, Auec son retour en Europe par la Perse & l'Armenie.* Paris: Sebastien Cramoisy et Gabriel Cramoisy.

Ricci, Matteo & Nicolas Trigault. 1615. *De Christiana Expeditione apvd Sinas. Suscepta ab Socjetate Jesu. Ex P. Matthaei Ricij eiusdem Societatis Commentarijs. Libri 5 ad S.D.N. Paulum 5. in quibus Sinensis Regni mores, leges atque instituta & nouae illius Ecclesiae difficillima primordia accurate & summa fide describuntur: Auctore P. Nicolae Trigautio Belga ex eadem Societate.* Augustae Vind. [Augsburg]: apud Christoph. Mangium.

Ricci, Matteo. 1603. *The True Meaning of the Lord of Heaven (Tianzhu shiyi 天主實義).* Translated by Douglas Lancashire and Peter Hu Kuo-chen, S.J.; revised edition by Thierry Meynard, S.J. Chestnut Hill, MA: Institute of Jesuit Sources, 2016.

Rodriguez, João. 1604–1608. *Arte da lingoa de Iapam composta pello Padre – Portugues da Cõpanhia de IESV diuidida em tres livros.* Nangasaqui: no Collegio de Iapão da Companhia de IESV.

Rodrigvez, João. 1620. *Arte breve da lingoa Iapoa tirada da Arte Grande da mesma lingoa, pera os que começam a aprender os primeiros principios della. Pello Padre – da Companhia de Iesv Portugues do Bispado de Lamego. Diuidida em tres Livros.* Amacao: no Collegio da Madre de Deos da Companhia de Iesv.

Rodrigues, João. c.1620–1622. *História da Igreja do Japão.* (part I, books 1 and 2) Ms. Lisbon: Library of the Ajuda Palace, *Jesuítas na Asia* series, 49-IV-53. The original work has been lost and the Ms is not completed. See Cooper (2001; secondary sources).

Ruiz de Montoya Hispalensis à Societate IESV, Didacus. 1625. *Commentaria ac disputationes in primam partem sancti Thomae. De Trinitate.* Lvgdvni [Lyon]: Lvdovici Prost.

Serrurier, Josephus. 1718. *Oratio funebris in obitum viri celeberrimi Hadriani Relandi, antiquitatum Sacrarum & Linguarum Orientalium Professoris Ordinarii recitata ipsis nonis Martis MDCCXVIII.* Trajecti ad Rhenum [Utrecht]: Apud Guilielmum vande Water, Academiae Typographum.

Thévenot, Melchisédec. 1696. *Relations de divers voyages curieux.* 2 vols. (second edition). Paris: Thomas Moette. (First edition: 1663–1672).

Trigault, Nicolas. 1626. Xiru ermuzi 西儒耳目資 ("Aid to the Eyes and Ears of Western Literati"). Hangzhou. Reprints: Beijing: Wenkui tang, 1933; Shanghai: Shanghai guji chubanshe, 2002.

Valignano, Alessandro. 1586. *Catechismvs christianae fidei, in qvo veritas nostrae religionis ostenditur, & sectae Iaponenses confutantur.* Olyssipone [Lisbon]: Antonius Riberius.

Valignano, Alessandro. 1944 [1584]. *Historia del principio y progresso de la Compañía de Jesús en las Indias orientales (1542–64).* Herausgegeben und erläutert von Josef Wicki. Roma: Institutum Historicum.

Varo, Francisco. 2006 [between 1677–1687]. *Vocabulario de la lengua Mandarina con el estilo y vocablos con que se habla sin elegancia. Compuesto por el Padre fray – ord. Pred. Ministro de China consumado en esta lengua escriuese guardando el orden del A.B. c.d. Francisco Varo's Glossary of the Mandarin Language. Vol. I: An English and Chinese Annotation of the Vocabulario de la Lengua Mandarina. Vol. II: Pinyin and English Index of the Vocabulario de la Lengua Mandarina* ed. by W. South Coblin. Nettetal: Sankt Augustin.

Varo, Francisco. 2000 [1703]. *Arte de la lengua mandarina.* Canton: [publisher unknown]. *Francisco Varo's Grammar of the Mandarin Language (1703). An English translation of 'Arte de la lengua mandarina'.* (With an introduction by Sandra Breitenbach) ed. by W. South Coblin & Joseph A. Levi. Amsterdam & Philadelphia: John Benjamins.
https://doi.org/10.1075/sihols.93

B.   Secondary sources

Blue, Gregory. 2001. "Xu Guangqi in the West: Early Jesuit sources and the construction of an identity". *Statecraft and Intellectual Renewal in Late Ming China. The Cross-Cultural Synthesis of Xu Guangqi (1562–1633)* ed. by Catherine Jami, Peter Engelfriet, & Gregory Blue, 19–71. Leiden Boston & Köln: Brill.

Bonnet, Maxime. 2019. *L'Ars grammaticae iaponicae linguae* (Grammaire de la langue japonaise de Didacus Coladus (Diego Collado). Mémoire de MA2. Paris: Université Paris Sorbonne.

Brockey, Liam Matthew. 2003. "The Death and 'Disappearance' of Nicolas Trigault". Part II: "Nicolas Trigault, SJ: A Portrait by Peter Paul Rubens" by Anne-Marie Logan and Liam M. Brockey. *Metropolitan Museum Journal* 38.157–167. https://doi.org/10.2307/1513105

Brockey, Liam Matthew. 2007. *Journey to the East. The Jesuit mission to China, 1579–1724.* Cambridge, Massachusetts & London: The Belknap Press of Harvard University Press. https://doi.org/10.4159/9780674028814

Brockey, Liam Matthew. 2014. *The Visitor André Palmeiro and the Jesuits in Asia.* Cambridge, Massachusetts & London: The Belknap Press of Harvard University Press. https://doi.org/10.4159/9780674735576

Coblin, W. South. 1997. "Notes on the sound system of late Ming guanhua". *Monumenta Serica* 45.261–307. https://doi.org/10.1080/02549948.1997.11731303

Cooper, Michael, ed. 2001. *João Rodrigues's Account of Sixteenth-century Japan.* London: The Hakluyt Society.

Demonet, Marie-Luce & Toshinori Uetani. 2008. "Les langues des Indes Orientales entre Renaissance et Âge Classique". *Histoire Epistémologie Langage* 30:2.113–139. https://doi.org/10.3406/hel.2008.3169

Duyvendak, J[an]. J[ulius]. L[odewijk]. 1936. "Early Chinese Studies in Holland". *T'oung Pao* 32.293–344. https://doi.org/10.1163/156853236X00155

Gaudio, Andrew. 2019. "A Translation of the *Linguae Annamiticae seu Tunchinensis brevis declaratio*: The first grammar of *quốc ngữ*". *Journal of Vietnamese Studies* 14:3.79–114. https://doi.org/10.1525/vs.2019.14.3.79

Jacques, Roland. 2004. *Les missionnaires portugais et les débuts de l'Église catholique au Vietnam: Các nhà truyền giáo Bồ Đào Nha và thời kỳ đầu của Giáo hội Công giáo Việt Nam*, Reichstett : Định Hướng Tùng Thư.

Jaski, Bart. 2021. "Appendix 2: The manuscript collection of Adriaan Reland". *The Orient in Utrecht: Adriaan Reland (1676–1718), Arabist, Cartographer, Antiquarian and Scholar of Comparative Religion* ed. by Bart Jaski, Christian Lange, Anna Pytlowany & Henk J. van Rinsum, 399–422. Leiden & Boston: Brill.

Klöter, Henning. 2011. *The Language of the Sangleys. A Chinese vernacular in missionary sources of the seventeenth century.* Leiden & Boston: Brill. https://doi.org/10.1163/9789004195929

Kornicki, P. F. 1993. "European Japanology at the End of the Seventeenth Century". *Bulletin of the School of Oriental and African Studies* 56:3.502–524. https://doi.org/10.1017/S0041977X00007692

Kuiper, Koos. 2005. "The Earliest Monument of Dutch Sinological Studies: Justus Heurnius's manuscript Dutch-Chinese dictionary and Chinese-Latin *Compendium Doctrinae Christianae* (Batavia 1628)". *Quaerendo* 35:1/2.109–139. https://doi.org/10.1163/1570069054094163

Loon, van der P[iet]. 1966. "The Manila incunabula and early Hokkien studies (part 1)". *Asia Major* 12.1–43.

Loon, van der P[iet]. 1967. "The Manila incunabula and early Hokkien studies (part 2)". *Asia Major* 13.95–186.

Lopes, Rui Oliveira. 2020. "Jesuit Visual Culture and the *Song nianzhu guicheng*. The *Annunciation* as a Spiritual Mediation on the Redemptive Incarnation of Christ". *Art in Translation* 12:1.82–113. https://doi.org/10.1080/17561310.2020.1769905

Luca, Dinu. 2016. "Figures, Hieroglyphs, and Ciphers". *The Chinese Language in European Texts. Chinese Literature and Culture in the World*, 73–135. New York: Palgrave MacMillan. https://doi.org/10.1057/978-1-137-50291-9_3

Lundbæk, Knud. 1986. *T.S. Bayer (1694–1738). Pioneer Sinologist.* (=Scandinavian Institute of Asian Studies, Monograph series, 54). London & Malmö: Curzon Press.

Luo, Changpei 羅常培. 2004. "Yesuhui shi zai yinyunxue shang de gongxian 耶穌會士在音韻學上的貢獻 (The contribution of Jesuits to phonology), in Luo Changpei 羅常培, Luo Changpei yuyanxue lunwen ji 羅常培語言學論文集, 251–358. Shangwu yinshuguan, Beijing.

Martin, Samuel E. 1953. *The Phonemes of Ancient Chinese. Supplement of the Journal of the American Oriental Society* 16.

Masini, Federico. 2005. "Chinese Dictionaries prepared by Western Missionaries in the Seventeenth and Eighteenth centuries". *Encounters and Dialogues, Changing perspectives on Chinese-Western exchanges from the Sixteenth to Eighteenth centuries* ed. by Xiaxin Wu, 179–193. Sankt Augustin: Monumenta Serica Institute/ The Ricci Institute of Chinese-Western Cultural History at the University of San Francisco.

Moran, Joseph F. 1972. A Comentary of the *Arte breve da lingoa Iapoa* of João Rodriguez S.J. With particular reference to pronunciation. Ph.D. dissertation. Oxford: Bodleian Library.

Norman, Jerry. 1988. *Chinese.* Cambridge: Cambridge University Press.

Paternicò, Luisa Maria. 2011. *Martino Martini's Grammar of the Chinese Language: The Grammatica linguae sinensis.* Tesi di Dottorato, Roma: Sapienza Università di Roma.

Pfister, Louis. 1932. *Notices biographiques et bibliographiques sur les Jésuites de l'ancienne Mission de Chine (1552–1773).* Vol. I. XVIe & XVIIe siècles. Chang-Hai: Imprimerie de la Mission Catholique, Orphelinat de T'ou-sè-wè.

Phạm, Thị Kiều Ly. 2018. *La grammatisation du vietnamien (1615–1919): Histoire des grammaires et de l'écriture romanisée du vietnamien.* Thèse préparée sous la direction de Dan Savatovsky et Xuyen Lê Thi. Université Sorbonne Paris Cité – Université Paris III – Sorbonne Nouvelle.

Phạm, Thị Kiều Ly. 2019. "The True Editor of the *Manuductio ad linguam Tunkinensem* (Seventeenth- to Eighteenth-Century Vietnamese Grammar)". *Journal of Vietnamese Studies* 14(2). 68–92. Chang-Hai (Shanghai): Imprimerie de la Mission Catholique/ Orphelinat de T'ou sé-wé. https://doi.org/10.1525/vs.2019.14.2.68

Phan, Peter C. 1998. *Mission and Catechesis. Alexandre de Rhodes and Inculturation in Seventeenth-Century Vietnam.* Maryknoll, New York: Orbis Books.

Pina, Isabel [Murta]. 2003. "João Rodrigues Tçuzu and the Controversy over Christian Terminology in China: The perspective of a Jesuit from the Japanese Mission". *Bulletin of Portuguese/ Japanese Studies* 6.47–71.

Pina, Isabel Murta. 2012. "Chinese and mestizo Jesuits from the China Mission (1589–1689)". *Europe-China: Intercultural Encounters (16th–18th Centuries)* ed. by Filipe Barreto, 117–137. Lisbon: Centro Científico e Cultural de Macau.

Pina, Isabel Murta. 2013. "Jesuítas de Macau: Intérpretes e Tradutores". *Para a História da Tradução em Macau* ed. by Luís Filipe Barreto & Li Changsen, 29–47. Lisboa: Centro Científico e Cultural de Macau-IPM.

Raini, Emanuele. 2010. Sistemi di romanizzazione del cinese mandarino nei secoli XVI-XVIII. Unpublished Ph.D. dissertation, Studi Asiatici, XXII ciclo, Facoltà di Studi Orientali, Sapienza – Università di Roma.

South Coblin, Walter. 1997. "Notes on the sound system of late Ming guanhua". *Monumenta Serica* 45.261–307. https://doi.org/10.1080/02549948.1997.11731303

Sun, Chaofen. 2006. *Chinese: A Linguistic Introduction.* Cambridge University Press. https://doi.org/10.1017/CBO9780511755019

Tollini, Aldo. 2018. "Translation during the Christian Century in Japan. Christian Keywords in Japanese". *Between Texts, Beyond Words. Intertextuality and Translation* ed. by Nicoletta Pesaro, 93–105. Venezia: Edizioni Ca'Foscari Digital Publishing. https://doi.org/10.30687/978-88-6969-311-3/001

Wen, Huiying. 2020. *Relative Clauses in Mandarin Chinese*. Queen Mary's Occoasional Papers Advancing Linguistics (OPAL, no. 46). On-line available at: https://www.qmul.ac.uk/sllf/media/sllf-new/department-of-linguistics/documents/Thesis-(Huiying-Wen,-20.11.2020).pdf

Weststeijn, Thijs. 2016. "«Sinarum gentes ... omnium sollertissimae»: Encounters between the Middle Kingdom and the Low Countries, 1602–1692". *Reshaping the Boundaries. The Christian intersection of China and the West in the Modern Era* ed. by Song Gang, 9–34. Hong Kong: Hong Kong University Press.

Wilkinson, Endymion Porter. 2000. *Chinese History: A manual*. Cambridge, Mass: Harvard University Asia Center for the Harvard-Yenching Institute.

Zwartjes, Otto. 2010. *Melchor Oyanguren de Santa Inés. Arte de la lengua japona (1738), Tagalysmo elucidado (1742) y "Arte chínico, o mandarín (1742)*. Estudio a cargo de Otto Zwartjes. 3 vols. Madrid: Agencia Española de Cooperación Internacional para el Desarrollo. In particular: "Arte chínico, ó mandarín" (1743) / "Arte Tagalog, Sinico, ó Sangley"/ "Gramatica china o mandarina", 183–209.

Zwartjes, Otto. 2011a. "Jacob Golius (1596–1667) and Martino Martini (1614–1661): The *Vocabularium Hispanico-Sinense* (Bodleian Library, MS Marsh 696) and the study of Chinese in the Netherlands/ Jiekao Koulinsi (1596–1667) yu Wei Kuangguo (1614–1661): Xi zhong cidian (Boduolaian tushuguan, MS Marsh 696*) yu hanyu yanjiu zai Helan". *The Sixth Fu Jen University International Sinological Symposium: "Early European (1552–1814) Acquisition and Research on Chinese Languages" Symposium Papers* ed. by Zbigniew Wesołowski, 305–345 [English version]; 347–381 [Chinese version]. New Taipei Xinzhuang qu: Fu Jen Catholic University Printing House.

Zwartjes, Otto. 2011b. *Portuguese Missionary Grammars in Asia, Africa and Brazil, 1550–1800.* (= *Studies in the History of the Language Sciences*, 117). Amsterdam & Philadelphia: John Benjamins. https://doi.org/10.1075/sihols.117

Zwartjes, Otto. [forthcoming]. *The Arte de la lengua mandarina (Libellus Hispanicus de pronuntiatione Characteribus Chinensium) appended to Francisco Díaz's Vocabularium Hispanico-Sinense (1640–1642) (Bodleian Library, MS Marsh 696): A fragment of the earliest extant grammar of Mandarin.*

Appendix

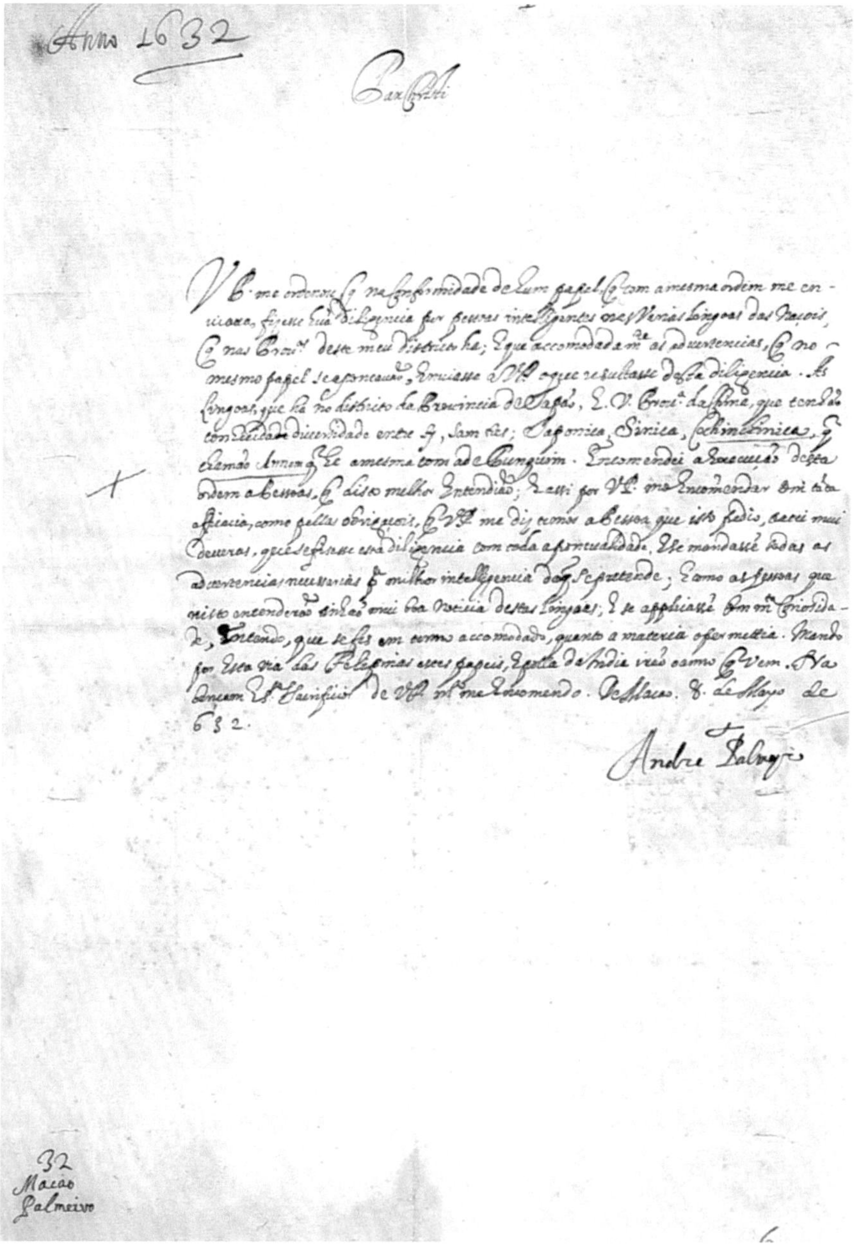

(f. 6r)

Anno. 1632

Trium linguarum specimina subjiciam sinicæ, Japonicæ et Annam quæ Tunkinum et Cocincinam complectitur, si pauca prius monuerim.
Primu sinicos characteres ut puto heroglyphicos, qui singulas dictiones singul...
proferant, communes quidem esse tribus his linguis eandemque rem ipsis significare diverso tamen idiomate proferri ut infra: sicuti et apud Europæos
sunt numerorum characteres 1. 2. 3. etc. Japones tamen alios etiam habent
characteres quibus vulgo utuntur, sed sinicos pluris faciunt, sic etiam fere
Annam. ideo solum sinicos subjicio qui omnibus sunt communes.
2.um vix posse nostris characteribus germanâ pronuntiatione harum linguarum exprimi
sinicæ præsertim et Annam, eo quod ex tono diverso qui literis diversis exprimi
non potest vocabulorum diversitas maxime pendeat: hanc tamen diversitatem
audentibus sinicæ linguæ acuto, gravi, et circunflexo utcunque exprimemus:
at si quis hanc diversitatem auribus non exigerit, vix ac ne vix quidem genuinam
diversitatem exprimere poterit: quoquo tamen modo imitabimur si vocabula
accentu acuto notata in modum falsæ musicæ proferat: gravi vero in modum
bassi, circunflexo denique vocem inflectendo ad modum interrogantis. Vocabla
nullo accentu notata absque ulla inflexione vocis sunt pronuntianda.
3.a aspirationes in his linguis sinica et Annam esse frequentissimas, et valdè asperas
ut in ph. kh. th æquivalent enim aspiratis φ, χ, θ, cum asperè pronuntiatur
ut a Germanis aut Belgis, in reliquis pronuntiatione ytalicâ secuti sumus plerique.

Oratio Dominica

	Japonicè	Sinicè		Annam
Pater	tenni	在	tsã trium æque hebreis ꝫ tradi	cia
noster	maximasu	天	thien	cium
qui	uareraga	我	ngò ng idem ægs hebreis ꝫ	toi
es	nonnoja.	等	ngain	ã diphtongus æ pronuntiabitur ut a Gallis in voce
in		父	tea	tlen œil oculus.
coelis.		者	fu	
		我	cé.	blai
sanctificetur	minauo		ngò	cium

(f. 7r)

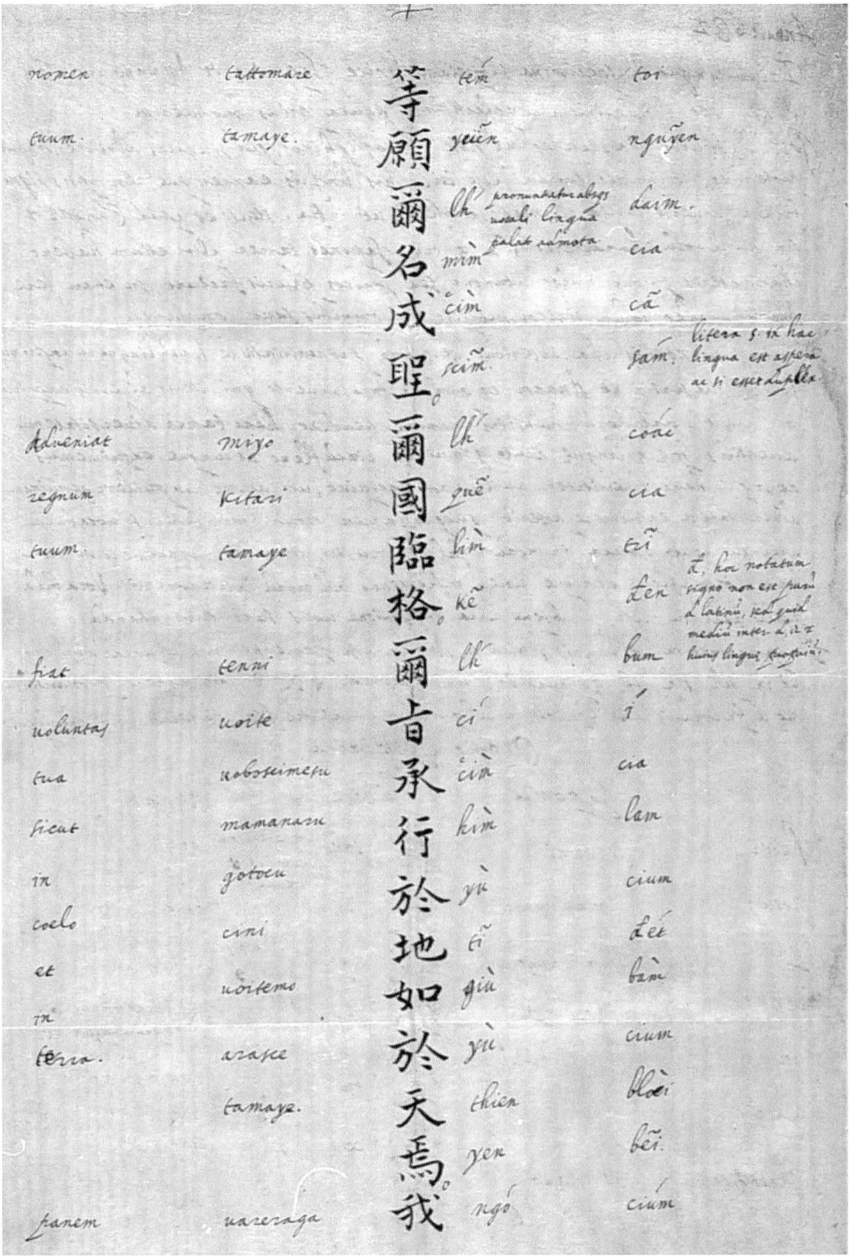

等
願
爾
名
成
聖
爾
國
臨
格
爾
旨
承
行
於
地
如
於
天
焉
我

Latin	Japanese	Chinese transcription		Latin note
nomen	tattomare	těm	toi	
tuum.	tamaye.	yeen	nguyen	
		lh	daim.	pronuntiabitur abijs quale lingua galica remota
		mĩm	cìa	
		cĩm	cã	
		sĩm.	sam	litera s in hac lingua est aspera ac si esset duplex
Adueniat	mizo	lh	coai	
regnum	kitari	gnẽ	cia	
tuum.	tamaye	hìm	cũi	ã, hoc notatum signo non esse punì a latinis, nec quali medin inter a, & e huius linguae proprium
		kẽ	den	
fiat	tenni	lh	bum	
uoluntas	uoite	cì	i	
tua	nobosuimesu	cìa	cia	
sicut	mamanaru	kìm	lam	
in	gotocu	yŭ	cium	
coelo	cini	cũ	dee	
et	uoitemo	yŭ	bam	
in		yù	cium	
terra.	arasexe	thiēn	bloei	
	tamaya.	yen	bei.	
panem	uareraga	ngò	cium	

(f. 7v)

nostrum	recipiciino	等	tem	toi
quotidianum	nonyaseinaius	望	iam	tiom
da	connieimo	爾	lh	cia
nobis	ataye	今	kin	zai
hodie.	tabi	日	gẽ	cio
	tamaye.	與	yn	ciun
		我	ngó	toi
		我	ngó	hàm
		日	gẽ	ngài
		用	yũm	lum
		糧	leam.	dũ
Et	nareraḡori	而	lh	mà
dimitte	ukenoytam	免	mien	tha
nobis	fitoni	我	ngó	noẽ
debita	yuruxei	債	chai ciẽ	cium
nostra	mosu	如	già	toi
sicut	gotocu	我	ngó	bàng
et	nareraga	亦	yẽ	cium
nos	noi takematsuru	赦	xẽ	toi
dimittimus	cotouo	負	fu	it tha
debitoribus	yuraxei	我	ngó	kẽ ciũ

(f. 8r)

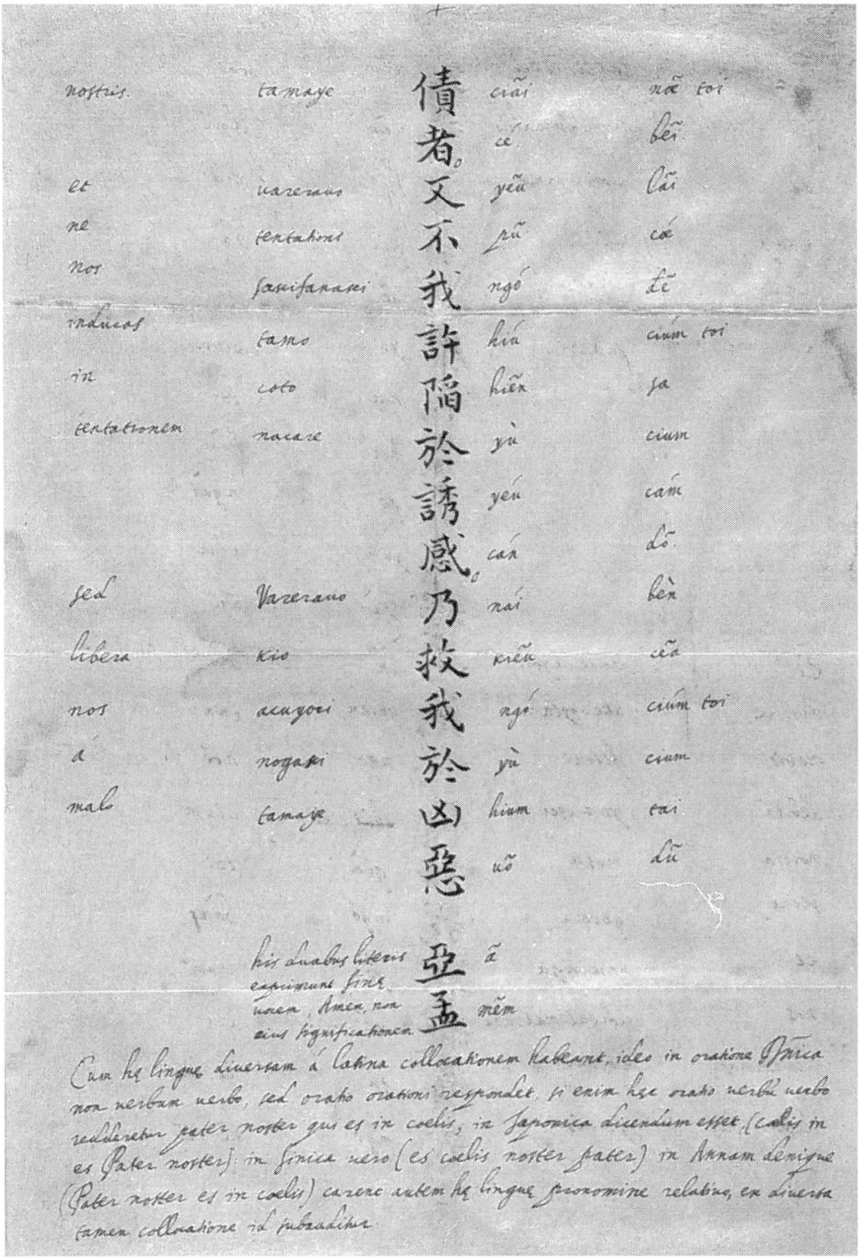

nostris.	tamaye	債	ciãi	nã toi
		者	ce	bẽi
et	varerano	又	yeũ	lãi
ne	tentationi	不	pũ	cõ
nos	saxifanasi	我	ngó	tẽ
inducas	tamo	許	hiú	cium toi
in	coto	陷	hiẽn	sa
tentationem	nacare	於	yù	cium
		誘	yeù	cám
		感	cán	dỗ
sed	Varerano	乃	nái	bẽn
libera	kio	救	kiẽu	cẽu
nos	acugoi	我	ngó	cium toi
a	nogaxi	於	yù	cium
malo	tamaye	凶	hium	tai
		惡	ŏ	dũ
	his duabus literis exprimunt finem orationis, Amen, non eius significationem	亞	ã	
		孟	mẽm	

Cum hę linguę diversam á Latina collocationem habeant, ideo in oratione Sinica non verbum verbo, sed oratio orationi respondet, si enim hęc oratio verbi verbo redderetur pater noster qui es in coelis, in Japonica dicendum esset (coelis in es Pater noster) in Sinica vero (es coelis noster pater) in Annam denique (Pater noster es in coelis) carere autem hę linguę pronomine relativo, ex diversa tamen collocatione id subauditur.

(f. 8v)

Nota sine apud Japones, sine apud Annam duplex esse idioma alterum proprium ut hæc pronomina quæ hic apponimus indicant, alterum mutuo accepta a Sinis, cum Sinicū compti quod omittimus, eo quod existimamus sufficere Sinicū proprium quo sunt in sua curia utuntur, et mandarinicū uocant lusitani si enim Sinicas dialectos subjiceremus unius cujusque prouinciæ Sinice uarietas etiam subjicienda esset, quod esset infinite, licet interdū non sit minor inter illas differentia quam inter Italicam et hispanicam harū tamen omniū origo est ista quā mandarinicū uocant, illā Japones et Annam simul cū characteribus acceperunt, sed non parū corruptam a sua lingua accomodatam. Illā tamen in uulgari sermone, nec illā uulgo intelligunt sine Japones sine Annam, sed soli qui literas didicerunt, et apud illos se habet sicut apud nos latina lingua, propria tamen quā uulgo utuntur sine Japones sine Annam, non magis a Sinica pendet quam Germanica a latina. Præterea cum in his tribus linguis nulla sit uox quæ unica nomen Dei explicet absque erroris periculo, ideo Deum explicamus ab effectu maxime noto cœlo nimirū et terra unā Magistrū sequuti Xūm Dominū qui ait confiteor tibi Pater Domine cœli et terræ Matt. 11. et iuxta illud Diui Pauli ad 17. hic cœli et terræ cum sit Dominus etc. sic igitur maxime apud Annam uerum cœli terræque Deum annuntiauimus, atque ita 4 characteribus Sinicis Dei nomen explicamus, qui suo modo ineffabili nomini tetragrammaton respondeant.

respondeant	Japonice		Sinice	Annam
Cœli	ten	天	thien	chàẽ
terra	cina	地	tĩ	ciuá
uerus	macotto	眞	chicin	blài
Dominus	aruji	主	cŭ	tế
homo	fito	人	giü	ngài
uir	uotoco	男	nàn	con blas
mulier	uonna	女	niù	con gai
maritus	uotto	夫	fu	ciaùn
uxor	tsuma	妻	tsi	bõ
Pater	cici	父	fŭ	cia
Mater	fafa	母	mũ	mẽ

(f. 9r)

	Japonicé		Sinice	Annam
frater maior, minor	Ani vototo	兄弟	hiam tŏ	aim em
soror ma. mi	ymoto ine	妹	muī	ci em
filius	co	男子	tsé	con nam
filia	musume	女子	niu tsé	con nũ
Auus		孫	sũ	em
Auus	vogi	祖	tsũ	om
Auia	uba	祖母	tsũ mũ	bà
Puer	Varabe	狨童	chom	con hai kẽ
Puella	coniusume	小女	nàn niũ	congai kẽ
Cælum	ten	天	thien	blời
Ignis	fi	火	hŏ	lũa
Aer	fuki	風	khĩ	khi
Aqua	midzu	氣	xui	nuôc
Terra	ci	水	tĩ	tét
Sol	fi	地	gẽ	mặt blời
Luna	tsuki	日	yuẽ	mặt blam
Stella	foxi	月	fim	sau
Mons	yama	星	suan	nui
flumen	caua	山	cioan	sum
Annus	toxi	川	niên	nam
Mensis	tsuki	年	yuẽ	tham
Dies	fi	日月	gẽ	ngài

(f. 9v)

	Japonice		Sinice	Annam
Nox	yoru	夜	yẽ	tem
Dominus	arugi	主	ciŭ	ciũa
seruus	figuan	僕	nŭ	toi
Vrbs	Iaixio	附	fŭ	thaim
Gladius	catana	住	kiển	guom
Panis	moci	劔	fim	baim
Vinum	sake	餅	tsiển	ruõu
Bonus	yoi	酒	xẽn	laim
Malus	nami	善	uõ	dũ
Mors	seisuru	惡	ßi	chết
Sacus	fueuro	冗	tài	tui
Edere	cus	袋	scẽ	an
Bibere	nomi	食	in	uấm
loqui	catari	飲	yŭ	nói
Niger	curoi	說	ßẽ	ßen
Albus	xiror	黑	fẽ	tlam
Croceus	kizro	白	hoàm	uàm
Ruber	acai	黃	ciễ	dõ
Viridis	auoi	紅	lõ	seiaim
Ceruleus	forayro	青藍	thien tsim	biếc

(f. 10r)

(f. 10v)

Non habent hæ linguæ nomina mensium communiter in usu, sed eorum loco utuntur numeris sequentibus ut in reliquis rebus: solu[m] in primo mense, utuntur hac litera 正 quæ Japonibus est sioguau finis (sinis [fin] yuè). Annã thám giam.

	Japonicè	Numeri Sinicè		Annam
1 Vnum	ichi	一	yě	nŏt
2 Duo	ni	二	lễ	hai
3 Tria	san	三	san	ba
4	xi	四	sũ	bón
5	go	五	ú	nam
6	roku	六	lô	sáu
7	xici	七	trẽ	bat
8	faci	八	pã	tám
9	cu	九	kiẽ	chín
10	giu	十	xẽ	muei
11	giu ici	十一	xẽ yě	muei nŏt
12	giu ni	十二	xẽ lễ	muei hai
13	giu san	十三	pẽ san	muei ba
14 20	ni giu	二十	lễ xẽ	hai muei
21	ni giu ici	廿一	lễ pẽ yě	hai muei mŏt
30	san giu	三十	san xẽ	ba muei
40	sei giu	四	sũ xẽ	bón muei

(f. 11r)

	Japonicè	Sinicè	Annam
50	go giu	五十 ǔ xě	nam muei
60	rocu giu	六十 lŏ xě	sáu muei
70	sici giu	七十 tsiĕ xě	bái muei
80	faci giu	八十 pá xě	tám muei
90	cu giu	九十 kiéu xě	cín muei
100	fiacu	一百 yĕ pŏ	mót tlam
200	ni fiacu	二百 lĭ pŏ	hai tlam
1000	xen	一千 yĕ tien	mót nghìn
10000	man	一萬 yŭ uẩn	mót muan

(f. 11v)

Jap.Sin. I. 200[74]
Anno 1632

[f. 6r] Pax Christi

Peace of Christ

VR. Me ordonou, que na conformidade de hum papel, que com a mesma me enuiara, fizesse huã diligencia por pessoas intelligentes nas varias lingoas das Naçois, que nas Prou[inci]as deste meu districto ha; e que accomdadam[en]te as aduertencias, que no mesmo papel se aponteauoã, enuiasse a VR o que resultasse desta diligencia. As lingoas, que ha no districto da Prouincia de Japão, e V. Prou[inci]a da China, que tenhão conhecida diuersidade entre sy, sam tres; Japonica, Sinica, Cochinchinica, que chamão Annam que he a mesma com a de Tunquim. Encomendei a execução desta ordem a pessoas, que disto melhor entendiaõ, e assi por VR. mo encomendar com tãta afficacia, como pellas obrigaçois, que VP me diz temos a pessoa que isto pedio, tratei mui deueras, que se fisesse esta diligencia com toda a pontualidade, e se mandasse todas as aduertencias necessarias p[ar]a milhor intelligencia do que se pretende, e como as pessoas que nisso entenderão tinhão mui boa noticia destas lingoas, e se applicassem com m[ui]ta curiosidade, entendo, que se fis em termo accomodado, quanto a materia o permettia. Mando por esta via das Felipinas estes papeis, e polla da India irão o anno que vem. Na bençam e S[an]to Sacrificio de VR. m[uit]o me encomendo. De Macao, 8 de Mayo de 632.
Andre Palmeyro

Your Reverence instructed me, in conformity with a paper that was sent to me along with the same mandate, to carry out an investigation among those competent in the various languages of the nations which are found in the Provinces of my district. And, conforming to the notes that were supplied on the same paper, that the results of this investigation be sent to Your Reverence. The languages that are found in the district of the Province of Japan and Vice-Province of China, which have a well-known diversity among themselves, are three: Japanese, Chinese, and Cochinchinese, which they call Annam, being the same as that of Tonkin. I delegated the execution of this task to people who were better informed about it, and because Your Reverence asked me to do it with such expediency and following the obligations that Your Reverence tells me that we owe to the person who asked for this, I saw to it honestly that this investigation be undertaken with all promptness, and that all of the necessary information for the best understanding was intended to be sent. And since the people who understood these things had a very good knowledge of these languages and applied themselves with much curiosity, I understand that as much as could be done with the material was accomplished in the appropriate time. I send these papers by way of the Philippines, and they will come via India in the coming year. I dearly request the blessing and [remembrance in the] Holy Sacrifice of Your Reverence. From Macau, 8 of May of [1]632.

(f. 7r) 1. Anno 1632
Trium linguaru[m] specimina subjiciam Sinicae Japonicae et Annam quae Tunkinum et Cocincinam complectitur, si pauca prius monuerim.

1. The year 1632
I will provide examples from the three languages, Chinese, Japanese and Vietnamese, which includes Tonkinese and Cochinchinese, even though I have pointed out certain indications before.

---

74. Today: MS Jap. Sin 194, 7–11v.

[1] Primu[m] Sinicos characteres utpote jerogliphicos, qui singulas dictiones singuli proferant, communes quidem esse tribus his linguis eandemque rem ipsis significare diverso tamen idiomate proferri, ut infra: sicuti et apud Europaeos numerorum characteres 1 2 3 etc. Japones tamen alios etiam habent characteres quibus vulgo utuntur, sed sinicos pluris faciunt, sic etiam feré Annam, ideó solum sinicos subjicio qui omnibus sunt communes.

[1] In the first place, the Chinese characters, in that they are hieroglyphics and each one of them carries a different concept/ idea, are common to these three languages and they have the very same meaning in the same three languages, even if they are pronounced differently, as follows below: just as with the European characters for the numbers 1, 2, 3, etcetera. The Japanese have different characters still which they use, but they mostly make use of the Chinese ones, and the same holds for Vietnamese. Therefore, I only use the Chinese characters which are common to all [three languages].

2[um]. Vix posse nostris characteribus germana[m] pronuntiatione[m] haru[m] linguaru[m] exprimi sinicae praesertim et Annam, eo quod ex tono diverso qui literis diversis exprimi non potest vocabuloru[m] diversitas maximé pendeat.

Secondly, our characters can hardly express the true pronunciation of these languages, the Chinese especially and the Vietnamese language, because the different meanings of the words depend heavily on the different tones, which cannot be expressed by our letters.

Hanc tamen diversitatem accentibus Graecae linguae acuto, gravi, et circu[m] flexo ut cunque exprimemus: at si quis hanc diversitatem auribus non excipiat, vix ac ne vix quidem genuinam diversitatem exprimere poterit: quoquo tamen modo imitabitur si vocabula accentu acuto notata in modum falseti musici proferat: gravi vero in modu[m] bassi, circunflexo denique vocem inflectendo ad modum interrogantis. Vocabula nullo accentu notata absque ulla inflexione vocis sunt pronuntianda.

However, we will express this difference with the accents of the Greek language, with the acute, the grave and circumflex accent. And if someone does not perceive this difference with the ears, he hardly will be able to express the genuine difference between them: However, in this way one will more or less imitate it if one pronounces the words which are marked by an acute accent like a falsetto in music, the grave like a bass and finally the circumflex by the manner of modulating the voice as in an interrogation. The words which are not marked by an accent must be pronounced without any modulation of the voice.

3[u[m]]. Aspirationes in his linguis sinica et Annam esse frequentissimas et valdé asperas ut in *ph, kh, th* aequivalent enim aspiratis φ, χ, θ, cum asperé pronuntia[n] tur ut á Germanis aut Belgis, in reliquis pronuntiatione Italica secuti sumus plerumque.
[Oratio Dominica]

Thirdly: Aspirations are very frequently used in the Chinese and Vietnamese languages, and they are pronounced with very rough breathing, as in *ph, kh, th* which are equivalent to the aspirated φ, χ, θ, which must be pronounced with rough breathing as in German and Dutch. In all the other pronunciations, we have mostly followed the Italian pronunciation.
[Oratio Dominica]

(f. 8v) Cum hae linguae diversam á latina collocationem habeant, ideo in oratione D[omi]nica non verbum verbo, sed oratio orationi respondet, si enim haec oratio verbu[m] verbo redderetur pater noster qui es in coelis, in Japonica dicendum esset, (coelis in es Pater noster) in Sinica vero (es coelis noster pater) in Annam denique (Pater noster es in coelis) carent autem hae linguae pronomine relativo, ex diversa tamen collocatione id subauditur.

Since these languages have a different syntax compared with Latin, the Oratio Dominica therefore does not correspond word for word, but sentence to sentence. If this sentence "pater noster qui es in coelis" ("lit. Father our, who art in heaven") would be literally translated, it would be in Japanese "coelis in es Pater noster" ("heaven in thou art Father our") and in Chinese it would in fact be "es [in] coelis noster pater" ("Thou art in Heaven our Father"), and finally in Vietnamese "Pater noster es in coelis" (Father our thou art in Heaven"); these languages lack a relative pronoun, however it is understood by a different word order.

(f. 9r) 2. Nota sive apud Japones, sive apud Annam duplex esse idioma alteru[m] propriu[m] ut haec specimina quae hic apponimus indicant, alteru[m] mutuo acceptu[m] a Sinis seu Sinicu[m] corruptu[m] quod omittimus, eo quod existimavimus sufficere sinicu[m] propriu[m] quo Sinae in sua curia utantur, et mandarinicu[m] vocant Lusitani si enim sinicos dialectos subjiceremus unius cujusque provinciae sinicae varietas etiam subjicienda esset, quod esset infinitu[m], licet interdu[m] non sit minor inter illos differentia quam inter italicam et hispanicam: haru[m] tamen omniu[m] origo est ista qua[m] mandarinica[m] vocant, illa[m] Japones et Annam simul cu[m] characteribus acceperunt, sed non paru[m] corruptam et suae linguae accomodatam.

2. Notice that the particular language of the Japanese and Vietnamese is twofold, partly a language of its own, as these examples indicated here demonstrate, and on the other hand, partly a language adopted from the Chinese or rather a corrupted Chinese, the one which the Chinese use in their court and which the Portuguese call Mandarin, would suffice. For if we would provide examples from the Chinese dialects of each province, we should have to provide an endless variation although sometimes the difference between these varieties is not smaller than the difference between Italian and Spanish. The origin of all these varieties however, is the language which is called Mandarin, The Japanese and Vietnamese have adopted this language together with the characters, but in a rather corrupt form and accommodated it to their own language.

Illa[sic] tamen in vulgari sermone, nec illa[m] vulgo intelligunt sive Japones sive Annam, sed solum qui literas didicerunt, et apud illos se habet sicuti apud nos latina lingua: propria tamen qua vulgó utuntur sive Japones sive Annam, non magis á sinica pendet quam Germanica a latina. Praeterea cum in his tribus linguis nulla sit vox quae unica nomen Dei explicet absque erroris periculo, ideó Deum explicamus ab effectu maximé noto coelo nimiru[m] et terra unu[m] Magistru[m] sequuti Xrūm Dominum qui ait "confiteor tibi Pater Domine coeli et terrae: Matt. 11* et iuxta illud Divi Pauli act. 17** hic coeli et terrae cum sit Dominus etc. sic igitur maximé apud Annam verum coeli terraeque D[omi]nūm annuntiavimus, atque ita 4. characteribus sinicis Dei nomen explicamus, qui suo modo ineffabili nomini tetragrammatωn respondeant.

In daily conversation or in general neither the Japanese, nor the Vietnamese understand this [Mandarin language], but only those who are educated, and among them it has the same status as Latin among us. Their own language, however, which the Japanese or Vietnamese use in general, does not depend more on the Chinese language than German depends on Latin. Besides this, since there is no unique word in these three languages which covers the word God unambiguously [lit. without the risk of an error], we therefore explain it most effectively with the well known heaven, of course, and earth, following one Master, Christ the Lord, who says "I confess to thee, O Father, Lord of Heaven and earth". Matt. 11:30 and next to this the Acts of Paul 17:31. Because he is master of heaven and earth, etc. So in such way we have made known among the Vietnamese with maximum effect the true Lord of heaven and earth, and thus we explain the word God with the four Chinese Characters, corresponding with the tetragrammaton of the unpronouncable name.

[Wordlist follows here]

[f. 11r] 3. Non habent hę linguę nomina mensium communiter in usu sed eorum loco utuntur numeris sequentibus ut in reliquis rebus solu[m] in primo mense, utuntur hac litera 正 quę Japonibus est scioguaci Sinis (cim, yuē), Anna[m] thám giam.***

3. These languages do not have common names in use for the months, but instead they use the following numbers, as in other matters. Only for the first month, they use this letter 正 which the Japanese pronounce as "scioguaci", the Chinese as "cim yuĕ" and the Vietnamese as "thám giam".

* Matthew (11: 25): "in illo tempore respondens Iesus dixit confiteor tibi Pater Domine caeli et terrae quia abscondisti haec a sapientibus et prudentibus et revelasti ea parvulis". [At that time Jesus answered and said: I confess to thee, O Father, Lord of Heaven and earth, because thou hast hid these things from the wise and prudent, and hast revealed them to little ones]. http://vulgate.org/nt/gospel/matthew_11.htm

** *Actus Apostolorum*, (17: 24) : "Deus qui fecit mundum et omnia quae in eo sunt hic caeli et terrae cum sit Dominus non in manufactis templis inhabitat". [God, who made the world and all things therein, he being Lord of heaven and earth, dwelleth not in temples made with hands]. http://vulgate.org/nt/gospel/acts_17.htm

*** *Zhēngyuè* 正月 is one of the terms, – there have been at least 15 other names for this month –, indicating the first month of the Chinese lunar year. The Chinese calendar was based on the observation of the rising and setting of the sun and the phases of the moon, the first lunar month of the year starts the first day of black moon of the new year. Months were named with progressive numbers followed by the term *yuè* 月 ['moon']. Today in China Gregorian system has been adopted, but months still are indicated with the number system, although following the western time. See also Wilkinson (2000: 170).

PART I

China

Eligio Cosi's (OFM; 1818–1885) "Nuovo metodo per scrivere la lingua volgare cinese" and its social impact

Teaching Chinese to Chinese peasants through the Gospel

Erica Cecchetti
Università per Stranieri di Perugia

1. Introduction

Eligio Cosi was an Italian Franciscan missionary who lived in China from 1849 until his death in 1885. While serving as Director of the Franciscan Seminary of Jinan, he invented a new system for transcribing the Chinese language using a 33-letter alphabet. This method spread through the Catholic communities of Shandong and Henan until the first half of the 20th century.

This paper is structured as follows: firstly, it introduces Cosi's life and work and the context shaping his decision to create a new system of romanization, hereafter referred to as "Cosi's script". This section will also outline the didactic principles upon which the system was based and the process by which Cosi's romanization of Chinese was diffused.

Secondly, it will describe and elaborate on the system itself, which has not yet been analyzed in linguistics literature,[1] drawing from this author's unpublished study of "古经略说, Gǔjīng lüèshuō" – a version of the Old Testament – as well as analysis of the book of prayers, "Mensis purgatorii" (in Chinese known as "炼狱称誉 Liànyù chēngyuè").

Next, the paper addresses criticisms of Cosi's script after it became widespread in China and, in particular, the reception of Cosi's method by Franciscan missionary Celestino Ibáñez (1873–1951). Ibáñez, a Spanish friar, was Apostolic Vicar of Shaanxi at the time, and drew from his criticism of several aspects of Cosi's script to develop another version of the Chinese alphabet, which he called "Zhonghua Zi mu" (1921).

---

1. See Cecchetti (2019).

https://doi.org/10.1075/sihols.130.02cec

In conclusion, the paper highlights the impact of Cosi's script on the lives of Chinese peasants belonging to his Catholic community. His work represents an attempt to spread the Gospel as well as literacy among the peasants living in China at the time. This research is based on the study of unpublished archival resources, such as letters and official documents Cosi exchanged with companions in China, the Order of Friars Minor in Rome, and the Director General of the Order. Books and letters published using Cosi's script are also analyzed in order to address the reactions of people belonging to his Catholic community in Shandong who bene-fitted from studying his transcription method. These written sources are preserved in Italian historical archives, such as the Propaganda Fide Historical Archive, the General Historical Archive of the Franciscan Order, and the Library of the Center of Chinese Studies at Urbaniana University.

Placing Cosi's script in the historical context of late Qing China, a period in which Mandarin Chinese was being defined as the national language and a standard for oral language was being debated across the country, is of interest for two main reasons. Firstly, it gives us new insight into the general contribution of missionaries to language diffusion through the Gospel at the local level (Malek 2015: 139), as well as into foreign and Franciscan missionary efforts to participate in the pro-cess of creating a national standard for Chinese language (Masini 2011: 621–662). Secondly, Cosi's script represents an attempt to create an easy and reliable method for teaching the Chinese language not only to foreign missionaries but also to illiterate local people.

The most interesting aspect of Cosi's script is that it was developed to teach the Chinese language to illiterate Chinese peasants without using the complex system of traditional Chinese characters. In analyzing texts containing Cosi's romanization of Chinese script in alphabetical characters, which were circulating among Catholic communities in China until the first two decades of the 20th century, this paper offers new insights on the general context of missionary linguistics in Asia during the late Qing China era.

Indeed, publications using Cosi's script were numerous (Streit & Didinger 1958: 347–348) and his method was adopted by several Franciscan communities operating in China. Cosi's method was received positively by those in need of a sim-pler method for learning Chinese. The method gained success not only among those working to spread the Gospel but also among lay people attending the Franciscan schools run by Cosi and his colleagues. At the same time, Cosi's script was criticized as incomplete, and this critique became the starting point for the development of a new Chinese alphabet by the Franciscan missionary Ibáñez.

The diffusion of Cosi's script in China confirms that debates among Chinese intellectuals about the need for a simpler version of the Chinese language and for a national literacy program (Masini 2011: 637) also involved foreign missionaries.

Cosi's script exemplifies how foreign religious sinologists contributed to this larger conversation about how to build a national language.

Moreover, the article foregrounds how and to what extent the diffusion of Cosi's script affected the lives of Chinese pesants in the Catholic communities where it was adopted. Indeed, Cosi's method was deeply influenced by his experience with the local community. Understanding how he approached language problems related to his apostolate reveals how he conceived of his activities in relation to the context of the Catholic missionary movement that arose in the second half of the 19th century.

Cosi's work was first discussed in the "ACTA" of the Franciscan Order in 1906 and some years later, his method was described in more detail by an unknown author in an article published in "Le Bulletin Catholique de Pékin." As mentioned above, Cosi's work was also studied at the beginning of the 20th century by Celestino Ibáñez O. F. M, a Spanish friar and missionary in China.

Cosi's script was diffused in Shandong and Henan provinces until the first two decades of the 20th century thanks to the publication of several books of prayers (Streit & Didinger 1958: 347–348), a Catholic catechism, and a version of the Old Testament called "古经略说, Gǔjīng lüèshuō". The text consists of excerpts from the Old Testament, and its first edition numbered 2,000 copies (Malek 2016: 140). Malek has compared the contents of Cosi's original translation of the Old Testament with the edition of "古经略说, Gǔjīng lüèshuō" published in 1905 by Joseph Hesser (1867–1920) of the Divine Word Missionaries Order S.V.D. in Yangzhou, Southern Shandong, noting that Hesser's translation is not a re-translation of Cosi's original work but a Chinese translation of a different text: the "Biblische Geschichte des Alten und Neuen Testaments" by Ignaz Schuster (1839–1869), which first appeared in Europe in 1847. This Chinese version of Schuster's compendium constituted a literal translation of Schuster's biblical histories, since "Hesser follows the original text whereas Cosi transcribes narratively" (Malek 2016: 145).

Moreover, the German missionary August Henninghaus (1861–1939) of the Divine Word Missionary S.V.D. order, who was appointed bishop of Southern Shandong at the beginning of the 20th century, stated in an article of 1911 that Catholic missions in China were in need of a complete translation of the Holy Books into Chinese. He found Cosi's script, among other translations of the Bible or of biblical stories circulating in China at the time, as a positive example of translation of holy texts into Chinese (Malek 2016: 139–140). Henninghaus was convinced that this need for the translation of religious texts and biblical materials should be a driving force for Catholic missions in China. He believed that Chinese versions of such texts were essential if Catholicism were to survive in China (Malek 2016: 139).

2. Cosi's life and work

Eligio Cosi was born in Pontassieve (Florence, Italy) in 1819 and in 1839 he became a friar in the Order of Minor Friars in the Italian Franciscan Province of San Bonaventura, Tuscany. Ordained a priest in 1843, he arrived in Shandong in 1849, like many other friars involved in the missionary movement promoted by the Catholic Church in China at the time. The Catholic missionary movement was facilitated by the introduction of privileged conditions for foreign missionaries guaranteed by the "Unequal Treaties" signed between the Qing Court and the Western powers. Cosi was assigned to a two-year-old Franciscan seminary near the city of Jinan and, like the majority of friars at the time, started learning the Chinese language after his arrival (Casacchia & Gianninoto 2012: 600–601). In 1865, Cosi was appointed Bishop and five years later, in 1870, he became Apostolic Vicar of Shandong, a role he held until his death in 1885 (de Moidrey 1914: 62–63).

As Walls (2002: 42) has noted, cross-cultural interactions in the encounter between foreign missionaries and local environments was deeply connected with "the need to live on someone else's terms, to make Christian affirmations within the constraints of someone's else language" and, for this reason, "the missionary movement is the learning experience of Western Christianity". From this perspective, the missionary movement can be "considered the very converse of the cultural imperialism" with which it is often "quite justifiably charged", since the movement unfolded as a "process of introducing Christian affirmations in other languages, and set them free to move within new systems of thought and discourse" (Walls 2002: 42).

As Rule (2007: 516) stresses, anthropological studies carried out in the mid-20th century promoted the idea that missionaries "had a bad name" because of their interference with local cultures and indigenous societies. Such studies of Catholic missionaries in China during the 19th century focused on the missionary movement's relation to Western imperialism and accentuated confrontational encounters between missionaries and local societies. However, Cosi's script and the reasons for its development reveal a missionary experience much more committed to profound cultural encounter with local Chinese people. Indeed, it constitutes an example of the effort some foreign missionaries made to help empowering illiterate people, which problematizes assumptions that missionaries were always mere agents of foreign imperialistic power (Giunipero 2017: 10–11).

Cosi intended his script to address three main problems affecting his missionary experience: the difficulty of learning Chinese for missionaries, widespread illiteracy among the Chinese people, and the slow diffusion of the Gospel in China. As will be described below, the script's social impact extended beyond these initial aims (De Francis: 1984) and facilitated the implementation of a wide variety of cultural and religious strategies for preaching the Gospel at the local level and helping it to spread within communities. In this sense, dissemination of the script is relevant to research on the strategies used by missionaries of different religious orders in China. Studying how missionaries dealt with language-related problems in their apostolates could lead us to a more comprehensive and multidisciplinary approach to understanding the strategies of evangelization adopted by different religious orders.

During his activities as Director of the Franciscan Seminary, Cosi developed a new romanization of the Chinese script in order to simplify the process of learning the Chinese language. His aim was twofold: he was moved by the need to teach the Chinese language to foreign friars and missionaries operating in China using an easy and reliable phonetic support. Secondly, and most importantly, he wanted to help local peasants to learn Chinese without using Chinese characters and to enable them to understand the Gospel. To reach these goals, Cosi created a system based on a new 33-letter alphabet.

In 1865, as rector of the Franciscan seminary, Cosi first informed Bernardino da Portogruaro –, Procurator General of the Reformed Friars and General Minister of the (1822–1895) Order at the time – of his creation of a new method called "Nuovo metodo per scrivere la lingua volgare cinese" ("a new method for writing the Chinese colloquial language"). The historical archive of the Franciscan Order in Rome preserves more than 20 letters Cosi wrote to Portogruaro between 1865 and 1880, which underline the importance of the diffusion of his method.[2]

In 1878, Cosi's letter to Portogruaro describes his reasons for romanizing Chinese and the objectives he had reached in implementing and diffusing the script within his Catholic community:

> L'unico mezzo comprovato dall'esperienza per l'incremento della missione e la diffusione del S. Vangelo, è la diffusione dei libri stampati secondo il nuovo metodo che, S. Eminenza ormai sa quanto il cinese sia contrario alle novità, ma nel vedere l'entusiasmo con cui il metodo è stato da tutti universalmente ricevuto, si comprende facilmente la somma utilità che il cinese abbia in questo, sì per l'anima che per il corpo. E infatti, questi poveri cinesi nelle scuole studiano gridando a squarciagola per quindici e anche diciotto ore al giorno, e dopo dieci e venti anni di assiduo studio restano scaldapanche. Ora questi scaldapanche, messisi a studiare il nuovo metodo, dopo un paio di mesi si sono trovati abili a leggere e capire i libri che ho stampato, e scrivere senza cacografie la lingua che parlano. Sua Eminenza può facilmente immaginare come questi restino trasecolati! Buttati da parte li antichi libri, leggono e studiano i libri che ho stampato, con grande utilità dell'anima loro, e mi dicono che i contadini vanno al campo col libro in mano, e nell'intervallo leggono e dopo, lavorando, ruminano ciò che hanno letto. […] Adesso poi uomini e donne d'ogni ceto, giovani e vecchi, ignoranti e letterati hanno imparato questo metodo.   (Agofm – Storico, Fondo M76, 1692–1860 Miscellanea Sinarum: 254)

---

2.   Agofm – Storico: SK 541: 422–425, 492, 495; SK 543: 625–627, 658–660; Agofm – Storico: Fondo M76, 1692–1860 Miscellanea Sinarum: 254.

[We have just one tool proven by experience that has given us results in terms of diffusion of the Gospel within our mission. The success is related to the diffusion of books translated with the new method. Dear Eminence, as you already know, Chinese people do not like new things but, if you could see the enthusiasm of those who have received the new system, you would immediately understand the great advantages it brings to their souls, and bodies too. Poor Chinese people who attend school spend 15 to 18 hours a day studying and shouting at the top of their lungs, but even 20 years later they remain idlers. Now those benchwarmers, after two months studying the new method, can read and understand the books I have printed, and they can also write without cacography the language they speak. Your Eminence, you can easily imagine their astonishment! Throwing away the ancient books, they read and study the books I have printed, and they benefit from the great advantages it brings to their souls. They tell me that peasants go to the cornfields holding my books in their hands. During breaks, they study, and during work, they repeat what they were studying before. Now, men and women of every class, old and young, illiterate and literate, have all learned this new method.]

In 1906, the "ACTA" of the Franciscan Order published a report on Cosi's script in which Cosi himself described his reasons for creating it:

Statim ut perveni ad Sinas incepi operam dare studio characterum. Videns autem quemlibet characterem multarum lineolarum complexione constare, sine sono, sine accentu, et sine aliquo signo quibus nos utimur in scriptura, ob parvitatem memoriae meae, inhabilem me iudicavi ad hoc difficile studium.

(*ACTA OFM* 1906: 98)

[Once I arrived in China, I began to study the Chinese characters. I saw that every character consists of a complex combination of lines, without any sound, accent; and without any sign we usually use in writing. Due to my terrible memory, I thought I was incapable of such hard study.]

…

Ego enim eram discipulus sine libris et sine magistro; quia sinenses nullam regulam agnoscebant, quae doceat bonam pronuntiationem […] Sudavi itaque per decem annos pro bona pronuntiatione acquirenda, sed postremo adhuc pauper balbutiens eram sicut in principio.   (*ACTA OFM* 1906: 100)

[As a Chinese language student, I did not have any book or teacher; since Chinese people didn't know any rule to teach good pronunciation […], I sweated for more than 10 years before learning how to pronounce Chinese, but at the end my confidence with the Chinese language was still as if I were at the beginning of my study: I was a stutterer.]

The friar decided to build a team of people including two Chinese seminarists, two women from the Third Franciscan Order, and some other foreign missionaries attending the same school to share knowledge, ideas, and skills and to create a new romanization (*ACTA OFM* XXV, 1906: 100). Cosi also underscored the results achieved by this structured, bilingual-team:

> Ad exequendum cogitatum opus, indigebam duobos Seminaristis, et duobos qui nullam linguae latinae cognitionem haberent. Extra Seminarium vero nullum iuvenem invenire potui; ast cum debita permissione Episcopi mei Superioris, quaesivi inter Moniales quae vivunt sub regula Tertii Ordinis, et inveni Catharinam et Filomenam Hu: de Seminaristis autem duos studentes philosophos elegi Paulum Siv et Ioannem Cin, ambos satis intelligentes et ad hoc opus a divina Providentia destinatos. (*ACTA OFM* 1906, XXV: 100)

> [In order to implement my idea, I involved two seminarists who did not know anything about the Latin language. Since I could not involve students from outside our seminar in the project, with the permission of our Bishop I asked the women of the Third Franciscan Order. I found Catherina and Filomena Hu, and two seminarist students of philosophy, Paul Siv and John Qin; they are both very smart, and they have been sent to me for this task by Divine Providence.]

Cosi wanted to disseminate Catholicism and Catholic religious texts through the community he was administering. A community of students, religious personnel, foreign friars, and, most importantly, illiterate people. Most, according to Cosi, were peasants and could not afford to spend years mastering Chinese ideographs. According to De Francis (1943: 225), "besides virtually excluding Occidentals from access to Chinese literature, the ideographic Script has also barred the written word to most of the Chinese people themselves". The importance of literacy to the Chinese population was a key concern for foreign missionaries at the time, who often addressed this issue in their aid and relief activities. As many missionaries stated at the time,

> The classical Character developed a privileged class. Where the ability to read and write in any nation is confined to a literary caste, it follows that the members of this caste obtain and hold the reins of governments.
> (Brewester 1901, cited in De Francis John 1943: 226)

The diffusion of Cosi's romanization system was linked to two key aspects of the friar's work: written publications and teaching in Catholic schools. The Bishop used the script when teaching the Chinese language not only in the seminary but also in the schools run by the friars in the Shandong Province (*ACTA OFM* 1906: 100). For this reason, not only did foreigners and Catholic Chinese learn the script but it was also introduced to non-religious people attending the missionaries' schools (Agofm – Storico, Fondo M76, 1692–1860: 254, *ACTA OFM* 1906: 133). As De Francis (1943: 227) highlights, "the systems of transcription developed by the foreigners for themselves were sometimes used to teach the Chinese to read their own language," and "missionary experiments in the romanization of the Chinese language awakened the interest of the Chinese themselves in this problem, particularly in the period of intellectual ferment from the 1890's on" (De Francis 1943: 228).

Between 1870 and 1917, many religious texts published in China adopted Cosi's script:[3] the first publication of a "Cosi's script version" of a religious text dates back to 1870 and other texts spread through the Catholic communities of Shandong and Henan until the first two decades of the 20th century. These published texts, all published in the typography of the Catholic Mission of Jinan, Northern Shandong, included a letter sent to Portogruaro from the seminarists of Shandong (Agofm – Storico: SK 541: 422–425), three prayers translated into script version (*Pater Noster, Ave Maria, Credo*,[4] a text for Catholic catechism (Bornemann 1976: 1095–1096), and four books of monthly prayers: the month of Mary, May (Streit & Didinger 1959: 347–348); the month of the Purgatory, November (Streit & Didinger 1959: 348), the month of Saint Joseph, March (F. H. 1918: 473); and the Month of the Holy Heart, June (F. H. 1918: 473). In addition, in Southern Shandong in 1894 a worship text was published, and in Eastern Shandong in 1917 Franciscan friars published a book on Saint Théres of Lisieux, edited by P. Irénée Frédéric. Finally, Cosi's "古经略说 (Gǔjīng lüèshuō)" was first published in Jinan in 1875 and included four volumes.

Another important example of the diffusion of Cosi's script at the time is offered by an Italian missionary in Henan. Emilio Anelli (1850–1924), a Xaverian missionary and the Apostolic Vicar of Henan Province at the time, wrote to Cosi in 1881 to confirm the success achieved by the diffusion of his method and the resulting spread of the Gospel in his Province. Anelli highlighted two important social impacts of the use of Cosi's script. First, the emergence of a different missionary strategy between the Jesuit and the Franciscan orders: the former taking a top-down approach, and the latter the opposite. Secondly, the improved literacy rates in his community. Anelli wrote:

> Grazie inoltre dei libri cinesi scritti nel nostro alfabeto, i quali mi giovano assai per la predicazione e la retta pronunzia delle parole, così tanto difficile, per noi Europei. Li mostrai al degnissimo mio Vescovo Mons. Volenteri, il quale lodò questo nuovo metodo, e sembra voglia Egli pure adottarlo nella nostra Missione. Se forse per i letterati non sarà di grande utilità, ma per gli idioti il Monsignore lo giudica utilissimo; poiché in poco tempo e colla massima facilità possono apprendere ciò che non senza gran difficoltà e dispendio di tempo imparano dai caratteri cinesi. Questa ragione è molto convincente, perché si sa che la maggior parte di quelli che si fanno cristiani non sono i letterati, né i ricchi, ma i poveri e i semplici, i quali generalmente non cognoscono caratteri, e molto meno sanno scrivere.

3. Agofm – Storico, Fondo M76, 1692–1860: f. 254, XXXII.
4. Agofm – Storico: SK 541 ff.: 492, 495, 496.

[I am very thankful for the books written in our alphabet, because they help me a great deal in my mission and also help me pronouncing the Chinese language properly, oh what a difficult language it is for us Europeans! I also showed your books to my superior, Bishop Volenteri,[5] who greatly appreciated this new method and said he would like to adopt it in our mission too. It might be useless for literate people but my Bishop thinks that for the "idiots" it will be very useful, since they can learn in an easier and faster way without facing the many difficulties related to learning Chinese characters. This reason is extremely persuasive, because it is well known that the vast majority of Christians are neither rich nor literate; they are poor and ordinary people who usually do not know characters, and even fewer know how to write.]

Io vedo tanti libri magnifici per dottrina e per stilo stampati dai Gesuiti; ma appunto perchè eleganti nessun cristiano i domanda, perché non i capirebbe. Or bene, col metodo ritrovato da V.E. anche un ragazzo, in un paio di mesi, può mettersi si in grado di leggere e scrivere. Ma perché l'opere buone, anche le ottime, trovano sempre dei critici e contradditore, così anche qua è chi disdegna tale suo metodo; ma sì risponde loro, che non è fatto per i dotti, e tantomeno per i critici, sibbene per gl'ignoranti e gli umili [...] Altro dice che le lettere non sono bene combinate, ne rendono l'accento cinese, cosa di tanta importanza per questa lingua, ma io rispondo loro quello che V.E. scrisse al P.N., cioè che questo metodo non è fatto per gl'europei, bensì per i cinesi, e perciò accomodano agl'orecchi e occhi cinesi.

(*ACTA OFM* 1906: 134)

[I see many books written with a magnificent style by the Jesuits, but they are so elegant that no Christian asks for them because they cannot understand them. Now with the method found by Your Eminence, even a boy, in a couple of months, would be able to read and write. Since good works, even excellent works, always receive critiques or generate conflicts, so in this case some do not appreciate your method. We answered that this new method is neither for literate people nor for critics. This method is for the ignorant and the humble. [...] Others say that the letters are not put together well and do not reflect the Chinese accent, which they consider such an important thing for this language. But I respond using the words you already used with P.N., that is, saying that this method is not for Europeans but rather for the Chinese, and the letters are suitable for their ears and eyes.]

(*ACTA OFM* 1906: 134)

---

5. De Moidrey (1914: 79, 81).

3. Description of the script

Analyzing the two written sources (*ACTA OFM* 1906; F. H. 1918) describing the script and together with excerpts from the "古经略说 Gǔjīng lüèshuō" and the "炼狱称誉 Liànyù chēngyuè," both written in Cosi's script, make it possible to outline the main characteristics of Cosi's romanization.

The original version of Cosi's 1875 edition of the "古经略说 Gǔjīng lüèshuō" (in Latin "Compendium Veteris Testamenti") is preserved in the Historical Library of the Center for Chinese Studies at Urbaniana University and consists of four volumes divided according to the content of each book. The original version of the "炼狱称誉 Liànyù chēngyuè" (in Latin "Mensis purgatorii", Cosi, Jinan 1878) is also preserved at Urbaniana University.

Cosi's 33-letter alphabet contains 23 letters belonging to the Latin alphabet – a, c, e, f, g, i, k, h, l, m, n, o, b, p, q, z, s, d, t, x, y, u, v – and 10 letters created by Cosi and his team. The alphabet includes 23 consonants and 6 vowels: a, e, i, o, u, y.

Archival sources do not include a phonetic description of this alphabet by Cosi himself, but the Chinese students who helped him create the system were from Lekou, a district near the city of Jinan. Cosi considered their skills in correctly pronouncing every consonant and vowel a sort of divine gift during the development of the script. This suggests that pronunciation of the script reflected the intonations found in that region.

> De seminaristis autem duos studentes philosophos elegi Paulum Siv et Ioannem Cin, ambos satis intelligentes et ad hoc opus a divina Providentia destinatos; nam cum essent ambo de districtu Lecoufu, clare secernebant omnes consonantes et vocales huic linguae proprias, quamquam hanc optimam proprietatem illarum gentium antea ignoraremus.   (*ACTA OFM* 1906: 100; F. H. 1918: 297)

> [I chose two seminarist students of philosophy, Paul Siv and John Qin. They are both very smart, and they were sent to me for this task by Divine Providence; they both come from the District of Lekou. They were able to properly pronounce vowels and consonants in Chinese although we did not know this great skill before.]

Table 1 represents Cosi's alphabet as it was published in China by Lazarist missionaries in 1918 (F. H. 1918: 502–503). It presents Cosi's 33 letters with an example of how to pronounce them in Latin as suggested by that article. This paper also provides an IPA and PIN YIN description of the letters.

For the use of tones and accents, Cosi does not include a specific rule. As will be discussed later, Cosi does not believe that accent was a necessary element in his method (*ACTA OFM* 1906: 216). In response to criticism for this choice (*ACTA OFM* 1906: 216–217, 299; F. H. 1918: 473, see 4.1), Cosi argues that only if the meaning of words are ambiguous in the context of a conversation should a user of

Table 1. Cosi's alphabet and its pronunciation

	Cosi's Script: Capital letters	Transliteration	Sound proposed by F. H. 1918	Word proposed by F. H. 1918	IPA	PIN YIN
1	A	a	A	A	[a]	A
2	[script]	[script]	ki	ki, (kia:ra)	[tɕ]	J
3	[script]	[script]	k'i	k'i	[tɕʰ]	Q
4	C	c	tch	Tche	[tʂ]	Zh
5	[script]	[script]	tch'	tch'e	[ʂ]	Sh
6	[script]	[script]	che	che	[ɕ]	X
7	[script]	[script]	ng	ngan	[ŋ]	-ng non final
8	F	f	f	fei	[f]	f
9	G	g	j	gi	[z̺]	r-
10	I	i	i	i	[i]	i
11	E	E	ai	ai	[e]	/ye/,/ie/, /yue/, /-üe/ like 也, 月
12	[script]	[script]	between "a" and "e"	ia	[ɛ]	en, eng
13	K	k	k	ka	[tɕʼiʼu]	g like 干
14	[script]	[script]	k'	k'a	[kʰ]	k like 口
15	H	h	h	ho	[x]	h
16	L	l	l	lai	[l]	l like 来
17	M	m	m	mai	[m]	m
18	N	n	n	nai	[n]	n
19	O	o	ao	o	[o]	o
20	[script]	[script]	ng	ang	[nk]	-ng
21	O	Ō	o	ngo	[ɔ]	o
22	B	b	p	pi	[p]	b
23	P	p	p'	p'i	[pʰ]	p
24	Q	q	gn	gni	[tɕ]	ng
25	Z	z	ts	tsi	[ō]	z
26	[script]	[script]	ts'	ts'i	[d͡z]	z
27	S	s	s	si	[s]	s
28	D	d	t	ti	[t]	d
29	T	t	t'	t'i	[tʰ]	t
30	X	x	hi	hi	[x]	h
31	J	y	y	Yy	[yu]	y
32	U	u	ou	ou	[u]	wu/u
33	V	v	yu	yu	[y]	yu/ü

his script decide to put a plain, acute, or low tone on the vowels. However, he does not specifically explain which accent should be used and when. For Cosi, vowels that do not present a specific understandable accent reflect the first or second tone. This position came from his reading of the book *U-fan-jven-in*. In all other cases, words can assume the third or fourth tones, corresponding to acute or low accents.

> Lingua vernacula sinensis, quae merito dicitur mater linguae characteristicae, tres tantummodo tonos admittit, uti ex ore vulgi manifeste patet, quam bene comparare possumus cum syllabis linguae latinae, quae alias syllabas habet planas, alias breves, et alias longas. Quapropter in libris, quos hactenus impressimus, usi sumus duobus dumtaxat accentibus, videlicet: acuto et demisso: nam syllabas, quae recte ac plane sonant, sine ullo signo seu accentu reliquimus.   (*ACTA OFM* 1906: 216)

> [The Chinese vernacular language, which is correctly said to be the mother tongue of the language, admits only three tones coming from the mouth of common people, which we can compare with Latin syllables that could be plain, short, or long. For this reason, in the books that I mentioned before, we made use of at least two accents, that is to say: the acute and the low tone. For syllables which sound correctly and plain, we do not use any indication for the accent.]

> …

> Ergo facile intelligitur vocales, quae sunt sine accentu, pertinere ad primum sive ad secundum tonum; nam in ore vulgi nulla soni differentia auditur inter primum et secundum tonum. Verum est enim, quod sunt plures voces, quas vulgus modo hoc, modo illo accentu pronuntiat, et secundum qualitatem accentus variat significationem; sed pro hac varietate duo supradicti accentus sufficiunt. […] Secundum U-fan-jven-in accentus acutus pertinet ad tertium tonum, et accentus demissus ad quartum.   (*ACTA OFM* 1906: 216)

> [Therefore, it is easily understood that vowels which are without an accent belong to the first or to the second tone, because in the mouth of the speaker we cannot hear any difference in the sound between the first and the second tone. It is true that there are many words that people pronounce in this or that way, and their meanings vary depending on the kind of accent used. However, for this variation the two abovementioned accents are sufficient. […] According to the book *U-fan-jven-in*, the acute accent reflects the third tone, and the low accent reflects the fourth tone.]

Table 2 describes Cosi's script based on analysis of a brief excerpt from the "古经略说, Gǔjīng lüèshuō" (Table 2, section a) as well as analysis of a brief excerpt from the "炼狱称誉 Liànyù chēngyuě" (Table 2, section b) using the IPA and Pinyin systems. The aim of the table is to highlight the script's main characteristics and shows its translation into different linguistic systems using some excerpts from his books. It presents five columns, which indicate Cosi's script in the original text, Cosi's script rewritten for a better representation of the letters, its IPA description, its Chinese characters in a Pinyin translation of the related text, and a translation in English.

Table 2, section a. Analysis of Cosi's script in the "古经略说, Gǔjīng lüèshuō"
(Cosi 1875: Frontpage)

Cosi's script	Transliteration	IPA	汉字 and Pinyin	English translation
KUⓈIⒶLJŌJŌ	KU + Ⓢ + I + Ⓐ	[kuˈtɕˈiˈtɕ]	古经 Gǔ jīng	Old histories
	Ljo + jō	[lˈɥˈɛ]	略 lüè	
	Ȼ + Ō	[ʂˈuˈɔ]	说 shuō	

The "炼狱畅月 Liànyù chàng yuè" (1878) is one of the four volumes of the monthly prayers written using Cosi's script that was published in Jinan between 1878 and 1880 (Streit & Didinger 1958: 348). It consists of 31 chapters: each chapter refers to the daily prayer to be recited during November, the month traditional Catholic ritual devotes to the worship and reparation of the souls of ancestors.

Table 2, section b. Analysis of some excerpts from Cosi's "炼狱畅月 Liànyù chàng yuě"
(Cosi 1878: Frontpage)

Cosi's script	Transliteration	IPA	Hanzi and Pinyin	Translation
LIENIV ꞼAⒶIVŌ *Lien yu cheng yue*	LIEN+ YU Ⓖ +A + Ⓐ + I + V+ Ō	[lˈiˈeˈnˈu] [ɕˈaˈnk] [iˈɥˈɔ]	炼狱 Liànyù 畅月 chàng yuè	Month of Purgatory (畅月= November)
KUANSJV SV-QEN	KU+AN + SJ +V SV – QEN	[kuˈanˈsˈyu][sˈu] [tɕˈeˈn]	关修 Guān xiū 死念 sǐ niàn	For the reparation (of souls) and commemoration of the dead
ꞼIU-IVŌ ꞼI-U-GI	Ⓢ+ I + U YV Ō Ⓖ + I + U – GI	[tɕˈiˈu] [yˈuˈɔ] [ɕˈi] [y] [ʐˈi]	九月十五日 Jiǔ yuè shíwǔ rì	On the fifteenth of September
ZE ꞼENDUⒶ ZINAENFU	ZE + Ⓖ + EN + DU + Ⓐ ZI + NA+ EN + FU	[d͡zˈe] [ɕˈen] [duˈnk] [d͡ʑˈiˈnaˈenˈfu]	在省都惊 Zài shěng dōu jīng 济南府 jǐnán fǔ	In the Capital of the Province, City of Jinan
ꞼENDUⒶ CUꞈⓄ KULIZIO CUIN	Ⓖ + EN+ DU+ Ⓐ CU +Ⓢ O KULIZIO CUIN	[ɕˈ enˈduˈnk] [tʂuˈtɕˈiˈu] [kuˈliˈnkˈo] [tʂuˈiˈn]	省都惊 Shěng dōu jīng 主教 Zhǔjiào 顾立爵准 Gù lì jué Zhǔn	With the permission of the Bishop of the Capital of the Province Eligio Cosi

4. Reception and criticism

As mentioned above, Cosi's work was first publicly recognized in a narrative description in the 1906 "*ACTA*" of the Franciscan Order and, some years later, Cosi's method was outlined in an article published in "Le Bulletin Catholique de Pékin". His system was also studied by the Spanish friar and missionary to China Ibáñez, who published his own romanization in 1921 taking Cosi's script as his point of departure.

According to how these three main sources described the script at the time, its diffusion through the Franciscan Catholic communities of Shandong, Henan (F. H. 1918: 473), and probably Shaanxi (Ibáñez 1921), was negatively received by some other missionaries. This section summarizes the main criticisms Cosi's script received, which were mainly related to its lack of a rule for the use of accents (F. H. 1918: 473), then addresses Ibáñez's view of Cosi's system.

4.1   Cosi's script and the use of accents and tones

With regard to the use of accents and tones, Cosi's script does not provide students with a specific approach and largely underestimated their importance. The development of the script does not include provisions for the use of tones and refers only to the adoption of two different tones, one raising and one falling, based on the rules contained in the book *U-fan-jven-in* (book of five accents or tones) that he considered an authority fot this issue (Casacchia & Gianninoto 2012: 513).

Cosi's script also received criticism for lacking a specific rule regarding the use of accents, which Cosi seemed to consider almost useless for the system itself (*ACTA OFM* 1906: 216).

The authors of the article published in "Le Bulletin Catholique de Pékin" and of the "*ACTA*" claimed that Cosi was highly censured for this choice and that his method was often considered incomplete.

> On a beaucoup discuté sur les accents et on a dit même du vivant de Mgr Cosi que son écriture était, du moins, défectueuse par les accents. L'inventeur incriminé répondait lui-même: « Quelques critiques voulaient que chaque syllabe eùt son accent particulier et disaient qu'il fallait adopter les 5 tons on accents tels qu'ils sont dans le livre U-fan-jven-in » (livre des 5 accents ou tons).   (F. H. 1918: 503)
>
> …
>
> Fuerunt aliqui critici, qui approbant quidem hanc novam methodum nostram scribendi linguam vulgarem, sed asserebant libros quos impressimus deficere pluribus accentibus. Volebant etenim unamquamque syllabam habere supra se suum peculiarem accentuum, dicentes esse adoptandos quinque tonos seu accentus uti sunt in libro *U-fan-jven-in*.   (*ACTA OFM* 1906: 216)

[There were some critics who approved our new method for writing the vernacular language but who also assumed that the books we printed had failed in representing many accents. They wanted every syllable to have its own accent and said that we should have adopted the five tones and accents contained in the book *U-fan-jven-in.*]

To reply to this critism, in 1881 Cosi started a process of reviewing the script involving other literate people from Shandong. He was convinced that they could point out problems related to tones and accents. He maintained that the review resulted in full appreciation for how the system had been conceived from all participants. He also found that they did not believe it needed improvement and instead proposed that it facilitated the writing of a plain, acute, or low accent.

> Nihil addendum vel demendum huic methodo, affirmantes duos accentus, acutum et dimissum esse sufficientes. Insuper asseruerunt etiam duos accentus pro hac scriptura non esse absolute necessarios, quia ex sensu sermonis, facile intellegitur significationem tam nominis, quam verbi.
> [...]
> Exemplum iuxta hanc nostram methodum.
> Accentus planus: a e i o u v – ē ō
> Accentus acutus: à é í ó ù – è ò
> Accentus demissus à è i ò ú v – è ō   (*ACTA OFM* 1906: 216)

[They all answered that the method was already good and did not need anything added or cut. They stated that two accents, one acute and one low, were enough. They also also assumed that accent was not necessary to the method because the meaning of every word or verb is very easily understood from the context of the conversation.
[...]
An example of our method.
Plain accent: a e i o u v – ē ō
Acute accent: : à é í ó ù – è ò
Low accent: á è i ò ú v – è ō.]

Cosi states that the accent should be used only for words whose meanings were ambiguous in order to avoid possible misunderstandings in the conversation. At the end of his discussion of accents and tones in the script, Cosi proposes the adoption of two signs that could be written on vowels if the words were characterised by a plain, acute, or low accent.

Cosi underestimates the importance of accents and tones and, despite receiving criticism for this approach, argued that spoken Chinese does not need a specific rule for tone and accent since in most cases Chinese words are understandable based on the context in which they are used. Though he seems to engage with this criticism and responds by organizing a team to review his method so as to find a solution with members of the community, he never actually acknowledges the importance of tones and their use in the language, and the solution he proposes for the use of accents remains incomplete.

The friar's priority, as well as that shared by all the missionaries at the time, was to save as many souls as possible and in the shortest time. This main goal may have affected the choice not to deepen some linguistic aspects preferring the quick achievement of their spiritual aims.

4.2   Ibáñez (1873–1951): An adaptation of Cosi's script

In 1921, Ibáñez published his own romanization of Chinese. His starting point was how Cosi's script had highlighted that learning Chinese characters was a privilege reserved for the rich upper classes and denied to the majority of the population (Ibáñez 1921: 4). Ibáñez had been bishop of Northern Shaanxi since 1911 and was a former missionary in Shandong; he would serve as apostolic Vicar in the city of Yan'an until 1949, when he was forced into exile in Shanghai and resigned (Camps & McCloskey 1995: 115).

Ibáñez assumes that using a romanised version of the Chinese language in primary schools would enable the Chinese population to learn the complicated Chinese writing system more easily. Without excluding the importance of Chinese characters in the Chinese education system, Ibáñez's romanization aims to give the poor an opportunity to learn how to write and understand their own spoken language, since most could not afford to attend school for the many years necessary to learn how to write traditional Chinese characters. Moreover, he wanted this new writing system to be a tool for Catholic religious and lay people in disseminating easier versions of the catechism and holy books (Ibáñez 1921: 5).

Ibáñez proposes his method to the students attending "l'école de Notre-Dame de Begoñâ, que notre Vicariat possède près de Yengaenfu, au lieu dit Ko-olkou" (Ibáñez 1921: 6). He maintains that all Chinese students attending the school achieved impressive results thanks to their study of the method and proposed:

> Il serait à désirer que les Missionnaires fissent connaitre cette méthode à leurs chrétiens et veuillent bien commencer dans leurs écoles; et ils verront par l'expérience sa facilité et son utilité qui peuvent la faire adopter peu à peu par les payens eux-mêmes.   (Ibáñez 1921: 8)

According to Ibáñez, the diffusion of his romanization, like Cosi's, had two main goals: increased literacy of the Chinese population and promotion of the Gospel. Another intention shared with Cosi (Ibáñez 1921: 43) was the intended target learner: Chinese people. As he states in his presentation of the method, "C'est le peuple chinois que nous avons eu directement en vue en écrivant cette méthod" (Ibáñez 1921: 43).

Ibáñez acknowledges that Cosi's script had been the departure point for his new alphabet, "CU♠HUA ZVMU, 中華字母 Zhōnghuá zìmǔ". To improve upon Cosi's version of the script, Ibáñez simplified and clarified some of its characteristics, modifying four main aspects. First, he excludes the vowels <ē>, [ɛ], and <ō>, [ɔ], because he believes their use was confusing and incomplete. Ibáñez maintains that their pronunciation depends upon the position of the vowel inside different syllables, as in other languages. For this reason, he removes the two redundant vowels in the new alphabet and introduces the diaeresis sign <ë> [ə] and <ö> [ø] to highlight the different pronunciation of these letters according to their position inside syllables.

Secondly, he modifies four letters invented by Cosi, replacing them with new versions resembling similar sounds in letters of the Latin alphabet. Ibáñez introduces the letters <k> [k], and <k> [kʰ] to substitute the two letters Cosi had used for sounds <k> without aspiration and sounds <𝒦> with aspiration. He also replaces <g> [z] with the letter <r> because of the similarity of the sound <r> in other language systems (French and Spanish) with the sounds Cosi had expressed with the letter <g>; he instead uses <g> only in syllables <go, ga, go> id. [ko],[ka], [ko] similar to those of the Latin system. Ibáñez also replaces Cosi's new letter "𝖃" [ɕ] with <x> and <q> with <ñ>, [ɲ], because of similarity of the sounds represented with these letters in the Spanish language. Finally, he applies some changes to the three groups of sounds represented by the syllables <a♠> [nk], <en> [ən], and <in> [in] when preceded by a consonant.

Ibáñez published his adaptation of Cosi's script in a table in 1921, showing some syllables with their corresponding Chinese characters and comparing them with their the romanised alphabetic version in Cosi's script, his own script, French, and English (Ibáñez 1921: 72–92).

5. Conclusion: Social impact

The social impact of the application of Cosi's script within the Chinese Catholic communities of Shandong and Henan included concrete results achieved by the first users of this new alphabet in two main fields: literacy and evangelization. Firstly, according to Cosi's letters and one letter sent to Rome by students at his seminary in Shandong (Agofm – Storico: SK 541: 422–425), the script was extremely useful for Chinese students attending schools directed by the Bishop.

The author of the introduction to the article published by the Lazarist missionaries in 1918 described in detail the benefit of Cosi's system for evangelization. The article highlights that the Chinese people would benefit from the diffusion of the method (F. H. 1918: 299). The author maintained that the script created uniformity and facilitated the learning process by simplifying written Chinese. For this reason,

Chinese people could learn to read and write their own language in an easier and more reliable way. Moreover, the article states:

> Nous avons demandé à un missionnaire du Chantoung oriental de faire pour les lecteurs du Bulletin un exposé de la Méthode Cosi pour la romanization de la langue chinoise. C'est ce travail que nous publions ici, et nous faisons volontiers nôtres ces réflexions de l'auteur des « Missions de Chine, pour 1917! »: Il est fâcheux que toutes les missions de Chine n'aient pas adopté ce mode d'écriture; car il seirat arrivé ce qui est arrivé en Indo-Chine, où les missionaires créèrent une langue qui est devenue langue officielle, en figurant la langue du pays avec les 24 lettres de l'alphabet européen. La vulgarization de ce procédé aurait singulièrement aidé à rsoudre le problème actuel de la simplification de l'écriture chinoise.
>
> (F. H. 1918: 296)

In addition, Emilio Anelli, saverian missionary in Henan, wrote to Cosi in 1881 to confirm the great success in terms of social impact achieved by Cosi's script in his Province. First of all, Anelli highlighted the improved literacy rates in his community and underlined the positive reception it achieved among Chinese people belonging to his community. Secondly, he appreciated the successful bottom-up missionary strategy carried out by the Franciscan order.

The impact of use of the script on evangelization was often enthusiastically highlighted by Cosi, who was eager to emphasise the success of his method. In 1880, he wrote:

> Adesso poi uomini e donne d'ogni ceto, giovani e vecchi, ignoranti e letterati hanno imparato questo metodo. Le madri di questi contorni mi portano le figlie di dodici quattordici anni e mi dicono: questa mia figlia sa leggere tutti i libri che ella ha stampato, adesso desidera imparare a scrivere, la prego dunque darle penne, carta e calamaio, imperocché con la tal maestria con cui ha insegnato loro a leggerle, possa insegnare loro anche a scriverle Agofm – Storico: Fondo M76, 1692–1860 Miscellanea Sinarum: 254–255).
>
> [Now men and women of every class, old and young, illiterate and literate, have all learned this new method. Mothers of this district bring me their daughters, 12 to 14 years old, in order to teach them reading and writing, and they beg me, saying "please, give her pens and paper and teach her how to write, too. With the same mastery you used to teach her how to read, we hope you could now teach her how to write".]

In conclusion, even if Cosi's script had a limited geographic and temporal diffusion and received both criticism (see 4.1) and revision (see 4.2), it achieved positive results in two main social aspects: evangelization – following the Franciscans' missionary strategy of targeting lay people – and the increased literacy of those who were taught, both missionaries and Chinese people.

Moreover, Cosi's method is a positive example of how missionary work built new systems for simplifying the traditional ideographic system of Chinese directly addressed the widespread illiteracy of the late Qing Chinese population. According to De Francis (1943: 239), the traditional system was also partially responsible for excluding the majority of Chinese people from access to Chinese literature. In addition, Masini (2011: 634–635), quoting Huang Zunxian (1848–1905), highlights the underlying influences of the foreign missionary presence in China on the larger ongoing debate about literacy that took place between the end of the 19th and the beginning of the 20th century.[6]

> La fioritura del cristianesimo è legata al Vecchio e Nuovo Testamento: quando questi furono tradotti nella lingua di ciascun paese, i seguaci di questa religione aumentarono enormemente. Infatti quando la lingua è separata dalla scrittura, pochi sono quelli che conoscono la scrittura, mentre quando la lingua e la scrittura concordano, molti sono quelli che sanno scrivere. [...]. Se desideriamo che i contadini e i mercanti, le donne e i bambini di tutto il paese siano in grado di conoscere l'uso della scrittura, saremo costretti a presentare un sitem più facile.
>
> (Masini 2011: 637)

> [The success of Christianity is connected to the Old and the New Testament: when their translation into the language of every country is completed, the number of followers grows tremendously. When language and writing are divided, those who can write are few. But when language and writing concord, many are those who can write [...] If we want peasants, merchants, women, and children to know how to write, we are obliged to present an easier system.]

Since the issue of the accessibility of the Chinese writing system was of interest at the end of the 19th century – especially since writing was a tool possessed by the powerful upper classes of literate Chinese, according to De Francis (1943: 225) – objections to romanization were presumably social rather than linguistic.

Cosi's script represents an example of how a national standard for written Chinese was constructed and how such a system could offer both literacy and the possibility of becoming an active part of the modernization process in China. The crisis of the traditional imperial system and the process of creation of a new modern identity that took place by the end of the 19th century had as protagonists the social and linguistic transformation of the country. That process was also highly influenced by the confrontation with the West.

---

6. Huang Zunxian (黃遵憲, Huángzūnxiàn, 1848–1905) best known in China for his "日本國志" (Rìběn guó zhì, 1890, Engl.: Japanese national ambitions, republished also in 1968 by 臺北縣永和鎮: 文海出版社, 民國, Táiběi xiàn yǒnghé zhèn: Wénhǎi chūbǎn shè, mínguó, 57, Taibei, Yonghe: Wenhai Publisher) was an active advocate of the need to modernization the Chinese writing system at the end of the 19th century.

Cosi's building of a bilingual team represents another attempt to involve local Chinese people in this process of creating an easy phonetic support to learn the language. As far as we know, Cosi above all appreciated the skills of these locals in correctly pronouncing every consonant and vowel, which also suggests that his script was meant to reflect the variety of Chinese spoken in that region. As mentioned above, such social impacts point toward the wide variety of cultural and religious strategies implemented by Franciscan missionaries to introduce and circulate the Gospel in their local communities. This suggests that further research into the missionary strategies promoted by different religious orders in China and elsewhere could afford a more comprehensive and multidisciplinary approach to the study of evangelization in the field of missiology (Buffon 2015; La Bella 2009).

Cosi's script represents an attempt to spread the Gospel as well as literacy among the peasants living in China at the time. This commitment had an impact on the lives of those who attended the schools run by the friars as well as on the general context of missionary linguistics studies. The creation of the method confirms the importance of the communication issue with Chinese peasants which became a major topic also debated among the Communist Party a few years later. The party-peasant relationship represented the key element of the Chinese transition towards modernization and language led empowerment of Chinese pesants had a crucial role in that process, too.

References

A.   Primary sources

ACTA OFM. 1906. "Dissertatio de lingua sinica ad discenda iuxta methodum Episcopi Cosi O.F.M.; ex codice mss. bibliothecae nostrae missionis in Zinanfu (China)". Quaracchi: Ad claras aquas ex tipographia collegii S. Bonaventurae. 25. 97–100, 133–134, 214–216.

Agofm – Storico (Archivio Storico dell'Ordine dei frati minori): SK 541 ff.: 405, 406, 422–425, 431, 441–442, 487–490, 492–494, 495–496; SK 542 ff.: 549–551, SK 543 ff.: 625–627, 658–660, 710–711. Fondo M127, Cina 1782–1869: ff. 494–520.

Cosi, Eligio. 1875. *Compendium Veteris Testamenti* (古经略说 Gǔ jīng lüè shuō). Jinan: Episcopus Eligio Cosi.

Cosi, Eligio. 1878. *Mensis purgatorii* – 炼狱畅月 Liànyù chàng yuè. Jinan: Episcopus Eligio Cosi.

Fondo M76 1692–1860 Miscellanea Sinarum: ff. 245–255 (f. 254), March, 20th, 1880: "Relazione della Missione, risposta ai 33 quesiti proposti dalla S. Congregazione della Propaganda di Roma ai vicari apostolici della Cina il 16.06.1878".

B.   Secondary sources

Bornemann, Fritz. 1976. *Der Selige P.J. Freinademetz 1852–1908. Ein steyler China-Missionar. Ein Lebensbild nach zeitgenössischen Quellen.* Roma: Analecta SVD; 36.1095–1096.

Brewester, William N. 1901. "China's intellectual thralldom and the way of escape". *Chinese recorder* 32:295 (cited in De Francis: 1943).

Buffon, Giuseppe. 2015. "Identità e missione: confronto tra forme tradizionali e nuove fondazioni in ambito francescano". *Svolta dell'innovazione* ed. by Roberto Fusco, Giancarlo Rocca & Stefano Vita, 69–78. Città del Vaticano: Urbaniana University Press.

Camps, Arnulf & Pat McCloskey. 1995. *The Friars Minor in China 1294–1955. Especially the years 1925–55.* St. Bonaventure, N.Y.: Franciscan Institute; Rome: General Secretariat for Missionary Evangelization, General Curia, Orders of Friars Minor.

Casacchia, Giorgio & Gianninoto, Mariarosaria. 2012. *Storia della linguistica cinese.* Venezia: Cafoscarina.

Cecchetti, Erica. 2019. "L'alfabeto del cinese di Eligio Cosi OFM (Firenze, 1818–Jinan, 1885): una proposta di romanizzazione alla fine del XIX secolo". *Associazione Italiana di Studi Cinesi. Atti del XVI Convegno 2017* ed. by Giunipero Elisa and Piccinini Chiara, 41–53. Venezia: Cafoscarina.

De Francis, John. 1943. "The Alphabetization of Chinese". *Journal of the American Oriental Society* 63:4.225–240. https://doi.org/10.2307/594356

De Francis, John. 1984. *The Chinese Language: Fact and Fantasy.* Hawaii: University of Hawaii Press. https://doi.org/10.1515/9780824840303

F. H. (author unknown). 1918. "Un essai de romanisation de la langue chinoise (Cosi). *Le Bulletin Catholique de Pékin* 5.296–299; 471–473; 502–504.

Giunipero, Elisa M. 2017. *Uomini e religioni sulla via della Seta.* Milano: Guerini e Associati.

Ibáñez, Celestino. 1921. *La Romanisation de la langue chinoise.* Beijing: Imprimérie de Lazaristes du Pe-t'ang.

La Bella, Gianni. 2009. "S. Sede e Cina nel pontificato di Pio 11°". *Sulle orme di Matteo Ricci. Chiesa e Cina nel Novecento* ed. by Elisa M. Giunipero, 125–143. Macerata: EUM.

Malek, Roman. 2015. *The Chinese Face of Jesus Christ. Annotated Bibliography.* London: Routledge.

Malek, Roman. 2016. "The Bible at Local Level. Notes on biblical material published by the Divine Word Missionaries SVD in Shandong (1882–1850)". *Monumenta Serica. Journal of Oriental Studies* 64.137–172. https://doi.org/10.1080/02549948.2016.1175779

Masini, Federico. 2011. "La riforma della lingua". *La Cina. Verso la modernità, La Cina III* ed. by Giorgio Samarani, 3.621–662. Torino: Einaudi.

Moidrey, Joseph [Tardif] de. 1914. *La hiérarchie catholique en Chine, en Corée et au Japon (1307–1914).* Shanghai: T'ou-sè-wè.

Rule, Paul. 2007. "Why Have Missionaries Got a Bad Name?" *A Lifelong Dedication to the China Mission: Essays presented in honor of Father Jeroom Heyndrickx, CICM, on the occasion of his 75th birthday and the 25th Anniversary of the F. Verbiest Institute K.U. Leuven* ed. by Noël Golvers & Saartje Lievens, 515–520. Leuven: Ferdinand Verbiest Institute K.U. Leuven.

Streit, Robert & Johannes Didinger. 1959. *Chinesische Missionsliteratur 1880–1884. Bibliotheca Missionum.* Vol. 12. Roma: Herder.

Walls, Andrew F. 2002. *The Cross-cultural process in Christian History: Studies in the transmission and appropriationof faith.* Maryknoll, New York: Orbis Books.

The Jesuits as translators between Europe and China (17th–18th century)

Noël Golvers
KU Leuven

> To publish books in Chinese is mostly nothing else
> but translate European books into Chinese
> (Verbiest 1680: 66–67)
>
> Translation is the performative nature of cultural communication
> (Bhabha 1994: 228)

1. Introduction

Missionizing in general is a communicative process *par excellence*, as it uses language – both spoken and written – as the preferred vehicle for converting people, even when it partly or occasionally relies on visual elements. In the China mission of the Jesuits, this verbal communication included also – mostly for strategic reasons – the transmission of the core of contemporary Late-Humanistic sciences, in domains ranging from philosophy to geography, medicine, technology and mathematics. This was a first particularity of the China mission: although the same sciences at random appeared also in other missions (such as in India and Arcadia), the scale on which it happened, and the central position of sciences in the communication in China was indeed unique. Another particularity was precisely the language – perceived as completely different from all other known languages – which made this mission in the perception of the missionaries the most difficult among the Jesuit missions, and constituted, together with its most remote position, one aspect of the martyrdom deliberately searched for by many candidates.

Communicating about the Gospel and European sciences happened in one particular register of Chinese – from the outset the *guānhuà* register, as we will see further – which required a systematic act of translation, in whatever form, which we can only trace back through the written output it had, namely Chinese texts, produced by the Jesuits. Afterwards, especially from the end of the 17th century

https://doi.org/10.1075/sihols.130.03gol
© 2021 John Benjamins Publishing Company

a new, academic incitement arrived from Europe, aiming for the acquisition of Chinese texts and their translations for a European public, either in Latin or in the vernacular. Therefore, in the next observations I would like to include both directions of this translation process, as I see them as each other's complement. Modern research on this phenomenon of inter-cultural communication or exchange was mostly limited to descriptive and / or statistical contributions, and rarely focused on the working methods: most interesting among them are the contributions of Tsien (1954: 306–313), Hsia (2007: 39–51) and Jami (2018). For a real understanding of the process of translation, its problems and solutions, one should enter in the detailed comparative research between particular *source* texts and its target text, as did, for example, Verhaeren (1935: 414–429) in the past, and more recently Kurtz (2008: 35–38), Engelfriet (1998) and Wu Huiyi (2017); as I am myself not a Sinologist, my approach is necessarily limited to testimonies in Western sources, taking into account three complementary aspects: that of (a) the source language, the Chinese *guānhuà*, with its particular problems for the Western Jesuits; (b) the method of working and (c) the instruments used.

2.   Translating from European languages into Chinese

It was actually Nicola Longobardo (1565–1655), who in May 1613, in Beijing, wrote a memorandum, unfolding – surpassing previous examples of translating and composing individual texts – a *systematic program* of translating Western knowledge, to be produced in complete or at least largely representative 'working libraries', with a central library in Peking and branches in the five other then existing Jesuit residences spread over China:

> Requerese hua livraria acabada de todos os livros, como qualquer das melhores (livrarias) de Europa. O nosso fim e traça que nisto temos he q(ue) posta esta livraria em Pekim, aonde se aiuntão a seus tempos // (fº 303v.) todos os mandarins e melhores letrados deste Reino, faça formar o conceito que se deseia de nos e de nossas cousas. E com isto demos occasião de nos pedirem a tradução dos ditos livros como se vio p(or) alguns poucos q(ue) ategora sairão o q(ue) nos faz estabalecer e perpetuar na China e confiamos q(ue) ha de ser ainda meio pera introduzir ca muitos sogeitos, q(ue) con autoridade real se occupem na tradução delles, q(ue) seria abrirse a porta q(ue) tanto deseiamos pera a pregação do Evang(eli)o neste Reino.
>
> (ARSI, Japonica Sinica 113, fº 303r.)

> [I required a 'complete' library of all (kind of) books, such as one of the better (libraries) in Europe. Our aim and project with this is that, when we have constituted this library in Peking – where at appropriate moments all the mandarins and the top of the Chinese 'literati' of this Empire arrive – it will shape their opinion

of us and our things. With this we give them the opportunity of asking us for a translation of our books, as one has seen so far for some few books. With this our presence in China is established and perpetuated, and we are entrusting that there must be now a way to introducing here (in China) many topics, which we can treat, with the authorization of the Emperor, in these translations, which will be the same as to 'open the gateway' for Evangelization in this Empire, as we desire so much.]

In 1615, Nicolas Trigault, SJ (1577–1628), procurator of the Jesuit mission in China sent to Europe in 1614 to implement this plan, again specifies this purpose:

> Et in singulis (sc. residentiis) expediat introduci lectionem unam publicam Mathematicae, aliam Philosophiae, aliam Theologiae, et si non omnes simul, paulatim tamen instituendae videntur. Id etiam videtur necessarium, ut singulae [residentiae?] possint esse capaces fundationis annuae cum propter distantiam locorum non possint facile alia aliis attribui et a se mutuo pendere. Quod si de omnibus hoc non placet, omnino tamen Nanquinensi et Pequinensi concedendum est, quia Nanquinensis in omni rigore constitutionum est Collegium, cum sit Seminarium nostrorum, qui linguam Sinensem ediscunt. Et Pequinense domicilium alere debeat eos qui librorum et Sacrae Scripturae versioni debent incumbere, praeter illas tres lectiones publicas quas ibi oportet inchoare.
>
> (ARSI: JS 100 ("*Sina, Memoralia – Responsa*"), f° 10ff)[1]
>
> [And it would be useful to introduce in each (residence) one public lecture of mathematics, another one of philosophy, another one of theology, and if they cannot be instituted all at once, they should be organized step by step. It seems indeed necessary, that each residence could be self-sufficient [capable (to get) its own annual funds], because due to the distance between the places it is hard to attribute things from the one to the other place and to be paid in return by them. And if this does not please for all of the residences, it should be completely granted to the Nanking and Peking College, because the Nanking residence is, in all the rigour of the Constitutions a College, as it is the seminary for our (novices), who are studying Chinese. And the residence of Peking should nourish / maintain those (fathers) who should devote them to the translation of books and the Holy Scriptures, in addition to these three public lectures, to be started there. And then the other residences could be connected to them.]

Also the Superior General, Muzio Vitelleschi (1563–1645), in his (lost) letter (*libellus supplex*) of 1615 to Pope Paul V, by which he requested for the constitution of a *bibliotheca pontificia* for the mission, mentions the translation of these books as the main target:

---

1.   "N. Trigault, Proposita R(everen)do P(atri) N(ostr)o Generali a Procuratore Missionis Sinensis, anno 1616", more precisely f° 11v. (col. B).

Notandum 5. …. Mutius Vitelleschius f(elicis) m(emoriae) olim obtulit libellum supplicem Pontifici Paulo V ad impetrandos omnis generis libros, et ad Sinas mittendos atque a Patribis Sinensibus in Sinicum idioma vertendos, uti expressis verbis declarat in dicto libello, quem hîc in archivio Vice-Provinciae servamus.[2]

[To be noticed. 5. Mutius Vitelleschi, of pious memory, once offered a request to Pope Paul V in order to obtain books of all kind, to be sent to China and to be translated by the Chinese Fathers into Chinese, as he explains in the said request, which we are preserving here in our archives of the Vice-Province.]

When this library was finally collected in Rome and largely extended throughout Europe, it bore the strong imprint of the particular interests of the *connoisseur* Johann Schreck Terrentius (1576–1630), polymath with skills in the domain of alchemy, iatrochemistry, botany, mathematics, astronomy and calendar making, and linguistics.[3] We retain here that these and other testimonies definitely establish that 'translation' was the main target of this enormous book acquisition program.

3.   The implementation of this translation program

First, we should make here three preliminary remarks: The first regards the source books themselves. Due to the heterogeneous composition of the staff of the 'Portuguese' mission in China – the French mission arrived since 1687 being homogeneously composed of French Jesuits – but also as a consequence of the rise of the vernacular book markets in Europe the library of the Xitang / Nantang, the 'central' college of the Portuguese mission in Peking represented in the 17th–18th century books in eight different European languages;[4] the basis of these translations was thus heterogeneous, and a battery of dictionaries were available to the translators.[5]

The concept of translation applied within this program was a very *elastic* one: it included various forms of 're-thinking' and 're-phrasing':[6] from translations *ex verbo ad verbum*, through summarizing and paraphrasing, often resulting in a patchwork produced by the technique of 'cut and paste', up to free compositions relying on personal reading and reading reminiscence. But, in general, as Ferdinand

---

2.   As the original letter of Vitelleschi to the Pope is no longer traceable, we know this only from Verbiest's reference in his *Postulata Vice-Provinciae Sinensis* (1680), who refers to a copy of this letter in the Jesuit archives in Peking: Golvers (2018: 64–65).

3.   On Terrentius's book search, see Golvers (2020).

4.   According to the extant items, books in Latin, Portuguese, Italian, French, German, Dutch, English, Slavonic, Ancient Greek: see Golvers (2015: 29–36).

5.   See Golvers (2015a: 444–455).

6.   See, among others Eco (2003).

Verbiest (1623–1688) in 1680 explains: "publish books in Chinese is mostly nothing else but translate European books in Chinese".[7]

Obviously this enormous program of producing translations and free compositions had also an institutional aspect within the Jesuit Society, more precisely with regard to the *ius* or *facultas imprimendi* ("right of printing") for these Chinese translations: as the European source texts had already received in Rome the *approbatio*, one argued in China that the procedure of a separate *approbatio* for a Chinese translation or paraphrase in Rome was superfluous and, as waiting for it had – because of the distance and the very time-consuming and risky intercontinental communication – a negative impact on the production process itself, it could better be conceded to the Jesuits in China, the only one who could evaluate the quality of the Chinese productions. But this request was not heard; in fact the answer on these proposals was negative, and even when in 1672 General Oliva had given a more differentiated answer, which distinguished between different situations, for the books of *iustae magnitudinis* ("with a fair volume") and *maioris momenti* ("of major importance") the decision remained entirely in the hands of the Roman authorities.

Turning now to the selection of what was translated, and for what reasons, there was a double imperative, namely the agenda of the Jesuits – obviously aiming in the end for the introduction of Teaching – which was crossed with the interest (and limits), curiosity, needs, if not orders from the Chinese public, which had in general other priorities than the Jesuits had. In answer to both imperatives, the selected source texts concerned:

a.   aspects of the Doctrine, also on moral philosophy;

b.   Western science, in the first place but by far not only those sciences related to 'Heaven', the latter offering an easy occasion to switch from dealing with the astronomical heaven to the Christian Heaven – but also aimed at the production of a calendar for China, a reliable prediction of eclipses for all the Chinese provinces, the application of Western medicine, and progressively the introduction of several 'new' techniques;

c.   Of the European source texts also *readers' digests* or *selections* were made and translated: see, for instance, Verbiest's project – probably never realized – of translating a selection from the proto-musicological treatise of Athanasius Kircher (1602–1680), titled *Musurgia*.[8]

---

7.   "Libros Sinico idiomate edere plerumque nihil aliud est quam libros Europaeos in Sinicum idioma vertere" Golvers (2018: 66–67).

8.   Golvers (2017: 647): "*Hanc ipsam ob causam ego modo ex Musurgia Patris Kircheri rariora aliqua tam theoretica quam practica in idioma Sinicum verto, et in exigui tractatûs libellum compono*" ["For the same reason I recently started the translation into Chinese of some curious parts, theoretical as well as practical ones, from Kircher's Musurgia, and to compose them in a small booklet".]

For an overview of the translated texts, I know only one up-to-date database, which pursues completeness, namely the CCT database of Ad Dudink and Nicolas Standaert (KU Leuven); still this describes only extant printed texts, and during my own research I could establish that, on the level of intentions and projects many more Western texts had been taken into consideration to be translated and were probably also (partly or completely) realized, without being printed, or preserved.[9]

The composition / translation of texts into Chinese was the commitment of most of the Fathers, when they arrived in China, especially in Peking but also outside. Yet, some of them were probably exclusively engaged as translators: such were, for instance, Manuel Osorio (1663–1710)[10] and (Francisco?) Pinto (1662–1731),[11] both mentioned as such in 1691,[12] and Alessandro Cicero (1639–1703)[13] – a physician – who helped Antoine Thomas (1644–1709) with the translation of his treatise on Algebra between 1692 and 1695, writing in the Palace, as the Emperor feared this precious knowledge would become more generally spread.[14]

Apart from some works originally written in Manchu (by Ferdinand Verbiest (1623–1688); Claudio Filippo Grimaldi (1638–1712); Dominique Parrenin (1665–1741); Joseph de Prémare (1666–1736), etc.) the target language of these translations was Chinese, and already Pope Paul V – donator of the aforementioned *bibliotheca pontificalis* ("Papal Library"), the real original nucleus of the Western libraries for China – specified this Chinese was the *lingua non vulgaris, sed erudita et litteratorum propria* ["not the 'vulgar' / colloquial (Chinese), but the erudite one,

---

9. A partial overview I gave in Golvers (2015: 575–581).

10. Dehergne (1973: no. 600): Osorio made his vows in Beijing on 15.08.1695 (ARSI, Lusitana, 11, 318).

11. Dehergne (1973: no. 642).

12. ARSI: JS 148, f° 535: "qui licet Mathematicas artes non callerent, erant tamen imprimis ad linguam discendam et vertendos libros Europaeos in linguam Sinicam idonei futuri: illi autem socii determinati sunt P(ate)r Emmanuel *Escovius (Osorius?) qui ab anno uno erat Macai, alter P(ater) Pinto, qui versabatur in Provincia Fokien, etc." ["Although they don't know the mathematical disciplines, they were nevertheless considered in the first place competent / suitable to learn the (Chinese) language and to translate European books into Chinese; for him were indicated the companions Emmanuel Escovius, who was since one year in Macau, the other one was Father Pinto, who remained in the province of Fujian".]

13. Dehergne (1972: no. 177).

14. ARSI: JS 149, f° 544: "1695 (May) Maio mense: "Imp(erat)or algebrae vacat": Lectiones Algebrae, quam (sic) eius iussu P(ate)r Alexander Ciceri et ego scribere linguâ Sinicâ coepimus anno praeterito (…)" ["The Emperor studies algebra. The lessons on algebra, which Father A. Ciceri and myself (Thomas) started last year to write in Chinese".]

proper to the literati"],[15] i.e. the *guānhuà*. This basic option, which remained afterwards unaltered, dictated also the language-to-be-studied by the Jesuit newcomers.
On the other hand, this logic preference involved some problems on the terrain,
as *guānhuà* was not throughout China the common language of oral communication, the natural vehicle of the missioning practice, especially not in Southern
China. In addition, there was the enormous typological difference between the linguistic systems of European (source) languages and the Chinese target language:[16]
a difference with many aspects, such as the (supposedly) exclusively monosyllabic
character of Chinese; the absence of any morphological and flectional system; the
'limited' lexicon, in terms of words (ca. 350 lexical 'roots'); the role of the five tones
supported in the oral communication by 'body language', e.g. by writing characters
by gestures in the air, an aspect which was lost in a written communication. But
especially the secular, cumulative literary background of the *guānhuà* tradition,
and its interplay of internal cross-references, etc. only to be acquired after many
years of study and devotion, constituted a concomitant difficulty for newcomers,
as the Jesuits were. Revealing is a text written by Francisco de Benavente (OSA;
1646–1709) in 1701, who described in precise terms the linguistic context in which
the Jesuits in China had to work, and the problems involved. Many of these problems are explained in the next comprehensive assessment of the linguistic situation
for the missionaries-in-the-field:

> Quibus alia difficultas accrescit…, videlicet linguae generalis difficultas, quae sic
> gravis est, ut V(estris) E(minent)iis in puritate et veritate loquar, ut post studium
> plurimorum annorum et exercitium improbo labore comparatum vix inveniatur,
> nec superioribus temporibus inventus sit homo Europaeus (nisi unus aut alter)
> qui ore proprio valeat Sinensem mediocriter catechizare, et forte nullus satis in-
> strueretur, nisi librorum ope et catechistarum iuvamine […]. Obsecro V(estras)
> E(minentias), ut in hoc mihi fidem adhibere velint, nam intra Sinam tam quoad
> linguam, quam quoad characteres (qui diversam a vulgari linguam [sic] efformant)
> nullus est, qui aliud iactare de se audeat. Vidi enim multos missionarios ex illis, qui
> videbantur columnae propter tempus studio et exercitio in Sina consumptum, et
> licet alios aliis minus ignaros invenerim, doctiores tandem satis pauperes in lin-
> gua et characteribus, sicut me ipsum expertum sum. Verum altissima providentia
> fit ut, adiutorio Christianorum literatorum libri satis faciliter componantur, nam

---

15. "Praeterea regularibus (sc. sacerdotibus) praefatis, ut Sacra Biblia in lingua(m) Sinarum,
non tamen vulgarem sed eruditam et litteratorum propriam transferre illisque translatis uti; ita
tamen ut in huiusmodi translatione summam et exquisitam exhibeant diligentiam, ut translatio
fidelissima sit" (published in Bontinck 1962: 412).

16. Summarized by Duhalde (1735: 2, 224) as follows: "La langue chinoise n'a rien de commun
avec les langues 'mortes' [Latin; Greek] ou vivantes que nous connaissons".

praedicti literati assueti nostro communi barbarismo nostros conceptus tandem non sine labore percipiunt, et Sinensi rhetoricâ explicant. Impressio deinde librorum facillima est, ita ut vili pretio non modo, papyrus et opera, sed etiam tabulae aperiantur, quae non semel sed perpetuo ad libros excudendos deserviunt.

(ARSI: Fondo Gesuitico, 723 / 7)

[To these (difficulties) came another one (…), namely the problem of the 'general' language, which is a so serious difficulty – as I will say to Y. Em. in sincerity and truth – that after a study of many years and a training acquired with heartless effort, there is – and was in the past – barely one European to be found (except one or other individual exception) who with his proper mouth could catechize in Chinese on an average level, and probably there is no-one sufficiently instructed, if not with the support of a book or the help of a catechist. (…) I have indeed seen many among those missionaries, who were seen as 'columns' because of the time they spent in China to study and exercise – even when some of them I found less ignorant than others – even those who are rather well instructed are in the end rather 'poor' in language and characters, as I have experienced myself. Yet the Almighty Providence makes that, with the help of Chinese literati rather easily books can be composed, because the aforementioned literati are accustomed to our shared 'barbarisms' and in the end they are perceiving our concepts, not without efforts, and they explain them in Chinese rhetoric. After that, the printing of books is very easy, so that not only the paper and the work, but also the wood blocks are opened at a cheap price, which are serving not once but permanently to print books.]
[…]

C[a]eterum maior difficultas non est in lingua generali, quae dicitur *koan hoa*, nam missionarii improbo labore tandem illa taliter qualiter utuntur; sed quia in hac provincia (idemque est in omnibus Australibus) praefata lingua generalis non est communis, praecipue inter populares et agrestes; nam in diversis locis diversimode corrupta est, ita ut intra spatium sex milliorum Italicorum homines diversorum vicorum et maxime feminae prorsus ad invicem non se intelligant; quia lingua Sinica omnino componitur ex 350 vocabulis monosyllabis, vel saltem diphtongis cum sono dissimili, qui ea diversificat et multiplicat. Ideo quaelibet minima corruptio linguam prorsus diversam constituit, quae intellegi nequit nisi ab oppidanis.

(*ibid.*)

[In addition, the major difficulty is not located in the general language, which is called *guānhuà*, because the missionaries, after an excessive effort, in the end use it in whatever way, but because in this province (and it is the same in all the Southern provinces) the aforementioned general language is not shared, especially not amongst common people and farmers; in the different places it is deformed in different ways, so that within a space of six Italian miles people from various hamlets, and especially the women do not understand each other mutually. Because the total Chinese language consists of 350 monosyllabic words, or at least diphthongs with a different sound, which diversifies these words and multiplies them. Therefore whatever minimal corruption constitutes a truly different language, which cannot be understood, unless by the locals ….]

For this reason, the phase of learning / acquiring[17] the language and scripture was tiresome and perceived as *taedium* ["weariness"], and one aspect of the 'martyrdom' the Jesuits were looking for in China. More practically, the basic study asked two years and the further refinement some 20 years, as Verbiest repeats in his *Postulata*; therefore there were no *tirones* ("candidates") older than 40 sent from Europe to China (acc. to Buenaventura Ibáñez, (OFM; 1610–1691), referring to the Jesuits).[18]

Even after an about 30 year long experience in China, a Jesuit like Francesco Brancati (1607–1671) – one of the Jesuits present in Canton in 1665–1671, and one of the most accurate and methodic philologists writing a clear Latin – expresses the problematic mutual comprehension, both with regard to the written and spoken language in the following terms:

> Dico igitur, cum Sinicum idioma sit valde ambiguum et perplexum, Sinici vero libri valde etiam sint obscuri et intellectu difficiles, contigit aliquando ut, quando nos Europaei Sinice loquimur propter verborum improprietatem et accentuum discrepantiam non bene et lucide sensus noster a Sinis percipiatur, nec nos Sinarum animi sensa absolute & perfecte penetrare possimus; atque adeo, quando solummodo verba Sinensium referuntur, debet illorum sensus valde nobis est perspectus et clarus, ut possit illorum auctoritas firmas habere radices.
>
> (Brancati 1700: I, 272)
>
> [So I say: because the Chinese language is very ambiguous and intricate (cryptic), and Chinese books are also very obscure and hard to be understood, it sometimes happened that, when we Europeans are speaking Chinese, because of the misusage of words and the discrepancy of the tones, our meaning (intention) was neither well nor clearly understood by the Chinese, and we could not penetrate absolutely (totally?) and perfectly into the thought of the Chinese. And so, when only (loose?) Chinese words are referred, their meaning should be very clearly perceived and clear to us, so that their authority can get firm roots.]

The problem for the translators did not come from the side of the target language only, but also from the source language, more precisely from the specific, and specialized *terminology* of several sciences used in the source texts, scientific and theological alike. In China – where the Jesuits had, all well considered, a primarily 'Teaching' commitment – this concerns in the first place the many – delicate – theological concepts, to begin with the transposition of the name of 'God' / 'Heaven',

---

17. On the learning process: Brockey (2007: 243ff.); Pina (2011); Hsia (2011: 211–229). Outside the Society see Girard (2008: 109–124).

18. "Hermano nuestro, escuse V.C. lo posible de mandar a esta mision religiosos de 40 años de edad para adelante, que de quantos sé que en esta mision entraron de [mas de 40 años] de los Padres de la Compañia nunca supieron lengua. Porque esta lengua, por su dificuldad, quiere sujetos de menor edad" (Ibáñez, cited in Alcobendas 1933: 125).

since the beginning of the mission,[19] but concerned also many other Christian liturgical and devotional terms, as well as the whole Aristotelian philosophical terminology (later: Cartesian, Newtonian, etc.) and the professional vocabulary of technology, mathematics, anatomy, not to mention particular proper names, geographical and personal alike (e.g. Aristotle; Galileo, etc.), which were an integral part of the contents transmitted. The Chinese neologisms which the Jesuit translators created in answer to this challenge[20] constituted within the Chinese language absolute oddities, both in semantic and lexicological sense, and remained therefore mostly obsolete, without finding a true reception. This was for instance the case with some individual attempts in the field of Western philosophy (Francisco Furtado [1589–1653] with Aristotelian categories)[21] as well as with theological concepts (Ludovico Buglio [1606–1682] in his translation of Thomas Aquinas's *Summa*)[22] and mathematical terms, especially with regard to Euclidean geometry.[23]

These translations and other free compositions were rarely isolated productions, and mostly they were situated within a wide-ranging program or project, and there are even indications of a planned division of the workload.

A first project was the so-called Astronomical Encyclopedia (*Chongzhen Lishu* [1629]) and its revised edition, titled *Xiyang sin-fa li-shu* [1645], the result of teamwork, consisting in the end of ca. 150 *juan* ("volumes") produced in the *Liju* ("Western Academy").[24] Another project concerned the *Corpus Aristotelicum*, starting from Porphyrius's *Isagoge* ('Introduction); an enterprise spanning a period from the 1620s until Verbiest finished it in 1683, when it was presented as *Qiongli xüe,* relying on the *cursus Conimbricenses.*[25]

In 1680, Verbiest, making the balance of 60 years of Jesuit translating activities concluded that in science, Western meteorology was the only domain not

---

19. To my knowledge a comprehensive and systematical historical overview of this aspect of the Rites Controversy is still lacking.

20. This process of lexicological innovation is perfectly parallel with what happened, when in the 1st century b.C. Cicero (and some earlier Latin writers) 'transposed' Greek philosophy and science into Latin; see on this process the inspiring observations of Nicolas (2000).

21. See Kurtz (2008: 35–57).

22. For theological terms in Martino Martini's (1614–1661) *Zhenzhu lingxing lizheng,* see Yuan in Paternicò (2000: 363–386).

23. For lexicological innovations in the field of mathematics, in order to render Euclidean geometry, see Engelfriet (1996: 164–167; 1998: 283–285).

24. See on this Bernard (1938 and 1940); Hashimoto (1988).

25. See the contributions of Dudink, Standaert and Golvers (1999).

yet covered by 'Western' publications in Chinese,[26] while in the domain of religious writings there was a lack of 'ascetical', i.e. 'spiritual' books for the common Christians, and he feared that – if the General would not concede the *ius imprimendi* to the Chinese Vice-Provincial – in the near future such books should be no longer produced, to the great damage of the missionary activity.[27]

A convincing proof of the systematic and planned character of Jesuit scholarly work in China we find among the French Jesuits, in a letter of Jean de Fontenay (1643–1710) to Marquis de Louvois (Jean-Baptiste Colbert, 1619–1683) of 16 November 1687, at the start of this 'academic' and 'scientific' mission par excellence,[28] organized, advized and paid by the *Académie des Sciences* in Paris:

> Mémoire / des instruments et livres que les Jesuites mathematiciens du Roy (….) supplient Mons(ieu)r le Marquis de Louvoy de leur faire donner. 1687.
>
> Pour le P(èr)e de Fontanay [responsible for astronomy/geography]
>
> 1° Deux pendules: 2° instr.; 3° instr.; 4° Les livres nouveaux de mathematiques qui sont estimez, et en particulier ceux des Mess(ieu)rs de l'Académie;
> Pour le P(ère) Visdelou [responsible for Chinese history; linguistics]
> 1° Un bon dictionnaire comme celuy de Danet pour le mettre peu à peu en Chinois; 2° La Grammaire raisonnée; 3° Trigault et Martini, de l'Histoire de la Chine, et ce qu'il a décrit sur cette histoire.
>
> Pour le P(ère) Le Comte [responsible for the 'artes liberales" and mechanics]
>
> 1° Le Dictionnaire des arts, et s'il y a quelque autre livre françois, qui apprenne les termes propres des arts; 2° Un bon livre d'architecture. Nous avons Vitruve, mais on en demande qui parle en detail de toutes les parties du batiment; 3° Un livre des aqueducs et fontaines, la maniere de conduire les eaux; 4° Quelque livre qui traite de la fonte des canons et des bombes, et s'il y a quelque chose sur le vernis, la verrerie etc.
>
> Pour le P(ère) Bouvet [responsible for natural history and medicine]
>
> 1° Ce que M(essieu)rs de l'Académie Royale ont fait jusques a present sur l'histoire naturelle des animaux et des plantes, car parmi les ouvrages qu'on nous avoit donnéz, il ne s'est trouvé qu'une seule feuille de leurs mémoires sur l'histoire naturelle, ce qui nous fait soupçonner que nous pouvions bien avoir perdu une quaisse de livres a Brest, car il nous manque aussi d'autres livres que nous croyions avoir; 2° Divers petits traitez de M(onsieu)r Du Verné; 3° L'Hortus Malabaricus, pour voir ce qui y manque; 4° L'histoire des animaux de Bauhin, ou quelque autre histoire

26. Dunyn-Szpot (1700: 2, 128–129).

27. Golvers (2018: 62–65).

28. Ample literature exists on the 'scientific' mission of these '5 *mathématiciens*'; here I only refer to the contribution of Landry-Deron (2001) and Jami (1995).

universelle des animaux; 5° Quelque traité des arbres et des plantes en françois pour apprendre les termes propres de la Botanique en nostre langue; 6° L'anatomie des plantes; 7° La micrographie de M(onsieu)r Hook; 8° Quelques instruments propres a faire des dissections; 9° Des echantillons des diverses drogues et mineraux avec leurs etiquettes pour les connoitre // (p. 40) 10° Le dictionnaire Tartare de M(onsieu)r Thevenot, s'il est imprimé; 11. Un dictionnaire et une grammaire Syriaque; 12. Un dictionnaire et une grammaire hebraique. Le P. Bouvet a désiré ces derniers livres, ayant envie de travailler sur la langue Tartare, a cause de la connoissance qu'il a deja de l'hébreu.

Pour le P. Gerbillon [responsible for Chinese 'politics' and social customs, and for some parts of physics, including mineralogy] Un estat present de la France, et un de l'Europe.[29]

4.   The working method and instruments

Most interesting is the question of *how* these translations were produced, taking into account the various possible degrees of respect / distance with regard to the model: depending of the case, there is indeed evidence for a scale of attitudes, going from an "*verbum ex verbo*", i.e. a 'literal' translation, to a translation respecting the general 'idea' / intention of the author ("*ad mentem auctoris*"). The instruments played an important role, viz. wordlists and bilingual dictionaries / vocabularies.[30]

4.1   European wordlists

In several situations, a first, very rough and preliminary translation was prepared. On this level personal wordlists and other tools were used, made by individual Jesuits in the first place for their private purposes; such instruments are mentioned, for instance, on the name of (in chronological order): Matteo Ricci (1552–1610) and Nicolas Trigault;[31] Alvarez Semedo (1586–1658);[32] Gaspar Ferreira

29. Archives des Missions Etrangères de Paris, 479. Chine – Jésuites (1687–1691: 32–33).

30. In the passages I researched, the terms "dictionarium" and "vocabularium" were used indiscriminately.

31. "Clavis…nemo nostrum illâ utitur; quia inutilis" ["Nobody of us uses it, as it is useless"]: Couplet to Daniel Papebrochius [(1628–1714) in Antwerp, on 03.02.1687 (Brussels, Museum Bollandianum, ms. 64, n° 217).

32. Bernard (1945: 41): "Habebat manibus duplex Dictionarium longe exactissimum, alterum Sinico-Lusitanicum, alterum Lusitano-Sinicum, sed mors antevertit" ["He worked on a twofold, very accurate dictionary, one a Chinese-Portuguese one, another a Portugues-Chinese one, but his decease anticipated it"] Cf. Barbosa Machado (1741: 114).

(1571–1649);[33] Manuel Dias (1574–1659);[34] Julien-Placide Hervieu (1671–1746) and Joseph de Prémare (1666–1736);[35] Dominique Parrenin (1665–1741);[36] Florian Bahr (1706–1771);[37] Luigi Cipolla (1736–1805?).[38] Several of these personal 'word

---

33. Barbosa Machado (1747: 351).

34. Barbosa Machado (1752: 246–247).

35. Jean-Placide Hervieu, from Macau in a letter to General Retz of 3 Nov. 1733: "Videns ego juniores Sinenses Latinis litteris instituendos suscipi, tum a Sacrae Cong. Missionariis, tum ab aliis ne dictis candidatis deesset auxilium ad minimum perutile ac prope necessarium, cogitavi de parando in eorum usum dictionario Latino Sinico. Novissime absolutum est operâ Patris Jos(ephi) de Premare et meâ, nec Latinam vocabularii partem typi Sinenses nec Sinicam Europaei admittunt, adeoque typis non destinatur opus – cumque non ita multi sint ejusmodi candidati, sufficient ad finem intentum si dictum vocabularium exscribant qui potuerint ac voluerint, vel sibi ab aliis excribi current. Nos quod sine fictione didicimus, sine invidia communicabimus, modo non displicuerit Sacrae Congregationi, cui nostra quantulacumque probari percupimus" ["Seeing that young Chinese were accepted to be instructed in Latin, and in order to prevent that the candidates of both the missionaries of the Holy Congregation of the Faith and of other (congregations) would lack a support, at minimum useful and almost necessary, I was thinking of preparing for their practice a Latin-Chinese dictionary. Very recently it was finished by Father J. De Prémare and myself. The Chinese printing press does not admit printing the Latin part, neither do the European presses (accept) the Chinese part. Therefore the work is not destined for printing; and, as there are only a few candidates, these (texts) will sufficiently reach their intended aim, when those who are able or willing can transcribe it, or look for someone else to do it for them. We will communicate without any envy the things we have taught without any pretence, if it does not displease the Holy Congregation, by which we greatly desire that our minimal works would be approved" (ARSI: JS 184, ff. 119–124). This dictionary is still extant in the Royal Library of Stockholm; see Cordier (1901: 1635–1636): "*Vocabulaire latin-chinois, 2 vol, in 4°, le premier contient 936 pages, le second autant, sur la première page de chaque volume, on lit: Auteur de ce dictionnaire le R P Jul(ien)-Plac(ide) Hervieu, traduit du latin de Danet*".

36. The dictionary of Parrenin, mentioned in Pfister (1932–1934: 514); Lundbaek (1986: 165, n. 25, etc.). This copy is preserved in Glasgow, University Library, Hunterian Ms., no. V.2.12, now Ms. 392, 877 pages; the title page says: "*Petri Daneti Lexicon Latinum Sinice conversum in Usum Gymnasii Pekinensis a R(everendo) P(atre) Dominico Parrenin S. J. missionario Pekinensi*" ["The Latin dictionary of Pierre Danet, translated into Chinese, to the behalf of the Peking school by Father Dominique Parrenin, SJ, missionary in Peking'".]

37. Discovered in the Palace Shou'an gong in Peking: Fuchs (1933: 68–72).

38. Cf. ARSI: JS 184, f. 255v. (16.09.1771): "*Il P. Cipolla avendo inteso che i P(atri) Francesi a Pekino sono molti, e senz'occupazione (!), ed istesso sentii un paragrafo di una lettera scritta dal P. Gramont francese al P. Lefebvre, in cui dice che tutta la sua occupazione è in Pekino trascrivere un dizionari cinese*" ["Father Cipolla had heard that the French fathers in Peking were numerous and without occupation, and the same had read a paragraph from a letter written by the French Father Gramont (1736–1812?) to Father Lefbvre (1706–1783), in which he said that his entire occupation in Peking consisted in transcribing a Chinese dictionary".]

lists' may have got some larger circulation, for instance within the residence of their 'owners': cf. during the Canton detention, when several *Dictionaria Sin(ic)o-lusitanica* and *Vocabularia Europaea-Sinica* were mentioned,[39] circulating within the Jesuit compound, where the fathers were working on their translating / writing program in seclusion; this not only included the CPF translation but also an intensive program of writing apologies on Domingo Fernández de Navarrete's (c.1610–1689) invectives. Inevitably, due to the limited space where ca. 25 fathers lived together for some years within the same buildings of the Canton Jesuit college, some exchange and mutual consultation will have existed.

Others were sent to Europe, where they are stored in historical collections, in general without a visible further reception.[40] From these individual wordlists, one arrived slowly to the idea, and even the production of a really comprehensive bilingual dictionary, a project which was entrusted to the Austrian Jesuit Christian Herdtrich (1625–1684), who had been intensively involved in the Confucian translation project in Canton, and who had almost finished it and prepared it for the printer, when he unexpectedly died on 17 July 1684:

> Quâpropter omnes V(ice)-Provinciae moderatores vocabularii Sinici revisendi et emendandi curam Patri commiserant; iamque novum vocabularium Latino-Sinicum Pater pr[a]elo paratum habebat, quod brevi tamquam opus posthumum in lucem prodibit.   (Golvers (2017: 600))

> [Therefore, all the 'moderators of the Chinese Vice-Province conceded the responsibility of the revision and emendation of a Chinese vocabulary to Father Herdtrich; the Father had already prepared the new Latin-Chinese vocabulary for the printing press; it will shortly appear as a posthumous work.]

From the few extant testimonies on this dictionary, it remains unclear whether it was a Latin-Chinese or a Chinese-Latin dictionary, but most probably it was a 'double' one: anyway, ca. 1684 Philippe Couplet (1622–1693) expressed from Europe – where he was travelling at that moment – great expectations for the imminent printing; the manuscript, however, seems to have been lost afterwards.

For some of these European word lists or dictionaries of Chinese, a pre-existent Latin dictionary had been the model, in the same sense as Jeronimo Cardoso's (1508–1569) *Dictionarium latino-lusitanicum (…)*, Coimbra, 1569 (etc.) the basis of Ruggieri-Ricci's first Chinese dictionary (James 2004); Pierre Danet's (1650–1709) *Lexicon Dictionarium Novum Latinum et Gallicum*, Paris, 1673 (French: *Nouveau dictionnaire françois et latin*, Paris, 1683), which already in November 1687 Jean

---

39. Dictionaria Sin(ic)o-lusitanica, used in Canton during the detention (1665–1671): cf. references for instance in Brancati (1700: II, 69; 70; 80; 107) and Lefaure (1700: 425 and 457–458).

40. See Standaert (2001: 871). A complete inventory is, as far as I know, still a desideratum.

de Fontaney requested from Ningbo in his letter of 16.XI.1687 to the Marquis de Louvois (i.e. Colbert): "un bon dictionnaire comme celuy de Danet pour le mettre peu à peu en Chinois".[41] Afterwards it was really used by Jean-Placide Hervieu and Joseph de Prémare. Another Latin model had been the Latin *Calepinus*, in one of its many editions, which was used for the composition of a tri-lingual Latin-Portuguese-Japanese dictionary.[42]

Because these personal lists and vocabularies were very precious material, several of them were posthumously stored in the local Residence library, where they could be consulted applied by the successors. This seems to have been the case with Augustin von Hallerstein (1703–1774) – I have to return to this – and, after the suppression and exceeding the inter-confessional border, with the Anglican Robert Morrison (1782–1834).[43]

Obviously, the Jesuits were aware of the difficulties involved in describing Chinese in a Western way, and some – like Verbiest – denied even the possibility *überhaupt* to make a dictionary / grammar of Chinese (this clearly despite Martini's attempt (1650), about which he was probably unaware.

Others did admit the difficult classification of 'terms' and meanings:

> Scimus quae voces in vocabulariis Europaeo-Sinicis strictius usurpatae sint, quae vero latius, defectu proprii vocabuli Sinico respondentis, in rebus quae vel supra Sinarum captum posita, vel procul a nostro modo loquendi modo dissitae sunt.[44]

> [We know which 'entries' in the Euro-Chinese dictionaries *are used in a more strict sense, which on the contrary are used in a more broad sense*, by lack of a proper Chinese word corresponding (to the model / source term), in things which are far from the understanding of the Chinese, or are far from our (Western) way of saying].[45]

In the last phase of the Jesuit presence in Peking, Augustin von Hallerstein – who was at the end of the line of Jesuit 'keepers of the Observatory' and could dispose of a large set of previously prepared dictionaries – in his letter to Dr. Mortimer of the *London Missionary Society* recognizes the qualitative difference between the aforementioned European word lists and Chinese and authentic Chinese dictionaries:

---

41. Archives des Missions Etrangères de Paris 479. Jésuites (1687–1691: 39).

42. Kishimoto (2006: 17–26).

43. For Morrison's dictionary and its predecessors: Yang (2014: 299–322).

44. Lefaure (1700: 425): "'sum hien' offeruntur, atque in iisdem ipsis discis seu lancibus çu quas vocabularia Europaeo-Sinica appellant 'vasa sacrifitii (sic)'".

45. This remark is true for bilingual monodirectional vocabularies which translate from Chinese into European vernaculars, such as Spanish: see Zwartjes (2014: 57–100).

> Chinese vocabularies, which interpret the Chinese words in Latin or any other
> European language, are very scarce, and for the most part very defective. Nor is
> there any one as yet brought to a sufficient degree of perfection, to deserve printing,
> or the expenses attending it. Those, which we use the first years after our arrival,
> were either left by our predecessors, or written with our hands with infinite effort.
> And even these are not of any great use to us, except the first two or three years,
> to read and understand some easy books of the Christian doctrine, composed by
> our Fathers.   (Hallerstein 1751: 322–323)

Therefore, for the following stage, namely the lexicological, idiomatic and stylistic
'Sinicization' the support / revision of Chinese assistants was fundamental. This is
commonly known and should not be further supported by examples here, but it is
rarely as clearly expressed as by the aforementioned friar Francisco de Benavente,
OSA, who in 1701 writes to his Superiors, that "they (i.e. their Chinese assistants)
could understand the typical (Western) 'barbarisms' and were able to transmit them
into current Chinese"; several of these Chinese assistants had also studied Latin
(Peking; Hangzhou), in order to understand better the 'errors' of the European
Sinologists.

4.2   Chinese dictionaries

Yet, indispensable was the access to, and use of native *Chinese-Chinese dictionaries*, even when also this I found rarely mentioned *expressis verbis* in the Western
sources. I may refer here again to Verbiest, who ca. 1680 mentions in Peking a –
further unspecified – *vocabularium commune*, which he quotes, with regard to the
radical "y" (i.e. *ji*), with its 164 meanings.[46]

Most explicit was, 80 years later, Augustin von Hallerstein (1703–1774) indeed
confirms the complementary use of the lexicological instruments he found in the
library of his Peking college:

> In order to read more difficult Chinese books and particularly their Classics, we
> are using Chinese dictionaries which explain their characters in Chinese lan-
> guage, but in a simple way, similar to Latin dictionaries of Stephens (i.e. Estienne),
> Nizolius etc.   (Hallerstein 1751: 323)[47]

Eager to know which Chinese (-Chinese) dictionaries precisely the Jesuits used, one
can only turn to a patient analysis of the Western sources, which unfortunately are
stingy with information on this point. A first cross-section through my Western
evidence of the 17th and 18th century brings 7 titles to the fore, namely:

---

46. Verbiest in his *Postulata*: Golvers (2018: 60–61).

47. Saje (2009: 105).

- *Eulh-ya*, i.e. *Erya*, one of the 13 Classics (3rd cent. b. Chr.: Matthews, 275): "qui date de plusieurs siècles avant l'incendie des livre" (Cibot 1778, vol. 3: 455)
- *Shuowen jiezi*: a dictionary going back as far as the 2nd C. B. C.; "le plus ancient dictionnaire chinois rangé par classifiques, 10.600 charactères divisés en 540 classifiques". (Simon 1970: 516)

The following 5 references speak about *personal use*:

- *Cu Guei*, i.e. *Zihui (Tzu)hui?)*, the only Chinese dictionary – apart from "*nostra dictionaria* (or: "*vocabularia*") *Sinicolusitanica*" – explicitly, profusely and precisely quoted by the Jesuits in Canton (Brancati: 1700; Intorcetta: 1700) in their apologies against De Navarrete, composed in 1668 and 1669, simultaneously with the *Confucius Sinarum Philosophus*. Also Philippe Couplet – between 1665 and 1671 part of the same group of translators (and transcribers) – preferred this dictionary before the following title *Zhengzi tong*.[48] He refers to a full copy in 12 volumes and more than 33,000 characters, a copy which he left in Rome in the *Collegio de Propaganda Fide*. On the same place he refers also to a "short or abridged version" of it, in only 8 small volumes, with a selection of the most frequent meanings and words; he compared it to – and also called it – *Calepinus Sinicus*. This was what he used during his European tour (according to other references in his correspondence in Berlin). An indirect echo of Couplet's presentation we also find in the correspondence of Emanuel Schelstrate (1649–1692), librarian of the Vatican Library (Ceijssens (1949: 182–183).
- *Zhengzi tong*, in 17th century transcription *Chim çu tum*, indicating a dictionary of the Ming dynasty: a copy Couplet ordered in 1682 'ordered' to be sent from Macau / China on behalf of Theodor Sas, Sr., Protestant 'minister' in Batavia, 1682: JA 49-IV-6, f° 37r./v.); it was edited by Ming scholar 張自烈 ZhāngZìliè and has 33,549 entries; it is considered as an amplified version of the former one;
- *Hai pien*, i.e. *Haipian*: translated as "Oceanus" (i.e. Tzu Hai): with 60,000 characters, abbreviated for the convenience of the Westerners to 6,000, 8,000 or 10,000 characters;[49]

---

48. "Ceterum Cu guei mihi magis placet quam Chim çu tum, quam hîc (i.e. in Paris) relinquo, etsi hoc posterum (?) habeat plures significationes et eruditiones. Habeo in Lusitania parvum çu guei, cum praecipuis significationibus constans octo tomulis, nam pleraeque significationes non sunt nisi rarissimae in usu, uti quoque in nostris Calepinis; multae sunt quae tantum semel (…) adhibentur" (1687).

49. Müller (1672: passim).

- *Pin çu çien*, i.e. *(Xie sheng) pin zi jian;* mentioned, among others, as the source of a note on the meaning of 'tian' ("Heaven"), which was kept in the archive of the Portuguese college in Peking (Xitang / Nantang);[50]
- *Kangxi zidian,* the so-called Kangxi dictionary, finished in 1716, with 214 'radicals' and ca. 49,000 characters (Simon 1970: 517).

But even in using these 'native' dictionaries, the Jesuits – including such philologists *pur sang* as Francesco Saverio Filippucci (1632–1692) – encountered serious difficulties, due to their always incomplete character, as Chinese characters needed a context to be exactly understood:

> Illa (sc. Vocabularia) quidem non esse numeris omnibus absoluta, nec (ut linguam et literas Sinicas apprime callentibus videtur) omnino perfecte fieri ullo modo posse; ratio est, quia Europaeae voces, ut plurimum vel unam aut paucas et determinatas habent significationes; Sinicae vero litterae, si solitariae sumantur, plerumque plurimas habent et saepe indeterminatas et contrarias significationes; si complexim cum aliis inveniantur, multa plura significant, et saepe saepius (sic) a singularis litterae significatione longissime disparatae.   (Filippucci (1700: 64–65)

> [These vocabularies are not fully 'complete', and can by no means become completely perfect (as the first learners of Chinese language and literature have in the beginning the impression); the reason of this is: that European words mostly have one or a few determined meanings; Chinese characters, on the contrary, when taken separately, have mostly several and often undetermined and opposite meanings; if one finds them in combination with other (characters), they mean many more things, and very often very far away from the meaning of the separate character.]

5.   Translations of Chinese texts into European languages

Complementary with the painful production of Chinese texts, to a lesser extent original Chinese texts were also translated into a European language, either Latin or one of the vernaculars, especially French. The incitement to this activity – which shifts the perspective of the missionaries' activities from the Chinese public of literati-to-be-converted to a European public – came from different angles. First, the China missionaries themselves understood the need of an appropriate preparation of the future novices for the mission, if possible already before they left Europe; these *tirones* are already mentioned as a target group of Martini's Chinese grammar (Paternicò 2000); Verbiest's *Elementa Linguae Tartaricae* (Aalto 1976,

---

50. Lisbon-Ajuda, Jesuitas na Asia, 49-V-25, f° 74ff., n° 89;

1977); Gabriel de Magalhães's (1610–1677) (lost) treatise on the Chinese language (De Magalhães 1688: 84–107; Pih 1979: 366), and – outside the linguistic domain – of *Confucius Sinarum Philosophus*, witness Intorcetta's introductory letter in the manuscript.[51] Besides, also many non-Jesuit individual scholars in Europe were expecting accessible Chinese texts: obviously these scholars were in the first place linguists, such as Andreas Müller (1630–1694) and Christian Mentzel (1622–1701); Hebraists like Louis Picques (Sorbonne, 1637–1699), etc. and others, who were looking for the 'universal' or the 'Adamic' language; in addition there were general *curiosi*, such as Christopher Arnold (Nurnberg, 1627–1685); Jan Theodore Royer (The Hague, 1737–1807), etc., astronomers and chronologists. Finally, also official academies, in the first place the French *Académie des Sciences* incited to a systematic collecting of Chinese texts to be sent to France, with the ultimate goal to be translated. Until the 19th century, however, translations from Chinese texts into European languages were made exclusively in China, by (mostly) Jesuit scholars.

Apart from individual attempts, such as Michael Boym's (c.1612–1659) translation of Chinese medical texts (*Specimen Medicinae Sinensis*, etc.), some particular contexts appear to have been particularly stimulating. The best known example is the 'Canton detention' (1665–1671), which was – despite the relative isolation of the fathers during a period of ca. 6 years within the Canton college and with regard to the rest of China, let alone Europe (1665–1671) – a fertile period for the production of translations and original texts;[52] among them I refer here to the Confucian treatises and their translations, which were certainly prepared by Ignacio da Costa (1599–1661) and Prospero Intorcetta (1625–1696; arrived in 1659 in Macau), and probably benefited from the individual 'exercises' of other Fathers. We are sufficiently well informed on the progress of this teamwork of translation (and transcription) of 3 of the 4 Classics (Mencius put aside, to 'save energy'; later resumed by François Noël), to which collaborated Philippe Couplet, François de Rougemont (1624–1676) and Christian Herdtrich (1625–1684).

Almost unknown is the 'hard' work made in the same context on Chinese medical texts by an "*anonymus eruditus Europaeus*", whom I could recently identify as Couplet, who worked for the Dutch physician Andreas Cleyer (1634–1698) in Batavia.

Outside the Canton context were produced also Chinese technological treatises and some literary texts. In addition, also documentary texts, such as petitions / decrees etc. (to be found, as supporting evidence in *Innocentia Victrix*; the Red Manifesto [Hongpiao (紅票)], etc.); Imperial diplomata (cf. the promotions of

---

51. The manuscript is in Paris, Bibliothèque nationale de France, Ms. 6277/ 1 and 2.

52. Golvers (2015).

Verbiest, inserted and translated in Latin in chap. 11 of his *Astronomia Europaea*);[53] testimonies of Chinese Christians for the Jesuit archives in Rome (Filippucci, etc.);[54] fragments of newspapers (inserted in the *Litterae Annuae*[55]); letters from Chinese correspondents;[56] eclipse maps (such as De Fontaney's Latin translations of some of Verbiest's eclipse maps).[57]

In the 18th century, especially the French Jesuits were active here. Wu Huiyi discovered, on the basis of a 'cahier' of Jean-François Foucquet (Borgia latino 523) how the 'translational' techniques of the French Jesuits were derived from the didactical practices in the French Jesuit colleges, more precisely the 'techniques' used to learn Latin and Ancient Greek.[58]

A particular problem in translating Chinese realities into Latin or any other European language, apart from the lexicological question, was of a grammatical character, namely the distance between a inflectional (Latin) and a completely non-inflectional language as Chinese was (is).

For adopting Chinese names and terms to Latin morphology, the Jesuit authors applied 6 different 'strategies':

Strategy 1: phonetic romanizations, basically emerging as transliterations of the original scripture of the Chinese word / name. Since the early days of the China-mission, especially since ca. 1600 various types of transcription systems were developed for this purpose, which I will not discuss here (Ricci; Trigault; the 'Portuguese' system; the French system). This looks too schematizing, and one must take into account many (also 'individual') differences, as the research of Raini (2009–2010) has proven.

Strategy 2: foreign names were 'assimilated' / integrated as *indeclinabilia*; for this Classical Latin gave many examples, of Punic and other (Asian) names, integrated in a Latin syntactical cluster as such:
  – anthroponyms: e.g. 'Cam Hy', referring to the Kangxi Emperor; Uming-Huen, equalling Wuming Xuan, etc.;

53. Golvers (1993: 83–87; 238–242; 382–388).

54. Standaert (2012).

55. Examples are to be found in Couplet, cited in Barten (1970: 113–116) and Intorcetta (1672: 38–76).

56. A very rare example is the letter of "*Taiso*" (i.e. *Qu Taisu* = *Qu Rukui*) to Longobardo (1701: 12–18).

57. De Fontaney, in Golvers (1999: 294–296).

58. Wu (2017).

- geographical names: Huquang, i.e. Huguang; Su Chuen, i.e. Sichuan Prov.; Xensi for Shaanxi and Xansi for Shanxi etc.); Peking and Pekim,[59] versus Pekinum, Nankinum (cf. infra); the many toponyms in Martino Martini, *Novus Atlas Sinensis*;[60]
- functions: "*Tum fum ta fu*", i.e. *tongfeng dafu* and several other similar examples, to be found e.g. in Johann Adam Schall von Bell's (1582–1666) and Verbiest's Latinized *diplomata*.

Strategy 3: more sophisticated was the morphological adaptation to Latin declensions by adding suffixes, or restyling an authentic Chinese character into a Latin ending. Here the examples are legion, regarding especially Sino-Manchu names, Chinese Emperors' names (e.g. in Martini's *Historiae Sinensis Prima Decas*; geographica; therefore at least two 'techniques' were applied, viz.:

(3.1) by (re-)interpreting the final part of the Chinese name in Latin morphological schemes:

e.g.: Guang*dong* > Cant*on*: (a) by substituting the province name for that of its capital, and (b) associating the –*dong* name with Graeco-Latin toponyms of the type *Chalcedon, -onis*; as a result this becomes *Canton, Cantonis*; this in its turn delivers the basis for further derivations such as: *Canton-ia* > adj. *Cantoni-ensis, Quanton-iensis*.[61] Another example is given in the placename Macao, interpreted as a Latin ablative locative on -o, from which was 're-invented' the nominative *Macaum*; a last example concerns the personal name *Patrocum*, for *paturu-kung*, itself a cluster of two terms, in which -*cum* is the phonetic transposition of the Chin. title *kung/-kum*);[62]

(3.2) By adding a Latin ending, creating thus a morphologically more 'operational' name form; here various forms can be recognized:

- (i)us: Kǒng fūzi > Con(g)fuci-us; Yang Guangxian > Yangkuangsen-*ius* (adding the normal Latin suffix of 'nomina gentilicia', viz. – ius, of the type *Jul-ius*, etc.);

---

59. On this double rendition of the final consonant cluster, with -ng (..) versus -m (Port.), see, for instance, Martini (1655: 17).

60. See the tables of correspondence in: Bertuccioli (2002: 917–1129).

61. Gabiani (1673: 474): "In Quam Tum provinciae Urbe primaria Quam Cheu, vulgari nomine Cantonia dicta"; cf. 399; 579, etc.; De Rougemont (1673: 173).

62. Golvers (1993: 183).

- us: Sunkovam-us, i.e. Sunko Wam / Wang: 'prince of the Sunko area";[63] Quesing-us, i.e. Guoxing, in a similar romanization *Coxinga* (i.e. Quoxing ye);
- a: cf. the dynasty name of the Ming: *Taiming-a* (passim), passing to the catgeory of names of the 1st declension;
- ia: cf. Cantonia (supra)
- um: Nanking / Nankim > *Nankim-um > (by dissimilation -m-m- > n-m-) Nankinum; Peking / Pekim > *Pekimum > Pekinum;

Strategy 4:   Substitutions of 'foreign' names / terms etc.:

i.e. replacing the Chinese terms by pre-existing, more or less corresponding terms with a Classical origin: type: gelao > *praefectus;* bu > *tribunal,* etc.: these Latin terms were thus metaphorically adapted to Chinese realities, receiving themselves by this a 'new', particular meaning.

Strategy 5:   Translation in the proper sense of the word:

These are not always immediately recognizable but in several cases are revealed by mutual comparison. It concerns:

- Geographical names: Verbiest's *Montes Occidentales* (used passim) are translating the Chinese model *Xishan*, indicating a small mountain group West (*Xi-*) of Peking; *Decem mille fontes* rendering Chin. *Wanquan*, i.e. literally 'Ten-thousand Wells'; etc. Occasionally this translation reveals some wrong interpretation, due to a wrong identification of a Chinese character: a similar confusion could be at the origin of the translation "*Filius Maris*" (since Martini) for the Chinese river name Yangzi, continued afterwards as a consequence of the authoritative position of Martini's *Atlas;*[64]
- Nominal loan translations are less evident, but see probably Latin expressions as *specula astroptica* for Chin. *guan xiang tai*, with the characters 'look/watch'; 'star' and 'platform; tower', and neologisms such as *anemo-dicticum*, i.e. a 'wind-direction-indicator' as a Latin transposition of Chinese *xiangfen chu*; the use of *Curia* for the Court city of Peking, i.e. Pei ('North') – jing: 'Court'; etc.[65]

Strategy 6:   Omission:

Complementary to this, there was a trend in many literary, printed Western works on China to drop the Chinese terms and names, or to replace them by Latin, Christian names, etc. This happened, I suppose,

---

63. De Rougemont (1673: *passim*).

64. De Rougemont (1673: 41): "*Yamzinkiam, id est maris filium non immerito Sinae vocant*".

65. For more examples: Golvers (1995: 339–345).

for a double reason, namely the obvious absence of any understanding of Chinese in Europe, but also for stylistic reasons, as part of the *toilette littéraire* to which texts from China were subjected by their European editors, always concerned to produce a 'harmonic' result, also by the purification of elements in the text felt as 'too strange'.[66]

A more systematic and comprehensive classifying of this type of examples – together with a complete overview of the 'translated' texts / compositions in Chinese, will certainly contribute to getting a deeper insight into the working methods of the Jesuit translators, who by doing so made accessible to the Western reader for the first time a world which completely fell beyond the classical schemata.

6.   Conclusive remarks

Communication, in oral or written (and sometimes figurative) form was the most elementary aim of the mission in general. For the China mission the circumstances were very particular, as the Jesuits (with a Late-Humanistic formation) were confronted with a very old and rich 'literary' tradition, and a complex linguistic situation, which made the China mission, acc. to their own perception, as the 'most difficult' in the world. Right from the beginning, ca. 1612/1613 a strategy was expanded to transfer to Chinese *literati* the core of 'Western Learning' (*xixue*), by establishing 'complete' (representative) libraries of Western books and a systematic translation program. So far unexploited manuscript sources, mostly without a direct 'linguistic' aspect or focus and being of general character, show the particular difficulties the 'translators' (or rather: transmitters) in China had to overcome: after the problems related to the language study itself, these regarded mainly (a) the choice of the right register for their literary compositions, for which the *guānhuà* was selected, and a correct idiomatic and stylistic use use of it, and (b) the creation, for a series of typical terms and concepts in the Western model of Chinese 'technical' neologisms (theological and philosophical concepts; technological, medical and mathematical terms…).

Apart from theology and Aristotelian philosophy (which were both related to the Jesuits' own agenda), the main domains of the *xixue* the Chinese were interested in were: (a) the year calendar(s) (and all the mathematical, astronomical and observational / instrumental aspects connected to it), as the warrant of the social life and dynastic stability; (b) technology, for public works and private pleasure, including

---

66. For this 'toilette littéraire', see: Brou (1934: 551–566).

artillery for the nation's internal and external safety; (c) medicine-pharmacy for the individual health.

In addition, the same manuscript sources contain also several explicit 'auctorial' remarks on the methods they applied to create the various forms of translating, which represent a broad specter from (rarely) literary translating through paraphrases (mixed with commentaries and personal observations) to the crossing of various different sources into one new composition. The working method was also largely relying on external support, first from the part of (poorly documented) Chinese re-writers; revisers, etc), whose assistance, where revealed with some more details, seems to have been quite substantial in 'upgrading' the first draft translation, by selecting the true Chinese counterpart and in adding the necessary 'literary (stylistic) flavor. For this first 'draft' the Jesuit authors had at hand handwritten wordlists made by Europeans and printed Chinese dictionaries, of which the Jesuit sources are mentioning a series by name.

This evidence presents not only a more precise idea about the process of translation and the Jesuits' own perception of it. Represented, albeit more indirectly is also the counterpart, namely the problems they met with the transmission of the many Chinese names, terms and concepts to Europe: these regarded the phonetical 'romanization' (the transcription systems) and the morphological-syntactical appropriation of the terms and concepts to a (mostly) Latin context, for which I could recognize six different techniques.

A more systematic investigation of this kind of references, spread throughout missionary archives will enable us, to get a still more sharp idea of this very voluminous and two-faced project, in close connection, of course, with the analysis of the very texts they produced, compared to their source texts.

References

A.   Primary sources

ARSI (=Archivum Romanum Societatis Jesu)

Barbosa Machado, Diogo. 1741. *Bibliotheca Lusitana historica, critica e cronologica*. Lisboa: A. Isidoro da Fonseca.

Barbosa Machado, Diogo. 1747. *Bibliotheca Lusitana historica, critica e cronologica*. Lisboa: Ign. Rodrigues.

Barbosa Machado, Diogo. 1752. *Bibliotheca Lusitana historica, critica e cronologica*. Lisboa: Ign. Rodrigues.

Brancati, Francesco. 1700. *De Sinensium Ritibus Politicis Acta*. Paris: N. Pepié.

Cibot, Pierre-Martial. 1778. "Notices de quelques plantes et abrisseaux de la Chine". *Mémoires concernant l'histoire, les sciences, les arts, les mœurs, les usages, &c. des Chinois, par les missionnaires de Pé-kin*. Vol. 3. 437–498. Paris: Chez Nyon l'aîné, Librairie.

Couplet, Philippe. 1687. Ms. in Staatsbibliothek Berlin: Preussisches Kulturbesitz, acc. ms. 1938, 48, f° 29.

Duhalde, Jean-Baptiste. 1735. *Description geographique, historique, chronologique, politique et physique de l'Empire de la Chine et de la Tartarie Chinoise (…)*. Paris: P. G. Le Mercier.

Dunyn-Szpot, Thomas. 1700. *Collectanea Historiae Sinensis ab anno 1641 ad annum 1700 ex variis documentis in Archivo Societatis existentibus excerpta*. Ms. in Rome: *Archivum Romanum Societatis Jesu* 104–105.

Filippucci, Francesco Saverio. 1700. *De Sinensium Ritibus Politicis Acta (…). Praeludium ad plenam disquisitionem an bonâ vel malâ fide impugnetur opininiones et praxes*. Paris: N. Pepié.

Gabiani, Giandomenico. 1673. *Incrementa Sinicae Ecclesiae a Tartaris oppugnatae*. Viennae Austriae: L. Voigt.

Hallerstein, Augustin von. 1751. "A letter from the Revd. Father Augustin Hallerstein (…)". *Philosophical Transactions* 47.322–323.

Intorcetta, Prospero. 1672. *Compendiosa narratione dello stato della missione cinese, comminciando dall'anno 1581 fino al 1669*. Roma: Tizzoni.

Lefaure, Jacques. 1700. *De Sinensium Ritibus Politicis Acta*. Paris: Pepié.

Longobardo, Nicola. 1701. *Traité sur quelques points de la religion des Chinois*. Paris: L. Guerin.

Magalhães, Gabriel de. 1688. *Nouvelle relation de la Chine*. Paris: Claude Barbin.

Martini, Martino. 1655. *Novus Atlas Sinensis*. Amsterdam: J. Blaeu.

Muller, Andreas. 1672. *De Invento Sinico Epistolae Amoebaeae*. s.l.

Rougemont, François de. 1673. *Historia Tartaro-Sinica*. Lovanii: M. Hullegaerde.

Verbiest, Ferdinand. 2018 [1680]. *Postulata Vice-Provinciae Sinensis in Urbe proponenda* ed. by Noël Golvers. Leuven: Ferdinand Verbiest Institute.

Verbiest, Ferdinand. 1687. *Astronomia Europaea sub Imperatore Tartaro Sinico Cam Hy appellato ex umbra in lucem revocata*. Dillingen: C. Bencard.

B.   Secondary sources

Aalto, Pentti. 1976. "The Elementa Linguae Tartaricae by F. Verbiest, SJ". *Tractata Altaica Denis Sinor sexagenario (…) dedicata* ed. by W. Heissig, 1–10. Wiesbaden: O. Harrassowitz.

Aalto, Pentti. 1977. "The Elementa Linguae Tartaricae by Ferdinand Verbiest, S.J. Translated". *Zentralasiatische Studien* 11.35–120.

Alcobendas, Severiano. 1933. *Las misiones Franciscanas en China. Cartas. Informes, y Relaciones del Padre Buenaventura Ibáñez (1650–1690)*. Madrid: Estanislao Maestre.

Barten, J. 1970. "Hollandse kooplieden op bezoek bij concilievaders". *Archief voor de geschiedenis van de Katholieke kerk in Nederland* 12.75–120.

Bernard, Henri. 1938. "L'encyclopédie astronomique du Père Schall". *Monumenta Serica* 3.441–527. https://doi.org/10.1080/02549948.1938.11745078

Bernard, Henri. 1940. "Ferdinand Verbiest continuateur de l'oeuvre scientifique d'Adam Schall". *Monumenta Serica* 5.103–140. https://doi.org/10.1080/02549948.1940.11745123

Bernard, Henri. 1945. "Les adaptations chinoises d'ouvrages européens: bibliographie chronologique". *Monumenta Serica* 10.1–57. https://doi.org/10.1080/02549948.1945.11744860

Bhabha, Homi K. 1994. *The Location of Culture*. London & New York: Routledge.

Bontinck, François. 1962. *La lutte autour de la liturgie chinoise aux XVIIe et XVIIIe siècles*. Louvain & Paris: Ed. Nauwelaerts.

Brockey, Liam Matthew. 2007. *Journey to the East. The Jesuit Mission to China, 1579 – 1724*. Cambridge, Massachusetts – London: Belknap Press of Harvard University Press. https://doi.org/10.4159/9780674028814

Brou, Antoine. 1934. "Les jésuites sinologues de Pékin et leurs éditeurs de Paris". *Revue d'histoire des missions* 11.551–566.

Ceijssens, Lucien. 1949. *La correspondance d'Emmanuel Schelstrate, préfet de la bibliothèque vaticane (1683–1692)*. Bruxelles & Rome: Academia Belgica.

Cordier, Henri. 1901. *L'imprimerie Sino-européenne en Chine. Bibliographie des ouvrages publiés par les Européens au XVIIe et au XVIIIe siècle*. Paris: Imprimerie nationale.

Dehergne, Joseph. 1973. *Répertoire des Jésuites de Chine de 1552 à 1800*. Roma: Institutum Historicum S.I. – Paris: Letouzey & Ané.

Eco, Umberto. 2003. *Dire quasi la stessa cosa. Esperienze di traduzione*. Milano: Bompiani.

Engelfriet, Peter. 1996. *Euclid in China. A survey of the historical background of the first Chinese translation of Euclid's Elements (Jihe yuanben; Beijing, 1607)*. Leiden, Boston & Köln: Brill.

Engelfriet, Peter. 1998. *Euclid in China: the Genesis of the first Chinese Translation of Euclid's Elements in 1607 & its reception up to 1723*. Leiden, Boston & Köln: Brill.

Fuchs, Walther. 1933. "Was wussten die Chinesen von Deutschland im 17. Jahrhundert?" *Jubiläumsband, hrsg. von der Deutschen Gesellschaft für Natur- und Völkerkunde Ostasiens anlässlich ihres 60 jährigen Bestehens, 1873–1933* ed. by Petzold Bruno, et al., 256–262. Tokyo: im Selbstverlag der Gesellschaft.

Girard, Pascale. 2008. "L'apprentissage et la connaissance du chinois par les religieux ibériques aux XVIIe et XVIIIe siècles". *Impérios, Religiosidades e Etnias* ed. by Adriana Campos, Gilvan Ventura da Silva & Sebastião Pimentel Franco, 109–124. Vitoria (Brazil): UFES.

Golvers, Noël. 1995. "Latin treatises of F. Verbiest, S.J. (…). Some linguistic considerations", *Humanistica Lovaniensia* 44.305–369.

Golvers, Noël. 1999. *Ferdinand Verbiest and the Chinese Heaven. The Composition of the Astronomical Corpus, its Diffusion and Reception in the European Republic of Letters*. Leuven: Leuven University Press.

Golvers, Noël. 2015a. *Libraries of Western Learning for China. Circulation of Western Books between Europe and China in the Jesuit Mission (ca. 1650–1750)*. Leuven: F. Verbiest Institute.

Golvers, Noël. 2015b. "The Canton-Macau area as a 'lieu de savoir': the Western missionaries' detention in the Canton Jesuit residence (1665–1671) and their written and editorial output". *Macau past and present* ed. by Luis Filipe Barreto & Wu Zhiliang, 215–227. Lisboa: Centro Científico e Cultural de Macau.

Golvers, Noël. 2020. *Johann Schreck Terrentius, SJ. His European network and the origins of the Jesuit Library in Peking*. Turnhout: Brepols.

Golvers, Noël, ed. 1993. *The Astronomia Europaea of Ferdinand Verbiest*. Nettetal: Steyler Verlag.

Golvers, Noël, ed. 1999. *The Christian mission in China in the Verbiest era: some aspects of the missionary approach*. Leuven: Leuven University Press.

Golvers, Noël, ed. 2017. *Letters of a Peking Jesuit. The correspondence of Ferdinand Verbiest, SJ (1623–1688) Revised and Expanded*. Leuven; F. Verbiest Institute.

Golvers, Noël, ed. 2018. *F. Verbiest. Postulata Vice-Provinciae Sinensis in Urbe proponenda. A blueprint for a renewed SJ mission in China*. Leuven: F. Verbiest Institute.

Hashimoto, Keizo. 1988. *Hsü Kuang-ch'i and astronomical reform. The process of the Chinese acceptance of Western astronomy 1629–1635*. Osaka: Kansai University Press.

Hsia, Po-Chia Ronnie. 2007. "The Catholic Mission and Translations in China, 1583–1700". *Cultural Translation in Early Modern Europe* ed. by Peter Burke and Ronnie Po-chia Hsia, 39–51. Cambridge: Cambridge University Press. https://doi.org/10.1017/CBO9780511497193.003

Hsia, Po-Chia Ronnie. 2011. "Language acquisition and missionary strategies in China, 1580–1760". *Missions d'evangélisation et circulation des savoirs – XVIe – XVIIIe siècles* ed. by Charlotte de Castelnau-L' Estoile, Marie-Lucie Copete, Aliocha Maldavsky, Ines G. Županov, 211–229. Madrid: Casa de Velázquez.

James, Gregory. 2004. "Culture and the Dictionary: Evidence from the first European Lexicographical work in China". *Historical Dictionaries and Historical Dictionary Research. Papers from the International Conference on Historical Lexicography and Lexicology, at the University of Leicester, 2002* ed. by Julie Coleman and Anne McDermott, 119–136. Tübingen: Max Niemeyer. https://doi.org/10.1515/9783110912609.119

Jami, Catherine. 1995. "From Louis XIV's court to Kangxi's court: An institutional analysis of the French Jesuit mission to China (1662–1722)". *East Asian Science: Tradition and Beyond. Papers from the 7th International Conference on the History of Science in East Asia, Kyoto, 2–7 August 1993*, ed. by Keizo Hashimoto, Catherine Jami & Lowell Skar, 493–499. Osaka: Kansai University Press.

Jami, Catherine. 2018. "Les traductions de traités scientifiques européens en Chine au XVIIe siècle: enjeux des langues et des disciplines." *La Révolution Française* 13. https://journals.openedition.org/lrf/1898#text

Kishimoto, Emi. 2006. "The Process of Translation in 'Dictionarium Latino-Lusitanicum ac Japonicum'". *Journal of Asian and African Studies* (Tokyo) 72.17–26.

Kurtz, Joachim. 2008. "Anatomy of a textual Monstruosity: dissecting the Mingli tan (De logica, 1631)". *Linguistic Exchanges between Europe, China and Japan* ed. by F. Casalin, 35–58. Rome: Tiellemedia Editore.

Landry-Deron, Isabelle. 2001. "Les Mathématiciens envoyés en Chine par Louis XIV en 1685". *Archive for History of Exact Sciences* 55.423–463. https://doi.org/10.1007/s004070000033

Lundbaek, Knud. 1986. *T.S. Bayer (1694–1738). Pioneer Sinologist*. London & Malmö: Curzon Press Ltd.

Nicolas, Christian. 2000. "La néologie technique par traduction chez Cicéron et la notion de verbumexverbalité'. *La création lexicale en latin* ed. by M. Fruyt & Chr. Nicolas, 109–146. Paris: Sorbonne.

Paternicò, Luisa. 2000. *When the Europeans began to study Chinese. Martino Martini's Grammatica Linguae Sinensis*. Leuven: F. Verbiest Institute.

Pfister, Louis. 1932–1934. *Notices biographiques et bibliographiques sur les Jésuites de l'ancienne mission de Chine. Variétés sinologiques* 59–60, 514. Shanghai: Imprimerie de la mission catholique.

Pih, Irene. 1979. *Le Père Gabriel de Magalhães. Un jésuite portugais en Chine au XVIIe siècle*. Paris: Fundação Calouste Gulbenkian. Centro cultural português.

Pina, Isabel. 2011. *Jesuitas Chineses e mestiços da missão da China (1589–1689)*. Lisboa: Centro Científico e Cultural de Macau.

Raini, Emanuele. 2009. *Sistemi di romanizzazione del cinese mandarino nei secoli XVI–XVIII*. Tesi di dottorato, Sapienza Università di Roma.

Saje, Mitja. 2009. *A. Hallerstein – Liu Songling. The Multicultural Legacy of Western Wisdom and Piety at the Qing Dynasty Court*. Maribor: Association for culture and education Kibla.

Simon, Renée. 1970. *Le P. Antoine Gaubil S.J. Correspondance de Pékin 1722–1759*. Genève: Droz.

Standaert, Nicolas. 2012. *Chinese voices in the rites controversy. Travelling Books, Community Networks, Intercultural Arguments*. Rome: Institutum Historicum Societatis Jesu.

Standaert, Nicolas, ed. 2001. *Handbook of Christianity in China. Volume One: 635–1800*. Leiden, Boston & Köln: Brill. https://doi.org/10.1163/9789004391857

Tsien, Tsuen-Hsuin. 1954. "Western Impact on China through Translation". *The Far Eastern Quarterly* 13:3.306–313. https://doi.org/10.2307/2942281

Verhaeren, Hubert. 1935. "Aristotle en Chine". *Bulletin Catholique de Pékin* 22.414–429.

Wu, Huiyi. 2017. *Traduire la Chine au XVIIIe siècle. Les jésuites traducteurs de textes chinois et le renouvellement des connaissances européennes sur la Chine (1687–ca.1740)*. Paris: Honoré Champion.

Yang, Huiling. 2014. "The Making of the first Chinese-English Dictionary". *Historiographia Linguistica* 41.299–322. https://doi.org/10.1075/hl.41.2-3.04yan

Yuan, Xi. 2000. "Una ricerca terminologica sull'opera teologica Martiniana Zhenzhu lingxing lizheng". *Martino Martini. Man of Dialogue* ed. by Luisa Maria Paternicò, Claudia von Collani & Riccardo Scartezzini, 363–386. Trento: Università degli Studi.

Zwartjes, Otto. 2014. "El vocabulario de letra china de Francisco Díaz (ca. 1643) y la lexicografía hispano-asiática". *Boletín Hispánico Helvético: Historia, teoría(s), prácticas culturales* 23.57–100.

The *Vocabolario Italiano-Cinese* of Joseph M. Pruggmayr (OCD; 1713–1791)

Miriam Castorina
Università degli Studi di Firenze

1. Introduction

This paper aims to shed light on the contribution made to the field of missionary linguistics by an Austrian missionary, Joseph Maximilian Pruggmayr OCD (Order of Discalced Carmelites) (1713–1791) who spent almost fifty years in China in the second half of the 18th century. Jesuits played the leading role in mediating between the Chinese court and Europe in those years and their contributions sometimes eclipse the works of other missionaries belonging to different religious orders. Pruggmayr is among them and compiled a very complete Italian Chinese dictionary entitled *Vocabolario Italiano-Cinese* (from now on also indicated as VIC). The dictionary made a long journey from China to Europe and although it is mentioned in some sources (always as anonymous) it has never been studied. This dictionary seems to have been neglected by scholars, which is difficult to understand, since – as will be demonstrated below – it deserves our attention, not only because of its richness, but also its features. Though compiled within a very well-established missionary tradition, the dictionary is in fact based on the *Vocabolario degli Accademici della Crusca* and makes use of a specific romanization Pruggmayr based on the Spanish-Portuguese system adapted to Italian orthography. This paper highlights Pruggmayr's contribution in the field of lexicographical material and focuses on the features this dictionary possesses compared with other sources, also given the value it possibly has since it was compiled in a span of time which 'recorded' the passage from Nanjing-based Mandarin to Beijing-based Mandarin.

After a brief account on the Carmelites in China and some biographical data (Section 2), based on the current state of the art, Section 3 illustrates Pruggmayr's language skills and works mostly on the base of archival material collected in Rome. Section 4 concentrates on the description of the Italian Chinese dictionary, where excerpts of his work will be given together with a few examples. This preliminary study on the *Dictionary* cannot be considered conclusive, and further studies will

https://doi.org/10.1075/sihols.130.04cas

be necessary in the future on the phonological and lexical aspects of the work and also in the perspective of a better understanding of the changes occurring in the linguistic panorama of the Celestial Empire at the end of the 18th century.

2.   Joseph M. Pruggmayr (OCD; 1713–1791)[1]

The foundation of the Sacred Congregation for the Propagation of the Faith in 1622 (*Sacra Congregatio de Propaganda Fide*, now The Congregation for the Evangelization of Peoples) apparently gave a new boost to the work of evangelization, providing new financial resources to different Catholic orders and allowing them to set up their communities in China more easily. This is the case of the Order of Discalced Carmelites (*Shengyihui* 聖衣會). Like other orders in China, the life of the Discalced Carmelites in the celestial Empire was neither easy nor smooth. On the contrary, mainly due to economic problems and the lack of that intellectual energy which characterized many Jesuits, the priests belonging to this Order had to face many difficulties. They often lived in poverty and had very little financial support from Rome itself, and begged for money over and over again.[2] The Carmelites first established their mission in Haidian 海甸 (now written as 海淀), then a poor village near the Capital city (today one of Beijing's livelier districts), whose administration passed from hand to hand and to (religious) order to order until the arrival of the Joseph M. Pruggmayr in 1745.[3]

Joseph Maximilian Pruggmayr was born on December 13th, 1713, in the city of Graz (land of Stiria, Austria). In 1733, he took his vows in the order of the Discalced Carmelites in Linz and chose the religious name of Joseph Mary a S. Theresia (Giuseppe Maria di S. Teresa). It is not possible to know whether he learned Italian in Linz or elsewhere. Maybe he learned it at home, assumingthat his family was partlyfromthe Peninsula. What is certain, however, is that he had a good proficiency in

---

1.   Not much is known about Pruggmayr's life. After some research conducted in the General Archive of the Discalced Carmelites in Rome, I have not been able to collect any new data with respect to what Father Ambrosius a Sancta Teresia has already published about his family and his educational background (Sancta Teresia 1940: 217–220). These first biographical notes, therefore, are mostly taken from this source, unless otherwise indicated. Other details on his life can be drawn from his correspondence with other missionaries, which will be treated below. A reconstruction of Pruggmayr's life through his letters can also be found in Aparicio Ahedo (2018) whose contribution mainly aims at analyzing Pruggmayr's political views and role at the time.

2.   For a first attempt to write a history of this Order in China, see Margiotti (1963) even though documents related to the Carmelites in China and the communities they established are still not comprehensive.

3.   On the history of this first community see Margiotti (1963) and Iannello (2012).

Italian as his letters and works prove. In fact, he chose to communicate with Rome in Italian and not in Latin and, as can be seen from the very title of this paper, he compiled a dictionary not in German, as one would have expected, but in Italian. In China he also taught European music in the court, but, once again, it is still not possible to know where he had studied it and what kind of musical instruments he could play.

In 1743, he was sent to the Chinese Mission where he began his apostolate work arriving in the city of Macau on September 29, 1744, after a journey of seven months. He traveled with other missionaries (cf. Margiotti 1963: 105, n. 47) on a French ship where the group had some troubles due to the "scanty treatment and of the little esteem and respect towards the missionaries" (Macau, January 8, 1745. APF; SOCP, 46: 144r).[4]

On July 14, 1744, he moved to Beijing where he fell ill for more than a month (Haidian, November 14, 1745. APF; SOCP, 46: 413v). On the 24th of February 1745, he was received by Emperor Qianlong 乾隆 (r. 1736–1795) together with other three Jesuits who were to work inside the imperial palace. On these three Jesuits, information can be found in one letter by Pruggmayr to *Propaganda* (January 8, 1746, is in APF, *SOCP*, 46: 144–145), where he writes that he was able to enter the court also thanks to the efforts of "F. Kegler" (Ignaz Kögler, Chinese name Dai Jinxian 戴進賢, 1680–1746) who "put my name with other three of his [men], of which one is my fellow countryman, [who entered] with the title of first-class [*eccellente*] painter, and the other two with the title of Mathematicians" (Macau, January 8, 1745. APF, SOCP, 46: 144v).

Despite having been accepted by the Court, Pruggmayr had to live in Haidian with Father Sigismundo, a Discalced Augustinian, instead of residing with Teodorico Pedrini CM (Congregation of the Mission) (De Lige 德理格, 1671–1746) because, according to what he writes,[5] Pedrini did not want him to stay in

---

4.   In other documents, more details are given regarding Pruggmayr's arrival in China. It has been attested that *Propaganda* justifies the "expedient" of sending Joseph M. to China in order to "prevent the danger to which the Residences of the Sacred Congregation are exposed to". See: "Memorie e Varie occorrenze del 1744" in Miralta (1744; APF, SOCP, 46: f. 13r). This *Relazione* also states that the missionary was introduced to the Emperor together with "three Fathers of the Company, i.e., a German, a Frenchman and a Portuguese man. According to the date, the Frenchman is probably Michel Benoist (Jiang Youren 蔣友仁, 1715–1774), even though I did not find any evidence of this, apart from the fact that he arrived in China in the same year as Pruggmayr. The German is maybe Ignatius Sichelbart (Ai Qimeng 艾啟蒙, 1708–1780), who is the only Jesuit matching the date and the nationality in Pfister (1932–1934, II: no. 383, 830–832).

5.   "While Mr. Pedrini, as I am told, did everything he could to prevent me from entering Beijing, with little dignity for this Holy Congregation, claiming that I stayed here for at least a year, to make me pass through *ignem & acquam*, in accordance with his distorted ideas" (Macau, January 8, 1745. APF, SOCP, 46: 145r).

Beijing. When Father Sigismondo died, Pruggmayr moved to Xitang 西堂 (Western Church) on October 4, 1746, with Pedrini, to return to Haidian soon after the latter died.[6] Pruggmayr settled then in the area of Haidian, where he worked towards a new foundation of the previous congregation. He succeeded in obtaining a formal approval in 1754 in the church of St. Joseph (Margiotti 1963: 107) and then he remained the only priest in Haidian until 1762.

In addition, from 1750, Pruggmayr began to teach Western music in the court together with "two Fathers of the Society" [of Jesus] since, as he writes in 1745, "they have not taught European Music in the Court for two years" (Haidian, November 14, 1745. APF, SOCP, 46: 414r). This new office 'obliged' him to stay in Beijing during working days and return to Haidian every holiday and Sunday "to say Mass to the Christians of this church" (November 15, 1750. APF, SOCP, 49: 374v). Pruggmayr's letters are a very precious source, since they allow a better understanding of how hard and challenging it was to live in China for the priests of *Propaganda*.

Pruggmayr would have tried to ask permission to return to Europe many times[7] but his voice remained almost unheard until 1767. In that year, he received a letter from *Propaganda* which authorized him to leave China. Unfortunately, he would not be able to do so, mainly for three reasons, according to what Pruggmayr writes. The first was the lack of money for the journey back to Europe; the second was the fact that working at court, he needed written approval from the Emperor to travel and it would take some time to obtain it; and, last but not least, the poor Chinese language skills of the other two missionaries working in Haidian made him unconfident of entrusting them with the local community. These two new missionaries were Arcangelo Maria Bellotti da S. Anna CM (1729–1784) and Eusebio da Cittadella OFM (1716–1766) (Metzler 1985: 123). As Pruggmayr writes to Propaganda in 1767:

> Therefore, I have considered extending my stay in this Mission for a further year, so as not to leave these Christians of mine deprived of the word of God and to give these two successors, taking care of this Christianity, time and incentive to apply themselves with greater commitment to the study of the Chinese language during this period,[8] ...   (Haidian, September 20, 1767. APF, SOCP, 55: 592v)

---

6.   The news of Pedrini's death is documented in a letter by Pruggmayr to Procurator Miralta. Cf. Pedrini, cited in Galaffi; Tarsetti, eds. (2018: xlvii).

7.   See, for example, the letter from Haidian, dated September 27, 1764 (APF, SOCP, 55: 67–68). As a matter of fact, Pruggmayr asked permission to leave in almost every letter he would send to *Propaganda*. The tone of these 'pleas' is very touching and sheds light on a side of the mission that does not often emerge in books and articles.

8.   All the translations from Italian to English are by this author if not otherwise specified.

He would never have this opportunity again and, according to other sources, he would agree to remain in China in exchange for the administration of the diocese of Beijing.[9] As a matter of fact, he held some important positions for *Propaganda* in the following years,[10] and also had a role in the controversy against the Society of Jesus until its suppression, a role that will not be treated in detail in these pages.[11] Actually "during the time following the suppression of the Society of Jesus in Beijing much depended on one man: Joseph M. a S. Theresia". who, however, according to Krahl (1964: 235) "certainly did not possess the extraordinary talent that the unusually difficult situation demanded". He at least succeeded in one aspect: to maintain a "relative peace".

Pruggmayr died in Beijing on October 31st, 1791 and he is probably buried in the Zhalan cemetery in the capital, though his grave his unknown (Margiotti 1963: 106, n. 47).

3.   Pruggmayr's language skills and works

As far as we know, Pruggmayr is the editor of a book in Chinese entitled *Shengmu shengyihui enyu* 聖母聖衣會恩諭, an Italian-Chinese Dictionary, a translation of an *Ars bene moriendi* into Chinese and many letters. These letters can be found in the Historical Archive of the *Propaganda Fide*, while I couldn't find anything written by him in the archives of the Carmelites in Rome.[12]

Soon after his arrival in China, Pruggmayr began to commit himself to the study of the Mandarin language. He could probably have begun this study while in Macau, nonetheless, he was there "subject to a severe illness" (Macau, January 8, 1745. APF, SOCP, 46: 144v) so that the first mention of his commitment to the study of the language can be read only later, in a letter to *Propaganda* dated November 14, 1745. "For now, – he writes – my only study and occupation is in learning this difficult Chinese language, so to soon be able to work hard for the salvation

---

9. This can be read in a letter dated Beijing, July 15, 1769, by Giovanni Damasceno Salusti OAD (安德義, 1727–1781). APF, SOCP, 56: 18–23.

10. In 1768, for example, he moved to Beijing after being appointed as Vice Procurator of the Chinese Mission. Later he would be appointed as *Delegatus Episcopi Nankinensis pro dioecesi Pekinensi* and, in 1775, as *Vicarius Episcopi Nankinensis pro dioecesi Pekinensi*, a position he would occupy until 1780. For further details see Ambrosius a S. Teresia (1940: 220).

11. This role is briefly treated in Aparicio Ahedo (2018: III.3).

12. According to Ambrosius a S. Teresia (1940: 219–229), Pruggmayr's collection of letters from China consists of 35 letters, all kept in the *Propaganda*'s Historical Archive.

⸱of these souls and make the exercise of my Evangelical ministry fruitful" (APF, SOCP, 46: 413v). No other detail reveals how he studied and how fast his progress was at least until 1764. In that year, having already spent twenty years in China, he implored *Propaganda* to give him permission to leave for Europe in order to "prepare for a good death", about which he had written a book in Chinese which "is currently in press" (Haidian, September 27, 1764. APF, SOCP, 55: 68v) and to which Ambrosius a S. Teresia (1940: 219) gives the generic title of *Ars bene moriendi*, a genre treated by many missionaries in China (Standaert 2001: 629–630). According to the sources (Margiotti 1963: 60; Iannello 2012: 355), the priest also edited and published a book by his predecessor Wolfgang Thumsecher (Na Yongfu 那永福 1693–1772), entitled *Shengmu shengyihui enyu* 聖母聖衣會恩諭 ("Graceful Instruction of the Discalced Carmelites").

Further information on Pruggmayr's language skills can also be found in other missionaries' letters. In 1773, for instance, the Procurator Nicola Simonetti (1773: 128r) would affirm that Pruggmayr "is currently the only one of ours in Beijing in the Science of the Chinese characters". For this very reason, in 1770 the Procurator of *Propaganda* in Macau, Emiliano Palladini (1733–1793), would ask him to translate into Latin the much-discussed[13] book by the French Jesuit Alexandre de la Charme (Sun Zhang 孫璋, 1695–1767) entitled *Xingli zhenquan* 性理真詮 ("Complete Explanation of Nature and Principle"). As the Carmelite would write to Palladini on October 28th of the following year, he only translated the sixth (and last) volume with the title of *Philosophiae Genuinae explicatis*[14] since "it is the only one that can be criticized", while the other five "merely deal with the Chinese philosophy and [...] if translated in the Latin language, would never be understood by the European philosophers".[15]

---

13. On de la Charme see Pfister (1932–1934, II: n. 324, 721–724). The book was at the center of the so-called Rites controversy. It was, in fact, used as a pretext to accuse the Jesuits of considering Confucius as a Saint and to propagate ideas opposed to the doctrine of the Roman Church. For further details, see also Krahl (1964: 186–189).

14. The translation by Pruggmayr, dated August 4, 1771, is now kept in the National Library of Rome, Mss Orientali 175.

15. Pruggmayr's words are reported by Palladini himself in the annual report to *Propaganda*. See Palladini (1771: 104r).

4.   The *vocabolario Italiano-cinese* (VIC)

4.1   Physical description

The copy kept in the Vatican library consists of one manuscript volume. Originally, there were three volumes, but the sinologist Antonio Montucci (1762–1829) bound them as one (see the next paragraph), as a manuscript note by Montucci himself attached inside the tome certifies.

The first volume is numbered 1–148; the second volume, clearly the continuation of the previous one, begins however with a folio numbered 174 and ends with f. 328; the third one is not numbered. In total, the three-in-one volume consists of 148 + 155 + 170 folios or leaves, i.e., almost 500 pages. The ostensible mistake in the numbering of pages can be explained by the fact that, as mentioned by Pruggmayr in the letter quoted below (November 4, 1784), he prepared a second and better copy. Presumably, then, the dictionary kept in Rome gathers together different volumes of these two copies. It is still to be verified if the other copy is still extant. Three labels on f. 1v are glued on the original paper and state that the original three-volume vocabulary had belonged to "Sir George Staunton Bar" also explaining the ambiguous page numeration;[16] while inside the volume two of Montucci's *ex libris* can be found (149v and 328r).

4.2   The history of the manuscript

Together with Pruggmayr's unique experience in China, his dictionary also has a very fascinating story. A first hint that Pruggmayr was writing a dictionary comes from his letters, and, through the years, he often mentions it in his correspondence to his superiors in Rome. He first announces his intention to compile a dictionary in 1768:

> [...] while in this time I will not be idle but I will work as far as my poor talent will allow for the good of the Mission, and for the ease of present and future Missionaries, using this time to compose and finish a good Italian and Chinese dictionary, which is missing here among our Italian Missionaries and with which they will soon learn the Chinese language well; I will leave this work of mine with them in China – since it is God's will that I leave my feeble body in this Mission – I hope to be able to compensate for my personal lack, and partaking in the Spiritual fruit

---

16. "The beginning of this Volume was marked with p. 174 by mistake, for the alphabetical order shows that from the last page of Vol. I which is 148 to the beginning of the page 174 nothing is wanting".

of the Missionaries, who, through my dictionary, will learn the language and thus will be in a position to carry out their Apostolic ministry, for which it is necessary to have a good grasp of the Chinese language.

(Beijing, September 19, 1768. APF, SOCP, 56: 34v)

In 1770, having to stay in China for one more year, he writes that he hopes "to accomplish the compilation of the Italian Chinese Dictionary I've been compiling for about three years" (Beijing, July 12, 1770. APF, SOCP, 57: 52r). The following year he would ask *Propaganda* permission to move to Macau and to "stay there for a year, free from other activities", as to be able to devote himself "exclusively to the composition and the accomplishment of this Dictionary" (Beijing, October 16, 1771. APF, SOCP, 59: 292r). The translation of the above-mentioned book by de la Charme, in fact, had taken much of this time, taking his mind off this work for more than six months. His request would not be accepted and, as already mentioned, he had to remain in the capital.

His commitment to this work can also be read in other missionaries' letters. In 1776, for instance, the Franciscan Eusebio da Cittadella writes to *Propaganda* that "he is [...], so constantly applied to his Chinese Dictionary, that it seems he cannot see anything else but this" (Beijing, September 21. da Cittadella 1776).

Finally, in September 1780, Pruggmayr reports to *Propaganda*: "after 13 years, I have finally finished the Italian Chinese Dictionary" (Beijing, September 17, 1780. APF, SOCP, 62: 646v). "Consequently, – he adds – having completed the task for which the Congregation decided to let me stay in this mission, I would like to leave this confusing Babylonia and retreat into a convent of my religion so as to quietly prepare myself for a good death".

As can be inferred by a later letter, someone in Rome had thought he wanted the dictionary to be published. Replying to *Propaganda*, we learn from Pruggmayr that the Prefect had already informed him about the impossibility of printing the dictionary in Rome because of the "lack of Chinese characters [i.e., types]" (Beijing, November 4, 1784. APF, SOCP, 61: 511r). But as he explains soon after:

> Reading this paragraph, I was somewhat surprised: when did I ever write anything to the Holy Congregation for the printing of this Dictionary, nor did it ever occur to me to want it to be printed, neither here nor in Europe and, least of all, printed in Chinese characters? How voluminous would this *Calepinus* [vocabulary] be, which written with only European letters, fills three large volumes? [...] Now I pray the Lord to give me two more years s̶o̶ to finish the second copy, which will be a little better than the first one, and which I am preparing in case the Holy Congregation will keep one [copy] in its Archives and keep the other one here in the Vice-Procuracy.   (Beijing, November 4, 1784. APF, SOCP, 61: 511r)

The dictionary was then sent to the Procurator in Macau. But, after he promised to send it to Rome, no other references to the dictionary can be found in the archives. What happened to it? At this point, it has been necessary to follow another path to reconstruct the story of this volume and consult other sources to discover that a *Vocabolario Italiano-cinese* (Borg. Cin. 407) has been in the Vatican Library for years, but has remained almost unknown and never described in detail. Moreover, it has been left unauthored in many repertoires. Cordier (1924: col. 3908/09) and Pelliot and Takata (1995: 44), for example, recorded it as anonymous. Both of the repertoires, however, underline that the volume belonged to the Italian linguist Antonio Montucci and, prior to him, to Sir George Thomas Staunton (1737–1801).

The first scholar to reconnect the dictionary to his original author is Ambrosius a S. Teresia on the basis of three pieces of evidence: the handwriting; the continuous references to the compilation of such a dictionary in Pruggmayr's as well in other Propagandists' letters; and the correspondence with the description given by Pruggmayr and the dictionary itself (1940: 128).

Once the authorship is established, the legitimate question is understanding how the work ended up in the Vatican Library. After having finished the *Vocabolario*, Pruggmayr sent it to the Procurator of *Propaganda* in Macau, as can be read in a letter from Macau to *Propaganda* by Procurator Giambattista Marchini (1757–1823)[17] dated February 12th, 1789 (Marchini 1789: 270v). From Macau, we can only infer that it was given to or bought by George Staunton since the Lord Macartney embassy stopped in Macau and saw the office of *Propaganda Fide*.[18] In 1811, as a letter attached to the copy kept in the Vatican library attests, the dictionary was sold to Montucci while he was in Berlin and, from there, it finally arrived in Rome in 1826.[19]

A few years after its compilation, the French sinologist Jean-Pierre Abel-Rémusat (1788–1832) had the chance to look at this dictionary from Montucci immediately recognizing that, though anonymous, it was "une traduction chinoise du *Vocabulario della Crusca*" (Abel-Rémusat 1825–1826, II: 67).

---

17. He was the Procurator of *Propaganda Fide* between 1786 and 1823. See Metzler (1985: 95–97).

18. Staunton speaks of a French and of an Italian clergyman in Macau that he must have met since he describes them "both of exemplary worth and piety, who are superiors of, and agents for, several of the missionaries in Eastern Asia" (Staunton 1797: II, 587). As reported in Peyrefitte (2013: 472), the German tutor of Staunton's son, Johann Christian Hüttner (1766–1847), recorded in his diary a description of the Office of Propagation of the Faith, headed by an Italian priest which they visited between January 13 and February 1, 1794.

19. Between 1824 and 1828, in fact, Montucci sold all of his book collection and of his Chinese printing materials and manuscripts to the Congregation of Propaganda Fide who put them in the Museo Borgiano, which eventually ended up in the Vatican Library in 1902 (Cherubini 2017: 68).

4.3   Contents and nature of the work

The dictionary opens with an introduction (*Avvertimenti*) of three folio pages (ff. 0r-1r) while the list of words, given in alphabetical order, begins at folio 2r. Inside the dictionary, words are arranged in two columns, starting with A B: *A Babboccio* ("haphazardly") and followed by the Chinese translation in transcription. In addition, entries are usually followed by a synonym or a phrase in Italian or, rarely, by a Latin expression in order to give a word's meaning and usage followed again by a Chinese translation. Each Italian word, synonym and phrase is followed by a transcription in the Chinese language with no Chinese characters (there is in fact no Chinese character in the text). Each part of the volume is clearly written by a single hand: that of Pruggmayr.

As James (1994: 188–189) points out, Pruggmayr's dictionary is an "early example of the *bilingualized* dictionary within Chinese" where *bilingualized* stands for a dictionary "which was not originally conceived of as a bilingual work". In fact, as stated in the above-quoted letter of November 4th, 1789, the dictionary is based on the last edition of the *Vocabolario degli Accademici della Crusca*.[20] According to the date, the author refers to the 4th edition of the work, which had been published in six volumes between 1729 and 1738, and this is confirmed by the first expression inserted in the work, *A babboccio*, which is present only in the 4th edition of *La Crusca* (1729–1738, vol I: 4).[21] This kind of macrostructure obviously creates some problems for users because the dictionary is, *de facto*, intended for Italian speakers or, at least, for missionaries with a high level of the Italian language.

To better understand which guidelines the compiler followed in his work, his letters and the three introductory pages, entitled *Avvertimenti agli Studenti della Lingua Mandarina, che vorranno impararla su questo Vocabolario* [Notes to Mandarin language learners, who wish to learn from this dictionary] can serve as a compass. As the author states in a letter, he had in mind to fulfil a precise need for specific users:

20. The five editions of the *Vocabolario* (1612, 1623, 1691, 1729–1738, 1863–1923) have been digitized and can be consulted in: "Accademia della Crusca. Lessicografia della Crusca in rete", http://www.lessicografia.it/index.jsp (accessed January 15, 2021).

21. It has yet to be discovered if such a work was kept in Beijing, in Haidian or elsewhere; where it was kept and, in addition, if it had been brought to China by Pruggmayr himself or by other Italian Propagandists. Until now I have simply checked the catalogue of Beitang Library only to discover that the six-volume dictionary is not listed there, so further research in this field would be needed.

This *Calepinus* is properly composed for Europeans who want to learn to speak Chinese and do not know the Chinese characters, so it is superfluous to add them to the Dictionary: to learn to read Chinese books, there are other Dictionaries. In this Dictionary of mine, on which I have worked for over 13 years, there are all the Italian Verbs, and many other words of the last *La Crusca*, with all their different meanings, with various phrases and different expressions: in truth this dictionary can be used to learn the Italian language better [*sic!*].

(Beijing, November 4, 1784. APF, SOCP, 61: 511r)

The Italian Carlo Orazio da Castorano OFM (1673–1755) had followed the same methodology for his *Dictionarium latino-italico-sinicum* (manuscript, compiled in 1732), basing his list of words on a *Calderino*[22] and a *Calepino* (Li 2014–15: 133; 162) though not specifying what edition he had used.

4.3.1   *The Chinese language*

In his three introductory pages, Pruggmayr briefly illustrates the Chinese language (Table 1) and explains how to read words and use the dictionary. Clearly inspired by previous descriptions of Mandarin, he begins by stating:

Table 1. The Chinese language

Original text	English translation
Essendo in questo Vocabolario le parole Cinesi scritte con certi Accenti, è da sapersi, come la lingua cinese è molto limitata, e composta di 364 sole voci, che per altro niuna di esse senza Accento, o inflessione della voce proferita, ha significato alcuno; onde volendo i Cinesi esprimere con sì poche voci una moltitudine sì grande e sì varia di cose, che nell'Universo Mondo si trovano, inventarono diversi Accenti, o siano Tuoni, de' quali ogn'uno da per se nella pronuncia, e diversifica il significato. (Pruggmayr 1780: f. 3r)	[The Chinese words in this dictionary are written with certain accents; it must be known that the Chinese Language is very limited and consists of only 364 voices,* none of which, however, has any meaning without accent or inflection of the voice; so the Chinese people, wishing to express with so few words such a wide and varied multitude of things, which are found in the Universe, created several accents, or tones [*tuoni*], each of which differs in pronunciation and distinguishes the meaning.]

* To be intended as words represented by the same letters with no diacritics.

---

22. The "Calderino" owes its name to Cesare Calderino Mirani (*fl.* 1586), author of *Dictionarium tum latini* (1586). He revised with others the Calepinus with the title *Perfectissimus Calepinus parvus, sive correctissimum dictionarium Caesaris Calderini Mirani* (with many editions from the 17th and 18th centuries), which served as a model for the compilation of other vocabularies.

As can be seen from this brief presentation, the authors generally refer to a "Chinese language" not going into details specifying who speaks this language and where or if there are differences inside this language community. At the same time, it is interesting to notice that the Austrian missionary lists "364 *voices*" like Francisco Varo (1627–1687) (Varo 2000 [1703]: 16–17) and unlike many other compilers of Chinese work of grammars of his time.[23]

4.3.2   *The Chinese 'Accents'*

The compiler explains that the tones of the Mandarin language are five and the Europeans "write them in this way": 1.mo ˉ ; 2do ^; 3° `; 4° ´, and 5° ˇ.[24] He then goes into detail explaining what these tones are called in Chinese and giving indications on how to pronounce them (Table 2).

Looking at this description it is possible to summarize the five tones system as explained by Pruggmayr as follows (compare with the summary of Varo's tones made by Coblin 2006: 26, and with Martini's tones system in Martini, n.d.: 7).

1. *Pingsheng* 平聲 or *shangping* 上平, Level tone or upper level, marked with a macron, e.g., ā.
2. *Zhuoping* 濁平 or *xiaping* 下平, Lower level tone, marked with a circumflex accent, e.g., â.
3. *Shangsheng* 上聲, Rising tone, marked with a grave accent, e.g., à.
4. *Qusheng* 去聲, Departing tone, marked with acute accent, e.g., á.
5. *Rusheng* 入聲, Entering tone, marked with breve, e.g., ă.

This kind of explanation by Pruggmayr is present in other missionary works on the Chinese language, but it is interesting to notice that, apart from the first tone, Pruggmayr's technical terminology closely follows the explanation of simple tones in Francisco Varo's *Arte de la lengua mandarina* (1703) (Varo 2000 [1703]: "Paragraph 1: On the Simple Tones", 33–39), which records the tones of early Qing

---

23. Just to mention the works written in 18th century, Joseph Henri-Marie de Prémare's (1666–1736) *Notitiae Linguae Sinicae*, compiled around 1730 and published in 1831, lists 487 *sounds* (Prémare 1831: 36); the *Museum sinicum* by Gottlieb Siegfried Bayer (1694–1738) enumerates around 350 monosyllables (Bayer 1730: I, 5); while in 1742 Étienne Fourmont (1683–1745) wrote in his *Grammatica sinica* that the number of all the possible (mono)syllables of the Chinese language is around 326,328 (Fourmont 1742: 5).

24. It must be noticed that the fourth tone is drawn more like a vertical line on the syllable [|] while the fifth tone, in Pruggmayr's handwriting, often tends to resemble a small circle [°] more than the mark [ˇ] given in his instructions. For this reason and because of typing difficulties, in the examples given in these pages, over the letter *y* the fifth tone will be marked with a small circle.

Table 2. On the Chinese Accents

Original text	English translation
Il 1mo Accento: ¯ : si pronuncia prolungando la voce egualmente, senza abbassarla, né alzarla, come quando ad una persona duole qualche cosa, e lamentandosi suol dire: <u>ai</u> i pronunciandolo con suono eguale. Questo Tuono o Accento si chiama: *p^cîm scīm* [平聲]; e anche: *sciám p^cîm* [上平].	[The first accent ¯ is pronounced by prolonging the voice equally, without lowering it or raising it, as when a person has pain, and complains saying: *ai*, pronouncing *i* with equal sound. This tone or accent is called *p^cîm scīm* [平聲], and also *sciám p^cîm* [上平].
Il 2do Accento: ˆ : si pronuncia abbassando un poco la voce nel fine, e non si prolunga tanto la voce, quanto nel primo Accento, come si suol pronunciare in lingua italiana la parola <u>No</u>, volendo negare una cosa. Questo Accento si chiama: *ciŏ p^cîm* [濁平], vel, *hiá p^cîm* [下平].	The second accent ˆ is pronounced by slightly lowering the voice at the end without prolonging it too much as for the first accent, like in the Italian language the word *No* is usually uttered as a negation. This accent is called *ciŏ p^cîm* [濁平], or *hiá p^cîm* [下平].
Il terzo Accento: ` : si pronuncia alzando la voce un poco, e subito abbassarla con modo imperativo: questo Accento si chiama: *sciám scīm* [上聲].	The third accent ` is pronounced by slightly raising the voice and suddenly lowering it with an imperative mood. This accent is called *sciám scīm* [上聲].
Il 4° Accento: ´ : si esprime con modo interrogativo, dal tuono alto terminando col tuono basso, prolungato un poco. Questo Accento s chiama: *k^ciú scīm* [去聲].	The fourth Accent ´ is expressed with the interrogative mood, from a high tone ending with a low tone, slightly prolonged. This accent is called *k^ciú scīm* [去聲].
Il 5° Accento: ˘ : devesi pronunciare quasi come il 4°, però senza protrazione della parola in fine; cioè, con soavità senza violenza; troncando colla voce in un colpo. Questo Accento si chiama: *giŭ scīm* [入聲]. (Priggmayr 1780: f. 3r)	The fifth Accent ˘ must be pronounced almost like the fourth one, but without prolonging the word at the end; that is with sweetness without intensity, cutting off the voice in one go. This Accent is called *giŭ scīm* [入聲].]

guānhuà 官話 (Coblin 1998), a court language used by imperial officials, commonly known as "Mandarin" in the European languages. The five tone marks were created by Matteo Ricci SJ (1552–1610) and Lazzaro Cattaneo SJ (1560–1640) and were immediately adopted both by missionaries in China and European scholars. In Table 3 the number and terminology for tones in the works of Chinese grammars are compared with the ones in VIC. Please note that the nomenclature for the tones is here in Pinyin in order to avoid confusion.

As can be seen, the nomenclature of Pruggmayr's tones is very close to that of Martini apart from the order in which they are presented and from the fact that the Austrian missionary also uses alternative denominations for the first and second

Table 3. Tone system in 17th and 18th missionary works on the Chinese language

Author	Title and date of composition/ publication	Tones nomenclature	Tone marks
Martini	*Grammatica Sinica* (1696 [1653])	*qu* 去	`
		shang 上	´
		ru 入	ˇ
		ping 平	–
		zhuo 濁	^
Varo	*Arte de la lengua mandarina* (1703 [c.1682])	*pingzhuo* 平清* (*shangping* 上平)	–
		zhuoping 濁平 (*xiaping* 下平)	^
		shang 上	`
		qu 去	´
		ru 入	ˇ
Prémare	*Notitiae Linguae Sinicae* (1728, 1831)	*ping* 平 (*qing* 清 and *zhuo* 濁),	– ^
		ze 仄 (*shang* 上 and *qu* 去),	` ´
		ru 入	ˇ
Bayer	*Museum sinicum* (1730)	*qu* 去	`
		shang 上	´
		ru 入	ˇ
		ping 平	–
		zhuo 濁	^
Fourmont	*Grammatica sinica* (1742)	*ping* 平 (*shangping* 上平 or *qingping* 清平)	–
		zhuoping 濁平 (*xiaping* 下平)	^
		shang 上	`
		qu 去	´
		ru 入	ˇ
Pruggmayr	*Vocabolario Italiano-Cinese* (1780)	*ping* 平 (*shangping* 上平)	–
		zhuoping 濁平 (*xiaping* 下平)	^
		shang 上	`
		qu 去	´
		ru 入	ˇ

* To be read as *qingping* 清平 (Varo 2000 [1703]: 34, n. 1).

tone and almost identical to those of Varo and Fourmont. All these similarities do not help to clearly identify what sources Pruggmayr used but reinforce the idea of a semi-established practice among missionaries in 18th China.

Being a work of grammar, *Arte de la lengua mandarina* of course elaborates on the explanation of tones, dividing them into four categories: "simple, guttural or aspirated, with dot, and guttural with dot", a subdivision that is only briefly mentioned in VIC. Pruggmayr, in fact, makes only a basic distinction between simple and guttural tones:

> The Accents or Tones can be divided into simple and guttural:[25] the simple ones are written as the ones we have explained so far; the guttural ones are marked with one *c* put next to the simple Accent, as can be seen in the following words of all the five Accents: *Tᶜiēn* [天], the Heaven; *tᶜaǒ* [逃], escape; *kᶜý* [起], to rise; *kᶜiú* [去], go; *kᶜě* [客], guest; etc.
>
> (Pruggmayr 1780: f. 3r)

In any case, even if in these introductory notes the author may have been inspired by previous works by missionaries, a further study is necessary to carefully explore the coherence within the dictionary in terms of transcriptional conventions and lexical choices.

4.3.3 *The romanization system*

As the author writes, the dictionary makes use of the Italian orthography, "so that an Italian [...], must read them and pronounce them as if he would pronounce such Italian words when reading an Italian book" (f. 3v). But Pruggmayr also adds some instructions to French and Portuguese missionaries on how to read his romanization. It has to be noticed that also Varo and Martini gave similar indications to their readers in their works. Martini, for instance, adds marginal notes for Italian, French, Portuguese (Lusitan) and Spanish readers to his "Catalogus dictionum Sinensium" (Martini n.d.: 2–6). Varo too devotes a section to his French readers since his romanization is based on the Castilian pronunciation but not for the Italians since for them the "difficulty is minimal" (2000 [1703]: 7–8). On the other hand, Fourmont gives pronunciation examples only taking into consideration French and German sounds (1742: 3–4) and Prémare also considers French, Spanish and Portuguese missionaries when giving instructions on how to correctly pronounce the sounds of the Chinese language (1831: 11–14).

The explanation by Pruggmayr goes on to illustrate the complete romanization system used in the dictionary. To indicate aspiration, for example, Pruggmayr inserts a sort "spiritus asper" or superscript *c* after the initial:

> Of these guttural Tones, the first letter is pronounced with aspiration or rather, with greater strength, precisely as we do when we want to pronounce a word written with two *c*-s: i.e., Caccia, where the syllable *ccia* is pronounced with more strength than this other one: *cia*, written with a single *c*. So the word *Tᶜiēn* [天] is pronounced as it was written with an *h*: i.e. *Thiēn*; *tᶜaǒ* [逃] as *thaǒ*; *kᶜý* [起], *kᶜiú* [去] and *kᶜě* [客], as they were written as *khý, khiú, khě*, etc.
>
> (Pruggmayr 1780: f. 3r)

---

25. These terms correspond to the difference between unaspirated (simple) and aspirated (guttural).

The author also explains how a dot is used to mark a variation in the syllable vowels *u, o* and *e*:

> In this Dictionary, many words are written with a dot over the Accent; this dot serves to denote that, being on the letter *u*, such a letter has to be pronounced as the French and the Milanese do; when it is put on the letter *o*, it must be pronounced between *o* and *u*; pronouncing it more as a *u* than an *o*; when it is on the letter *e*; it must be pronounced between *e* and *i*, as if it were an *i* and not an *e*.
> (Pruggmayr 1780: f. 3v)

This explanation, however, is not consistent with VIC's content since the only dotted vowel throughout all the dictionary is the final *u*.

The romanization used by the author is still partly based on Latin, Portuguese or Spanish, the most common in missionary materials (Masini 2019) but, as Pruggmayr writes:

> This being an Italian Chinese Dictionary, and expressly composed for Italian missionaries, I considered I should make use of the Italian orthography to write the Chinese words; so that an Italian, reading the Chinese words written in this Dictionary is able to read and pronounce them as he would pronounce such words when reading an Italian book.
> (Pruggmayr 1780: f. 3v)

Due to space limitations, it not possible here to further illustrate in detail this Italian adaptation of the romanization of Chinese, but here follows a brief account of the main traits of Pruggmayr's romanization.

In regard to initials and finals, Pruggmayr gives indications on how to read the Italian orthographic conventions, especially for Portuguese and French users. These indications are summarized in Table 4:

Table 4. Orthographic conventions in VIC (Pruggmayr 1780: f. 3v-4r)

Italian graphemes	Equivalent in Portuguese	Equivalent in French	Given examples (IT-PO-FR)
c (before -e and -i)	ch	tch	ciù/chù/tchù
z (or tsi)	ç	_____	zù/çù
sc (before -e and -i)	x	ch	sciāo/xāo/chāo
g (before -e and -i)	J or j (as in Jesus or Joannes)		gîn, giào, Giám/jîn, jào, jám

The author thus explains that all the Chinese "words starting or written with <ng> are to be read as they were written <gh>, e.g. <ngēn> [恩], favor, has to be read <ghēn>; <Ngān> has to be read <gān>; <ngái> has to be read <gái>" (Pruggmayr 1780: f. 3v). A final piece of advice to French and Italian readers regards the final <-m> which "has to be pronounced in the Portuguese way, without joining the lips, but as it was written <ng>, e.g. *tᶜâm* has to be read as *tᶜâng* [堂]" (Pruggmayr 1780: f. 4r).

Taking into consideration the reconstruction of initial consonants in Ming-Qing Mandarin *guānhuà* made by Raini (2009–2010: 42) and the reconstruction of Castorano's romanization in Li Hui (2014–2015), Table 5 briefly illustrates the initial graphemes used by some Italian missionaries in comparison with those used by Pruggmayr in VIC and their probable phonetic value (PPV) in square brackets:[26]

Table 5. Initial graphemes in the romanization systems by Italian speaking missionaries

PPV	RES	RLS	MM1	HZXY	DLIS	VIC
[p]	p	p	p	p	p	p
[p']	p	p'	p'	p'	p'	p'
[m]	m	m	m	m	m	m
[f]	f	f	f	f	f	f
[v][ʋ]	v	v	_____	ü (or v)	v	v
[t]	t	t	t	t	t	t
[t']	t	t'	t'	t'	t'	t'
[n]	n	n	n	n	n	n
[l]	l	l	l	l	l	l
[ts]	c	ç, c,	ç, c,	ç	z	z
[ts']	z	ç', c'	ç', c'	ç'	z'	z'
[s]	s	s	s	s	s	s
[tʃ]	c	ch	ch	ch	c	c (-e,-i)
[tʃ']	(cc)	ch'	ch'	ch'	c'	c'(-e,-i)
[ʃ]	sc(-i)	x	x	x	sc	sc(-i)
[ʒ]	g(-i)	g, j	g (or j)	j	g	g(-i)
[k]	c, ch, q	c, k, q	c, k, q	k, q	k	k (g?)
[k']	c, ch, q	c', k', q'	k, k'	k', q'	k'	k'
[ŋ]-[ʔ]	ng(-h); g	ng, g	ng, g	ng, g	ng (-a,-o); ngh (-e)	_____
[x]	h, sch	h	h	h	h	h
[ɣ]/[v] [ɣw]	_____	_____	_____	_____	g (-oei, -u)	g

26. Acronyms in Table 5 are taken for the most part from Raini (2009–2010) and stand for: RES, Ricci Early System; RLS, Ricci Late System; MM1 stands for the romanization by Martino Martini SJ (1614–1661) in his *Grammatica Sinica*; HZXY, *Hanzi xiyi* 漢字西譯 by Basilio Brollo (1648–1704); DLSI, *Dictionarium latino-italico-sinicum* by Castorano.

At a first look, VIC's romanization seems to share many features in common with other works by Italian missionaries, Castorano's *Dictionarium* being the closest. It can also be noted that initial graphemes in Ricci Early System, Castorano and Pruggmayr suggest a more italophone approach. From Table 5 another important piece of information can be inferred, that is the loss of the velar nasal initial [ŋ] in VIC. The phonetic value of <g> is maybe controversial and due to limited space will not be discussed here but can be compared with the use in transcription made by Varo and the hypothesis advanced by Coblin (1998: 263).

4.3.4   *On the different pronunciations of standard Chinese*
Unlike some of his predecessors (Ricci and Ruggieri, Varo and others) Pruggmayr does not focus on the different linguistic registers of Chinese and adds no information on the literary styles used in the written language. This 'omission' can be read in the light of four hypotheses: first, Pruggmayr's primary interest was the oral production of the language; secondly, he was not very familiar with the Chinese writing system, as the absence of characters in his dictionary seems to confirm; third, he simply believed that this kind of information would be of no use for a foreign missionary in China; four, he worked alone and none of his Chinese accolites were able to write down characters. Nonetheless, it is interesting to notice that the Carmelite is aware of the existence (and differences) between the Northern and the Southern pronunciation of the *guānhuà*, or Mandarin, of the period. He writes:

> This Dictionary is compiled according to the speaking and the pronunciation of the Chinese words used in the Boreal regions, and above all in the province of Beijing, which in many words is different from the pronunciation used in the Austral region, where the words and the Chinese characters are pronounced as they should be. It should be noted that the two words *voě* [物], which means thing, and *kuě* [國], which means kingdom, in the Boreal provinces are pronounced *vŭ* and *kuŏ*.
> (Pruggmayr 1780: f. 3v)

And again, he documents elsewhere: "Affair, the Austral Chinese call it *sú·*,[27] [while] in this area it is written and pronounced *scý* [事]".

This conscious change in the transcription of the sounds from the Southern pronunciation or Nanyin 南音 to the Northern one (Beiyin 北音), which is consistent inside the dictionary, can be considered as ~~an~~ evidence of the process which progressively led to the linguistic shift from south to north and, finally, to the birth of the modern national language.

---

27. In the original text, that I was unable to reproduce, the dot is right above the vocal *u* and just below the tone.

4.3.5   *One grammatical note and some examples*

Pruggmayr leaves a brief grammatical note in his *Notes*, stating that in his Dictionary:

> you can often come across the word *ciŏ* [著] which has different meanings, but many times it has no meaning at all and, for the most part, it is usually added to the neutral verbs, e.g. *zó* [坐], to sit, that can be also said as *zó ciŏ* [坐著], and means to sit, as the word *zò* alone. It must be noticed, though, that this particle *ciŏ*, when added to some verb and meaning anything, must be pronounced as it is written *cè* i.e., *zó cè*.   (Pruggmayr 1780: f. 4r)

Even lacking grammatical explanations, inside the dictionary it is possible to find examples of use which can help defining grammatical patterns. One of the first lemmas to open the work is "A bastanza" (enough), from which can be seen the use of particle *de* (now written as 得 and used to link a verb and the manner clause):

> A bastanza, o abbastanza; *keú leào* [夠了] = *fū zŭ* [富足] = *pŭ sciào* [不少] e.g., Mangiar a bastanza ["eat enough"]: *cᶜŷ pào* [吃飽, eat (one's) fill] = *cᶜŷ tŷ tám leào* [吃得當了, "eat properly"]. Piovuto a bastanza, vg. per poter seminare ["it rained enough", e.g., "to sow"]: *hiá tŷ iù˙ keú leào* [下的雨夠了, "it rained enough"]

Again, translating the lemma "Abbasso" [down], great use is made of the directional complement:

> Abbasso, in giù, *hiá* [下, "down"] = *vuàm hiá* [往下, "downward"]
> Andar abbasso, *hiá kᶜiú* [下去, "go down"]
> Venir abbasso, *hiá lâi* [下来, "come down"]
> Cascar abbasso, *tiáo hiá lâi* [掉下来, "fall down"]

5.   Some open questions and observations

As Klöter points out, for years a "monolinguistic view on China" has had "important implications" within the field of Chinese missionary linguistics (Klöter 2007: 193). Studying the linguistic variety documented by Pruggmayr, we can conclude that there are slight differences compared with previous works in terms of tone nomenclature, orthographic choices, use of diacritics. However, what differentiates the *Vocabolario Italiano-Cinese* from other works of those times can be found in the 'phonologic traces' it records. The study of early missionary dictionaries and grammars, in fact, demonstrates that these early materials, when not describing the local vernaculars of Southeast China, recorded the so-called Southern pronunciation or Nanyin. "Indeed, it was not until the mid 1800s that the northern standard or Beiying 北音 became the dominant form of Guanhua pronunciation"

(Coblin 2007: 108). Looking at the life and cultural background of the Carmelite, it is easy to imagine that the entries in the dictionary are based on the language he had learned in the field, i.e., among his Catholic community in Haidian and in the Imperial court. In other words, in his *Vocabolario*, Pruggmayr is one of the first European missionaries to record a Chinese variety which is closer to Northern *guānhuà*. This can be seen in the loss of the velar nasal initial [ŋ] (as illustrated in Table 5) and in the substitution in transcription of the final <u> with an <i> after the alveolar fricative /s/. Comparing VIC with other works like those by Martini, Varo, Brollo, and others, it is important to underline that Pruggmayr's dictionary is one of the earliest extant Italian-based material on the Chinese language together with the *Dictionarium latino-italico-sinicum* by Castorano. Of the works of the latter, I suspect that Pruggmayr is particularly indebted to the works of the latter, but only a more careful study of both sources will better reveal their connection.

Many questions are still open, but the most relevant ones, in my opinion, are to find out what kind of Chinese sources the author may have used while compiling the lexicon; the influence of Castorano's work on the dictionary must be further explored, and a more in-depth study on the lexicon and transcription is needed to establish more precisely to what extent the *Vocabolario* is based on the Northern variety of the *guānhuà*. Pruggmayr's work is rich and comprehensive and allows scholars to deepen their knowledge of phonology and word usage of the period. In other words, Pruggmayr's *Vocabolario Italiano-cinese* can be regarded as a complementary and useful tool for the study of the phonology, the lexicon of Northern varieties, and the changes occurring not only in the linguistic shift from Nanyin to Beiyin starting from the second half of the 18th century but also from Beiyin to modern varieties of the Chinese language.

References

A.   Primary sources

APF. *Archivio Storico della Congregazione per l'Evangelizzazione dei Popoli or de Propaganda Fide*. Vatican City.

Bayer, Gottlieb Siegfried (Theophili Sigefridi Bayeri). 1730. *Museum Sinicum in quo Sinicae Linguae et Litteraturae ratio explicatur*. 2 vols. Petropoli [Saint Petersburg]: Ex Typographia Academiae Imperatoriae.

Calderino Mirani, Cesare. 1586. *Dictiorarium d. Caesaris Calderini Mirani Veronensis. Tum latini, tum italici sermonis studiosis, apprime congruens*. Venetiis: apud Felicem Valgrisium.

Castorano, Carlo Orazio da. 1732. *Dictionarium Latino Italico Sinicum Tam vocum, quam Litterarum seu Characterum usualium Sinensium ad usum et commoditatem PP. Missionariorum in hanc Sinicam Missionem noviter adventantium*. Vatican Library, Vatican City. Vat.estr.or.4 [anastatic version in: https://digi.vatlib.it/view/MSS_Vat.estr.or.4].

Cittadella, Eusebio da. 1776. *Letter to Propaganda*. Beijing. September 21, 1776. APF, SOCP, 61. 390.

Fourmont, Étienne. 1742. *Linguae Sinarum Mandarinicae hieroglyphicae grammatica duplex, latinè, & cum characteribus Sinensium. Item Sinicorum Regiae Bibliothecae librorum catalogus*. Paris: Hippolyte-Louis Guerin, Rollin & Joseph Bullot, Ex Typographiâ Josephi Bullot.

Marchini, Giambattista. 1789. *Letter to Propaganda*. Macau. February 12, 1789. APF, SOCP, 66.276–270.

Martini, Martino. (n.d.). *Grammatica Linguae Sinensis*. (n.p.) [anastatic version in: http://www. archive.org/details/grammaticalingua0015p

Miralta, Arcangelo. 1744. "Memorie e Varie occorrenze del 1744". *Relazione dello stato in cui si ritrovano le Missioni della Sagra Congregazione de Propaganda nel 1744. SS.O P.o del Tumkino*. Ms. APF. SOCP, 46.

Palladini, Emiliano. 1771. *Memorie ed occorrenze delle Missioni delle Indie Orientali, che Emiliano Palladini Procuratore della S. Congregazione di Propaganda Fide in Macao umilia alla stessa per l'Anno 1771*. (Macau, December 31, 1771). Ms. APF, SOCP, 59.93–104.

Prémare, Joseph-Henri de. 1831 [c. 1730]. *Notitia Linguae Sinicae*. Malaccæ: Cura et sumptibus collegii anglo-sinensis. Printed in Thévenot (1696).

Pruggmayr, Joseph Maximilian. *Letters*. APF, SOCP, vols. 46, 55, 56, 57, 59, 61, 62.

Pruggmayr, Joseph Maximilian. 1780. *Vocabolario Italiano Cinese*. Ms. Borg. Cin. 407. Vatican Library, Vatican City.

Simonetti, Nicola. 1773. *Memorie per le Missioni dell'Indie Orientali, che all'Emo Sig.r Card. Castelli Pref.o della Sac. Cong.ne de Propaganda Fide, ed alla stessa Sac. Cong.ne si umiliano da Nicola Simonetti di lei Proc.re in Macao per l'anno 1773*. (Macau, December 31, 1773). Ms. APF, SOCP, 60.124–134.

SOCP. *Scritture Originali delle Congregazioni Particolari delle Indie Orientali*.

Thévenot, Melchisédec. 1696. *Relations de divers voyages curieux*, 2 vols. Paris: Thomas Moette.

Varo, Francisco. 2000 [1703]. *Arte de la lengua mandarina compuesto por el M.R°. Pe – de la sagrada Orden de N.P.S. Domingo, acrecentado, y reducido a mejor forma, por N° H. fr. Pedro de la Piñuela P[redicad]or y Comisario Prov[incial] de la Mission Serafica de China. Añadiose un Confessionario muy vtil, y provechoso para alivio de los nueos Ministros*. Canton: [publisher unknown]. *Francisco Varo's Grammar of the Mandarin Language (1703). An English translation of 'Arte de la lengua mandarina'* ed. by W. South Coblin & Joseph A. Levi (with an Introduction by Sandra Breitenbach). Amsterdam & Philadelphia: John Benjamins.

Vocabolario degli Accademici della Crusca. 1729–1738. Quarta impressione [fourth edition], 6 vols. Firenze: appresso Domenico Maria Manni. Available online: http://www.lessicografia. it/index.jsp

B.   Secondary sources

Abel-Rémusat, Jean-Pierre. 1825–1826. *Mélanges asiatiques, ou choix de morceaux critiques et de mémoires relatifs aux religions, aux sciences, aux coutumes, à l'histoire et à la géographie des Nations Orientales*, vol. 2. Paris: Librairie Orientale de Dondey-Dupré pèreet fils/Imprimerie-Librarie de la Société Asiatique.

Aparicio Ahedo, Óscar Ignacio. 2018. "Un carmelita descalzo misionero en China (1745–1791)". *Anuario de Historia de la Iglesia* 27.351–376. https://doi.org/10.15581/007.27.351-376

Cherubini, Donatella. 2017. *Una famiglia tra Siena e l'Europa: I Montucci 1762–1877*. Milano: FrancoAngeli.

Coblin, W. South. 1998. "Francisco Varo and the Sound System of Early Qīng Mandarin". *Journal of the American Oriental Society* 2.262–267. https://doi.org/10.2307/605899

Coblin, W. South. 2006. "Introduction". Francisco Varo (2006 [between 1677–1687]). *Vocabulario de la lengua Mandarina con el estilo y vocablos con que se habla sin elegancia. Compuesto por el Padre fray – ord. Pred. Ministro de China consumado en esta lengua esriuese guardando el orden del A.B. c.d., Francisco Varo's Glossary of the mandarin Language. Vol. I: An English and Chinese Annotation of the Vocabulario de la Lengua Mandarinaed*. by W. South Coblin, 11–36. Nettetal: Sankt Augustin.

Coblin, W. South. 2007. "Review of *Dicionário Português-Chinés / Pú-Hàn cídiǎn* 葡漢辭典 / *Portuguese-Chinese Dictionary by Matteo Ricci and Michele Ruggieri* ed. by John W. Witek. San Francisco and Lisboa: Ricci Institute for Chinese Western Cultural History (University of San Francisco) and Biblioteca Nacional Portugal, Instituto Português do Oriente, 2001". *Ming Studies* 56.106–111. https://doi.org/10.1179/014703707788762382

Cordier, Henri. 1924. *Bibliotheca sinica. Dictionnaire bibliographique des ouvrages relatifs à l'Empire chinois. Supplément*. Vol. 1. Paris: Librarie Orientaliste Paul Geuthner.

Iannello, Tiziana. 2012. "La missione in Cina di Rinaldo Romei O.C.D. nella corrispondenza da Pechino con il duca di Modena, Rinaldo d'Este (1720–1731)". *Scritture di Storia* 6.343–355.

James, Gregory C. 1994. "Towards a Typology of Bilingualised Dictionaries". *Meeting Points in Language Studies* ed. by Gregory James, 184–196. Hong Kong: HKUST Language Centre.

Klöter, Henning. 2007. "'Ay sinco lenguas algo difirentes': China's local vernaculars in early missionary sources". *Missionary Linguistics III / Lingüística misionera III. Morphology and Syntax* ed. by Otto Zwartjes, Gregory James, & Emilio Ridruejo, 191–210. Amsterdam & Philadelphia, John Benjamins. https://doi.org/10.1075/sihols.111.16klo

Krahl, Joseph. 1964. *China Missions in Crisis: Bishop Laimbeckhoven and His Times 1738–1787*. Roma: Gregorian University Press.

Li, Hui 李慧. 2014–2015. *Il Dictionarium latino-italico-sinicum di Carlo Orazi da Castorano O.F.M. (1673–1755)*. Ph.D. Dissertation, University of Rome La Sapienza.

Margiotti, Fortunato. 1963. "La confraternita del Carmine in Cina (1728–1838)". *Ephemerides Carmeliticae* 24.91–154.

Masini, Federico. 2019. "Chinese Language and Christianity". *The Routledge Handbook of Chinese Applied Linguistics*, ed. by Chu-Ren Huang, Zhuo Jing-Schmidt & Barbara Meister-ernst, Chapter 3, 44–57. Hong Kong: Routledge. https://doi.org/10.4324/9781315625157-4

Metzler, Josef. 1985. "Das Archiv der Missionsprokur der Sacra Congregatio de Propaganda Fide in Canton, Macao und Hong Kong". *La conoscenza dell'Asia e dell'Africa in Italia nei secoli XVIII e XIX* (Collana 'Matteo Ripa', IV), ed. by Ugo Marazzi and Carlo Gallotta vol. 2, 75–139. Napoli: Istituto Universitario Orientale.

Pedrini, Teodorico. 2018. *Son mandato à Cina, à Cina vado: lettere dalla missione, 1702–1744*. ed. by Fabio G. Galeffi & Gabriele Tarsetti. Macerata: Quodlibet.

Pelliot, Paul & Takata Tokio. 1995. *Inventaire sommaire des manuscrits et imprimés chinois De La Bibliothèque Vaticane: A Posthumous Work*. Kyoto: Ist. Italiano di Cultura.

Peyrefitte, Alain. 2013. *The Immobile Empire*. New York: Vintage Books.

Pfister, Louis. 1932–1934. *Notices biographiques et bibliographiques sur les Jésuites de l'ancienne mission de Chine: 1552–1773*. 2 vols. Chang-Hai: Imprimerie de la Mission Catholique, orphelinat de t'ou-sè-wè.

Raini, Emanuele. 2009–2010. Sistemi di Romanizzazione del cinese mandarino nei secoli XVI–XVIII. Ph.D. Dissertation, University of Rome La Sapienza.

Sancta Teresia, Ambrosius a. 1940. *Bio-bibliographia Missionaria Ordinis Carmelitarum Discalceatorum (1584–1940), collecta et ordine chronologico digesta a p. fr. Ambrosio a s. Teresia.* Romae: apud Curiam Generalitiam.

Standaert, Nicolas. 2001. *Handbook of Christianity in China. Volume One: 635–1800.* Leiden, Boston & Köln: Brill. https://doi.org/10.1163/9789004391857

Staunton, George. 1797. *An authentic account of an embassy from the King of Great Britain to the Emperor of China…*, 3 vols. London: G. Nicol.

PART II

Japan

Politeness in João Rodrigues's grammars of Japanese
A terminological analysis

Olivia Yumi Nakaema
Universidade de São Paulo

1. Introduction

Portuguese missions in Japan started with Jesuit Francisco Xavier (1506–1552) in 1549 and developed some missionary linguistic works published in Japan and Macau. The most outstanding works are the two grammars of Japanese composed by the Portuguese Jesuit João Rodrigues:[1] *Arte da Lingoa de Iapam* (Nagasaki, 1604–1608) and *Arte Breve da Lingoa Iapoa* (Macau, 1620).[2]

According to Tadao Doi (1971: 8), Rodrigues followed the Latin model of Manuel Álvares in his *Arte da Lingoa de Iapam,* using eight Latin parts of speech (noun, pronoun, verb, participle, preposition, adverb, interjection and conjunction) and expanded the system with two more, aiming to describe Japanese language's particularities: the article and the particle ("artigo" and "particula").[3] Tae Suzuki (1987: 117) highlights that in the first half of *Arte da Lingoa de Iapam,* Rodrigues follows Manuel Álvares's[4] Latin model, and in the second half he describes linguistic elements that he considered typical of Japanese. Maruyama (2009: 8) explains that *Arte da Lingoa de Iapam* is organized similarly to the traditional Latin model

---

1. Born in Sernancelhe, Portugal, around 1561 or 1562, João Rodrigues died in Macau, around 1633 or 1634. He served as an interpreter, missionary and professor. He was known for his excellent Japanese language proficiency.

2. For more information about the linguistic works written by Portuguese Missionaries in Japan, see Zwartjes (2011: 93–142).

3. In fact, Rodrigues uses different models, not only the Western model inspired by Álvares, but also the Japanese classification of three parts of speech (Zwartjes 2011: 104).

4. Portuguese humanist Manuel Álvares (1526–1582) was a Jesuit Father who wrote a very influential Latin Grammar titled *De Institutione Grammaticae Libri Tres* (1572). In Japan, Álvares's grammar was printed in Amakusa in 1594, adapted to Japanese students.

https://doi.org/10.1075/sihols.130.05nak

(morphology,syntax, orthography, prosody), as in Antonio Nebrija's (c.1444–1522) and João de Barros's[5] (1496–1570) grammars. However, the Japanese language, its morphology and vocabulary related to 'politeness', do not lend themselves to analyses entirely based on Latin. In fact, these European sources could hardly provide a framework in order to satisfactorily describe politeness in Japanese.

However, Doi (1971: 9) considers that Rodrigues's description of politeness was influenced by models present in different Japanese works. Also, Suzuki (1987: 122) emphasizes Rodrigues' originality in describing the typical linguistic forms of the Japanese language without using the Latin model. In these *Artes*, Rodrigues used the expressions *honra* ['honour'] and *humildade* ['humility'] to describe politeness in Japanese. Therefore, as a peculiarity of this language, Rodrigues develops an 'innovating metalanguage' which are 'expansions of Latin terminology' (Zwartjes 2011: 136). The missionary uses an original terminology which cannot be found either in Latin nor in Portuguese grammars of his time.

João Rodrigues highlights the importance of politeness in the Japanese language and presents and describes it in detail in his *Proemio* ['Preface'], the section entitled *Algumas Advertencias* ['Some warnings'] at the beginning of *Arte da Lingoa de Iapam* (1604–1608). In his *Advertencias*, he emphasizes that politeness is a peculiarity of elegant speech in the language, using the following words:

> mas no que esta lingoa se assinala, & he diuersa de quantas temos noticia, he na maneira de respeitos, & cortesias que inclue nos modos de falar quasi universalmente: por que tem verbos acõmodados para falar de pessoas, & com pessoas baixas, & altas, & tẽ varias particulas que se ajuntam aos verbos, & nomes, respeitando sempre à pessoa cõ quẽ, de quẽ, & de q̃ cousas fala, para usar das taes particulas, & verbos conforme a calidade de cada hũ; de modo que se não pode aprender sem juntamente se aprender a falar com honra, & cortesia.
>
> (Rodrigues 1604–1608 (AG): *Advertencias*, no numbered folios)[6]

> [but what in this language is signalled, distinct from others of which we have knowledge, is the means of [showing] respect, and courtesy that is included almost universally in the way of speaking: because it has verbs accommodated to talking about people and with lower and higher people, and it has many particles that are joined to verbs, and nouns, always respecting the person with whom one speaks, about whom [one speaks] and about which matters one speaks, to use these particles, and verbs according to the quality of each one; so that it is not possible to learn [that language] without learning how to talk with honour and courtesy.]

---

5. Portuguese historian João de Barros was born in Viseu, Portugal, in 1496. His most famous works about the language were *Cartinha para aprender a ler* (Lisbon, 1539) and *Grammatica da lingua portuguesa* (Lisbon, 1540).

6. In the following, abbreviated as AG (Arte "Grande") (1604–1608) and AB (Arte Breve, 1620).

Mastering politeness was necessary in the missionary work, as in any other context. In the Japanese language and culture, politeness plays a prominent role and is culture-specific (emic). Rodrigues warns his learners that if they do not use the honorific particles correctly, interpersonal relationships would be considered odd and unnatural with such erros. Rodrigues points out, for example, the priests' way of speaking:

> Tambem se cometem muytos erros no vso das particulas de honra assi dos nomes como dos verbos. Item no vso dos verbos honrados & no dos humildes, & no verbo simples: de modo que da muyto nas orelhas dos ouuintes, porque ou se honram assi mesmos demasiadamente, ou aos companheiros, & igoais, ou dam honra a gente baixa como a moços, & criados que a nam merecem. Primeiramente hum Padre falando de outro em presença diante dos de fora o honra demasiadamente vsando de, *Sama, Vôxeraruru, Nasaruru,* &c. devendo soomente falar delle como de igoal pois sam da mesma familia, & de igual grao: antes falando com gente de fora ainda do mesmo superior o nam deve honrar mais que com, *Raruru,* pois fala o subdito de seu superior, o discipulo de seu mestre, o filho do pay, assi como o criado de seu senhor com os de fora, quãdo sam pessoas de respeito. (AG: 172r)

> [Also, many errors are made using honorific particles, and nouns and verbs. The same applies in the use of honorific and humbling verbs, and in the simple verb: so that it [is very common] in the ears of listeners, because either they honour themselves too much, or [they over-honour] companions and equals, or they give too much honour to low people, such as boys and servants, who do not deserve it. Firstly, a Father talking about another in front of others that come from another place, gives him too much honour using *Sama, Vôxeraruru, Nasaruru,* etc., he should talk about him as an equal, since they are from the same family, and have an equal rank: talking with outsiders about the same superior person we should only honour them with Raruru, because the vassal talks about their superior, the disciple [talks about] their master, the son [talks about] his father, in the same way that the servant talks about their lord to outsiders, when they are people of respect.]

In this example, Rodrigues explains that a priest should not express honour referring to hierarchical superiors or equals in front of 'outsiders' of the religious community since this would cause some embarrassment. Since *Sama,*[7] *Vôxeraruru,*[8] *Nasaruru*[9] are expressions used when the speaker speaks to the addressee with honour, these cannot be used among themselves in front of outsiders.

---

7. According to *Vocabvlario da Lingoa de Iapam* (1603: 217r), *Sama* means "palavra, que se usa pera honrar no cabo dos nomes das pessoas como merce, senhoria, etc." [Word that is used to honour someone, used at the end of a person's name, as *sir, lordship*] (my translation).

8. *Vôxeraruru* is a verb that means "falar pessoa honrada" ['to speak, used to refer to an action of honoured people'] (*Vocabvlario da Lingoa de Iapam*, 1603: 285v).

9. The verb *Nasaruru* means "to do", used to refer to an action of honoured people.

Considering the above-mentioned, I shall investigate the 'technical layer' (Swiggers 2004) by analysing, semantically and epistemologically, Rodrigues's met-alanguage elaborated to describe politeness. For such purpose, I use the following classemic parameters proposed by Swiggers (2010: 18–19): the content of terms ("le contenu des termes"), the frequency of terms ("l'incidence des termes") and the cultural footprint of terms ("l'empreinte culturelle des termes"). In the following section (2) I shall describe hierarchical interpersonal relationship in the three layers identified by Rodrigues. Section 3 situates Rodrigues's approach to politeness in his *Artes* in its context, with focus on the analysis of the terms "honra", "humildade" and "abatimiento". In Section 4 investigates Rodrigues's approach to politeness in relation to the "cultural footprint" (Swiggers 2010), and finally, in the conclusion (Section 5), the most important results of this investigations are summarized.

2.   Hierarchical interpersonal relationships

Before analyzing the description of politeness, it is necessary to understand the hierarchical relationship established among people according to Rodrigues. For him, there are three degrees of hierarchical interpersonal relationship which have to be taken into consideration when others are addressed or referred to, and knowing one's place and status in society was one of the major topics in his teaching program: superiors, inferiors and equals.

Superior is, according to Rodrigues, someone *nobre digna de honra, & veneração* ['noble person who is worthy of honour and veneration'] (AG: 158v), who *excede a outra em alguma dignidade* ['exceeds the other in certain dignity'] (AB: 66). Rodrigues refers to superiors as *pessoas altas* ['high people'] (AG: 78v) or *honradas* ['honoured people'] (AG: 67v). For instance, those are: *anjos* ['angels'], *Santos* (Saints), *Apóstolos* ['apostles'] (AB: 66), *velhos* ['the elder people'], *religiosos* ['religious people'], *rapados honrados* ['Buddhist monks'; lit. 'honourable shaved'] (AG: 68), *Bonzos, & Eclesiásticos* ['Buddhist monks and clergymen'] (AB: 55v), and other expressions. Jesus Christ is also an "honoured person" which deserves to be addressed with respect (Cristo [Chris'']) (AG: 78v; AB: 66).

Inferiors are those referred to as *gente baixa* ['low people'] (AG: 68). Those are, for instance: *filho* ['a son, in relation to his father'] (AB: 63v), *criado* ['a servant, in relation to their lord'] (AB: 63v), *ínfimos* ['insignificant ones'] (AG: 67v), and others.

The difference between superior and inferior directions are remarkable in the following definition of the pronouns *honrado* and *baixo*:

> O Pronome assi derivativo como primitivo, ou he dessi honrado; ou bayxo: honrado he aquelle que soo pertence a pessoas altas, & meaãs bayxo aquelle, que só pertence a infimos, ou de que vsamos por causa de desprezar a outro. (AG: 67v)

> [The Pronoun, both derivative and primitive, can be either honoured or low: honoured is the one that only belongs to high people; and mediocre [and] low is the one that only belongs to irrelevant people, or the one we use to depreciate someone.]

Equals refer to people of similar hierarchical level. For example, the relationship between Jesuit priests and brothers (AG: 78v) as equals or 'insiders' of the same rank.

Rodrigues considers these three types of addressee, but he also indicates different *graos* ['levels'] inside superior and inferior directions. For instance, when Rodrigues defines particles used in plural, he distinguishes levels as *muyto honradas* ['very honoured'], *honradas* ['honoured'], *meãs* ['mediocre'] and *baixas* ['low'], *cousas inanimadas* ['inanimate things'] and *animaes* ['animals']:

> As particulas que servẽ de plural são, *Tachi, Xu, Domo, Ra*. As quais se poem immediatamẽte ao nome, & antepoẽ as particulas articulares; entre estas ha diversidade de graos de honra: porque, *Tachi* serve para segundas & terceiras pessoas muyto honradas, posto que entre gente baixa se usa às vezes; *Xu*, pera honradas & meãs, & baixas. *Domo*, pera primeiras, & segundas & terceiras baixas, ou quando abatemos, & pera cousas inanimadas, & pera animaes. *Ra*, serve pera primeiras, quando se humilhão, & pera desprezar & abater muyto as segundas, & terceiras.   (AG: 1v)

> [The particles used to indicate plural are: *Tachi, Xu, Domo, Ra*. These are placed immediately [after] the nouns and before the articulatory particles; among these particles there are several levels of honour, because *Tachi* is used for very honoured second and third very honoured people, but they are used among low people sometimes; *Xu*, for honoured, mediocre and low people. *Domo*, for first, second and third low people, or when we depreciate, and for inanimate things, and for animals. *Ra* is used for first person, when self-depreciating, and to greatly depreciate and subjugate second and third people.]

We cannot clearly define how many levels of superiority and inferiority Rodrigues defined in his *Artes*. Since there were so many hierarchical levels in the Japanese society of his time, it is probable that he could not easily describe such a complex structure in his own grammar.

3.   Treatment of politeness in Rodrigues's *Artes*

3.1   Subject-controlled and object-controlled honorifics and Rodrigues's approach

Since politeness has many definitions in linguistics, it is important to clearly explain in what sense the term is used in this paper. In *A dictionary of linguistics and phonetics* (Crystal 2008), "politeness phenomena" are defined as "linguistic features mediating norms of social behaviour, in relation to such notions as courtesy, rapport, deference and distance" that "include the use of special discourse markers (*please*), appropriate tones of voice and acceptable forms of address (e.g. the choice of intimate *v.* distant pronouns, or of first *v.* last names)". Based on this definition, in this paper I use the term politeness to refer to the linguistic phenomena that express social behaviour related to the positive image of the subject in an interaction. To refer to the negative image of the subject in an interaction, we use the word "impoliteness", relating to discourtesy, bad rapport, non-deference and proximity. Thus, I adopt here the so-called "Scale of Politeness" proposed by Ide et al. (2005: 281) in which "'polite' refers to plus-valued politeness, 'impolite' means minus-valued politeness, and 'non-polite' marks the neutral or zero-valued center of the scale". As explained by Ide et al. (2005: 293), I also avoid the use of the terms "positive" and "negative politeness" because these have already been employed by Brown and Levinson (1978, 1987) and other scholars for many different purposes.[10]

According to Shibatani (1990: 375),[11] in the Japanese language politeness has two different kinds of honorification: addressee-controlled honorification; and referent-controlled honorification. The former is in the speaker-addressee axis called *teineigo*[12] ['polite language'] in Japanese, and the latter is in the speaker-referent axis, and is divided into *sonkeigo* ['respect language'] and *kenjôgo* ['humility/ humbling language'] in Japanese (Shibatani 1990: 375). Also, the author (Shibatani 1990: 376) classifies referent-controlled honorification in object-controlled honorifics and subject-controlled honorifics.

Regarding these two axes, Shibatani (1990: 376) highlights: "notice that the speaker-addressee axis and the speaker-referent axis are independent axes, though when the subject or the object of a sentence refers to the addressee or the speaker, the two merge. Being independently controlled, the polite and honorific forms can be used independently of each other."

---

10. Brown and Levinson's framework and the notion of "face" has been criticized in the context of Japanese Politeness, as Haugh & Obana (2011: 151) observe: "This equivocality about Brown and Levinson's (1987) notion of face on the part of those using or defending their framework is perhaps not surprising as it is face that has received the most criticism from scholars who favour *emically* motivated accounts of politeness in Japanese over Brown and Levinson's approach".

11. In this paper, I use Shibatani's description of politeness in modern Japanese as a framework to analyse Rodrigues's terminology. For an overview of studies on politeness in Japanese see also Haugh & Obana (2011).

12. In this paper, I use Hepburn Romanization System (Revised Hepburn) to write Japanese language using the Latin alphabet, except in quotations, where we prefer to keep the original Romanization system created by Rodrigues.

This classification is commonly used in Japanese language grammars, and currently accepted. Therefore, in this paper, I will use Shibatani's terminology to describe Rodrigues' approach to politeness and his descriptive metalanguage.

To describe politeness phenomena in the Japanese language, Rodrigues does not use the same terminology as Shibatani. Rodrigues also describes the speaker-addressee axis and the speaker-referent axis, however, he uses the same terms to indicate both axes. For Rodrigues, *honra* is the term used to indicate the form through which one may treat distinctively *quem fala, a quem se fala, diante de quem, e de que cousas* ['who speaks, to whom one speaks, in front of whom, and things spoken about'] (1604–1608: 158). In other words, expressions of honour are useful to confer respect on the speaker, on the addressee, on the audience, or on things related to the addressee or the audience. Under Shibatani's classification (1990), for Rodrigues, *honra* belongs to the speaker-addressee axis (*teineigo*, ['polite language']) and to the speaker-referent axis under the (*sonkeigo*, ['respect language']) category. This is because *honour* is the term used not only to refer to the addressee, but also to the referent (to whom or what is spoken about) in the conversation and include undervaluing the speaker or even self-deprecation.

For Rodrigues, there are two categories in the politeness system he describes: honour and humility. To address such system, he uses several metaterms, such as *partículas de honra* ['honour particles'] (AG: 158), *partículas honorativas* ['honorific particles'] (AG: 158), *partículas humiliativas* ['humbling particles'] (AG: 158), *verbos honrados* ['honour verbs'] (AG: 164v), *verbos humildes* ['humbling verbs'] (AG: 165v), *grao de honra* ['degree of honour'] (AG: 159v), etc. According to Rodrigues, honour and humility also have other denominations, such as *abatimento* ['demotion/subjugation'],[13] *respeito* ['respect'], *cortesia* ['courtesy'], etc. Since there are several terms used here, the descriptions developed by Rodrigues are often difficult to understand, it is necessary to comprehend their 'content' and 'incidence' (Swiggers 2010) grouping them into *honra* (3.1) and *humildade* or *abatimento* (3.2). In the following section, these three terms will be analysed in detail.

---

13. As will be explained later, for Rodrigues, *abatimento* is a synonym of humiliation. In modern Portuguese, *abatimento* is rarely used to refer to humility, but it often indicates depression or weakness. In Rodrigues, however, such metaterm stresses the act of someone 'demoting' or 'subjugating' oneself or someone to a lower position in relation to/about whom one speaks to. In other words, lowering oneself in a social ranking regarding to someone else. Hence, demotion, or subjugation. Therefore, although not strictly the same, 'demotion' or 'subjugation' were the closest English expressions to describe such noun of the 16th century's Portuguese used by Rodrigues.

3.2   Honra

According to *Dicionário Etimológico da língua portuguesa* (Cunha 2010), the etymological origin of the term *honra* ['honour'] is Latin *honōr, -ōris* and its derivations, as the verb (*honōrare*).[14] In Portuguese 'honrar' means 'to confer honour, to respect, to ignify, to give credit to someone'. In the same sense, the *Vocabulario Portuguêz e Latino* (1713) compiled by Father Rafael Bluteau of the Congregation of Clerics Regular of the Divine Providence (CR; 1638–1734) also considers *honra* as a synonym of "respeito & reverencia com que tratamos as pessoas em razão da sua nobreza, dignidade, virtude, ou outra excellencia" ['respect and reverence with which we treat people according to their nobility, dignity, virtue, or another excellence'].[15]

Honrar is extensively used in religious contexts. For example, in the *Ten Commandments*, it is written: "honour thy father and thy mother" (Exodus 20:12).[16] Also Barros (1539: 22v) uses "E a fé católica é ésta: que honremos hum deos em trindade, e a trindáde em unidáde" ['And the catholic faith is this: may we honour one god in trinity, and the trinity in unity'].[17]

As explained in the introduction of this paper, the Japanese language, its morphology and vocabulary related to 'politeness', do not lend themselves to analyses entirely based on Latin. Politeness, an important topic in modern linguistics, was not described systematically in the early modern Humanist grammatical tradition.

The word *honra* is used in in the *Grammatica da lingoagem portuguesa* (1536) by Fernão de Oliveira (1507–*post* 1581), and in the *Grammatica da lingua portuguesa* (1540), by João de Barros.

In Oliveira (1536), the term *honra* is documented, but he does not discuss how politeness is expressed in the Portuguese language:

> Hercoles lybio filho de Osiris rey do egipto veo morrer em esta terra desejãdo de viver sua velhice descãsada em ella por a virtude q̃ dela conhecia e os socessores deste edificarão em memoria e honrra do nome de seu capitão.
>
> (Oliveira 1536: 5)
>
> [Libyan Hercules, son of Osiris, king of Egypt, died in this land wishing to live his old age in it, because he knew the virtues of the land, and his successors will edify in memory and honour of their captain.]

---

14. The word *honrar* had already been registered in 13th century (Cunha 2010).

15. My translation.

16. In Portuguese: *Honrar pai e mãe* (Barros 1539: 12). In Latin: *honora patrem tuum te matrem tuam* (*Vulgate*, Exodus 20:12).

17. My translation.

Also, João de Barros (1540) used *honra* in his grammar to describe nouns that express nobility and honour, without describing politeness as a grammatical or linguistic topic which deserves particular attention:

> Os nóbres buscáram hũ termo que fosse sinal de nobreza, que os apartásse dos plebeos, como açerca de nós, Dõ, que ue deste nome. Dominus, que quer dizer senhor. Os Franceses tomáram Monseor, Os Italianos, Mister, Os aragoeses, Mos sem. E assy outras muitas nações tomáram hũ termo que denotásse honrra.
>
> (Barros 1540: 5v)
>
> [The nobles searched for a term that would be a sign of nobility, separating them from the plebeians. For us (Portuguese people), such expression is *Dõ*, originated from *Dominus*, which means Lord. French people use *Monseor*. Italians, *Mister*. Aragonese, *Mos sem*. Likewise, many other nations chose a word indicating *honrra* (honour).]

When Westerners started to describe the Japanese language, they came to the conclusion that 'politeness' in Japanese is expressed differently, compared with European languages: In his *Tratado em que se contêm muito sucinta e abreviadamente algumas contradições e diferenças de costumes entre a gente de Europa e esta província de Japão* (1585) Luis Fróis (1532–1597)[18] explains how "honra" operates in Japanese, compared with Portuguese:

> Nós pomos a honra nos nomes; o Japão a põe toda no uso dos verbos.
>
> (Fróis 1585: 166)
>
> [We (Portuguese people) put the honour in the noun. Japanese people put all of it in the use of verbs.]

Although politeness can be expressed in nouns, pronouns, intonation and other sort of expressions, according to Fróis, the remarkable difference between Portuguese and Japanese languages was the use of politeness in verbs, and not in nouns. Fróis uses the term *honra* ['honour'] to point out this difference.

However, João Rodrigues uses such a familiar term of his time to explain the Japanese politeness system, using the concept of *honra* ['honour'] as a metalinguistic term in various places and in various derivations (*honrado, honorativo*, etc.) in his *Artes*.

Rodrigues gives great importance to the subject *honra* ['honour'] in Japanese, attributing the origin of the elegance of that language to it:

---

18. The Jesuit missionary Luis Fróis was born in Lisboa, in 1532, arrived in Japan in 1563 and died in Nagasaki, after spending most his life in the Orient. He also composed the *Historia de Japam*, relating the history of the Christian Church in Japan from 1549 to 1593.

Toda elegancia desta lingua consiste em saber vsar de varias honras, & particulas que pera isso tem dando a cada cousa seu lugar. De tres sortes podemos tratar destas honras respeitando sempre, quem fala, aquem se fala, diante de quem, & de que cousas: por que tudo isto he necessario   (AG: 158)

[All the elegance of this language consists in knowing how to use the many honours and particles which have been giving to each thing its place. We can deal with these honours in three ways, always respecting: who speaks, who is spoken to, in front of whom, and about which things: because all those things are necessary.]

Here, Rodrigues innovates by describing politeness in three directions which are very similar to Shibatani's twofold classification: to the addressee (speaker-addressee axis), to the people who are not addressed directly by the speaker but referred to as outsiders (audience), and to the referent-object (speaker-referent axis). Rodrigues considers the audience, although Shibatani's classification does not include it. Thus, an innovative aspect of his description is the inclusion of this third axis, referring to the audience, i. e. people in front of whom one speaks.

According to Rodrigues, *honra* may be expressed through the employment of verbs, nouns and particles:

Esta lingua no vso dos verbos, & nomes; tẽ varios respeitos de honra, cortezia, & humiliaçam, por que todos seus verbos tem vozes particulares para todos os tempos, & modos com certo grao de honra, & abatimento falando de pessoas, & com pessoas altas & baixas. Tem tambem varias particulas, que juntas aos nomes, honram & abatem com grande artificio, & elegancia. No vso destes verbos, & particulas sempre se tem respeito à pessoa, com quem, de quem, diante de quem, & cousas de que se falla; de modo que he necessario aprender a fallar esta lingua com honra, & cortezia, ou sem ella vsando dos verbos, & particulas conforme ao que se requerer.
(AB 1620: 1)

[This language, in the use of verbs and nouns, has many respects of honour, courtesy and humiliation, because all its verbs have particular voices for all tenses and moods with certain degree of honour and demotion talking about and to low and high people. It has also several particles, that are joined to nouns, which honour and lower with great artifice and elegance. In the use of these verbs and particles there is always respect for the person we talk to, the person about whom we talk, the people in front of whom we talk and the thing we talk about; so that it is necessary to learn this language with honour and courtesy, or without it using the verbs and particles according to what is requested.]

While Rodrigues uses the traditional classes of words, he innovates by introducing the class of particles and articles.

The Portuguese Jesuit also innovates by describing the *grao de honra* ['degrees of honour'], according to social hierarchy:

Sonofô. Sonata. Conata. Tu, cortes & corrente, l. *Vos, Vt, Conataua coreuo gozonji naica?* Vos não sabeys isto?;

Quixo. Quiden. Quifen. Quifô. Gofen. Vos, honrado para escritura, ou pratica grave, & acrecentandolhes a particula de honra, *Sama*, servem para mais honrados.

(AG: 68)

[*Sonofô. Sonata. Conata. Tu*, polite and current, 1. *Vos, Vt, Conataua coreuo gonzonju naica?* Do not you know this?;

Quixo. Quiden. Quifen. Quifô. Gofen. Vos, honoured in writing or solemn practices, adding the honour particle, *Sama*, they serve for more honoured people.]

As quais se poem immediatamẽte ao nome, & antepoẽ as particulas articulares; entre estas ha diversidade de graos de honra: porque, *Tachi*, serue pera segundas & terceiras pessoas muyto honradas, posto que entre gente baixa se vsa às vezes;.

(AG: 1v)

[They are placed immediately next to the noun, and before articular particles;[19] among them there are various degrees of honour: because, *Tachi*, serves for second and third people that are very honoured, since it is sometimes used among low people.]

In the previous examples, Rodrigues alludes to the difference in Portuguese between *Tu* and *Vós*, in terms of the difference between less or more honoured people and low people.

The people to whom one speaks (addressee) are referred as *segundas pessoas honradas* ['second honoured people']. The people about whom we speak (referent), as *terceiras pessoas honradas* ['third honoured people']:

Tem esta lingoa alguns verbos que de sua natureza encluem em si certo grao de honra sem particula honorativa, os quais servem somente para segundas, & terceiras pessoas honradas. Outros verbos ha que tem certo grao de cortesia, & humildade dos quais usam inferiores respeito de superiores, estes honram à pessoa com quem, ou diante de quem se fala por elles, & humilham à pessoa sobre quem cayem os tais verbos, ou que delles vsa.   (AG: 164v)

[This language has some verbs that in their nature include in themselves some degree of honour without having an honour particle, these verbs serve only for second and third honoured people. There are other verbs that have a certain degrees of courtesy and humility which are used by inferior [people] to show respect to superior ones, they honour the person to whom or in front of whom one talks about them, and humiliate the person about whom the verbs refer to, or the person that use them.]

---

19. *Particle* is the term used by Rodrigues to indicate the tenth word class that includes many morphological expressions in Japanese as particles, cases, articles, terminations added to verbs, etc. *Particulas articulares* (articular particles) are particles that express cases to nouns, when added after them. As examples of articular particles, Rodrigues indicates *Va, No, Ga, Ye, Vo, Ni* (1604–08: 149), etc. that in Modern Japanese are the particles *Wa, No, Ga, He, Wo* and *Ni*.

> O verbo substantiuo, *Aru, Nai,* ou outro verbo substantiuo posposto à rayz de qual-
> quer verbo, precedēdo a a rayz algūa das particulas de honra, *Vo, vŏ, go,* supre todos
> os tempos, & modos da tal rayz conjugandose soomente o verbo substantiuo. Este
> modo he muy certo & vsado, & seu vso he soomente em segundas & terceyras pes-
> soas por causa da honra que tē. Vt, *Voaguearu, voague atte, voaguearŏ. Voagueare.*
> (AG: 9)
> [The substantive verb, *Aru, Nai,* or another substantive verb placed after any verb's
> root, [when] some of the honour particles *Vo, vŏ, go* precede the root, supplies all
> the tenses and moods of such root conjugating only the substantive verb. This way
> is very correct and used, and its use is only in second and third people due to the
> honour it has. Vt, *voaguearu, voague atte, voaguearŏ. Voagueare.*]

Throughout these fragments, Rodrigues uses the metaterm *honra* ['honour'] several
times, and typifies particles and verbs into *particulas honorativas* ['honorific particles'] or *particulas de honra* ['honour particles']. The Jesuit also uses the metaterm
verbos honrados ['honorific verbs or honoured verbs'] to indicate verbs that express
honour:

> Fallando com pessoas, ou de pessoas de respeito sempre se ha de fallar com verbos
> honrados compostos das particulas, que ha de varios graos de honra, ou por verbos
> de si honrados dado a cada hum o grao, que lhe couber de honra, de que se falla
> na rudimenta, & diffusamente na sintaxi da arte grande.   (AB: 66)
>
> [Talking to people, or about respectful people, one will always talk with honoured
> verbs composed by particles of many degrees of honour, or by verbs of honour
> themselves given to each one the honour degree that suits them, about which we
> talk in the *rudimenta*, and diffusely in the syntax of *Arte Grande*.]

3.3   Humildade or abatimento

According to the *Dicionário etimológico da língua portuguesa* (Cunha 2010), the
word *humildade* ['humility'] has its origins in the Latin term *humilitas, âtis*, meaning and means "modesty, submission, poverty, inferiority".[20] In Bluteau's *Vocabulario Portuguêz e Latino* (1713), *humildade* is defined as "virtue, which inclines
the intellectual creature to contempt of its prerogatives, to have low opinion of
itself, to magnify God".[21] For Bluteau, the Portuguese term *humildade* ['humility']
is related to Christianity, although in Classical Latin this word did not have the
same meaning.

---

20. In the original: *modéstia, submissão, pobreza, inferioridade.*

21. In the original: *virtude, que inclina a criatura intellectual ao desprezo das suas prerogativas,
& a ter baixa opiniaō de si, para engrandecer a Deos* (my translation).

Humildade has a similar origin as the word *humilhação* ['humiliation']. As stated by *Dicionário Houaiss da língua portuguesa* (2009), there were the Latin verbs *humilîto, as, âvi, âtum, âre* and *humilîo, as, âvi, âtum, âre*, had both the same meaning: *abaixar* ['lower'], *abater* ['depreciate, subjugate'], *humilhar* ['humiliate, depreciate']. In 13th century Portuguese, (Cunha 2010), the former originated the verb *humildar* ['make someone humble or subjugate'], the noun *humildade* ['humility'], and the adjective *humilde* ['humble']. The latter originated the verb *humilhar* ['to humiliate'], the noun *humilhação* ['humiliation'], and the adjective *humilhado* ['humiliated']. Therefore, as can be noticed, *humilhação* ['humiliation'] and *humildade* '[humble'] have the same Latin origin, but have considerably different derivations and meanings in Portuguese.

Humility is also used in a religious context. For instance, Barros (1539: 13) uses the term *Humildade* to refer to the 10th of the *12 Fruits of the Holy Spirit*: *Humildade nas obras* ['modesty'] (Galatians 5:23).[22] In addition, Barros uses the term *humildade* ['humility'] to indicate the *Seven Virtues* against the *Seven Deadly Sins*: *humildade* ['humility'], *largueza* ['gratitude'], *castidade* [chastity"], *paciência* ['patience'], *temperança* ['temperance'], *caridade* ['charity'] and *diligência* ['diligence'].

Synonym of *humiliation*, the term *abatimento* and its derivations have origins, according to *Dicionário etimológico da língua portuguesa* (Cunha 2010), in the Latin term *abbat(u)ēre* or *abbattere*, which means 'derrubar, prostar, fazer cair por terra' ['to overthrow, to fall, to fall to the ground'], among other meanings. In Portuguese, such word originated the verbs *abater* ['defeat or subjugate'] and *bater* ['hit or beat'], and to the noun *abatimento* ['subjugation, demotion, depression or weakness']), according to the *Dicionário Houaiss da língua portuguesa* (2009).

In João de Barros (1540: 8), the term *abatimento* is used to mean "despise someone or something":

> Destes nomes, Gregos, e Latinos nã tratã em suas Grammáticas por ôs nam terem, e casy todos se terminã em, am, e az, como, molheram, caualã, velha caz, ladrabaz e outros que sempre sam ditos ē desprezo e abatimento da pesoa ou cousa a que os atribuímos.
> (Barros 1540: 8)

> [Greeks and Latins do not refer to those words in their grammars since they did not have them. Almost all ended in 'am' and 'az', such as *molheram, caualã, velha caz, ladrabaz* etc., almost all used to [express] despise or to demote/lower the person to whom we address such terms.]

In this sense, in the Jesuit *Vocabvlario* (1603–1604), the term *abater* is commonly used as equivalent to *humilhar* ['humiliate/ depreciate'], *abaixar* ['to lower'] and *desprezar* ['to despise/subjugate/depreciate']:

22. In Latin: *modestia* (Vulgate, Galatians 5:23).

Sague, uru, eta. Abaixar. q. Atama uo saguru. Abaixar a cabeça humilhandose & sujeitandose, ou por outro respeito. *Fitouo saguru*. Humilhar, abaixar, ou abater a alguem.   (Anonymous 1603–1604: 215v)

[*Sague, uru, eta*. Lower. q. Lower the head. Lower the head humiliating oneself & subjugating oneself, or for another respect. *Fitouo saguru*. Humiliate, lower, or demote/subjugate someone.]

Sague iyaxime, uru, eta. Desprezar, ou abater a outro.
                                        (Anonymous 1603–1604: 215v)

[*Sague iyaxime, uru, eta*. Despise, or demote/subjugate the other]

Merŏ. Molher, falando com desprezo, & abatimento.
                                        (Anonymous 1603–1604, *Suplemento*: 362v)

[*Merŏ*. Woman, speaking with scorn and subjugation.]

In the *Vocabvlario* (1603–1604), *abatimento* also means *humildade* ['humility']:

Gufô Vorocana fô. i. Minha ley, ou seita: falando humildemente, & como com certo abatimento.   (Anonymous 1603–1604, *Suplemento*: 354v)

[*Gufô Vorocana fô*. i. My law, or sect: speaking humbly, and with certain humility.]

In this sense, it is possible to notice that, in Rodrigues's times, *abater* used to mean *humilhar* ['humiliate'], *diminuir* ['lower'], *abaixar* ['lower'], *desprezar* ['despise']. *Abatimento* also indicated *humildade* ['humility']. With this in mind, I will observe the 'incidence' of the terms *humildade, humiliação, abatimento* and derived terms in Rodrigues's *Artes*.

When Rodrigues presents the *graos de verbos* ['degrees of verbs'], he clarifies that the use of particles *que humilham o supposto do verbo* ['which humiliate the subject of the verb'] does not modify the simple form (original form) of the verb to which it is connected to. In the following example, these particles confer respect to the addressee (speaker-addressee axis) or the referent to whom one speaks to (speaker-referent axis), i.e. upward respect through the humiliation of the subject of the verb (self-deprecation):

O verbo cõposto cõ as particulas, que humilham o supposto do verbo, & mostram respeyto a pessoa cõ q̃, ou diante de quem se fala, tambem não muda a significação do seu simplex: as particulas são, *Mairaxi, Moxi, Tatematçuri, Xexime, Soro, Nari, Famberi, Samburai*.   (AG: 69v)

[The verb composed with particles that humiliate the subject of the verb and show respect to the person whom we speak to, or in front of whom we speak, do not change the meaning of its simple form (of the verb): those particles are, *Mairaxi, Moxi, Tatematçuri, Xexime, Soro, Nari, Famberi, Samburai*]

When Rodrigues denominates these particles as *que humilham o supposto do verbo* ['which humiliate the subject of the verb'], he indicates the distinction between object-controlled honorifics and subject-controlled honorifics, as Shibatani's (1990: 376) classification indicates.

Regarding the particles, Rodrigues also elucidates that they have the function of *humilhar* ['humiliating'] the subject of the verb, expressing courtesy and reverence:

> *Sorō. Saburai, rō. Famberi, ru. Xexime, ruru.* Acompanham o verbo, & mostram cortesia.
> *Mairaxe, suru. Mōxi, su. Tatematçuru, ru.* Humilham mostrando reuerencia.
> (AG: 77)

> [*Sorō. Saburai, rō. Famberi, ru. Xexime, ruru.* Accompany the verb and show courtesy. *Mairaxe, suru. Mōxi, su. Tatematçuru, ru.* Humiliate showing reverence.]

> Outros verbos ha que tem certo grao de cortesia, & humildade dos quais vsam inferiores respeito de superiores, estes honram à pessoa com quem, ou diante de quem se fala por elles, & humilham à pessoa sobre quem cayem os tais verbos, ou que delles vsa. (AG: 164v)

> [There are other verbs that have certain degree of courtesy and humility which inferior [people] respect the superior ones, they honour the person to whom, or in front of whom one talks about, and humiliate the person to whom the verbs refer, or the person that uses them.]

Likewise, the use of the metaterm *humildade* ['humility'] is also related to an expression of reverence:

> As que se ajuntão a os verbos por causa de humildade, & reverenciasão, *Mairaxe, suru. Tatematçuri, ru. Mōxi, mōsu.* (AG: 10)

> [Those which are joined to verbs because of humility and reverence, *Mairaxe, suru. Taremaatçuri, ru. Mōxi, mōsu.*]

As observed above, *humildade* ['humility'], *abatimento* ['demotion/ subjugation'], *humilhação* ['humiliation'] are not only used to express the modesty in the speaker-addressee axis, but are also used in the speaker-referent axis.

Besides the humbling language, Rodrigues uses these metaterms meaning *humilhar* ['humiliate'] and *desprezar* ['despise'], expressing impoliteness to the addressee of the conversation or to the referent. Such use had already been cited in João de Barros (1540), as mentioned above.

Rodrigues uses, for example, the metaterms *humilhar* ['humiliate'] and *abater* ['lower, subjugate, defeat'] when referring to *partículas que servem de plural* ['particles which function as plural'] as mentioned above.

To summarize, from the observation of the 'incidence of the terms' (Swiggers 2010), it is possible to notice that the metaterms *abatimento* and *humilhar* were also used to express impoliteness by lowering the addressee or the referent (object or subject). Hence, those expressions were not only used in the sense of the humbling language (*kenjôgo*).

4.   Cultural footprint of the terms

According to Swiggers (2010), "linguistic terminologies carry a certain number of cultural values and presuppositions", such as the relationship of linguistics with a certain religion and/or ideology, hierarchical structures of a society, roles established under the law, social and professional role-sharing between men and women, etc.

Rodrigues's terminology carries a 'cultural footprint' related to Christianity. As we mentioned above, *honour* and *humility* were commonly used to nominate Christian values, as the *Ten Commandments* and the *Seven Virtues* against the *Seven Deadly Sins* in Portuguese in Rodrigues' time. Not only in Barros' *Cartinha para aprender a ler* (1539), but also in other works and in the Bible (Vulgate) it is possible to note that these two terms had a religious use. Also, as mentioned, in Bluteau's *Vocabulario Portuguêz e Latino* (1713), *humildade* is defined as 'virtue, which inclines the intellectual creature to contempt of its prerogatives, to have low opinion of itself, to magnify God'. Thus, in Rodrigues's *Artes*, he uses *honour* and *humility* as metaterms that carry implicitly religious values as well.

Likewise, Rodrigues uses the metaterm *honra*, which consists of conferring someone a positive quality distinctive from the others, as well as stresses different degrees of honour, describing a complex social hierarchy. *Honra, humildade, abatimento* and other terms used by Rodrigues to make the values of a hierarchical society divided into clearly distinct social groups visible. The king (emperor) is above everyone. Below, the *Shogun* (*Taikun*) and the nobles. At the bottom of the pyramid are servants, women, children, sons and daughters. In the case of the religious group, the use of politeness has been amply brought to light. Rodrigues points out that honour may not be excessively used between religious people of the same hierarchical level (insiders) in front of people considered 'outsiders' of the community. This is because it would be a mistake to over-honour a superior before a person that does not belong to the same community and should be treated respectfully.

In summary, the use of politeness reveals the complexity present in the Japanese society at that time. Besides the vertical hierarchy (superior, inferior, equal) of such society, Rodrigues also describes horizontal relationships (outsiders –,insiders)

among members of different social groups. In this sense, from the "cultural footprint of the terms", it is possible to observe that there was a great complexity in
the Japanese society. Such facts highlight the importance of the politeness system
treated in this paper.

5.   Concluding remarks

Rodrigues's politeness system includes the two different kinds of honorification indicated by Shibatani (1990: 375): addressee-controlled honorification and
referent-controlled honorification. Similarly, the Portuguese Jesuit points to the
distinction between the speaker-addressee and speaker-referent axes, indicating the
difference between *sonkeigo* ['respect language'] and *kenjôgo* ['humbling language']
inside the speaker-addressee axis, using the terms related to *honra* and *humildade*
(or *abatimento*). In addition, Rodrigues innovates by considering not only the politeness given to speaker and referent, but also to the audience (people in front of
whom one speaks). Also, the author uses the same terminology to denominate the
object and subject referents, indicating the distinction between object-controlled
honorifics and subject-controlled honorifics (Shibatani 1990: 376), and considers
the vertical relation, as he distinguishes types of politeness between 'insiders' and
'outsiders'.

In Rodrigues, the synonyms of *honour*, such as *respeito* ['respect'], *cortesia*
['courtesy'], *reverência* ['reverence'], etc., and the synonyms of humility, such as
abatimento ['demotion/subjugation'], *modéstia* ['modesty'], are used without a clear
distinction. The only metaterms that are clearly differentiated from each other are
honra and *humildade,* and their derivative adjectives, since the author separates
different sections for *partículas de honra* ['particles of honour'] (AG: 158), *partículas
humiliativas* ['humbling particles'] (AG: 158), *verbos honrados* ['honoured verbs']
(AG: 164v), *verbos humildes* ['humbling verbs'] (AG: 165v), as well as systematically
establishing *grao de honra* ['degree of honour'] (AG: 159v).

In relation to the use of *humildade* or *abatimento*, differently from what current grammarians denominate *kenjôgo* ['humility/humbling language'] not only
does Rodrigues describe their use as honorific expressions, but also as expressions
of impoliteness, because they are used to humiliate or express despise toward the
addressee or referent.

Through the analysis of the 'cultural footprint of the terms' (Swiggers 2010), it
is possible to notice the religious values related to Christianity and the relationship
between linguistics and society. Also, one can observe how linguistic terminology
carries a series of cultural values and presuppositions, reflecting the fact that the

politeness system is an instrument of social differentiation. As Rodrigues highlights, ⸳ without mastering such system, it is not possible to conduct missionary activity in the complex Japanese society of that time.

Acknowledgements

I would like to thank my supervisor Prof. Dr. Olga Ferreira Coelho Sansone and Prof. Dr. Cristina Altman from CEDOCH-USP for their orientation and support in my research.

References

A.   Primary sources

Álvares, Manuel. 1572. *De Institvtione grammatica libri tres*. Olyssipone [Lisbon]: Ioannes Barrerius, Typographus Regius.

Álvares, Manuel. 1594. *De Institvtione grammatica libri tres. Coniugationibus accessit interpretatio Iapponica*. Amakusa: In Collegio Amacvsensi Societatis IESV cvm facvltate svperiorum.

Anonymous. 1973 [1603–1604]. *Vocabvlario da Lingoa de Iapam com declaração em Portugues, feito por algvns padres, e irmãos da Companhia de Iesv*. Nangasaki: Collegio de Iapam da Companhia de IESVS. Facsimile of the Bodleian Library of Oxford University's version ed. by Kamei Takashi. Tokyo: Benseisha.

Barros, João de. 2008 [1539]. *Cartinha com preceitos e mandamentos da Santa Madre Igreja*. Lisboa: Luís Rodrigues. Edição crítica, leitura modernizada e reprodução fac-similar Gabriel Antunes de Araujo (org.). São Paulo: Humanitas/Paulistana.

Barros, João de. 1540. *Grammatica da lingua portuguesa*. Olyssippone [Lisbon]: apud Lodovicum Rotorigiu[m] Typographum.

Bluteau, Raphael. 1713. *Vocabulario Portuguez e Latino. Autorizado com exemplos dos melhores escritores portuguezes, e latinos, e offerecido a el-rey de Portugal, D. João V. pelo padre –*. Coimbra: Real Collegio das Artes da Companhia de Jesu.

Fróis, Luís. 1993 [1585]. *Tratado em que se contêm muito sucinta e abreviadamente algumas contradições e diferenças de costumes entre a gente de Europa e esta província de Japão (…)*. Apresentação de José Manuel Garcia. Fixação de Texto e Notas por Raffaella D'Intino. Lisboa: Comissão Nacional para as Comemorações dos Descobrimentos Portugueses.

Oliveira, Fernão de [Fernando Oliveyra]. 1536. *Grammatica da lingoagem portuguesa*. Lixboa [Lisbon]: casa d'Germão Galharde.

Rodrigues, João. 1604–1608. *Arte da lingoa de Iapam composta pello Padre Padre Ioão Rodriguez Portugues da Cõpanhia de Iesv diuidida em tres Livros*. Nangasaqui: Collegio de Iapão da Companhia de IESV.

Rodrigues, João. 1620. *Arte breve da lingoa Iapoa tirada da Arte Grande da mesma lingoa, pera os que comecam a aprender os primeiros principios della*. Amacao: Collegio da Madre de Deos da Companhia de Iesv.

Vulgate. n.d. The Holy Bible In Latin Language with Douay-Rheims English Translation. http://www.vulgate.org/

B.   Secondary sources

Altman, Maria Cristina. 2011. "A descrição das línguas 'exóticas' e a tarefa de escrever a história da linguística". *Revista ABRALIN* 10:3.209–230.

Crystal, David. 2008. *A dictionary of linguistics and phonetics.* 6ª ed. Blackwell Publishing Ltd. https://doi.org/10.1002/9781444302776

Cunha, Antônio Geraldo da. 2010 [1982]. *Dicionário etimológico da língua portuguesa.* 4ª ed. Rio de Janeiro: Lexikon.

Doi, Tadao. 1971. *Kirishitan Gogaku no Kenkyu.* Tokyo: Sanseidô.

Fernandes, Gonçalo & Carlos Assunção. 2018. "First gramatical encoding of Japanese Politeness (17th century)". *Boletim do Museu Paraense Emílio Goeldi. Ciências Humanas* 13:1.187–203. https://doi.org/10.1590/1981.8122018000100011

Haugh, Michael & Yasuko Obana. 2011. "Politeness in Japan". *Politeness in East Asia: Practice* ed. by Dániel Z. Kádár & Sara Mills, 147–175. Cambridge: Cambridge University Press. https://doi.org/10.1017/CBO9780511977886.009

Houaiss, Antônio & Mauro de Salles Villar. 2009. *Dicionário Houaiss da língua portuguesa.* Rio de Janeiro: Instituto Antônio Houaiss de Lexicografia e Banco de Dados da Língua Portuguesa S/C Ltda/ Objetiva.

Ide, Sachiko, Beverley Hill, Yukiko M. Carnes, Tsunao Ogino, Tsunao & Akiko Kawasaki. 2005. "The concept of politeness: An empirical study of American English and Japanese". *Politeness in Language: studies in its history, theory, and practice* ed. by Richard Watts, Sachiko Ide & Konrad Ehlich. (Second edition). The Hague: Mouton de Gruyter.

Koerner, Konrad. 2014. "O problema da metalinguagem na Historiografia da Linguística". *Quatro décadas de historiografia da Linguística: estudos relacionados,* 75–90. Vila Real: Universidade de Trás-os-Montes e Alto Douro, Centro de Estudos em Letras. Originally published in 1993: "The Problem of 'Metalanguage' in Linguistic Historiography" *Studies in Language* 17:1.111–134. (Revised version in Koerner, *Professing Linguistic Historiography,* 27–46. Amsterdam & Philadelphia: John Benjamins, 1995.)

Maruyama, Toru. 2009. "Prólogo". *Melchor Oyanguren de Santa Inés, Arte de la lengua japona (1738).* Transcripción y edición preparada por Otto Zwartjes. 7–19. Frankfurt am Main: Vervuert; Madrid: Iberoamericana. https://doi.org/10.31819/9783964563026-001

Shibatani, Masayoshi. 1990. *The languages of Japan.* Cambridge: Cambridge University Press.

Suzuki, Tae. 1987. "Padre Ioão Rodriguez: suas Artes e a linguagem de tratamento da língua japonesa". *Revista Estudos Japoneses* 7.113–127. https://doi.org/10.11606/issn.2447-7125.v7i0p113-127

Swiggers, Pierre. 2004. "Modelos, Métodos y Problemas en la historiografía de la linguística. Nuevas Aportaciones a la historiografía linguística". *Actas del IV Congreso Internacional de la SEHL. La Laguna (Tenerife), 22–25 de October 2003* ed. by Cristóbal José Corrales Zumbado, Josefa Dorta Luiz, Antonia Nelsi Torres González, Dolores Corbella Díaz & Francisca del Mar Plaza Picón, Vol. 1. 113–146. Madrid: Arco/Libros.

Swiggers, Pierre. 2010. "Le métalangage de la linguistique: reflexions à propos de la terminologie e de la terminographie linguistiques". *Revista do GEL (Grupo de Estudos Linguísticos do Estado de São Paulo)* 7(2).9–29.

Zwartjes, Otto. 2011. *Portuguese missionary grammars in Asia, Africa and Brazil, 1550–1800.* Amsterdam & Philadelphia: John Benjamins. https://doi.org/10.1075/sihols.117

Romanization in early Japanese Christian texts
A comparison of manuscripts and prints of Jesuit and Spanish missionary texts

Atsuko Kawaguchi
Mie University

1.   Introduction

In the history of the Japanese language, Late Middle Japanese (from the 15th to the 17th century) was the era of transition from classical to modern Japanese. However, it is hard to reconstruct the historical pronunciation through Japanese characters: *Kana* and *Kanji*. It was in that era that the Europeans first arrived in Japan, using phonograms which were different from Japanese *Kana*, namely the Roman alphabet. The European missionaries, especially the Jesuits, studied the Japanese language through their missionary works and used romanized Japanese. Nowadays romanized Japanese is called *Rōmaji* 'Roman alphabet' in Japanese. The earliest romanization system of Japanese was developed by Jesuit missionaries. The early Japanese Christians from late 16th to the 17th century are called *Kirishitan*, so that the texts made by the missionaries in Japan in this era are called *Kirishitan* texts. Some of the *Kirishitan* texts include Japanese words written in *Rōmaji*, not Japanese characters, and provide a lot of information about Late Middle Japanese. After Francisco Xavier (1506–1552) came to Japan in 1549, the Jesuits started their missionary work in Japan. From around 1591, the Jesuits opened a printing press in Japan and published more than 30 books for Japanese Christians, the earliest of printing of European style in Japan. The *Rōmaji* of Jesuit prints was based on Portuguese orthography, which became canonical in the Far East.

Later, the Franciscans came to Japan in 1593 and the Augustinians and the Dominicans in 1602. The Dominicans published some books in Japanese and printed these in Manila, such as Juan Rueda de los Ángeles's (*fl.* 1622) translation

https://doi.org/10.1075/sihols.130.06kaw

into Japanese of the rosary *Rozario kiroku*[1] (Binondoc, Manila, anonymous 1622), the *Rozario no kyō*[2] (Binondoc, Manila, anonymous 1623) and a Spanish edition by Jacinto Esquivel del Rosario (1595–1633) of the Japanese-Portuguese dictionary (Anonymous 1630). These works are usually referred to as "The Manila Press".

In 1632, three books were published by the Propaganda Fide Press in Rome, composed by the Spanish Dominican Diego Collado (c. 1589–1641), a grammar of Japanese written in Latin *Ars Grammaticae Iaponicae Linguae*, a trilingual Latin-Spanish-Japanese dictionary entitled *Dictionarium sive Thesauri Linguae Iaponicae Compendium*, and a confession book *Niffon no cotobani yô confesion*. The *Rōmaji* system used in these Dominican printings is generally similar to that in earlier Jesuit works, so it is obvious that the Dominicans were familiar with the Jesuit prints. Even in the texts written in Spanish, the Dominicans adopted the Portuguese spelling conventions for romanized Japanese. Since the production of Jesuit printed works on Japanese outnumber those of the Spanish Dominicans, studies have been primarily focused on the former. This paper concentrates on the latter.[3] There are some studies on the Dominicans' linguistic production, the so-called Manila Press, and Collado's three books published by the Propaganda Fide Press and his manuscript, housed in the Vatican (Collado 1632 a; b; c and BAV Borg. Cin. 501).

Comparing the Jesuit printed works and other manuscripts, some discrepancies or "irregularities" are documented in the Spanish corpus, which deserve attention in this paper. These "irregular" romanizations can be explained as being a personal habit of the author, or even as "errors", but, as will be demonstrated below, often belong to a certain Spanish orthographical tradition, – shared by more authors –, to be taken into consideration. Also I would like to show the influence of the Spanish manuscripts on other Spanish (non-Jesuit) texts.

---

1.   According to the catalogue of the digital archives of Sophia University including the "Manila Press", the work *Virgen S. Mariano tattoqi rosario no xuguioto,* disappeared from the Franciscan convent: "In 1939 the original had certainly disappeared [from the Franciscan convent] or hopelessly misplaced. Even if it had not been lost before the war, it was certainly destroyed with the convent and the entire library during the fighting in and around Manila. There is, however, a copy of the present volume in the archives of the Dominican Convent in Manila, which happily escaped the ravages of the war". https://digital-archives.sophia.ac.jp/laures-kirishitan-bunko/view/kirishitan_bunko/JL-1622-KB52-51-40

2.   The work *Virgen S. Mariano tattoqi Rosariono jardin tote fanazononi tatoyuru qio* is according to the catalogue of the digital archives of the Sophia University, "an enlarged new edition of Rueda's book on the rosary, or rather, an altogether new work on the same subject", (idem, Kirishitan bunko/ JL-1623-KB53-52-41).

3.   Although there are some studies that focused on Spanish sources, such as Doi (1982) and Kawaguchi (2016).

2. Romanized Japanese: Printed works and manuscripts compared

The modern *Rōmaji* is based on the traditional Japanese syllabary table and the Modern English system. There are three major Roman letter transcription systems used in modern Japan: the *hebon-shiki* 'Hepburn-style' system (1885) which is based largely on English spelling conventions, the *nihon-shiki* 'Japan-style' system (1881) which is modeled on *Kana*, and the *kunrei-shiki* 'official-directive-style' system (1937) which is slightly modified form of *nihon-shiki*. Today, both *hebon-shiki* and *nihon-shiki* would be permitted (Irwin & Zisk 2019: 115). On the other hand, the *Rōmaji* in Jesuit printings is based on the Portuguese of the late 16th century. For example, the *Rōmaji* for /se/, /tu/, /ha/ is realized orthographically as <xe>, <tçu>, <fa> in the Jesuit printings, but as <se>, <tu> (or <tsu>), <ha> in modern *Rōmaji*. The *Rōmaji* in Jesuit printings shows us the difference in pronunciation between Late Middle Japanese and Modern Japanese.

However, it should be noted that the *Rōmaji* in Jesuit manuscripts differs from *Rōmaji* in Jesuit prints in certain ways. We can see some examples in handwritten letters, annual reports, and the Barreto Manuscript (BAV Reg. Lat. 459). The Barreto Manuscript is a Japanese miscellany written in 1591 by the Portuguese Jesuit Father Manoel Barreto (1564–1620), who worked in Japan from 1590. For example: <ça> or <ssa> for /sa/, *baptizmouo çazzucari* ['be baptized'] (Damião 1564: 177v), *Cazzuça* ['*Kazusa* town'] (Ferreira 1628: 76–24), *tacassa* ['height'] (Barreto 1591: 459, 1r); <ccu> or <ççu> for /tu/, *futaccu* ['two'] (Barreto 1591: 1v *et passim*); <jji> for /dzi/, *nanjji* ['you'] (Barreto 1591: 8r, *et passim*). The existence of such variation in the *Rōmaji* in the manuscripts shows that the *Rōmaji* style in the Jesuit works are meant to be obvious for reading.

As for the Spanish (non-Jesuit) texts, the *Rōmaji* notation in the printed works of the Manila Press and Collado's books are generally similar to those of Jesuit prints. For example:

(1) *DAISAN. Rosarioua futatçuno Oracioni quiuamaruto yŭcoto.* ['Number three'. Rosary is summarized as two prayers.] (*Rozario no kyō*,[4] p. 8)

(2) *Itçu, vel itçŭgòro confession vo mòxi àtta ca?* ['When, or about when did you make confession?'] (Collado 1632a: 4)

On the other hand, there are some irregularities in the notations found in the Spanish manuscripts. In the copies of *Relacion del Reino de Nippon* by Bernardino de Ávila Girón,[5] there are some irregular spellings, such as <ça> and <za> as /sa/,

---

4. AFIO 1014-3.

5. Born in Mérida, but the date of his birth is unknown. He travelled to Manila in 1590. After having killed his wife and her lover, he escaped to Japan in 1594. Not much is known about his life (see Hsu 2007: 228).

<tzu> as /tu/, <ba> and <gua> as /wa/ (Doi 1982). In Jesuit printed works, these are written as <sa> as /sa/, <tçu> as /tu/, <ua> or <va> as /wa/. Doi (1982) considered the difference between this text and Jesuit prints as explaining that these irregular notations depended on Ávila Girón's personal orthography habits. Contrariwise, Kawaguchi (2016) claims that these irregular spellings also exist in texts written by other Spanish authors, such as the report about the persecutions of the Christians in Edo (Tokyo) and Arima between 1612 and 1614 by Franciscan Father Diego de Chinchón[6] (?-1617) (Chinchón 1614: 23-1). For example: *Zamuray* ['Samurai'] (Chinchón 1614: 23-1, 12r, *et passim*); *futzuca* ['second day'] (Chinchón 1614: 18r); "en vna ciudad que se llama Guaca Yama" ['in a city which is called *Wakayama*'] (Chinchón 1614: 10r). These spellings, labelled as "personal habit" by Doi (1982: 276–277) are both used in Bernardino de Ávila Girón's and Diego de Chinchón's texts. It is evident that such discrepancies are not unique cases. In the following section, some more specific cases will be discussed.

3.   The influence of the romanization in Spanish manuscripts

In this section, I will show that Spanish missionary texts reveal some hitherto un-explained discrepancies in the romanization of Japanese generally which deserve more attention. Firstly, I shall summarize the findings of Kawaguchi (2018) with additional insights from Morita (1993) and then focus on the comparison between printed works and manuscripts.

The pronunciation of consonant coda <-t> of Sino-Japanese words in *Kirishitan* prints has been already pointed out in former studies, and it has been considered that the spelling <-t> shows the real pronunciation in Late Middle Japanese (Imaizumi 1951: 22–23, Cooper 1976: 428).

As will be demonstrated below,[7] – which has been pointed out in Kawaguchi (2018) –, the irregular notations in Collado's texts (e.g., <-tç> as consonant coda for closed syllable '-t' and <zu> as /tu/) are not errors, but the result of the influence of the romanization found in the Spanish manuscripts.

---

6.   Probably born in Chinchón (Madrid), but the date of his birth is unknown. In 1610, he left Spain to Philippines and stayed in Mexico until early 1611. He worked as missionary in Japan from 1612 to 1614. After leaving Japan, he stayed in Manila and was elected as Provincial min-ister of the Province of San Gergorio. He died in Manila (see for a transcription of the *Relación* Sánchez Fuertes 2015: 499–541).

7.   The Sections 3.1. to 3.3 are partial summaries of Kawaguchi (2018), published in Japanese.

3.1 The consonant coda for closed syllable '-t' of Collado's texts

The consonant coda for closed syllable '-t', which is called *Nisshō-on* in pre-modern Japanese, was the special pronunciation for the Chinese characters, and in some words it has changed to the open syllable /tu/ ([tsu]) in Modern Japanese. It is hard to identify the pre-modern pronunciation of the closed syllable '-t' relying on Japanese characters, because Japanese *Kana* or *Kanji* characters cannot strictly express a consonant,[8] so that the notation of *Rōmaji* is crucial for understanding how the closed syllable was in fact pronounced in Japanese. Morita (1993: 196–204) mentions that the notations in the Japanese-Portuguese dictionary *Vocabulario da Lingoa de Iapam* (anonymous 1603–1604) show that the closed syllable '-t' was already beginning to change to the open syllable. In the Jesuit texts and Spanish prints, the notation for closed syllable '-t' is <-t>. If we use the Jesuit texts and the printed work of Domincans, it seems that the pronunciation of the closed syllable '-t' would be [t], but if we consider the notation <-tz> as spelling for the closed syllable '-t' in the Spanish manuscripts, the reasoning and the result would be different.

The *Rōmaji* notation of Collado's texts basically follows that of Jesuits' printed works, so the notation of closed syllable '-t' is spelled as <-t> in general. However, there are examples of the irregular digraph <-tç> as the closed syllable '-t' in Collado's manuscript Spanish-Japanese dictionary *Vocabulario de la lengua Japona* (BAV Borg. Cin. 501).

> (3) *xòcubùtç* 'comida' ['food']   (Collado s.a.: 15r16)[9]
>
> (4) *cùguàtç* '9.o mes' ['ninth month' ('September')].   (76v23)

If the spelling conventions of the Jesuits works would have been followed, Example (3) should be spelled as <xocubut> and Example (4) as <cuguat>. In fact, there are also two examples spelled as <xòcùbùt> in the *Vocabulario de la lengua Japona* (Collados.a.: 15r22, 28v29). And also in Collado's printed dictionary *Dictionarium sive Thesauri Linguae Iaponicae Compendium*, the closed syllable '-t' is spelled as <-t>. It occurs in seven different lemmas in Latin with the meaning of 'food' translated in Japanese as *xocubut*:

---

8. The Japanese *Kana* syllable has the pattern consonant-vowel (CV), where a consonant nearly always must be followed by a vowel.

9. The second number after the folio number refers to the line. This information is needed because the lemma is not in Alphabetical order.

Table 1. *Final -t in Collado's dictionary* (Collado 1632b)

Lemma in Latin	Spanish	Japanese
cibus (20) ['food']	comida	*xòcubùt*
cibalis, vel cibarius (184) ['pertaining to food']	cosa de comer	*xòcubùt*
daps (200) ['meal']	vianda	*xòcubut*
esca (221) ['food']	comida	*xǒcubùt*
ferculum (230) ['food']	vianda	*xǒcubùt*
pabulum (296) ['food']	pasto	*xòcubùt*
victus (349) ['sustenance, nourishment']	sustento	*xǒcubut*

As for <guat>[10] in *cuguat* is generally spelled in the closed syllable style as <guat> <guet> or in the open syllable style <guachi> in *Vocabulario de la lengua Japona*, such as *Xoguat* 'primero mes a que hazen gran fiesta' ['the first month when they have a big party' ('January')] (Collados.a.: 73v07), *jitget ni voyobigatai* 'inexplicable', ['hard to reach to the sun and moon'] (Collados.a.: 25r37), and *goguachi* 'el 5 mes' ['the fifth month' ('May')] (Collados.a.: 76v19). The two examples *Xòcubùtç* (3) and *cùguàtç* (4) written with the final digraph <-tç> for the closed syllable '-t' are the irregular notations even in the *Vocabulario de la lengua Japona*.

The irregular notation <-tç> as the closed syllable '-t' is not explained as a simple misspelling of the open syllable <tçu>. If it is a simple error, <-tç> should be explained as an omission of <u> from <tçu>, so that the expected spelling of <-guatç>, meaning 'month' or 'moon', would be <-guatçu>. However, I cannot find the example of <-guatçu> in other *Kirishitan* texts.

In Jesuit texts, the common spellings are <-guat> and <-guachi>. For example: <-guat> and <-guachi> in the *Vocabulario da Lingoa de Iapam* (*Gogutat*. l. *goguachi*. 'a quinta lũa do anno de Iapão' ['the fifth month in Japan' ('May')] 354r, etc.), <-guachi>; in the Barreto Manuscript *fachiguachi* ['the eighth month' ('August')] (Barreto 1591: 226r13, 292v14), *goguachi* ['the fifth month' ('May')] (Barreto 1591: 325r17, 363v17), and <-guat> in Jesuits manuscripts: *conguatno* ['of this month'] (Gonçal et al. 1621?; ARSI Jap. Sin. 34, 178r26), *Cuguat* ['the ninth month' ('September')] (Anonymous 1604; ARSI Jap. Sin. 33, 76r,12), *guoguat* ['the fifth month' ('May')] (Damião 1564; ARSI Jap. Sin 5, 177a.v02), *Rocuguat* ('the sixth month ('June')] (Casai & Matçumoto 1617; ARSI Jap. Sin. 17, 317r20, etc.). Also, in Collado's printed dictionary, there are examples of <-guat> *Nanban no cuguàt* 'Septiembre mes' ['September'] ['the ninth month in *Nanban*'[11] ('September')] (Collado 1632b: 328).

---

10. Japanese pronunciation of *Kanji* which means 'month' or 'moon'.

11. *Nanban* means 'the Southern countries'. In the Edo period, *Nanban* included Europe because the Europeans came to Japan via Southern Asian countries.

On the other hand, in the manuscripts of Spanish non-Jesuit texts, the closed syllable '-t' is generally spelled as <-tz>, not as <-t>. For example: *xichinguatz* ['the seventh month' ('July')] (Chinchón 1614: 23–1, 25v25; 26–3, 94v26, BNE Mss. 19628, 173r154, etc.).

Besides, in the manuscript text by Father Diego de Chinchón (AFIO 23–1), there are also some irregular notations of the closed syllable '-t', such as <tzu> and <tcu>.

(5)   *isatzu* '(una) escriptura' ['a document']   (Chinchón 1614: 23–1, 18r05)

(6)   *xichiguatcu* 'la luna septima' ['seventh month' ('July')] (Chinchón 1614, 24r11)

Example (5) and (6) are the alternative romanizations in the open syllable style, both not commonly used in the manuscripts of Spanish (non-Jesuit) texts.

3.2   The comparison with the manuscripts of Spanish non-Jesuit texts

In the manuscripts of Spanish non-Jesuit texts, such as Father Chinchón's report and Ávila Girón's *Relacion del Reino de Nippon*, the open syllable /tu/ is spelled as <tzu> or <tz>. Example (7) and (8) are <tzu>, Example (9) is as <tz>.

(7)   *tzucamatzuri* ['do, serve']   (Chinchón 1614: 23–1, 15v14, Chinchón
                                          1614: 26–3, 94v24–25, BNE Mss. 19628, 173r12),

(8)   *futzuca* 'los dos dias' ['the two days']   (Chinchón 1614: 23–1, 18r08)

(9)   *futzca* 'los dos dias' ['the two days']
                                          (Chinchón 1614: 26–3, 96v02, BNE Mss. 19628, 175v10)

Considering that the spelling <tz> is used mainly for the closed syllable '-t', the general spelling of /tu/ is presumed to be <tzu>. In Table 2, the romanization of '-t' in a closed syllable and open syllable /tu/ in *Kirishitan* texts is explained:

Table 2. The notations of closed syllable '-t' and open syllable /tu/ in Kirishitan *texts*

	Jesuit texts		Spanish (non-Jesuit) texts		
	Prints	Manuscripts	Prints	Manuscripts	
				Collado's *Vocabulario de la lengua Japona*	Ávila Girón's *Relacion del Reino de Nippon*, and Chinchón's text
/tu/	tçu	tçu (tcu), ççu (ccu)	tçu	tçu	tzu (tz)
closed syllable '-t'	-t	-t	-t	-t (-tç)	-tz (-tzu, -tcu)

Table 2 shows the correspondence between the notation <-tz> and the irregular notation <-tç> as the closed syllable '-t'. In Medieval Portuguese, <ç> and <z->, <-z->
were not confused in writing (Ikegami 1984: 113–114). By contrast, in Castilian
in 16th and 17th centuries, <z> and <ç> were confused because /z/ was devoiced
(Yamada, ed. 1996: 112; Terasaki 2011: 203). Therefore, it was possible to write
<tzu> as <tçu> according to the Spanish orthography of those days. It means that
the notation <tzu> in Spanish manuscripts is the equivalent for the Jesuit spelling
<tçu>. In the same way, it was possible to represent <-tz> as <-tç>.

For Diego Collado, it should be easier to spell <tzu> as open syllable /tu/ and
<-tz> as closed syllable '-t'. Nevertheless, he used the Portuguese style <tçu> and
<-t> which was commonly used in *Kirishitan* texts. Example (3) and (4) can be
explained as misspellings or errors, made when transcribing <-tz> in Spanish to
<-t> in Portuguese style, because of the similarity of the relation of the notations
<tzu> in the Spanish style and <tçu> in the Portuguese style as /tu/. From this it is
plausible to assume that Collado's spelling in these cases followed the romanization
of Spanish manuscripts, not only that of Jesuit printed works.

3.3   Collado's spelling of /tu/

The notations in the Spanish manuscripts make it possible to identify the pronunciation of pre-modern Japanese. Morita (1993: 202–203) considers the word *Mitçu*
'honey' in *Kirishitan* texts as an early example which changed from the closed
syllable '-t' (/mit/) to the open syllable /tu/ (/mitu/). In Japanese, /mitu/ has different meanings: 'three' and 'honey', both written identically in *Kirishitan* texts. For
example:

(10)   Mitçu. *Mel.*   (Collado s.a.: 162r)

(11)   Mitçu. *Tres.*   (ibid. 363r)

Collado spells *mitçu* for the word meaning 'three' (see Example (12) and (13)), but
the Japanese equivalent of *mel* ['honey'] is not spelled as such, but as <mizu> (see
Examples (14), (15), (16), (17) and (18)).

(12)   tres *mitçu.*   (Collado s.a.: 9r08)

(14)   miel. *mizu.*   (Collado s.a.: 71r01)

(15)   panal de abejas. *mizu bachi.*   (Collado s.a.: 84v10)

(16)   *Mel, is: miel*, mizu.   (Collado 1632b: 80)

(17)   *Fauus mellis* ['honey-comb'] 'panal de abejas'. *mizu bàchi.* (Collado 1632b: 48)

(18)   *mizu, significat mel* ['meaning honey']   (Collado 1632c: 4)

As these examples illustrate, in Collado's books and his manuscript *Vocabulario de la lengua Japona*, the word /mitu/ meaning 'honey' is surprisingly spelled as <mizu>,[12] not as <mitçu>. The assumed spelling should be <mitçu> in the Portuguese style or <mitzu> in the Spanish style, so the spelling <mizu> seems to be a strange spelling choice for *Kirishitan* texts. Even though Collado distinguished the notations <zu> as /zu/ and <tçu> as /tu/ in his Japanese texts and generally used the notation <tçu> as /tu/, he used the irregular notation <zu> as /tu/ only in this case, the Japanese word meaning 'honey' (see Table 3).

It is reasonable to assume that this kind of confusing spelling error occured because there was the notation <zu> as /tu/ in other Spanish manuscripts. As I observed, this notation is very unusual in the *Kirishitan* printings, but it is not a unique case here. There is an example of notation <zu> as /tu/ in the copy of *Relacion del Reino de Nippon* (Doi 1982: 284), so that it could be explained that this 'irregular' notation is the result of the influence of the notation from other Spanish manuscripts. Additionally, Doi (1982) also mentions irregular notations in *Relacion del Reino de Nippon* by the texts of the copies in Biblioteca Nacional de España and Real Biblioteca del Monasterio de San Lorenzo de El Escorial, such as <zu>, <çu> and <su> as /zu/ (Doi 1982: 280), <tzu>, <tz>, <zu>, <zçu>, <z> and <çu> as /tu/, <tzu>, <tz>, <zu> and <çu> as /dzu/ (Doi 1982: 283), and there is also the example of notation <ntzu> as /dzu/: *zacantzuqui* /sakadzuki/ ['sake cup'] (BNE Mss. 19628, 182v06, 188vr23).

Table 3. Notations of /tu//zu//dzu/ (based on Kawaguchi 2018: 9)

	Jesuit texts		Spanish (non-Jesuit) texts			
	Prints	Manuscripts	Prints		Manuscripts	
			Manila press	Collado's books	Collado's Esp.– Jap. dictionary	*Relacion del Reino de Nippon*, etc.
/tu/	tçu	tçu (tcu), ççu (ccu)	tçu	tçu		tzu, tz, zu, zçu, z, çu
				zu (only *mizu* 'honey')		
/zu/	zu	zu	zu	zu		zu, çu, su
/dzu/	zzu, dzu	zzu	zzu	zzu		tzu, tz, zu, çu, ntzu

---

12. *Mizu* (/mizu/) means 'not looking' in pre-modern Japanese.

4. Conclusion

In previous studies, it has generally been accepted that the romanization used in Collado's texts are mainly based on the Portuguese romanization system, used by Jesuits in their printed works. I have demonstrated that at least some hitherto unexplained "irregularities", "discrepancies" or even "erros", can be explained as a direct influence from Spanish texts on Collado's work.

This conclusion considers a new side of the story that we couldn't recognize by only comparing these with Jesuit printed works. Through this comparison of Jesuit texts and Spanish texts, not only the comparison of prints, new questions emerge regarding the development of *Rōmaji* and the pronunciation of Late Middle Japanese.

There are few studies regarding the influence between Jesuit manuscripts and Spanish manuscripts. For example, there is a copy of *Relacion del Reino de Nippon* in the Roman Jesuit Archives (ARSI Jap. Sin. 49, 149r-221v, Jap. Sin. 58, 167r-273r). Although the main text of this copy is written in Spanish, the notation of romanized Japanese is a rescript of the Portuguese style. This will be the focus of future studies.

A. Abbreviations

AFIO	Archivo Franciscano Ibero-Oriental, Madrid
ARSI	Archivum Romanum Societatis Iesu, Rome
BAV	Biblioteca Apostolica Vaticana, Vatican
BNE	Biblioteca Nacional de España, Madrid
BNP	Biblioteca Nacional de Portugal, Lisbon
RBME	Real Biblioteca del Monasterio de San Lorenzo de El Escorial, San Lorenzo de El Escorial

Funding

This work was supported by JSPS KAKENHI; Grant Numbers JP15K02564 and JP19K00643.

References

B. Primary sources

Anonymous. 2013 [1603–1604]. *Vocabvlario da lingoa de Iapam com adeclaração em Portugues, feito por algvns padres e irmãos da companhia de IESV. [Nippo jisho].* Nangasaqui: no Collegio de Iapam da Companhia de IESVS. Facsimile edition: Bensei Corp. 2013. *Kirisitanban Nippo jisho: karā eiinban* ['Japanese-Portuguese Dictionary Nagasaki Japan 1603–4 VOCABVLARIO DA LINGOA DE IAPAM Nagasaqui 1603–4 Color Facsimile'], The original is housed in the Bodleian Library in Oxford. Tokyo: Bensei Publishing Co.

Anonymous. 1604. "Letter by a Japanese Christian". ARSI Jap. Sin. 33, 76r.

Anonymous. 1622. *Rozariyo kiroku. Virgen S. Mariano tattoqi Rosario no xuguiŏto, vonajique Iesusno minano Confradiani ataru riacuno qirocu. Core Predicadoresno Monpano uchi Padre Fr. Juan de los Angeles no fonyacu nari. Ordinariono yuruxiuo comuri.* ['A brief account of the holy rosary of the Blessed Virgin Mary and of the confraternity of the holy name of Jesus. Translated by Father Juan de Rudea de los Ángeles, of the Order of Preachers. Printed with permission of the Ordinary in the Hospital of St. Gabriel at Binondoc, in 1622'] Binondoc [Manila] no S. Gabrielno Hospitalni voite fanni firaqu mono nari.

Anonymous. 1623. *Rozario no kyō. Virgen S. Mariano tattoqi Rosariono jardin tote fanazononi tatoyuru qio Vonajiqu Iesusno Cofradiano regimientono riacu. Core Predicadoresno mompano uchi Fr. Joan de los Angeles no fonyacu nari. Supperiorto, Ordinariono yuruziuo comuri. Binondoc no S. Gabriel no Hospitalni voite fanni firaqu mono nari. Goxuxxe yori 1623.* ['A book comparing the holy rosary of the Blessed Mary to a flower garden, as it were, and also a summary of the rules of the confraternity of the name of Jesus. Translated by Father Joan de los Angeles, of the Order of Preachers. Printed with permission of the Superior and thew Ordinary in the Hospital of St. Gabriel at Binondoc in the year of the Lord, 1623'] Binondoc, Manila. AFIO 1014-3.

Anonymous. 1630. *Vocabvlario de Iapon declarado primero en portugves por los padres de la compañia de IESVS de aquel reyno, y agora en Castellano en el Colegio de Santo Thomas de Manila.* Manila: Tomas Pinpin, y Iacinto Magaurlua.

Ávila Girón, Bernardino de. s.a. *Relacion del Reino de Nippon.* AFIO 26–3, BNE Mss. 19628, RBME O-III-19.

Barreto, Manoel. 1591. "Barreto Manuscript". Japan. BAV Reg. Lat. 459.

Casai, João & Nizayemŏ João Matçumoto. 1617. Martyrdom report in Father Porro's report. ARSI Jap. Sin. 17, 317r–319r.

Chinchón, Diego de. 1613. *Relación cierta y verdadera de los ocho Mártires de Arima, cuyo martirio fue a siete de actubre de este año de 1613.* [Japan]. AFIO 23–1 (fols. 36r–47v). A transcription of this text is published in Sánchez Fuertes as "Documento 2" (2015: 542–554). A transcription of Japanese letters of this text is published in Kawaguchi (2016).

Chinchón, Diego de. 1614. *Relación de la persecución de los cristianos de Yedo en 1612–14.* [Japan]. AFIO 23–1 (fols. 1r–35v). A transcription of this text is published in Sánchez Fuertes as "Documento 1" (2015: 499–541). A transcription of Japanese letters of this text is published in Kawaguchi (2016).

Collado, Diego. s.a. *Vocabulario de la lengua Japona.* BAV Borg. Cin. 501. Facsimile edition: Mitsunobu Ōtsuka & Yukie Kojima ed. 1985. *Koryādo jihitsu Sei-Nichi jisho: fukusei, honkoku, sakuin oyobi kaisetsu.* ['Collado's handwritten Spanish-Japanese dictionary: facsimile, transcription, index and commentary']. Kyoto: Rinsen Books Co.

Collado, Diego. 1632a. *Niffon no cotobani yô confesion.* Romae: Typis & impensis Sacr. Congreg. de Propag. Fide.

Collado, Diego. 1632b. *Dictionarivm sive Thesavri Lingvae Iaponicae Compendium.* Romae: Typis & impensis Sacr. Congr. de Prop. Fide.

Collado, Diego. 1632c. *Ars grammaticae Iaponicae linguae.* Rome: Typis & impensis Sacr. Congr. de Propag. Fide.

Damião (Irmão). May 24, 1564. Letter to Rome from Meaco (Japan). ARSI Jap. Sin. 5, 177–179v.

Ferreira, Christovão. 1628. *Relação da perseguição contra nossa Santa fé, q[ue] de nouo se leuantou no Tacaqu este anno de 1627.* BNP Mss. 76-24.

Gonçal (Irmão), Pedro (Irmão), Antonio (Irmão) and Miguel (Irmão). 1621(?). *Letter to Father Jerónimo Rodríguez.* ARSI Jap. Sin. 34, 188r.

C. Secondary sources

Cooper, Michael. 1976. "The Nippo Jisho". *Monumenta Nipponica* 31:4.417–430.
https://doi.org/10.2307/2384310

Doi, Tadao. 1982. "Abira hiron Nihon ōkokuki no nihongo [Japanese Language in *Relacion del Reino de Nippon* by Ávila Girón]". *Kirishitan ronkō* ['Study on *Kirishitan*'], 275–297. Tokyo: Sanseido.

Hsu, Carmen Y. 2007. "El japón de Bernardino de Ávila Girón". *Las dos orillas: Actas del XV Congreso Asociación Internacional de Hispanistas, Monterrey, México, del 19 al 24 de julio de 2004* ed. by Beatriz Mariscal and María Teresa Miaja de la Peña. Vol. 2, 227–243. México: Fondo de Cultura Económica.

Ikegami, Mineo. 1984. *Porutogarugo to Garishiago: Sono seiritsu to tenkai* ['Portuguese and Galician: Its Establishment and Development']. Tokyo: Daigaku Shorin.

Imaizumi, Tadayoshi. 1951. "Nippo jisho wo tōshite mita jion to gohō to" ['The Japanese Sounds for Chinese Characters and Japanese Syntax in Vocavlario da Lingoa de Iapam']. *Kokugogaku* 6.11–28.

Irwin, Mark & Matthew Zisk. 2019. *Japanese Linguistics*. Tokyo: Asakura Publishing.

Kawaguchi, Atsuko. 2016. "Furanshisukokai ibero orientaru monjokan shozō Diego de Chinchon hōkokusho no nihonmoji to rōmaji gaki nihongo" ['Japanese Characters and Romanized Japanese in Diego de Chinchón's Report, Archivo Franciscano Ibero-Oriental']. *Mie daigaku nihon gogaku bungaku* 27.1–11.

Kawaguchi, Atsuko. 2018. "Koryādo no t-nissho hyōki to /tu/ hyōki: Supein-kei shahon tono hikaku kara" ['The notations of closed syllable -t and /tu/ by Collado: Comparing with other Spanish manuscripts']. *Mie daigaku nihon gogaku bungaku* 29.1–10.

Morita, Takeshi. 1993. *Nippo jisho teiyō* ['Study on the Vocabulario da lingoa de Iapam']. Osaka: Seibundō.

Sánchez Fuertes, Cayetano. 2015. "Relaciones de Diego de Chinchón OFM sobre la persecución de los cristianos de Edo (Tokio) y Arima (1612–1624)". *Archivum Franciscanum Historicum* 108.485–554.

Terasaki, Hideki. 2011. *Supeingoshi*. ['History of the Spanish Language']. Tokyo: Daigaku shorin.

Yamada, Yoshiro, ed. 1996. *Supein no gengo* ['Language of Spain']. Kyoto: Dōhōsha Shuppan.

PART III

Vietnam

Some remarks on Alexandre de Rhodes's linguistic works on Vietnamese

The influence of João Rodrigues's Japanese grammars

Emi Kishimoto
Osaka University

1. Introduction

The Jesuit Alexandre de Rhodes (1593–1660), a French-speaking Jesuit missionary, born in Avignon, is famous for his missionary activities in Vietnam and especially for his linguistic works on Vietnamese. The romanization system of Vietnamese is described in detail in his grammar (*Brevis Declaratio*, de Rhodes 1651b) and applied in his *Dictionarium Annamiticum Lusitanicum, et Latinum* (1651a) and the *Catechismus* (1651c). These works printed by the Propaganda Fide Press had a great impact on the establishment of the romanization system of Vietnamese as it exists today (*quốc ngữ*). His work on Vietnamese has been described and studied in recent publications, like Jacques (2002), Zwartjes (2011: 290–295), Fernandes & Assunção (2014) and Pham (2018). De Rhodes wrote his letters in many different languages, Latin, Italian, Portuguese, Spanish and French, his native tongue. As a Jesuit scholar, he did not only know Latin, but also Greek and Hebrew. In his grammar, we find references to these languages, as in his description of the special symbol <ƀ>, which is "is almost pronounced as the Greek β" ("pronunciatur ferè vt β Græcum"; de Rhodes 1651b: 2–3)[1] and some other sounds which are compared with Hebrew.

De Rhodes lived and worked for many years in Macau. He lived there for a short period in 1623, before leaving for Cochinchina and after he was expelled from Tonkin in May 1630, and later from Cochinchina in september 1640, he returned to Macau where he worked as professor of Theology at the Jesuit College. He reports that he was able to understand Chinese, although admitting that his proficiency was not sufficient for preaching in Chinese. He was forced to make use of interpreters for that purpose:

---

1. See Van Rooy's paper in this volume for further information regarding the Greek sources.

https://doi.org/10.1075/sihols.130.07kis

> Parce que encore que i'entendisse fort bien la langue Chinoise, ie n'en sçauois
> pas pourtant assez, pour la parler dans vn discours continué, de sorte que i'estois
> contraint de prescher auec vn interprete.   (de Rhodes 1653: 114)

> [although I understood the Chinese language very well, I still did not know it
> well enough to make a long speech in it, so that I was forced to preach through an
> interpreter.].   (Translation by Phan 1998: 45)

It is also documented that de Rhodes started learning Persian when he arrived in
Isfahan in 1655 at the end of his life.

It is less commonly known that de Rhodes original destination was not
Cochinchina but the mission in Japan, and for the sake being well prepared, he
started to learn Japanese in Macau, as he reports in his *Divers Voyages.*

> *Mon seiour d'vn an, dans Macao ville de la Chine tenue par les Portugais.* Chap.
> XIIII. Estant arriué en ce beau Royaume mon premier sejour fust à Macao, où l'on
> me retint vn an, pendant lequel ie m'emploiay de tout mon pouuoir à me rendre
> familiere la langue du Iapon, où ie prentendois d'aller au plustost.
>   (de Rhodes 1653: 57)

> [About my stay for a year in the Chinese town Macau, held by the Portuguese:
> Chapter 14: Before I arrived in this beautiful Kingdom, my first stay was in Macau,
> where I was held-up for a year. Over this period, I focused to all my abilities on
> getting familiar with the language of Japan, where I attempting to go as soon as
> possible.]

His desire to missionize in Japan was never realized, as a consequence of the persecution of the Christians there, which started in 1614 when the Tokugawa authorities
issued the decree of expulsion. It is unknown how de Rhodes studied Japanese
during his first stay in Macau. Did he study this language as an autodidact, or from
a teacher or a Japanese refugee? Was João Rodrigues (1562–1633) his teacher, or
was someone else? It is likely that he has seen a copy of the second edition of João
Rodrigues Japaneese grammar, printed in Macau in 1620, but we dot not know
if he had already seen the first edition, the Jesuit dictionaries or any other works
in or about Japanese. After the expulsion of the Christians, the study of Japanese
remained an important activity of missionaries, who took care of the Japanese
convert refugees in Macau. The main purpose of this paper is to discuss a possible
influence of João Rodrigues's Japanese grammar(s) on the work of Alexandre de
Rhodes on Vietnamese. Secondly, we shall give a brief account of the presence
of Japanese words in the trilingual Vietnamese-Portuguese-Latin dictionary. This
paper is an extension and continuation of some earlier publications. Kishimoto's
paper written in Japanese (2018) indicates that it is possible that de Rhodes referred
to the Japanese grammar books written by João Rodrigues when he edited his
short Vietnamese grammar *Brevis Declaratio*, appended to the *Dictionarium*. In this

paper, some more evidence will be provided, analysing de Rhodes's statements about the Japanese and Chinese languages, and showing resemblances with Rodrigues's *Arte Breve da lingoa Iapoa* (1620). What is important for the history of linguistics is that the Jesuits working in Macau not only came from different European nations, bringing together different linguistic descriptive traditions, but working in Macau also presented an extra dimension, since specialists in Vietnamese, Japanese and Chinese worked together closely, wile at the same time, native speakers of Chinese and Japanese and exiled Vietnamese Christians were living in the same community, which motivated missionary linguists to benefit from each in turn.[2] In their texts, just as in de Rhodes's grammar, we find, as I shall demonstrate below, similar views of the native languages of East Asia. In the second place, Kishimoto (2019), – also published in Japanese –, demonstrates that several Japanese words such as *catana* "Japanese sword" in Rhodes's *Dictionarium* are used to explain the Vietnamese entries, not because Rhodes found them in Japanese dictionaries printed in Japan, but because the Jesuit Fathers actually needed to use such Japanese words in their daily life in Vietnam, where many Japanese people also lived. This paper includes more details on these Japanese loanwords in the dictionary of de Rhodes.

This paper is organized as follows. Firstly, I would like to introduce Father Alexandre de Rhodes' *Dictionarium*. Next, I will provide some more details about his learning of the Japanese language, including an overview of Japanese loan-words included in his *Dictionarium*. Thirdly, I will compare Rodrigues's Japanese grammar books with de Rhodes's Vietnamese grammar, and finally, I will present a brief conclusion.

2.   *Rhodes's* Dictionarium Annamiticum Lusitanum et Latinum *(1651)*

According to Phan (1998), de Rhodes was born in Avignon, on March 15, 1591, and became a Jesuit in Rome in 1612. He dreamed of working in Japan, for which purpose he began studying Japanese. However, the Japanese government banned Christianity and issued decrees starting a severe religious persecution around 1614. Instead of Japan, de Rhodes was sent to Cochinchina, which is in central Vietnam. He arrived there in 1624 and remained there until 1626. Between 1627 and 1630, de Rhodes lived in Tonkin, in northern Vietnam. He taught theology in the Jesuit College in Macau between 1630 and 1640, then returned to Cochinchina in 1640, where he lived until 1645. After a journey to Rome, where he arrived in 1650, he published several books about Vietnam, such as his *Divers voyages* and religious works, such as the *Cathechismus*, a bilingual Latin-Vietnamese Christian doctrine.

---

2.   See also Zwartjes & de Troia's paper in this volume.

The *Dictionarium* was published in 1651 in Rome by the Sacra Congregatio de Propaganda Fide press, and has 591 pages in three main parts: *Dictionarium Annamiticum seu Tunkinense cum Lusitana, & Latina Declaratione*, the body of the Vietnamese-Portuguese-Latin dictionary (450 pages);[3] *Index Latini Sermonis*, an index of Latin entries (100 pages); and *Linguae Annamiticae seu Tunchinensis Brevis Declaratio*, a basic grammatical sketch of Vietnamese (31 pages). In the preface de Rhodes indicates two aims for the dictionary: for anyone to easily understand and translate Vietnamese, and for native Vietnamese speakers to learn Latin and Portuguese.[4]

Moreover, in the preface, Rhodes writes that the Portuguese Jesuit Francisco de Pina (1585–1625) had taught him Vietnamese, and that he added the Latin parts of the dictionary using two previous Vietnamese dictionaries, a Vietnamese-Portuguese dictionary written by Gaspar do Amaral (1594–1643) and a Portuguese-Vietnamese dictionary compiled by António Barbosa (1594–1647), both considered to have been lost. Although de Rhodes was a French-speaking missionary, the *Dictionarium* includes Portuguese and Latin because Latin was the official language of the Catholic Church and Portuguese was the language most commonly spoken and written among the Jesuits in Asia. Regarding the *Brevis Declaratio*, Jacques (2002) indicates that de Rhodes's linguistic texts were inspired or influenced by the *Manuductio ad Linguam Tunkinensem* ("Initiation to the Tonkinese language") by Francisco de Pina, which is according to his view the earliest extant grammar of Vietnamese, but recently, Pham (2018 and 2019) demonstrates that this work was written much later, probably by the German Jesuit Philipp Sibin (1679–1759). I agree with Pham and consider de Rhodes's the earliest extant full-fledged account of Vietnamese.

3.   Rhodes as a learner of the Japanese language

As I have stated in the previous section, de Rhodes studied Japanese in the Jesuit college of Macau in 1623 as preparation for missionary work in Japan. It is known that the Jesuits had been offering Japanese classes at the Jesuits' college in Macau since 1620 (Takase 2001: 435–437), and de Rhodes was probably one of the Japanese students there.

---

3.   In fact, the dictionary as no page numbers but numbered columns. The pages are arranged in two columns on each page.

4.   "…. Tum etiam quia sic facilius poterit quilibet libros Annamiticos intelligere & interpretari: praterquam quod pro ipsis Annamitis erit utilius, ut possint tam lusitanam quam latinam linguam addiscere" (de Rhodes 1651a: Ad lectorem", no numbered pages).

Even after his stay in Macau, de Rhodes had the opportunity to learn and use Japanese in Vietnam. He worked with several native Japanese Jesuits who were sent from Japan to Macau or Vietnam, and he stayed at least twice in *Nihon-machi* "Japan-town" Hội An in Cochinchina, where several hundred Japanese people lived, including many Christians. In the seventeenth century, the Japanese dominated the port's trading activities, as Brockey observes:

> The mission's center was Faifo, where in 1628 and 1629 there were four priests and a coadjutor. Since the missionaries lived among foreigners in this port, the Visitor [Palmeiro] took care to send the remaining Japanese priests and brothers from Macau to serve among their countrymen there, with the objective of reclaiming the exiles who had apostatized.   (Brockey 2014: 338)

When de Rhodes began learning Japanese in Macau, he possibly used books printed by the Jesuits. As regards grammar, there were (1) *Arte da lingoa de Iapam* (*Arte Grande*), a Japanese grammar by João Rodrigues, printed in 1604–1608 in Nagasaki in Japan, and (2) *Arte Breue da lingoa Iapoa*, a concise Japanese grammar by João Rodrigues, printed in 1620 in Macau. João Rodrigues came to Japan in 1577 and engaged in missionary work in Japan for around thirty years, and after leaving Japan in 1610 he stayed in Macau and China.

It is likely that the Jesuits in Macau could have seen and used the Latin-Portuguese-Japanese dictionary printed in 1595 in Amacusa, entitled *Dictionarium Latino Lusitanicum, ac Iaponicum*, and the Japanese-Portuguese dictionary printed in 1603–1604 in Nagasaki (*Vocabulario da lingoa de Iapam*). As Kishimoto (2019) indicates, de Rhodes' *Dictionarium* has little in common with the two printed Japanese dictionaries, except that they are trilingual. In the first place, the languages are arranged in a different order: de Rhodes starts with Vietnamese, and gives translations or (near) equivalents first in Portuguese and finally Latin, whereas the anonymous dictionary of the Jesuits describing Japanese starts with Latin, followed by Portuguese, and finally, the Japanese translation is given. As we can see in Example (1), when comparing the Portuguese-Latin parts in the *Dictionarium* with the Latin-Portuguese-Japanese dictionary, we see that the Latin verb "ludo" is translated into Portuguese as "brincar" and "folgar", whereas the Latin-Portuguese-Japanese translates it as "iugar". In general, we do not find many identical pairs of translations.

> *ác, chơi ác:* [to play]
> Rhodes' *Dictionarium* (1651)
> *ác, chơi ác:* 'brincar', 'folgar' [to play, enjoy]: ludo, [play].
> Latin-Portuguese-Japanese (Anonymous 1595)
> Ludo, is, si, sum. Lus. 'Iugar'. [play or gamble] Iap. *Asobu*, l, *caqemonouo xite bacuyeqiuo nasu.* [play, or gamble …]

Besides the Japanese dictionaries, there is the possibility that de Rhodes added the Latin parts using Portuguese-Latin dictionaries printed in Portugal, where trilingual dictionaries were published as well, such as Bento Perreira's (SJ; 1605–1681) *Prosodia in vocabularium trilingue latinum lusitanum et castellanum digesta* (1634), but also other sources could have been available to him, maybe not during his stay in Asia, but when he was in Europe, preparing his publications on Vietnamese between 1649 and 1652. In the following Example (2) some comparisons are provided, extracted from the Portuguese-Latin dictionary *Dictionarium Latino Lusitanicum et vice versa Lusitanico Latinum* published after 1562 by Jerónimo Cardoso (1508–1569), Agostinho Barbosa's (fl. 1590–1649) *Dictionarium Lusitanico Latinum* (1611) and Bento Pereira's (1605–1681) *Thesouro da lingoa Portuguesa* (1647). I demonstrate that the Portuguese and Latin translations in the Vietnamese dictionary of de Rhodes do not correlate with Portuguese-Latin dictionaries.

> Cardoso's Portuguese–Latin (1592)
> 'brincar' *ludo is*, [to play]
> 'folgar', *gaudeo, es* [to enjoy]

> Barbosa's Portuguese-Latin (1611)
> 'brincar'. *ludo, is. lusi, lusum.* [to play]
> 'folgar'. *gaudeo, es, gauisus sum. Lętor, aris. laetatus sum.* [to enjoy] *Triumpho, as.* [return in triumph]

> Pereira's Portuguese–Latin (1647)
> 'brincar'. *ludo, is. colludo, is.* [play together]
> 'folgar'. *gaudeo, es. Laetor, oris.* [enjoy] *Triumpho, as.* [return in triumph].

This comparison is far from comprehensive, and more research is needed in order to trace the possible sources of inspiration of Alexandre de Rhodes's trilingual dictionary. These examples demonstrate that the Latin verbs 'gaudeo', 'laetor' do not occur in de Rhodes.

Another aspect to be highlighted in this paper is the presence of Japanese loanwords in de Rhodes's dictionary, which were not taken from any European example.

– *Catana* (刀) is documented in the Portuguese translations of the following 14 Vietnamese lemmas. One of these is as follows: *bọc gươm, ßỏ gươm, chè, bánh chè gươm, đánh, giá, gươm, khâu, lếy, lười gươm, nhọn, rọn, đẽao rọn, sóũ, sút, tót.*

The lemma *gươm* is as follows:

> *gươm: catana* (刀): gladius contortus ex vna tantum parte acutus. alij *cừơm. ßỏ gươm*: bainha da *catana*; gladij vagina, *chuoi gươm*: cabo da *catana*: gladij capulus. *bánh chè. gươm*: guardas de *catana*. gladij scutum. *tüót gươm ta. desembainhar a*

catana: gladium è vagina extrahere. *rút gươm ra, idem. xỏ gươm βĕào: meter na bainha.* gladium mittere in vaginam. *tra βĕaò*, idem.   (de Rhodes 1651a: 300)

[*gươm: catana* (刀): a twited sword, sharp only on one side. Others [say] *cươm. βỏ gươm:* 'bainha da *catana*'; sheath of the sword, *chuoi gươm*: 'cabo da *catana*': hilt of the sword. *bánh chè. gươm:* 'guardas de *catana*': shield of the sword. *tüót gươm ta.* 'desembainhar a *catana*': to unsheathe the sword. *rút gươm ra,* the same [meaning]. *xỏ gươm βĕaò: meter na bainha.* 'to sheathe the sword'. *tra βĕaò,* the same.]

– *Bonzo* (坊主) is documented in 11 lemmas as follows in Portuguese translations oft he Vietnamese: *mũ, ni vãi, quạt vã, sãi, sám hối, tăng, đi tu, thĩ kiép ngưởita, tu, đi tu, uà, lù và, uả, quạt vả, uãi.*
  sãi: bonzo (坊主): sacrificulus, i (de Rhodes 1651a: 671). [*sãi: bonzo* (坊主): priest.]

– *Bonza*, which is a female form of *bonzo*, is documented in three lemmas in Portuguese translations of Vietnamese *ni vãi, tăng, đi tu, uãi.*
  uãi: bonza: sacrificula, ae. *sãi vãi: bonsos e bonzas:* sacrificuli & sacrificulae (Rodrigues 1651a: 856). [*uãi: bonza:* priestess. *sãi vãi: bonsos e bonzas:* priests & priestesses.]

– *Xaca* (釈迦) occurs in one lemma as follows in Portuguese and Latin.
  Thíc ca: Xaca (釈迦); Xaca, ae. is, primus fuit idolorum inuentor in Indijs orientalibus, natus est in ea Indiae parte quam sinae *thien trúc cŏắc* vocant, patrem habuit *tịnh phặn vương,* matrem *mada phu nhên,* vxor illi fuit *da du phu nhên con lí thien vương,* filius eius vocabatur *ca haù la.* duos habuit diabolos qui illum artem magica[m] docuerunt Alala scilicet & Calala, in montibus *đàn đạt* vbi primum se recepit, cum reliquit vxor[em] post aliquot cohabitationis annos & seipsũ fecit bụt idest, idolum, suis praestigijs innumeros decipiens vsque ad octuagesimum aetatis annum quo mortuus est in sylua dicta, Sala, mille circiter annis ante Christi Domini Natiuitatem, tempore Regis Sinarum dicti *βua Chu.* (de Rhodes 1651a: 761)
  [*Thíc ca: Xaca* (釈迦); Xaca, ae. He was the first inventor of the idols in the East Indies and he was born in that region of India that the Chinese call *thien trúc cŏắc.* His father was *tịnh phặn vương,* his mother *mada phu nhên,* his wife was *da du phu nhên con lí thien vương,* and his son was called *ca haù la.* He had two demons, Alala & Calala, who taught him magic in the mountains *đàn đạt* where he first retired, when he left his wife after a few years of cohabitation, and then he rendered himself one, that is a demon, beguiling countless people with his sorceries, until he was 80 years old and he died in the forest called Sala, a thousand years or so before the birth of Christ, during the time of the chinese King called *βua Chu.*]

–   *Missò* occurs in one lemma in Portuguese and Latin and *xiru* is seen in the same lemma in the Latin part.

   tương: certa massa de feijoẽs cozidos e pilados, a qual os Iapoẽs chamão missò (味噌): massa quaedam ex fasiolis coctis & pistis confecta quam Iapones vocant, *missò* (味噌), hac praecipuè vtuntur ad condiendos cibos praesertim iusculum quod, *xiru* (汁), vocant Iapones, & vix sine illo orizam comedunt. (de Rhodes 1651a: 846). [*tương: certa massa de feijoẽs cozidos e pilados, a qual os Iapoẽs chamão missò* (味噌): a kind of mass made of cooked and crushed beans that the Japanese call *missò* (味噌). They use it especially to season food, in particular a broth that the Japanese call, *xiru* (汁), without which they hardly eat any rice.]

–   *Fuxi* is seen in the lemma *mẵn* (rice), as follows in Portuguese and Latin.

   mẵn: arròs do Iapão chamado fuxi: oriza ex Iaponia, quam *fuxi* (フシ) vocant. (de Rhodes 1651a: 451). [*mẵn: arròs do Iapão chamado fuxi:* rice from Japan, called *fuxi* (フシ).]

4. De Rhodes's grammar and Rodrigues's Japanese grammars compared

In this section, I shall compare de Rhodes's and Rodrigues's grammars. De Rhodes's *Brevis Declaratio* consists of eight chapters:

1. letters and syllables,
2. accents and other diacritics,
3. nouns,
4. (honorific) pronouns,
5. other pronouns,
6. verbs,
7. other indeclinable parts of speech,
8. some syntactical precepts.

In the *Brevis Declaratio*, de Rhodes often compares Vietnamese with other languages, especially when describing the pronunciation in Chapters One and Two. However, most of them are not the native Asian where the missionaries worked, but languages used or known in Europe, such as Greek, Latin, Hebrew, Italian, Portuguese, and French, but some comparative remarks are included regarding Chinese and Japanese. Regarding the beginning of the introduction and in Chapter One; both are similar to Rodrigues's books, especially in his *Arte Breve* where we find references to Japanese.

4.1 Grammatical similarities between Japanese and Vietnamese

At the beginning, as we can see in the Example (3), de Rhodes summarizes the characteristics of the Vietnamese. De Rhodes writes that the verbs in Vietnamese are not inflected for tenses and moods, and nouns are not inflected for gender and number, just as in Japanese. This is almost the same observation as Rodrigues's statement in the *Arte Grande*. We also find similar comments in the *Arte Breve*, except that it lacks the statement about gender. De Rhodes claims that the three languages, Vietnamese, Chinese and Japanese share these features, which are diametrically different from European languages. In fact, there are no conjugations nor declensions:

> VICINIORA Orientali plagae idiomata praecipuè verò Cinense & Tunchinense, & ex parte etiam Iaponense, artem illa addiscendi habent à nostratibus linguis longè diuersam: carent enim omninò generibus: declinationes etiam non habent propriè neque numeros; Tunchinica certè lingua, de qua nunc agimus, nullas habbet coniugationes, tempora nulla aut modos.   (De Rhodes 1651b: 1)

> [When learning the neighbouring languages of the east coast, but especially Chinese and Vietnamese, and also some parts of Japanese, they have a very different grammar from our languages: they entirely lack, for instance, genders; they also have neither declensions properly nor numbers; certainly Vietnamese, which we are now considering, has no conjugations, tenses, or modes.]

> *Arte Breve* (1620)
> Os nomes desta lingoa saõ indeclinaueis, seruindo hũa sò voz ao singular, & plural.
>   (Rodrigues 1620: 1v)

> [The nouns of this language (Japanese) have no declensions and have only one form for both the single and the plural.]

> e posto que esta lingoa ẽ algũas cousas seja defectuosa por carecerẽ os nomes de variedade de casos, & não terẽ distinção de numero plural, & singular, nem de genero.   (Rodrigues 1604–1608: 'Advertencias')

> [This language is imperfect in some ways because the nouns have no variation in cases, distinction between plural and singular, or gender distinction …]

4.2 Pronunciation

The statement about declensions, gender, and number by itself is not clear evidence that de Rhodes had lifted his organization from Rodrigues; however, another comment on pronunciation is more convincing, as is illustrated in the following example:

L, Est in vsu maximè in principio vt lá, folium; hac autem litera omninò carent
Iapones, sicuti Cinenses carent r.   (de Rhodes 1651b: 5)

[L is used especially at the beginning of words, for instance, *lá* (leaf). The Japanese
language lacks this letter entirely, just as the Chinese lacks the letter R.]

Carece sua pronunciaçam da letra, L, & tambem de, R, dobrado; & os Chinas ao
contrario tem, L, & nam tem, R.   (Rodrigues 1620: 9v)

[The Japanese pronunciation has neither the letter L nor the double R. On the
contrary, Chinese has the letter L, but not R.]

os Iapões pronūciam a seu modo, imitando aos Chinas quanto podem por carece-
rem em sua pronunciação de muytas letras & syllabas que tem os Chinas, que os
Iapões não podem pronunciar. Como he, L.   (Rodrigues 1604–1608: 58v)

[The Japanese people pronounce Chinese characters in their own way, imitating
the Chinese as much as possible, because the Japanese pronunciation lacks many
letters and syllables that Chinese has, and the Japanese cannot pronounce, for
instance, the letter L.]

When de Rhodes discusses the letter L in Vietnamese, he refers to both Japanese
and Chinese; the Japanese language lacks the letter L, while, conversely, the Chinese
language lacks the letter R. This is quite similar to what Rodrigues wrote in the
Arte Breve, saying that "the Japanese pronunciation has neither the letter L nor the
double R. On the contrary, Chinese has the letter L but does not have the letter
R." In the *Arte Grande*, Rodrigues also wrote that the Japanese language lacks the
letter L, which the Chinese language has; however, he does not mention the letter
R. De Rhodes obviously added the information about Japanese and Chinese based
on the *Arte Breve*. However, there remains the possibility that he came to similar
descriptive conclusions independently from Rodrigues, or that he had been taught
by others, but it is likely that he knew the work of Rodrigues well.

5.   Conclusion

In the preceding sections we have highlighted some aspects of de Rhodes's connection with the Japanese language. In the first place, he studied Japanese himself
during his stay in Macau, before he started his mission in Vietnam. When he was
a professor of Theology over his 10-years stay in Macau from 1630 until 1640,
he worked together closely with missionaries who were language specialists in
Japanese, Chinese and Vietnamese and many expelled Japanese Christians who
lived in Macau. Multilingual Macau was the ideal place for linguistic comparisons,
which could have inspired de Rhodes continuously, always eager to hear and learn
about the language of the mission of his dreams, Japan. Later in Vietnam, he also

worked together closely with missionaries with experience in Japan and Japanese Christian refugees, expelled from Japan. This particular situation had the consequence of de Rhodes including Japanese loanwords in his trilingual dictionary.

Although it appears difficult to find any hard evidence that de Rhodes was influenced by Japanese dictionaries previously printed by the Jesuits in his Vietnamese dictionary, what he wrote about the Japanese language in his *Brevis Declaratio* shows that he was familiar with Rodrigues's grammars of Vietnamese.

Funding

This paper was supported by JSPS KAKENHI Grant Numbers JP20H01267, JP19K00626, JP17H02341, JP 17H02392, JP15K02573.

References

A.   Primary sources

Anonymous. 1595. *Dictionarium Latino Lusitanicum, ac Iaponicum.* Amacusa: Collegio Iaponico Societatis Iesu.

Anonymous. 1603–1604. *Vocabulario da lingoa de Iapam.* Nangasaqui: Collegio de Iapam da Companhia de Iesus.

Barbosa, Agostinho. 1611. *Dictionarium Lusitanico Latinum.* Bracharae [Braga]: typis, & expensis Fructuosi Laurentij de Basto.

Cardoso, Jerónimo. 1592. *Dictionarium Latino Lusitanicum et vice versa Lusitanico Latinum.* Olyssiponem [Lysbon]: excussit Alexander de Syqueira, expensis Simonis Lopezij, bybliopolae.

Pereira, Bento (=Benedicto Pereyra). 1634. *Prosodia in vocabvlarium trilingve latinvm, lvsitanicvm, & hispanicum digesta.* Eborae [Évora]: Apud Emmanuelem Carualho Academiae Typographum.

Pereira, Bento. 1647. *Thesouro da lingoa Portuguesa.* Lisboa: na officina de Paulo Craesbeeck, & à sua custa.

Rhodes, Alexandre de. 1651a. *Dictionarium annnamiticum [sic] lvsitanvm, et latinvm op Sacrae Congregationis de Propaganda Fide.* Romae: Typis & sumptibus eiusdem Sacr. Congreg.

Rhodes, Alexandre de. 1651b. "Lingvae annamiticae sev Tvnchinensis Declaratio". Grammatical compendium, appended to the *Dictionarium.* (de Rhodes 1651a).

Rhodes, Alexandre de. 1651c. *Cathechismvs pro ijs, qui volunt suscipere Baptismvm in Octo dies diuisus. Phép giảng tám ngày cho kẻ muấn chiụ phép rửa tọi, ma ɓẽáo đạo thánh đức Chúa blời.* Romae: Typis Sacrae Congregationis de Propaganda Fide.

Rhodes, Alexandre de. 1653. *Histoire dv Royavme de Tvnqvin, et des grands progrez qve la predication de l'evangile y a faits en la conuersion des Infidelles. Depuis l' Année 1627, iusques à l'Année 1646. Composée en Latin par le R.P. Alexandre de Rhodes, de la Compagnie de IESVS et tradvite en François par le R.P. Henry Albi, de la mesme Compahnie.* Lyon: Iean Baptiste Devenet.

Rodrigues, João. 1604–1608. *Arte da lingoa de Iapam composta pello Padre – Portugues da Cõpanhia de IESV diuidida em tres livros*. Nangasaqui: no Collegio de Iapão da Companhia de IESV.

Rodrigues, João. 1620. *Arte Breve da Lingoa Iapoa tirada da Arte Grande da mesma lingoa, pera os que começam a aprender os primeiros principios della. Pello Padre – da Companhia de Iesv Portugues do Bispado de Lamego. Diuidida em tres Livros*. Amacao: no Collegio da Madre de Deos da Companhia de Iesv.

B.   Secondary sources

Brockey, Liam Matthew. 2014. *The Visitor André Palmeiro and the Jesuits in Asia*. Cambridge, Massachusetts & London: The Belknap Press of Harvard University Press. https://doi.org/10.4159/9780674735576

Fernandes, Gonçalo & Carlos Assunção. 2014. "Cuốn Từ Điển Tiếng Việt Đầu Tiên (Rome 1651): Đóng Góp Từ Chế Độ Bảo Trợ Của Bồ Đào Nha Đối Với Ngôn Ngữ Học Phương Đông" [The First Vietnamese Dictionary (Rome 1651): Contributions of the Portuguese Patronage to Eastern Linguistics]. *Journal of Foreign Language Studies* 41.3–25.

Jacques, Roland. 2002. *Pionniers portugais de la linguistique vietnamienne*. Bangkok: Orchid Press.

Kishimoto, Emi. 2018. "Kirishitan-gogakusho no tenkai: João Rodrigues to Alexandre de Rhodes" [Developments of Jesuits' Linguistics in the East Asia: João Rodrigues and Alexandre de Rhodes]. *Gobun* 110.1–15.

Kishimoto, Emi. 2019. "Alexandre de Rhodes Vietnam-go, Portugal-go, Latin-go jisho (1651) no Nihongo" [Japanese Words in the *Dictionarium Annamiticum Lusitanum et Latinum* (1651) Compiled by Alexandre de Rhodes]. *Kokugo goishi no kenkyu* 38.1–18.

Pham, Thi Kieu Ly. 2018. "La grammatisation du vietnamien (1615–1919): Histoire des grammaires et de l'écriture romanisée du vietnamien". Ph.D. dissertation (Sorbonne Paris Cité).

Pham, Thi Kieu Ly. 2019. "The True Editor of the *Manuductio ad linguam Tunkinensem* (Seventeenth- to Eighteenth-Century Vietnamese Grammar)". *Journal of Vietnamese Studies* 14:2.68–92. https://doi.org/10.1525/vs.2019.14.2.68

Phan, Peter C. 1998. *Mission and Catechesis: Alexandre de Rhodes and Inculturation in Seventeenth-Century Vietnam*. Maryknoll, N.Y.: Orbis Books.

Takase, Koichiro. 2001. *Kirishitan-jidai no bunka to shoso* [Culture and the Various Aspects in the Christian Century in Japan]. Tokyo: Yagi Shoten.

Zwartjes, Otto. 2011. *Portuguese Missionary Grammars in Asia, Africa and Brazil, 1550–1800*. Amsterdam & Philadelphia: John Benjamins. https://doi.org/10.1075/sihols.117

Vietnamese grammars composed by missionaries from the *Missions Étrangères de Paris* during the 19th century

Thi Kieu Ly Pham
Vietnam National University, Hanoi

1. Brief overview: The historical context of Vietnamese grammar

The work on Vietnamese missionary grammar can be divided into three main periods. The initial period coincided with the first attempts by the Jesuits to provide a reasoned description of the Vietnamese language after their arrival in Cochinchina on the eighteenth of January 1615. Other missionaries also joined the mission at Cochinchina, including Francisco de Pina[1] in 1617, Christoforo Borri[2] in 1618 and Alexandre de Rhodes[3] in 1624, amongst others. In conjunction with their evangelical activities, they began to study the local language. Among these missionaries, Francisco de Pina compiled a vocabulary of Cochinchinese as early as 1619 (ARSI, Jap-Sin 71: 002). His report of 1623 confirmed that he had completed a description of the tones of the Cochinchinese language (BA, J.A, vol. 49-V-7: 414v.). However, influenced by Matteo Ricci's opinion (Brockey 2007: 247), Francisco de Pina assumed that, similar to Chinese, Vietnamese had no 'grammar' (Pham 2019). Another Portuguese Jesuit, Gaspar do Amaral,[4] announced in a report dated 1634 that he had transcribed a rich vocabulary, but made no mention of a grammar (BA,

---

1. Francisco de Pina (1585–1625), a Portuguese Jesuit, joined the company in 1605 and was sent to Cochinchina in 1617. He is considered to be the first missionary to have mastered the Annamite (Vietnamese) language.

2. Christoforo Borri (1583–1632) entered the Society of Jesus in 1601, went to Cochinchina in 1616 and remained there until 1621.

3. Alexandre de Rhodes (1593–1660) came from Avignon, Papal States, joined the Society of Jesus in 1612, and was sent on a mission to Asia in 1619. He arrived at the port of Tourane (now Dà Nẵng) in 1624.

4. Gaspar do Amaral (1594–1646), a Portuguese Jesuit, first arrived in Tonkin in 1629 and returned there in 1631.

https://doi.org/10.1075/sihols.130.08pha

JA, vol. 49-V-31: 307v–308r). It was not until 1651 that Alexandre de Rhodes published the first Annamite grammar, *Linguae Annamiticae seu Tunchinensis Brevis Declaratio* as a separate section in his *Dictionarium Annamiticum Lusitanum et Latinum* (published in Rome). In general, this period was a continuation of the great movement of grammatization of vernacular languages in Europe, and of the development of missionary linguistics in the New World – a movement that was based on the widespread use of the conceptual framework of the Graeco-Latin grammatical tradition.

The foundation of the *Missions Étrangères de Paris* (MEP) in 1658 and the subsequent dispatch of French missionaries to Vietnam transformed the practical conditions of such evangelization and the nature of the missionary linguistic work that took place from the end of the seventeenth century until the middle of the nineteenth century. During the age of the Jesuits, the majority of the missionaries in Vietnam were Portuguese. The number of French missionaries increased following the arrival of the MEP (Marillier 1995). Despite these changes, the priests of the MEP continued to compile their dictionaries and grammars in Latin for nearly two centuries after the start of their mission in Vietnam, having French as their mother tongue (for example, Taberd's grammar in *Dictionarium anamitico-latinum*, published in 1838).

Following the attack on the port of Tourane (Đà Nẵng) in 1858, the French gradually occupied Cochinchina, leading to increasing collaboration and confusion between the two processes of evangelization and colonization. The new political landscape had a strong impact on various aspects of Vietnam, particularly the field of linguistics. The French language was introduced in some schools. Adran College, founded in 1861, was considered to be the first school at which learners outside of the Church were taught *quốc ngữ* – Romanised Vietnamese script (DeFrancis 1977: 69–81). Another result was the emergence of many Vietnamese grammars written in French by missionaries, colonial administrators and Vietnamese people.

2. Choice of the corpus

A careful selection of material is essential given the large number of books – grammars written in Latin during the period 1651–1877 (written manuscripts and printed versions) of which the first grammar of Vietnamese, *Linguae Annamiticae seu Tunchinensis Brevis Declaratio,* was printed in 1651. Moreover, 83 grammars had been written in French since 1855, and 57 grammars in Romanised Vietnamese script, the first of which was published in 1867 (Pham 2018: 514–517). Thus, I compiled a selected corpus of some of the most representative grammars to conduct a comparative analysis in chronological order to demonstrate the evolution and transfer of theoretical models to the reasoned description of Vietnamese throughout the period under examination (Vietnamese grammars until 1900).

An analysis of the *Grammaticae compendium* attached to the *Dictionarium anamitico-latinum* (1838) published by Jean-Louis Taberd (1794–1840) and the *Proœmium*, part of the *Dictionarium anamitico-latinum* (1877) by Joseph-Simon Theurel (1829–1868) and the translation of Taberd's grammar published in 1861 by Gabriel Aubaret (1825–1894) reveals the importance of the role of the Latin grammatical tradition and the influence of Latin grammar textbooks used for teaching in France on descriptions of the Vietnamese language. The *Vocabulaire français-annamite, précédé d'un abrégé de grammaire et d'un traité des particules annamites* was published in 1861 by Gabriel Aubaret. It is, in fact, a translation of Taberd's grammar, although the description of nouns and verbs was modified to conform more closely to French grammar.

The grammars by Trương Vĩnh Ký[5] (1837–1898) published in 1883 served the same purpose as those of the colonial administrators, namely to explain the basic concepts of the Vietnamese language. With regard to the two grammars by Jourdain (1812–1871) printed in 1872 and Gabriel Vallot (1866–?) published in 1897, these works demonstrated quite clearly the influence of the grammar textbooks used to teach in France at that time and the contemporary linguistic trends used to describe Vietnamese (for example, the ten parts of speech, comparative linguistics and the like).

3.   Grammars written in Latin

3.1   Taberd's grammar

In 1838, Jean-Louis Taberd[6] published the *Dictionarium anamitico-latinum*, which contained 46 pages of grammar as an introduction. This is the first grammar of Vietnamese to be published by a missionary from the MEP. This grammar was divided into the following four parts:

---

5.   His baptismal name is Jean-Baptiste Petrus, therefore Trương Vĩnh Ký known as Petrus Ky and Jean-Baptiste Petrus.

6.   Jean-Louis Taberd (1794–1840), a priest from the Missions Étrangères de Paris, was sent on a mission to Cochinchina in 1820. In 1827, he was appointed Bishop of Isauropolis and Apostolic Vicar of Cochinchina.

- *Litterarum anamiticarum ex ordine disposita series*
- *Proœmium*
- *Grammaticae compendium*
- *Tractatus de variis particulis et pronominibus ad elegantem linguae anamiticae elocutionem utilissimis.*

The structure of Taberd's *Grammaticae compendium* differed significantly from the structure of *Linguae Annamiticae seu Tunchinensis Brevis Declaratio* by Alexandre de Rhodes (1651). Alexandre de Rhodes relied entirely on cases and on the distinction between declinable and indeclinable categories to organise the chapters of the *Brevis Declaratio* (Pham 2019), while Taberd approached number, gender and case in separate chapters in his grammar, which contains twelve chapters in total.

There are nine parts of speech in Taberd's book:

> Omnes voces variarum linguarum ad novem genera ordinarie reduci possunt; scilicet, Nomen, Adjectivum, Pronomen, Verbum, Participium, Adverbium, Praepositio, Conjunctio, et Interjectio. (Taberd 1838: ix)

> [In various languages, all words can usually be reported in nine categories, namely: noun, adjective, pronoun, verb, participle, adverb, preposition, conjunction and interjection.][7]

The fact that Taberd mentioned adjectives as being among the nine categories can be considered as the long-term result of the changes that gradually affected the theory of parts of speech, and as the immediate legacy of the *Elémens de la grammaire latine à l'usage des collèges* (1780) by Charles-François Lhomond (1727–1794) (Savatovsky 1997: 597) – the influence of this work remained strong at the beginning of the nineteenth century in terms of Latin pedagogy (Bazin 1940: 132–149).

Unlike De Rhodes (1651), who assumed that there is no participle in Vietnamese, Taberd clearly included the participle among the parts of the speech in Vietnamese, deciding in favour of a ranking that appeased in Lhomond, who is his main inspiration. On the one hand, Lhomond considered a participle "as a kind of word in its own right" (Lhomond, as cited in Colombat 1999: 183). On the other hand, Lhomond conceived of the participle as a subcategory of the infinitive, probably because both are invariable and thus appear as nominal forms of the verb. Taberd presents the Vietnamese equivalent of the present Latin participle, *amans: kẻ mến,* and the future participle, *amaturus, a, um: kẻ sẽ mến.* Another factor that explains the existence of the participle in Taberd's grammar is the method chosen: De Rhodes translated the Vietnamese words into Latin, while Taberd followed the opposite path. The Vietnamese verb that De Rhodes presented as an example is not conjugated; thus, its syntactic forms are not distinguished (Pham 2020).

---

7. All translations are by the author unless stated otherwise.

Although Taberd points out that the Vietnamese language doesn't have cases as Latin does, his analysis nevertheless applies the case system to the description of the noun, again in the pure tradition of Latin grammar, based on which the author respects the order of cases (nominative, genitive, dative, accusative, vocative and ablative).

Taberd discusses the issue of the noun followed, in order, by considerations of gender, number and case. As Bouard (2007) pointed out with regard to the grammars of French published at the same time, "the chapter on case follows the chapters on nouns, number and gender as an additional change affecting nouns and indicating the various relationships that things have with each other" (Bouard 2007: 188). Therefore, in the paragraph that Taberd devoted to the noun, we can see a double reference: the Latin reference to the case system and the French reference to the classification of the properties of the noun (Pham 2020).

3.2 Aubaret's (1861) grammar – Taberd's grammar translated into French

Gabriel Aubaret[8] composed the *Vocabulaire français-annamite, précédé d'un abrégé de grammaire et d'un traité des particules* in 1861, which was printed in Bangkok. With the *Abrégé de grammaire* added to its vocabulary, the work is considered to be the first grammar written by a colonial administration official, and reflects a state of transition between two linguistic traditions: one that uses Latin and one that uses French as a metalanguage.

However, this was not a sudden break with the past: As Théophile Legrand de la Liraÿe (1819–1873) points out (1868: 9), Aubaret translated Taberd's *Compendium* from Latin into French. Nevertheless, it was not a faithful translation because, depending on the passages, Taberd's text is either made more complex or is simplified, particularly with regard to the parts of the speech.

Concerning the properties of the Vietnamese language, he remarks:

> La grammaire annamite se réduit à très peu de chose, l'absence de déclinaison et de conjugaison en rend la première partie très simple. La syntaxe sera plus particulièrement apprise dans le traité des particules.　　　　(Aubaret 1861: ix)
>
> [The Annamite grammar is reduced to very little, the absence of declension and conjugation makes the first part very simple. Syntax will be more particularly learned in the treatise on particles.]

---

8. Louis Gabriel Galdéric Aubaret was a French naval officer and diplomat. After graduating from the Naval Academy, he participated in the China campaign and the Cochinchina campaign in 1858 as a lieutenant. He is also the author of various historical and linguistic works.

The first section of the word discusses the origin of the Vietnamese language, followed by an explanation of its tones (pp. i–iii), which precedes the description of vowels (pp. iii–v) and consonants (pp. v–viii), a summary of the grammar (pp. ix–xvi) and a repetition of the treatise on particles (pp. xvii–xcv). Aubaret wrote seven pages reflecting on the parts of the speech (pp. ix–xvi), which include the study of nouns with remarks about how gender, number and case, as they are distinguished morphologically in Latin, are expressed in Vietnamese (pp. ix–xi). He then focused on adjectives and pronouns (pp. xi–xiii). Verbs occupy two pages (pp. xiv–xv), and adverbs, prepositions, conjunctions and interjections are discussed together at the end of the work (pp. xv–xvi). In this initial work, Aubaret did not translate Taberd's chapter on verbs accurately. There is no mention of the past subjunctive, the future subjunctive, the perfect infinitive, the gerund or the supine in the chapter. Nor is there any exposition of the participle because, according to the author, "[C]e sont là des formes peu employées, les temps principaux suffisent pour l'intelligence du discours" [These are forms that are rarely used, the main tenses are sufficient for the intelligence of the discourse] (Aubaret 1861: xv).

In general, the interesting fact about the *Abrégé de grammaire* is that, in his description, the author takes a contrasting view from the outset, noting that, unlike French, there are no articles in the Vietnamese language.

> L'article n'existe pas dans cette langue. […] Les substantifs n'ayant pas d'article forment d'eux même le singulier.   (Aubaret 1861: ix–x)
>
> [The article does not exist in this language. […] Nouns with no article form the singular by themselves.]

Aubaret's grammar is a linguistic work that represents the moment of transition between the use of Latin and French as the metalinguistic language. This translation of Aubaret's work was partly influenced by the characteristics of French grammar (for example, the remarks about articles or the absence thereof in Vietnamese).

3.3   Theurel's grammar

Joseph-Simon Theurel[9] completed the Latin grammar in Vietnamese begun by Pierre-André Retord (1803–1858) (Burel 1998: 38). Considering that there are very few copies of Taberd's dictionary remaining and that he omits the usual vocabulary of the Tonkinese, Theurel, assisted by Vietnamese catechists, began to write his dictionary during a time in which Christian prohibition was strict. Theurel was

---

9. Joseph-Simon Theurel (1829–1868), a missionary from the MEP, departed for Tonkin in September 1852. Since 1855, Theurel had been in charge of management and had teaching duties at Tonkin College and at the mission's printing office.

able to complete a large portion of his work before he died in 1868. His colleague Émilie-Charles Lesserteur (1841–1916) added a few new words to the manuscript and published the book *Dictonarium anamitico-latinum* in 1877 (Theurel 1877: v).

This 30-page grammar consists of three sections: In the first part (*Prooemium*, pp. i–v), there are brief explanations of the origin of the Annamite language and the creation of the *quốc ngữ* (Vietnamese written in romanised script), as well as the context of the publication of the *Dictionarium anamitico-latinum*. The second section (Caput I, *De singulis vocum speciebus*, pp. vi–xiv), reveals the parts of speech and the particularities of the Annamite language, while the third section (Caput II, *Ad notantur quadam, Ad perfectam lingua anamitica intelligentiam juvantia*, pp. xiv–xxx) presents some strategies for speaking the Annamite language fluently. The author includes the last part of Taberd's grammar in its entirety.

The structure of this grammar is not similar to the model of classical grammar, which traditionally contains two parts, namely the letters followed by the parts of the speech. The grammar by Theurel has no section relating to 'letters'; that is, phonetic-orthographic elements.

Theurel mentioned eight parts of speech in the Annamite language, namely nouns such as *nhà* (*domus*), adjectives such as *tốt* (*bonus*), pronouns such as *nó* (*ille*), verbs such as *làm* (*facere*), adverbs such as *lâu* (*diu*), prepositions such as *vuối* [sic] (*cum*), conjunctions such as *nếu* (*si*) and the interjection *ôi trời ôi* ! (*o coelum*).

Theurel (1877) dit not mention participles (listed as a part of speech in Taberd's grammar) among the eight parts of speech in his grammar. Theurel presented adjectives as an autonomous class among the parts of speech and reserves an independent chapter for it.

> Nec genera, nec numeros, nec casus habet adjectivum, et in hoc eadem sorte gaudet a substantivum. Ordinarie sequitur substantivum, quandoque tamen antecedit.
>
> (Theurel 1877: viii)
>
> [The adjective has no gender, no numbers, no cases; neither does the noun. Usually, it follows the noun; however, in some cases, it precedes the noun.]

It should be recalled that Alexandre de Rhodes's (1651) grammar included adjectives in the same chapter as nouns. For a long time, although being seen as a subcategory of nouns, adjectives were distinguished from nouns based on morphological criteria (Colombat 1999: 193–206). The inclusion of adjectives as a part of speech in French grammar became clearer in the eighteenth century (Julien 1992). In Lhomond's Latin grammar, an adjective is definitely considered to be "a kind of word" among the "nine categories of words" (Lhomond (1780, as cited in Colombat 1995: 11). Since the grammar by Lhomond is one of Taberd's direct sources, followed by Theurel, these two missionary authors considered the adjective to be a part of speech.

4. Trương Vĩnh Ký's grammars

Trương Vĩnh Ký (1837–1898), often known as Petrus Ký, was trained at the General College of Missions Étrangères de Paris in Penang (Malaysia). He was a great polyglot scholar and author of hundreds of linguistic or historical books and textbooks. In 1867, Trương published the *Abrégé de la grammaire annamite* in Saigon (131 p.). Some years later, in 1883, Trương published another more voluminous grammar (304 p.) entitled *La grammaire de la langue annamite*. When reporting on the changes he had made to the *Abrégé* in 1867, Trương remarks:

> Grâce aux comparaisons avec les grammaires des autres langues que nous connaissons, nous avons publié, pour la première fois en 1867, l'*Abrégé de grammaire annamite*. Nous offrons aujourd'hui au public une autre édition plus étendue sur les notions précises de (la langue annamite) pour la rendre plus abordable aux étrangers.   (Trương 1883: 17)

> [Thanks to comparisons with the grammars of the other languages we know, we have published, for the first time in 1867, the *Abrégé de grammaire annamite*. We are now offering the public another more extensive edition about the precise notions of the Annamite language to make it more comprehensible to foreigners.]

In a review of the book, the orientalist Émile Gaspardone (1932) – a resident at the École française d'Extrême Orient (Hanoi branch) at the time – confirmed this change of perspective by considering that the grammar by Trương is "built on Lhomond, with a view to the theme for French students". Gaspardone (1932) declared:

> Cette grammaire est restée le meilleur exposé de l'annamite de Cochinchine; elle offre un trésor d'exemples de consultation facile, notamment pour les particules.

> [This grammar remained the best presentation of the Cochinchine Annamite; it offers a treasure of examples for easy reference, especially for particles.].

Unlike other grammars, the book has no introduction and is divided into two main parts, namely preliminary concepts (the presentation of language and writing) and the grammar itself (the eight parts of speech). Trương often characterised the noun as follows.

> Le substantif en annamite n'a pas de terminaisons variables. Il peut être précédé de son article défini ou de son appellatif ou de son numéral ou (être) suivi de son complément (substantif, adjectif, verbe).   (Trương 1883: 18)

> [The noun in Annamite has no variable endings. It may be prefixed with its definite article or appellative or numeral, or (be) followed by its complement (noun, adjective, verb).]

Influenced by French syntax, Trương (1883) insisted on the mandatory use of an article, such as the definite article *cái*, to determine the noun. Nevertheless, he still referred to the system of Latin declensions: "L'annamite n'a pas de cas. [...] Pour représenter ces différents cas, on emploie des particules *ad hoc*" [The Annamite language has no cases. [...] To represent these different cases, we use *ad hoc* particles] (Trương 1883: 68–69). This remark shows the challenge that Trương experiences with regard to abandoning the mental framework of the borrowed (Latin) system entirely in the description of the noun. His book indicates the revival of the two reference models, the Latin model and the Franco-Latin model, since Taberd (1838). Trương divided the Vietnamese temporal system into primitive and derived periods. In order to accomplish this end, he adopted a comparative point of view by presenting the tenses and modes of French verbs in relation to the corresponding Vietnamese words in tabular form. When attempting to teach Vietnamese to the French people, Trương Vĩnh Ký believed that it was best to use concepts familiar to French people to facilitate their learning. Trương Vĩnh Ký was one of the first grammarians in Vietnam to describe his native language. However, this does not mean that his model was fundamentally different from that of his native French-speaking predecessors. Once again, it was the linguistic tools used that mainly decides the metalanguage, not the first language of the grammarian. The grammar by Trương Vĩnh Ký (1883) is the last book to retain traces of the Latin influence in the description of Vietnamese.

5. The grammars by Jourdain (1872) and Vallot (1897)

5.1 Jourdain's grammar

The *Grammaire française-annamite* was published in 1872, one year after the death of the author, Denis Jourdain.[10] This missionary from the MEP had already produced a two-page annotated grammar that was published as a supplement to Saigon's Courrier in 1865. Jourdain (1872) stated that he followed the method of English grammar proposed by Théodore Robertson (1803–1871).[11]

---

10. Denis Jourdain (1812–1871), ordained in 1836, entered the seminary of the Foreign Missions of Paris in 1846. He left for the General College (Penang – Malaysia) in the same year. After many years in Asia, he returned to France in 1857 and then left for Cochinchina in 1859. He died in Saigon on the 1st of July 1871.

11. This refers to Robertson's book *Cours pratique, analytique, théorique et synthétique de langue anglaise,* which was published for the first time in Paris in 1837 and was reprinted several times during the second half of the nineteenth century (Fischer 1999).

> Tous les mots employés dans cet ouvrage sont expliqués dans des vocabulaires particuliers placés après chaque partie du discours. [...] M. Robertson, dans sa grammaire anglaise, s'est servi avantageusement de cette méthode pour inculquer à ses élèves les règles de la langue dont il donnait des leçons.   (Jourdain 1872: 5)

> [All words used in this book are explained in appropriate vocabularies placed after each part of the speech. [...] Mr. Robertson, in his English grammar, made good use of this method to instill in his students the rules of the language he was teaching.]

Robertson's method aimed to teach words and sentences first, with the rules being inferred later.

It is important to remember that two phenomena mark the nineteenth century: (1) The advent of school grammars as a completely autonomous genre (Chervel 1977), and (2) the beginnings of comparative linguistics in the academic field (Chevalier 1994). Jourdain's grammar follows these two trends: While his book belongs to the field of comparative linguistics, it is also a learning manual with pronunciation guides and a vocabulary list in each chapter to facilitate reading.

The grammar begins with the introduction, which is extremely interesting because it opens with Humboldt's comments[12] about the Chinese language[13] (including Vietnamese, as it has similar characteristics to Chinese). Humboldt claimed that Chinese was devoid of grammar. Jourdain expressed two criticisms of European grammarians, with particular reference to Humboldt's criticism of the Chinese (or Vietnamese) language: according to Humboldt, Chinese or Annamite has no termination system and contains a limited number of sounds (Humboldt, as cited in Jourdain 1872: 2). Jourdain believed that Chinese had a concise and sentinel style and this style stemmed largely from Chinese education, and that Chinese taste was probably not well formed (Jourdain 1872: 3); what was easy to understand seemed to be too simple for a composition or a book for Chinese people. This defect of the Chinese language (according to Humboldt) can also be found in Solomon's proverbs. Jourdain admitted that each language has its peculiarities, but maintains that languages had the same origin in "God's punishment" (Jourdain 1872: 4).

> Aussi est-ce une belle étude que la comparaison des langues entre elles; on y voit souvent les mêmes règles, les mêmes figures, les mêmes images et tournures de phrase. On voit que c'est l'ouvrage du même ouvrier, l'homme.
>
> (Jourdain 1872: 5)

---

12. Jourdain recited this remark by Humboldt in Alphonse Gratry's work *Connaissance de l'âme* (1857).

13. These are the discussions between Wilhelm von Humboldt (1767–1835) and the sinologist Jean-Pierre Abel-Rémusat (1788–1832) from 17 January 1822 to 7 August 1831 (See Jacques-Philippe 2001).

[So it is an excellent study to compare languages with each other; we often see the same rules, the same figures, the same images and turns of phrases. We see that it is the work of the same worker, man.]

Jourdain's grammar contains 17 chapters, but a numbering error occurred between Chapter 15 and Chapter 17; thus, there are actually 16 chapters in his book. Jourdain lists eight parts of speech, namely nouns, pronouns, verbs, adverbs, prepositions, conjunctions and injections. The final chapters explain syntax (Chapter 14), particles and Annamite poetry (Chapters 15 and 17).

The first chapter aimed to explain pronunciation and writing. The second chapter aimed to teach foreign students to pronounce Annamite correctly. According to Jourdain, this was imperative because, once flawed, pronunciation is difficult to correct.

After introducing the two types of nouns (simple and compound) in Chapter 3, Jourdain presented examples of compound nouns in French, English and Italian in order to reiterate his stance, as expressed in the introduction, that all languages have the same origin.

Jourdain sought to convince readers about two or more languages having the same origin, particularly the equivalence between Vietnamese and French, in the other chapters.

5.2　Vallot's (1897) grammar

The work *Grammaire annamite à l'usage des Français de l'Annam et du Tonkin* by Pierre-Gabriel Vallot,[14] published in Hanoi in 1897, became the main textbook used in Annam and Tonkin schools as soon as it appeared.

This grammar is published in a considerable tome (viii–208 pages). In the preface, Vallot informs the reader that he has consulted previously published grammars in order to write a work that explains the rules of the language more clearly and provides a great service to learners:

> En publiant une nouvelle grammaire, l'auteur ne manque presque jamais de passer en revue tous les ouvrages de ce genre qui ont paru jusqu'à son époque […]. Jusqu'à présent ceux qui ont précédés dans ce pays se sont bornés à rédiger sur la langue annamite des notions trop succinctes et par conséquent incomplètes.
>
> (Vallot 1897: i)
>
> [In publishing a new grammar, the author almost never fails to review all the books of this type that have appeared up to his time […]. Until now, those who preceded in this country have confined themselves to writing too succinctly and therefore providing incomplete ideas about the Annamite language.]

---

14. Pierre-Gabriel Vallot (1866–?) was ordained as a priest in 1890; he was sent to the mission in Western Tonkin in the same year.

In the introduction, Vallot discusses the origin of the Annamite language and quốc ngữ (Vietnamese written in romanised script). His explanations are similar to those of Theurel (1877) and Trương Vĩnh Ký (1883) to some extent. Grammar is divided into two main parts: The first part is reserved for the parts of speech, while the second analyses the syntax of the language.

Vallot believed that there were ten categories of words or parts of speech in Vietnamese, and that the article and the noun should constitute two independent chapters.

> Il y a dix espèces de mots ou parties du discours: le substantifs, l'article, l'adjectif, les pronominaux, le pronom, le verbe, la préposition, l'adverbe, la conjonction et l'interjection.
> (Vallot 1897: 31)
>
> [There are ten categories of words or parts of speech: the noun, the article, the adjective, the pronominals, the pronoun, the verb, the preposition, the adverb, the conjunction and the interjection.]

A new chapter pertaining to a new part of speech that appeared in this grammar discussed pronominals:

> Les pronominaux génériques sont des mots qui jouent le rôle soit d'articles soit de pronoms par rapport à des catégories déterminées d'êtres ou d'objets [...]. Ils sont articles lorsqu'ils accompagnent un substantif, pronoms lorsqu'ils le remplacent.
> (Vallot 1897: 54)
>
> [Generic pronominals are words that play the role of either articles or pronouns in relation to specific categories of beings or objects [...]. They are articles when they accompany a noun, pronouns when they replace it.]

Thus, these words, which were classified as 'particles' in previous grammars, are identified as 'articles' by Trương Vĩnh Ký (1883); examples are *cái bánh*, bread, and *con dao*, knife. Pronominals are words that are used to determine the noun by agreeing with it in terms of gender and number.

In the chapter on nouns, Vallot ceases the use of declensions completely. The chapter on verbs reflects the organization specific to the modes and tenses of French. Vallot also used the categories of French grammar *in absentia* to draw a comparison with Vietnamese language.

> Il n'y a point en annamite de verbes auxiliaires, c'est-à-dire de verbes servant à former les temps des autres verbes. C'est par imitation des grammaires françaises [...] que nous voulons indiquer brièvement ici la façon de les rendre en annamite.
> (Vallot 1897: 74)
>
> There are no auxiliary verbs in the Annamite, i.e. verbs used to form the tense of the other verbs. It is by imitating French grammars [...] that we want to briefly indicate here how to render them in Annamite.

This strategy was intended to facilitate school translation exercises using a method borrowed from the Franco-Latin theoretical model. In the nineteenth century, this model had been adapted to version and theme exercises specific to the learning of modern languages, in which word-for-word translation remained important:

> Nous croyons utile de rappeler que le but de ce tableau est le même que celui des explications qui précèdent : c'est de faire voir comment l'on pourrait traduire mot-à-mot les temps français. (Vallot 1897: 82)

> [We believe it is useful to recall that the purpose of this table is the same as that of the previous explanations: to show how the French times could be translated word-for-word.]

Thus, Vallot paired French verbs and words from Vietnamese to make them correspond fully to all the elements of French grammar. All the aforementioned grammarians attempted to account for the morphological properties of Vietnamese by focusing on the differences from French: They are explicitly contrasting grammars.

6. Conclusion

With the mass arrival of the French missionaries from the MEP from 1663 and, later, of the French colonisers in 1858, the grammar of Vietnamese adopted the French grammar textbooks being published in France (Lhomond and Humboldt) as its primary reference model, gradually moving away from the Greek-Latin tradition in terms of the description of French whereby it is envisaged. Accordingly, Taberd (1838) and Theurel (1877), having chosen to compose their grammars in Latin, were influenced by the characteristics of their first (French) language, hence the use of French for a description of the contrasts in the object language. When Aubaret translated Taberd's Latin book into French in 1861, he added reflections on the French article and, by contrast, treated Vietnamese verbs according to the French verb model.

During the French colonial era, Vietnamese grammars were all written in French – examples include works by Aubaret (1861) and Trương Vĩnh Ký (1883) – but they also included designations from Latin cases to describe the Vietnamese noun system. Such grammars also contained a Franco-Latin theoretical approach. Jourdain's (1872) grammar forms part of comparative linguistics, one of the two trends in France in the nineteenth century. In the grammars by Jourdain (1872) and by Vallot (1897), the traces of Latin declensions disappeared completely, and the authors were influenced by the French grammar textbooks being published in France at the time.

Acknowledgements

This article relates (in part) the results of the thesis entitled "La grammatisation du vietnamien (1615–1919) : histoire des grammaires et de l'écriture romanisée du vietnamien" that the author defended in November 2018 at the Université Sorbonne Nouvelle – Paris 3. I would like to thank Otto Zwartjes for his helpful suggestions.

References

A.   Primary sources

Abel Rémusat, Jean-Pierre. 1822. *Élémens de la grammaire chinoise ou principes généraux du Kou-wen ou style antique et du Kouan-Hoa, c'est à dire, de la langue commune généralement usitée dans l'empire chinois*. Paris: Imprimerie royale.

ARSI. *Archivum Romanum Societatis Iesu (ARSI)*, Jap-Sin 71, fol. 002.

Aubaret, Gabriel. 1861. *Vocabulaire français-annamite, précédé un abrégé de grammaire et d'un traité des particules annamites*. Bangkok: Impr[imerie] de la Mission catholique.

BA. Biblioteca da Ajuda. Jesuítas na Ásia, vol. 49-V-7, fol. 414v; vol. 49-V-31, fols. 307v–308r.

Bazin, Antoine-Pierre-Louis. février 1840. "Critique littéraire". *Journal Asiatique* 132–149.

Gratry, Alphonse. 1857. *De la Connaissance de l'âme*. Paris: C. Douniol.

Humboldt, Wilhelm von. 1827. *Lettre à M. Abel Rémusat, sur la nature des formes grammaticales en général et sur le génie de la langue chinoise en particulier*. Paris: Dondey-Dupré. https:// gallica.bnf.fr/ark:/12148/bpt6k5469694j/f8.item.texteImage

Jourdain, Denis. 1865. "Grammaire annamite: introduction". [no page numbers]. *Supplément au courrier de Saïgon*.

Jourdain, Denis. 1872. *Grammaire français-annamite*. Saïgon: Impr[imerie] du gouvernement.

Legrand de la Liraÿe, Théophile. 1868. *Dictionnaire élémentaire annamite-français*. Saigon: Imprimerie impériale.

Lhomond, Charles-François. 1780 [1779]. *Élémens de la grammaire latine à l'usage des collèges*. Paris: Colas.

Rhodes, Alexandre de. 1651. *Dictionarium Annamiticum Lusitanum et Latinum*. Rome: Typis et sumptibus ejusdem Sacr[a] Congr[egatio].

Robertson, Theodore. 1839 [1837]. *Cours pratique, analytique, théorique et synthétique de langue anglaise*. Paris: Derache.

Taberd, Jean-Louis. 1838. *Dictionarium anamitico-latinum, primitus inceptum ab illustrissimo et reverendissimo P. J. Pigneaux, episcopo adranensi, vicario apostolico Cocincinae, &c*. Fredericnagori vulgo Serampore: Ex typis J.-C. Marshman.

Theurel, Joseph-Simon. 1877. *Dictionarium anamitico-latinum, ex opere Ill. et Rev. Taberd constans*. Ninh Phu: Ex typis missionis Tunquini occidentalis.

Trương, Vĩnh Ký. 1867. *Abrégé de grammaire annamite*. Saigon: Imprimerie impériale.

Trương, Vĩnh Ký. 1883. *Grammaire de la langue annamite*. Saigon: Bản in nhà hàng C. Guilland et Martinon.

Vallot, Pierre-Gabriel. 1897. *Grammaire annamite à l'usage des Français de l'Annam et du Tonkin*. Hanoi: F.-H. Schneider.

B. Secondary sources

Bouard, Bérengère. 2007. Structure de la proposition et construction verbale : régime, complément et transitivité, dans les grammaires françaises, 1651–1863. Ph.D. dissertation, Université Paris-Diderot – Paris VII.

Brockey, Liam Matthew. 2007. *Journey to the East: The Jesuit Mission to China 1579–1724*. Cambridge, Massachusetts: The Belknap Press of Harvard University Press. https://doi.org/10.4159/9780674028814

Burel, Laurent. 1998. "La paroisse vietnamienne au XIXème siècle: un compromis entre commune traditionnelle et modernité". *Péninsule* 36:1.31–54.

Chervel, André. 1977. *Et il fallut apprendre à écrire à tous les petits Français: histoire de la grammaire scolaire*. Paris: Payot.

Chevalier, Jean-Claude. 1994. *Histoire de la grammaire française*. Paris: Presses universitaires de France.

Colombat, Bernard. 1995. "A propos de la *grammaire latine étendue*. Quelques remarques sur les contrecoups subis par le modèle latin lors de son adaptation au français". *Archives et Documents de la SHESL* 11.7–11. https://doi.org/10.3406/hel.1995.3397

Colombat, Bernard. 1999. *La grammaire latine en France à la Renaissance et à l'âge classique. Théorie et pédagogie*. Grenoble: ELLUG-Université Stendhal.

DeFrancis, John. 1977. *Colonialism and Language Policy in Viet Nam*. The Hague, Paris & New York: Mouton. https://doi.org/10.1515/9783110802405

Fischer, Denise. 1999. "Les idées pédagogiques de Soler y Arqués. Leur application dans sa 'méthode analytique-synthétique'". *Documents pour l'histoire du français langue étrangère ou seconde* 23.329–345. https://doi.org/10.4000/dhfles.3057

Gaspardone, Émile. 1932. "Truong Vinh Tong : Grammaire de la langue annamite". *Bulletin de l'École française d'Extrême-Orient* 32.519–520.

Jacques-Philippe, Saint-Gérand. 2001. "Lettres édifiantes et curieuses sur la langue chinoise: un débat philosophico-grammatical entre Wilhelm von Humboldt et Jean-Pierre Abel-Rémusat (1821–183) et Pierre Joseph Proudhon, Écrits linguistiques et philologiques". *Romantisme* 111.138–141.

Julien, Jacques. 1992. "L'extension de la classe adjectivale en grammaire française". *Histoire Épistémologie Langage* 14:1.199–209. https://doi.org/10.3406/hel.1992.2348

Marillier, André. 1995. *Nos pères dans la foi, notes sur le clergé catholique du Tonkin de 1666 à 1765*, vol. 3. Paris: Eglise d'Asie.

Phạm, Thị Kiều Ly. 2018. La grammatisation du vietnamien (1615–1919): histoire des grammaires et de l'écriture romanisée du vietnamien, Ph.D. dissertation, Université Sorbonne Nouvelle, Paris.

Phạm, Thị Kiều Ly. 2019. "The True Editor of the Manuductio ad linguam Tunkinensem (Seventeenth- to Eighteenth-Century Vietnamese Grammar)". *Journal of Vietnamese Studies* 14:2.67–92. https://doi.org/10.1525/vs.2019.14.2.68

Phạm, Thi Kiều Ly. 2020. "Les deux premières grammaires vietnamiennes écrites en latin (1651 et 1838)". *Beiträge zur Geschichte der Sprachwissenschaft* 30:1.88–102.

Savatovsky, Dan. 1997. L'invention du français. Une histoire des exercices dans l'enseignement classique au XIXᵉ siècle. Ph.D. dissertation, Université Paris VIII.

How Greek is the Graeco-Latin model?

Some critical reflections on a key concept
in missionary linguistic historiography
through Alexandre de Rhodes's early description
of Vietnamese (1651)

Raf Van Rooy
KU Leuven

1. Introduction

> Applying terms and distinctions defined by Antonio de Nebrija […], missionary
> linguists employed the paradigms and methods of traditional European grammar,
> i.e., the Greco-Latin model.   (Klöter 2011: 84)

> The missionaries abroad needed to describe typologically different languages, and
> they often adapted the traditional Greco-Latin model drastically in order to ac-
> commodate linguistic features they were unfamiliar with.   (Zwartjes 2011: 7)

As the above quotes make abundantly clear, the concept of a "Graeco-Latin model"
is well-established in missionary linguistic historiography, and with good reason.
Most missionaries relied on their grammatical education for their descriptions of
the so-called exotic languages they were trying to lay down in rules. The traditional
parts-of-speech system and the terminology that went with it served as an almost
self-evident starting point, even though it could have both a "positive inspiring"
and a "negative blocking effect", to put it with Wolf Peter Klein's (2001: 39–40)
words. The Latin character of the model surely could not be denied by missionaries. Indeed, even in the early modern period, *grammar* often still equaled "Latin
grammar". When thinking this through, one is faced with several questions. Why
is the concept of "Graeco-Latin model" usually not defined by modern scholars?
How accurate is the label "Greek" here? Were missionaries truly aware of the Greek
origins of Latin grammatical education? If so, how did they conceive of the relationship between the two? If not, one could ask oneself: how tenable is the modern
historiographical concept of a seemingly monolithic "Graeco-Latin model"? Is it
desirable to continue using the phrase, acknowledging, however, that most scholars

https://doi.org/10.1075/sihols.130.09van

did not associate their model with the Greek language and that, by consequence, the concept is somewhat anachronistic? Or should we abandon the "Graeco" in "Graeco-Latin model" and simply speak of "the Latin model" instead? Also, could Greek grammar operate as a model separate from the Latin one and, perhaps, foster original approaches to thorny linguistic issues, in which the Latin framework proved unsatisfactory? In this contribution, I want to explore some of these pertinent questions by means of a case study. First, I will briefly elaborate on the historical reasons behind the phrase "Graeco-Latin model" (Section 2). Then, I will present a case study of a seventeenth-century Jesuit deliberately setting Greek tradition apart from the Latin one (Section 3). I will finish with a number of critical reflections in the fourth and final Section. Needless to say, as my analysis is based on a very limited source basis, the implications of my afterthoughts should be studied in more depth in follow-up investigations, considering both missionary grammars and other types of language manuals.

2.   The "Graeco-Latin model": A historical perspective

As an analytical concept in linguistic historiography, the "Graeco-Latin model" is a rather recent creation. It was coined by modern historians of linguistics in their attempts at analyzing the tensions between tradition and innovation in describing the grammar of a language. They were led to do so by their historical knowledge, as they were aware of the evolution of grammar in antiquity.[1] In the Western sphere of influence, the Greeks were the first to develop a full-fledged grammatical tradition sometime in the two centuries before the common era. Very soon, this model was taken over by the Romans, who did not only conquer Greece quickly after the emergence of grammar, but also absorbed Greek culture more broadly. Indeed, for many key aspects of their intellectual and artistic production, the Romans were very much indebted to Greek examples. However, since the Latin language was obviously different from the Greek, Roman grammarians had to adapt certain aspects of Greek grammar to the specificities of their own language. For instance, Greek had no ablative case, so Roman scholars had to fill this void. Yet, most of the adapting did not consist in expanding Greek grammar, but in narrowing it down; Latin had no article, optative, or aorist, for instance (cf. Law 2003: 59). To the Romans, however, taking over the Greek model must have seemed self-evident. W. Keith Percival has summed it up neatly:

---

1.   On this topic, numerous studies have appeared during the past century. See, among many other publications, Swiggers & Wouters (1996).

> Interestingly, there is little evidence of much theoretical discussion in the classical period on the feasibility of constructing a grammar of Latin on the Greek model, Latin being regarded by scholars at that time as a variety of Aeolic and hence basically Greek.
>
> (Percival 1995: 48)

Because of this historical evolution, today historiographers, particularly of missionary linguistics, tend to speak of "the Graeco-Latin model" when they assess a grammarian's traditionalism or innovativeness in describing a language other than the so-called classical ones.

One might therefore say that the modern concept of a "Graeco-Latin model" is historically justified. That would, however, imply ignoring an important turn in the history of the language sciences. After the fifth century, Greek was largely unknown in Western Europe, whereas Latin grammar remained widely studied. Even more, it became a core component of the medieval and early modern education system. The Greek grammatical tradition was rediscovered by Western scholars only from the late fourteenth century onward, an event of great momentum for the history of linguistics, as Percival (1995: 49) has rightly emphasized. The rediscovery of Greek grammar not only made Renaissance scholars increasingly aware that "grammar" was not confined to "Latin grammar", but it also served as a source of inspiration to describe linguistic features that had no place in Latin grammar, or a marginal one at best. For instance, several sixteenth-century French grammarians resorted to the Greek tradition to map out features of their native tongue, while trying to tie French to Greek historically. The categories of "article" and "aorist" proved particularly popular in this context. The French grammarian Jean Pillot (1515–1592), for instance, adopted a highly eclectic approach toward Greek and Latin grammar. Or in his own words: "I have partly imitated the Latins, partly the Greeks, in accordance with the variety of place and subject matter".[2] Most notably, Pillot followed Greek tradition in discussing the interjections among the adverbs, in distinguishing between a definite and indefinite ("aorist") perfect, and in positing the article as a French part of speech.[3] This major turn in the history of language studies has not yet received due attention from historians of linguistics. Through the present contribution, I aim to briefly explore a notable aspect of this neglected issue, namely the way in which some missionary grammarians sometimes consciously relied on the Greek rather than the Latin model. I will do so by concentrating on an early modern work on the Vietnamese language: Alexandre de Rhodes's (1593–1660) description of Vietnamese in his *Linguae Annamiticae seu Tunchinensis brevis declaratio*

---

2. Pillot (1550: ã.iiij^R): "Partim Latinos partim Græcos, pro loci ac rerum varietate sum imitatus".

3. Pillot (1550: ã.iij^{R-V} [aorist], 7^R [interjections among adverbs], 8^V [article], 20^V-21^R [definite vs. indefinite perfect]).

(de Rhodes 1651b), usually attached to his *Dictionarium Annamiticum* of 1651 (i.e. de Rhodes 1651a), but also found appended to another work by de Rhodes, printed a year earlier and discussing the Jesuit mission in Vietnam (i.e. de Rhodes 1650).

3.   An early description of the Vietnamese tonal system: Alexandre de Rhodes's *Brevis declaratio*

In what context did the earliest descriptions of the Vietnamese tonal system appear? It was Jesuit missionaries in Vietnam who first engaged in detail with the phenomenon. For my purposes, the case of Alexandre de Rhodes (1593–1660) is the most relevant. Before situating de Rhodes in history and analyzing his exposé on Vietnamese tones, however, I should clarify my stance vis-à-vis a language manual of disputed authorship and dating, namely the *Manuductio ad linguam Tunchinensem*. Following the convincing arguments recently advanced by Pham (2018, 2019), I regard this *Manuductio* as an eighteenth-century work, most likely composed by the German Jesuit Philipp Sibin (1679–1759).[4] In consequence, I do not consider de Rhodes's work to be dependent on the *Manuductio*.[5] Yet I will refer to the latter text in as far as it is relevant to my discussion.

De Rhodes is the author of a brief grammatical sketch of Vietnamese, comprising also a description of the language's tonal system.[6] This Avignonese Jesuit was of Spanish-Jewish ancestry and received his first education at the large Jesuit college in his hometown, where he no doubt learned Greek, as this was part of the standard curriculum of Jesuit colleges ever since the 1599 *Ratio studiorum*.[7] He most likely studied Greek using the standard Jesuit grammar by the German Jacob Gretser (1562–1625), first printed in 1593, with numerous editions across Europe, particularly in French-speaking areas, and containing many contrastive observations on Greek linguistic particularities vis-à-vis Latin. De Rhodes's Greek learning

---

4.   I sincerely thank Otto Zwartjes for drawing my attention to the most recent developments in research on the *Manuductio*.

5.   *Pace* Fernandes & Assunção (2017), where it is wrongly attributed to the Portuguese Jesuit missionary Francisco de Pina. Pina was, however, probably one of the first to compare Vietnamese tones to music notes, which also occurs in the *Manuductio*, but he was active in an area where Vietnamese was spoken with only five and not six tones (Pham 2018). The *Manuductio* consists of 22 pages and is divided into three main chapters, on the tones, the letters, and the nouns, which are followed by some other material such as short dialogues.

6.   Biographical information on de Rhodes is principally based on Collani (1994); Phan (1998: 28–68); Schatz (2015).

7.   See Compère & Julia (1984: 94), who specifically mention that Greek was taught at the Avignon college. On the *Ratio studiorum*, see e.g. Scaglione (1986).

seems to be reflected in his name as well. His original Spanish family name was *de Rueda* ("of the wheel"), which he restyled as *de Rhodes*, reminiscent of the Greek island in the Dodecanese. It seems that he wanted to mask his Jewish origin – *rueda* referred to the small disk medieval Jews were forced to wear on their clothes – and, perhaps, he wanted to evoke Greek culture at the same time, a practice fashionable in humanist circles.[8]

In 1612, de Rhodes entered the Society of Jesus in Rome with the intention of becoming a *missionarius apostolicus* of the *Sacra congregatio de propaganda fide* in Japan. He eventually wound up in Vietnam, undertaking three distinct missions in different regions and studying the local language for over a decade (Zwartjes 2011: 291). In mid-1645, de Rhodes journeyed back to Rome, a long and difficult trip that lasted four years. The next five years he worked for the church in Vietnam from Europe. His last years were devoted to the Jesuit mission in Persia, where he likewise studied the local language; he died there in 1660.

Three elements in de Rhodes's life deserve additional emphasis here. First of all, he was excellently trained in the ancient and vernacular tongues of Europe. Most importantly, he seems to have been acquainted with Greek grammar, even though the exact circumstances in which he learned the language remain somewhat obscure. Secondly, he did not limit his interest to European tongues, but grasped the opportunity to study non-European tongues during his missions. Thirdly, he thought it useful to put his mastery of the "tongue of Annam" to use by composing a brief handbook. De Rhodes's grammatical outline of Vietnamese, entitled *Linguae Annamiticae seu Tunchinensis brevis declaratio*, was incorporated into his well-known and much-studied *Dictionarium Annamiticum, Lusitanum et Latinum*, published in 1651 while he was back in Rome.

De Rhodes's *Brevis declaratio* discusses in 31 pages:

1. letters and syllables ("De literis & syllabis quibus hæc lingua constat"; pp. 2–7);
2. tones and other diacritics ("De Accentibus & alijs signis in vocalibus"; pp. 8–10);
3. nouns ("De nominibus"; pp. 10–14);
4. pronouns ("De Pronominibus"; pp. 14–20 & "De alijs Pronominibus"; pp. 21–23);
5. verbs ("De Verbis"; pp. 23–26);
6. indeclinable parts of speech ("De reliquis orationis partibus indeclinabilibus"; pp. 26–29), and
7. syntax ("Præcepta quædam ad syntaxim pertinentia"; pp. 29–31).[9]

---

8. Cf. e.g. Price (2003: 95); Aleksiejuk (2016: 444).

9. On de Rhodes's grammatical sketch, see e.g. already Zwartjes (2011: 292–295), where it is summarized.

The section in de Rhodes's outline which concerns me here is that on the tones, *accentus* in Latin. De Rhodes opened his chapter on this tricky matter as follows:

> Diximus accentus esse quasi animam uocabulorum in hoc idiomate, atque ideò summa diligentia sunt addiscendi. Vtimur ergo triplici accentu linguæ Græcæ, acuto, graui, & circumflexo, qui quia non sufficiunt, addimus iota subscriptum, & signum interrogationis nostræ; nam toni omnes huius linguæ ad sex classes reducuntur, ita ut omnes prorsus dictiones huius idiomatis ad aliquam ex his sex classibus seu tonis pertineant, nulla uoce prorsus excepta.   (de Rhodes 1651b: 8)
>
> [We have said that accents are as it were the soul of words in this idiom, and for this reason they are to be studied with the greatest diligence. We therefore use the triple accent of the Greek language, acute, grave, and circumflex, to which, because they do not suffice, we add the subscribed iota and our interrogation sign; for all the tones of this language are reducible to six classes, so that all words of this idiom entirely pertain to one of these six classes or tones, with no word at all excepted.]

De Rhodes was relying on his knowledge of Greek to spell out Vietnamese tones; indeed, his description of this feature of the language was for a large part – although not exclusively – based on the description of the accent in the Greek grammatical tradition.[10] These diacritics were more widely known and used by missionary grammarians, but normally without reference to the Greek language; de Rhodes is an exception, in that he consciously and repeatedly sought to tie his description to this classical tongue.

Let me briefly outline the description of the six tones by de Rhodes and its parallels with Greek grammar. The first tone is called *aequalis*, the neutral tone, which "is pronounced without any inflexion of the word".[11] It is not marked by an accent; *ba*, for example, means 'three'. The second tone is the *acutus*, "pronounced by giving an acute accent to the word, and by pronouncing the term as if someone would exhibit rage".[12] The word *bá*, for instance, means 'royal concubine'. The third tone is the *gravis*, "pronounced by pressing down the word, like *bà*, 'grandmother', or

---

10. In the *Manuductio*, one simply reads: "Accentus hac in Linguâ seu tonorum mutationes sunt sex, ex quibus solis multoties significationum diversitas sumi debet; unde patet hujusmodi tonos ex arte callendi necessitas [The accents or tone changes in this language are six in number, from which alone the difference of meanings must often be taken. And thence there is a clear necessity of being versed in tones of this kind through an art]". See [?Sibin] (ca. 1745: 313ᴿ). Cf. also Fernandes & Assunção (2017: 169).

11. "sine ulla uocis inflexione pronunciatur". This and the following quotes are all taken from de Rhodes (1651b: 8).

12. "profertur acuendo voce[m], & proferendo dictionem, ac si quis iram demonstraret".

'mistress'".[13] The fourth tone is the circumflex, "expressed by inflecting a word that is pronounced from the bottom of the chest and later resoundingly raised, like *bã*, 'a fist blow', or 'to box one's ears'".[14] The fifth tone is termed "weighty" or "heavy". It is expressed with a certain weight or burden, while the word is pronounced from the bottom of the chest (like the fourth tone). The subscribed iota is used as a symbol for this tone, as in *bạ*, 'abandoned thing'. Finally, the sixth tone is called "smooth" (*lenis*), since it is pronounced with a certain smooth inflexion of the voice. Here, a parallel is drawn with interrogative intonations in European tongues. Because of this parallel, the question mark is used to note this sixth tonal type, as in the word *bả*, which signifies a type of saffron-yellow silk. By consequence, in Vietnamese, the syllable *ba* can denote the most diverse things in accordance with the diversity of "accents".[15] In sum, tones two to four are described by means of typically Greek accentual signs, whereas tone five is expressed by means of another Greek orthographic symbol, namely the *iota subscriptum*. The sixth tone is termed *lenis*, perhaps suggesting yet another association with Greek grammar, since it evokes the concept of the smooth breathing (*spiritus lenis*) typical of Greek orthography. It does not seem a coincidence that the question mark symbol de Rhodes used resembles to a high degree the Greek *spiritus lenis* symbol ('). What is more, the Latin verbs and phrases used by de Rhodes in describing the Vietnamese tones remind of the terminology of early modern grammars of Greek, not in the least the Jesuit Jacob Gretser's (1593) popular work. The verbs *acuere* (for the *acutus*) and *deprimere* (for the *gravis*), for instance, both appear throughout Gretser's grammar. The use of other phrases like "ex imo pectore prolata" for descriptive linguistic purposes seem to be idiosyncratic to de Rhodes.[16]

De Rhodes proposed a parallel between the Vietnamese tones and musical tones, perhaps inspired by his predecessor, the Portuguese Jesuit missionary Francisco de Pina (1585/86–1625), or his colleagues in Macau working on Chinese, also a tonal language.[17] De Rhodes emphasized, however, that the similarity between Vietnamese and musical tones was not exact, and that it would be difficult

---

13. "profertur deprimendo uocem, ut bà, auia, uel Domina".

14. "qui exprimitur inflectendo uocem ex imo pectore prolatam, & postea sonorè eleuatam, ut bã, colaphus, uel colaphizare".

15. Today, still six tones are distinguished for northern Vietnamese (Phan 1998: 33; Zwartjes 2011: 293).

16. A query in Brepolis' Cross Database Searchtool conducted on September 30, 2019 (http://clt.brepolis.net/cds/pages/Search.aspx) shows that the phrase "ex imo pectore" is solely used by later Christian authors, principally to characterize deep breaths and sighs.

17. See Raini (2010: 67) for the early association of Chinese with musical tones.

to learn the Vietnamese tones through musical theory alone. Rather, one should learn them from a native speaker of Vietnamese. Remarkable is that de Rhodes did not perceive a further parallel between Greek and Vietnamese here. Although explicitly tying his description to Greek tradition, he failed to make explicit that Ancient Greek, too, had a tonal rather than a stress accent such as Latin and most other Indo-European languages. In the *Manuductio*, which is, as I have mentioned, most likely of a later date, it is also suggested that there is a parallel between the Vietnamese tones and musical notes. The treatise even contains musical staves to visualize this (see [?Sibin] ca. 1745: 313ᴿ-314ᴿ), but the link with Greek scholarship is much less prominent than in de Rhodes's account.

De Rhodes's description of the six tones, the parallel with musical tones, and the recourse to Greek descriptive terminology were the result of two decades of studying Vietnamese, as the manuscript evidence indicates. The earliest remarks of this kind date back to 1632.[18] De Rhodes also commented on the Vietnamese accent in a more rudimentary form in an Italian work printed in 1650, where the Greek element was, however, much more marginal (de Rhodes 1650: 114–118). Here, the reference to Greek was limited to the subscribed iota and the circumflex accent, and the parallel with the musical notes occupied a more central position; a brief comparison with the Chinese tonal system was likewise offered.

In conclusion, Alexandre de Rhodes was very original and relatively accurate in his description of the Vietnamese tonal system, an originality apparently at least partly triggered by his knowledge of Greek grammar. Indeed, as I have demonstrated, de Rhodes tied the description closely to the "triple Greek accent", a

---

18. See the quote in Pham (2018: 227, French translation at p. 567), where de Rhodes applies the three Greek accents to the romanization of both Vietnamese and Chinese already in a letter of 1632 (and also compares the Greek aspirates to Vietnamese and Chinese sounds; cf. infra): "2ᵘᵐ uix posse nostris characteribus germana[m] pronunciatione[m] haru[m] linguaru[m] exprimi Sinice pręsertim et Annam, eo quod ex tono diuerso qui literis diuersis exprimi non potest uocabuloru[m] diuersitas maximé pendeat: hanc tamen diuersitatem accentibus Gręcę linguę acuto, graui, et circu[m]flexo utcunque exprimemus: at si quis hanc diuersitatem exprimere poterit: quoquo tamen modo imitabitur si uocabula accentu acuto notata in modum falseti musici proferat: graui uero in modu[m] bassi, circunflexo denique uocem inflectendo ad modu[m] interrogatis. Vocabula nullo accentu notata absque ulla inflexione uocis sunt pronuntianda. 3ᵘ⁽ᵐ⁾ aspirationes in his linguis Sinica & Annam esse frequentissimas, et valdé asperas ut in ph, kh, th ęquiualent enim aspiratis φ, χ, θ, cum asperé pronuntia[n]tur ut á Germanis aut Belgis, in reliquis pronuntiatione[m] Italica[m] secuti sumus pleru[m]que". See also the contribution of Paolo De Troia and Otto Zwartjes in this volume for more details on this early writing by de Rhodes and other testimonies (e.g. from 1636) suggesting that his insights developed over a long period of at least two decades (1632–1651). For a similar application of Greek diacritical marks to Chinese, dating to 1687, see the anonymous Jesuit treatise translated in Lundbæk (1988: 39).

phrase he seems to have borrowed from his Jesuit school grammar of Greek.[19] The Avignonese Jesuit missionary seems to have been confident that Greek grammar was very adequate to describe the Vietnamese tonal system and offered a way out when traditional Latin grammar was not satisfactory. Admittedly, he could have found the terminology related to the Greek accent in Latin grammatical tradition, but he seems to have drawn directly from Greek tradition rather than through the intermediary of Latin grammar; this Hellenic inspiration is most clearly suggested by, among other things, de Rhodes's explicit reference to the *Greek* accent and his usage of the *iota subscriptum* as a descriptive device.

Elsewhere, de Rhodes apparently felt constrained by the traditional parts-of-speech model. For instance, before embarking on a sketch of the Vietnamese parts of speech, he made the following disparaging remark about the language:

> Tandem vt aliquam notitiam demus de partibus orationis de illis singillatim agemus, quantum hoc idioma permittit, ex quadam proportione cum lingua Latina: facilè tamen quis aduertet non poße assignari tantam uarietatem, non solum vt est in lingua Latina, sed neque vt in vulgaribus Europæis.   (de Rhodes 1651b: 10)

> [Finally, in order to give an idea of the parts of speech, we will discuss them one by one, in as far as this idiom allows it, through a certain analogy with the Latin language. Yet anyone will easily notice that it cannot be assigned such a variety, not only like there is in the Latin language, but neither as in the European vernaculars.]

So it may be clear that de Rhodes described at some length the tonal system of Vietnamese, primarily by relying on Greek rather than Latin grammar. I am, of course, not the first modern scholar to notice this missionary's detailed description of Vietnamese tones.[20] Yet I believe that the implications of this account and especially his usage of the Greek tradition have not yet been fully acknowledged. It seems to imply that, for de Rhodes, the Latin model was not entirely the same as its Greek source of inspiration. This mindset also emerges from other aspects of de Rhodes's early missionary work on Vietnamese. He repeatedly resorted to Greek letters in order to describe certain Vietnamese sounds (see de Rhodes 1651b: 3–5). Vietnamese had two [b]-like sounds, de Rhodes (1651b: 2–3) reported. The second one, which he wrote as ƀ, "is almost pronounced as the Greek β".[21] His familiarity with Greek grammar surfaces here as well, since he interpreted it as resembling a

---

19. Gretser (1593: 8): "Ad rationem legendi spectat quoq[ue] accentus; qui triplex est".

20. See e.g. Phan (1998: 33); Zwartjes (2011: 292–293); Fernandes & Assunção (2017: 167–173); Pham (2018).

21. De Rhodes (1650/51: 3): "pronunciatur ferè vt β Græcum". Interestingly, de Rhodes also drew a parallel with the pronunciation of Hebrew in the very same sentence.

[v] sound, just like most early modern grammars of Ancient Greek did for the beta, or vita rather. Indeed, the standard Jesuit school grammar presented β as "Vita" on its very first page (Gretser 1593: 1). De Rhodes's background as a Hellenist also enabled him to correctly identify some Vietnamese sounds as aspirated consonants and to claim that "this language therefore has three aspirated [letters] like the Greek language", namely [kʰ], [pʰ], and [tʰ], written in the Greek alphabet as χ, φ, and θ, respectively.[22] Here, too, his Jesuit school grammar likely resonates, in which these letters were also termed *aspiratae* (Gretser 1593: 7).

In conclusion, de Rhodes's case seems to indicate that at least some early modern grammarians did not have a monolithic Graeco-Latin model in mind when describing languages other than the classical ones.

4.   By way of conclusion: Some afterthoughts

In the present contribution, I have simply wanted to field the question as to whether the designation "Graeco-Latin model" can be maintained or whether it would be preferable to simply speak of the "Latin model" or the "traditional parts-of-speech model", given the fact that descriptions of Greek could serve as a clearly separate source of inspiration, as the case of Alexandre de Rhodes seems to suggest (just like Jean Pillot's sixteenth-century French grammar). One could moreover ask oneself whether it is desirable to evoke every time the Greek origin of the descriptive framework missionary grammarians used by speaking of the "Graeco-Latin model", when in most cases they did not refer at all to Greek grammar in their linguistic works (cf. also Peetermans 2020: 301), and only few of them had mastered this ancient language. What is more, historiographers speaking of the "Graeco-Latin model" often seem to presuppose that it is a kind of monolithic platonic idea or, at least, might convey this impression, whether they want to or not. This idealized model contrasts with the emphasis these same historiographers frequently put on the flexible usage of traditional grammar among missionaries. It seems more fruitful not to start from one such platonic model but to consider the circumstances under which missionary grammarians were confronted with, and educated in, the art of grammar, often at an early age. Their education, their confession, their native tongue, and the foreign language they described are all factors to be taken into account in trying to reach an adequate picture of what they considered to be their

---

22. De Rhodes (1651b: 4): "habet igitur hæc lingua tres aspiratas sicuti lingua Græca". See also the document from 1632, quoted in footnote 18 above, and the contribution of P. De Troia and Zwartjes in this volume.

grammaticographic model. The very fact that these circumstances were diversified suggests that even though they all started from a model in which the parts of speech took center stage, the specificities of this model could greatly vary among scholars of different backgrounds. As a result, the exact interpretation of the model acquired various shapes across different periods, regions, education practices, and confessional dividing lines. In other words, one should perhaps not speak of "*the* Graeco-Latin model" but rather assess for each author individually what they considered to be their model, a judgment that should be firmly grounded in a study of their background, education, and confession.

The issue at stake here is obviously not limited to missionary linguistics but is relevant to the historiography of linguistics as a whole. Nonetheless, the matter is particularly pressing in the case of missionary linguistics, where the model status of the parts-of-speech framework is a more obvious and almost inevitable issue. In order to counter the rather loose and ambiguous uses of the phrase "Graeco-Latin model", one could, for instance, take the pains to explicitly define how exactly one conceives of it. This practice would, I believe, lead to a more straightforward meta-historiographical discourse and would force the historiographer to reconsider how Greek the so-called Graeco-Latin model actually is.

Acknowledgements

I thank Otto Zwartjes for his detailed and helpful comments on earlier drafts of this paper.

Funding

This paper is an outcome of my junior postdoctoral fellowship funded by the Research Foundation –, Flanders (FWO), project 12V4818N, entitled "The cross-linguistic application of grammatical categories: The early modern genesis of a contemporary problem, with specific reference to the relevance of 'typically Ancient Greek' categories (ca. 1470–1800)".

References

A.   Primary sources

Gretser, Jacob. 1593. *Institutionum de octo partibus orationis, syntaxi et prosodia Græcorum, Libri Tres*. Ingolstadii: Excudebat Dauid Sartorius.

Lundbæk, Knud. 1988. *The Traditional History of the Chinese Script from a Seventeenth Century Jesuit Manuscript*. Aarhus: Aarhus University Press.

Rhodes, Alexandre de. 1650. *Relazione De' felici successi della Santa Fede predicata da' padri della Compagnia di Giesù nel regno di Tunchino [...]*. In Roma: per Giuseppe Luna.

Rhodes, Alexandre de. 1651a. *Dictionarium Annnamiticum [sic], Lusitanum et Latinum [...]*. Romae: typis, & sumptibus eiusdem Sacr. Congreg.

Rhodes, Alexandre de. 1651b. "Linguae Annamiticae seu Tunchinensis brevis declaratio". In de Rhodes (1650; 1651a).

[?Sibin], [Philipp]. ca. 1745. "Manuductio ad Linguam Tunckinensem", Lisbon, Biblioteca da Ajuda, collection "Jesuítas na Ásia", Codex Ms. 49-VI-8, 313ᴿ–323ᵛ.

B.   Secondary sources

Aleksiejuk, Katarzyna. 2016. "Pseudonyms". *The Oxford Handbook of Names and Naming* ed. by Carole Hough, 438–452. Oxford: Oxford University Press.

Collani, Claudia von. 1994. "RHODES, Alexandre de, SJ". *Biographisch-bibliographisches Kirchenlexikon* ed. by Friedrich Wilhelm Bautz and Traugott Bautz, vol. 8, 151–153. Hamm: Traugott Bautz.

Compère, Marie-Madeleine & Dominique Julia. 1984. "84 AVIGNON, collège de plein exercice". *Bibliothèque Historique de l'Éducation* 10:1.90–98.

Fernandes, Gonçalo & Carlos Assunção. 2017. "First Codification of Vietnamese by 17th-century Missionaries: The Description of Tones and the Influence of Portuguese on Vietnamese Orthography". *Histoire Épistémologie Langage* 39:1.155–176. https://doi.org/10.1051/hel/2017390108

Klein, Wolf Peter. 2001. "Die linguistische Erfassung des Hebräischen, Chinesischen und Finnischen am Beginn der Neuzeit: Eine vergleichende Studie zur frühen Rezeption nicht-indogermanischer Sprachen in der traditionellen Grammatik". *Historiographia Linguistica* 28:1/2.39–64. https://doi.org/10.1075/hl.28.1.05kle

Klöter, Henning. 2011. *The Language of the Sangleys: A Chinese Vernacular in Missionary Sources of the Seventeenth Century*. Leiden & Boston: Brill. https://doi.org/10.1163/9789004195929

Law, Vivien. 2003. *The History of Linguistics in Europe: From Plato to 1600*. Cambridge: Cambridge University Press. https://doi.org/10.1017/CBO9781316036464

Peetermans, Andy. 2020. The Art of Transforming Traditions: Conceptual Developments in Early Modern American Missionary Grammar Writing. Unpublished Ph.D dissertation (KU Leuven).

Percival, W. Keith. 1995. "The Genealogy of General Linguistics". *History of Linguistics 1993: Papers from the Sixth International Conference on the History of the Language Sciences (ICHoLS VI), Washington D.C., 9–14 August 1993* ed. by Kurt R. Jankowsky, 47–54. Amsterdam & Philadelphia: John Benjamins. https://doi.org/10.1075/sihols.78.09per

Pham, Thi Kieu Ly. 2018. *La grammatisation du vietnamien (1615–1919): Histoire des grammaires et de l'écriture romanisée du vietnamien.* Ph.D. dissertation (Sorbonne Paris Cité).

Pham, Thi Kieu Ly. 2019. "The True Editor of the *Manuductio ad linguam Tunkinensem* (Seventeenth- to Eighteenth-Century Vietnamese Grammar)". *Journal of Vietnamese Studies* 14:2.68–92. https://doi.org/10.1525/vs.2019.14.2.68

Phan, Peter C. 1998. *Mission and Catechesis: Alexandre de Rhodes and Inculturation in Seventeenth-Century Vietnam.* (= *Faith and Cultures Series.*) Maryknoll: Orbis.

Price, David Hotchkiss. 2003. *Albrecht Dürer's Renaissance: Humanism, Reformation, and the Art of Faith.* Ann Arbor: University of Michigan Press. https://doi.org/10.3998/mpub.17733

Raini, Emanuele. 2010. *Sistemi di romanizzazione del cinese mandarino nei secoli XVI–XVIII.* Ph.D. dissertation. Studi Asiatici, XXII ciclo, Facoltà di Studi Orientali, Sapienza – Università di Roma.

Scaglione, Aldo. 1986. *The Liberal Arts and the Jesuit College System.* Amsterdam & Philadelphia: John Benjamins. https://doi.org/10.1075/z.26

Schatz, Klaus. 2015. „… *Dass diese Mission eine der blühendsten des Ostens werde…*": *P. Alexander de Rhodes (1593–1660) und die frühe Jesuitenmission in Vietnam.* Münster: Aschendorff.

Swiggers, Pierre & Alfons Wouters, eds. 1996. *Ancient Grammar: Content and Context.* Leuven & Paris: Peeters.

Zwartjes, Otto. 2011. *Portuguese Missionary Grammars in Asia, Africa and Brazil, 1550–1800.* Amsterdam & Philadelphia: John Benjamins. https://doi.org/10.1075/sihols.117

PART IV

India

Mood and modality in 17th century missionary grammars of Tamil

The subjunctive and the imperative

Cristina Muru
University of Tuscia

1. Early missionary grammars of Tamil: State of the art

It is unnecessary to reiterate the value of missionary grammars and dictionaries for the History of the Language Sciences, or to provide references about the state of the art of missionary linguistics, with the most recent excursus offered by Zwartjes (2012) being more than comprehensive in this case. However, before discussing in detail the main topic of this contribution, it is useful to give a brief summary of the available scientific works on Tamil missionary grammars, which are presented here in chronological order.[1]

The pioneering work on the Western contribution to the description of Tamil is found in Meenakshisundaram (1974), while a broad perspective about the Portuguese descriptions of the languages of Asia, as well as of Africa and Brazil, between the 16th and the 18th century, is found in Zwartjes (2011: 28–45) who also provides detailed information about missionary grammars on Tamil.

Regarding missionary works on Tamil, in 1982 Vermeer published the earliest grammar available today, *Arte da lingua Malabar*,[2] written in Portuguese[3] by

---

1. The present state of the art as summarized here, is not comprehensive, since the focus here is only on Tamil grammars and does not take into consideration lexicographical works on Tamil for which I refer the reader to Thany Nayagam (1964; 1966), Chevillard (2015, 2017 and 2021), James (2000 and 2009), Van Hal (2019) and Zwartjes (2011: 270–276). For the descriptions of other Indian languages, see Van Hal (2016 and 2019), Fernandes (2019), Ciotti (2019), Mastrangelo (2018), and Pytlowany (2018).

2. This grammar, as well as many others composed between the 16th and 17th centuries remained unpublished. In Blackburn (2003) there is a detailed account of printed missionary works in India.

3. According to Thani Nayagam (1966) it corresponds to the manuscript Cod. 3141, Lisbon National Library.

https://doi.org/10.1075/sihols.130.10mur

the Jesuit Henrique Henriques (1520–1600). The same *Arte* was translated into English in 2013 by Heine (†) and Rajam. Bartholomäus Ziegenbalg's (1682–1719) *Grammatica Damulica* (1716) written in Latin was also translated into English by Jeyaraj in 2010,[4] while a semi-diplomatic edition of the Portuguese grammar by Balthasar da Costa (ca. 1610–1673) along with its annotated and commented English translation by the author of this paper will hopefully be published soon.

Apart from translations, different papers on various aspects of missionary works such as the treatment of the adjective, the noun, the description of the Tamil case system, verb classification and paradigms, aspect and mood auxiliaries have also been published recently (Chevillard 1992a; b, 2021; James 2007 and 2019; Muru 2010 and 2021).

This contribution aims to provide an insight into the description of the Tamil imperative and subjunctive in two missionary grammars within the Latin grammatical framework. One of the two *Artes* discussed here was composed by the Jesuits Balthasar da Costa (ca. 1610–1673). As regards the second, two missionaries should be mentioned: the Jesuit Gaspar de Aguilar (1548–?) and the Protestant Philippus Baldaeus (1632–1671). Since the authorship of this second text has not yet been fully ascertained, in the next sections, it will be referred with an acronym representing both fathers (i.e. GA/PB). Five manuscript copies are extant of the former, while only one manuscript is known of the latter.[5] Balthasar da Costa, who was Superior of the Madurai mission from 1649 to 1656, also composed a dictionary of Tamil along with the grammar which were printed in Ambalacat around 1680, but no copies are extant (James 2000: 96). Gaspar de Aguilar worked in Goa and in the Cardiva residence in Jaffna and according to Streit (1929: 210), he composed a grammar entitled *Arte Tamul, sive institutio grammaticae Malabaricae* which was frequently referred to by other grammarians. As I pointed out in Muru (2020: 60), Cod. Orient. 283 is a composite manuscript (74+8 folios) including: a title page (f. 1r), *Arte Tamul, sive institutio grammatica linguae marabaricae*; a *Preface* (f. 1v); a *Tamil Arte* which runs to 42 folios numbered by the same hand that wrote the year 1665 on the title page. The *Arte* includes *Letras* (Letter, ff. 2r–6r), *Declinações* ['Declensions', ff. 7r–18r'], *Verbos* ['Verbs', ff. 18r–42v']; *Arte de escrever Tamul* ['Art of writing in Tamil', ff. 42[43]r–49r'] ending with *1665 pilippi valateyucu* (Philippus Baldaeus). The remaining folios include bilingual Portuguese-Tamil texts, such as formulas and words used during Sacraments, prayers asked during Confession, followed by a list of numbers in Tamil, some

---

4.　For Ziegenbalg see also Jeyaray (2006) and Sweetman (2012).

5.　For detailed information about Costa's life and his impact on other works, consult Chakravarti (2014), Muru (2010, 2018, 2020: 60, footnote 6; in preparation). For Aguilar's life and manuscript Cod. Orient. 283 I refer to Francis (2011), Muru (2014 and 2020: 61–63), and Pytlowany (2018).

other prayers and – in a different hand – some folios for writing and practicing letters. Philippus Baldaeus was a pastor of the Dutch Reformed Church and appointee of the Dutch East India Company in Sri Lanka. According to James (2007: 173), Baldaeus authored also a work entitled "Prodromus Grammaticus" in 1672, included in his work *Naauwkeurige Beschryvinge van Malabar en Chromandel* (James 2007: 173; Muru 2020: 61).

This paper aims to highlight how these two missionaries extended the Latin model of reference in the description of verb mood with a focus on the imperative and the subjunctive, in order to point out how they contributed to the History of the Language Sciences in general, and the history of descriptions of the Tamil language in particular, and finally, their influence on later works, which also influenced the grammar of Giuseppe Costantino Beschi (1680–1747).

2. The Latin framework and the Tamil language

For the description of Tamil,[6] both Da Costa (henceforth BC) and Aguilar/Baldaeus (GA/PB) used the categories of the Latin grammatical model. Indeed, the Latin framework was applied by missionaries in their descriptions of non-European languages from the 16th century onwards, in the same way as European vernaculars had been described, like Greek grammar had been adapted to the *grammaticization* of the Latin language. The process of *grammaticization* during Humanism had led to what Law (2003: 232–241) considered as its main innovation: the awareness that any vernacular language could achieve the same 'perfection' of Latin through its codification within the Latin grammatical framework. At the same time, this had also represented the incipit for the most significant *technological revolution* (Auroux 1994), as it became the *Zeitgeist* within which grammars of many non-European languages all around the world were later composed through the lens of the Latin grammar. It also became the medium through which the Science of Language developed, since "the accumulation of knowledge of 'exotic' language structures led to a deeper understanding of language in general" (Bossong 2007: 141). The Portuguese missionary grammars are not an exception. They are written within the Latin framework, although it is sometimes difficult to find the sources of inspiration,

---

6. In this paper, when the main features of Tamil are discussed, I refer to the formal written variety of Modern Tamil. However, the reader should be aware of the fact that the Tamil language described by missionaries was never one single variety of Tamil, but rather elements from the spoken Tamil intertwined with those of the formal variety. Very few elements can be addressed to Classical Tamil, at least in the two grammars analysed in this article. For a detailed discussion of Tamil triglossia see Chevillard (2021: 2–5).

since missionary grammarians did not always mention them by name and many sources could have served as model.

Regarding India, as discussed in Muru (2020), both BC and GA/PB used Manuel Álvares's (1526–1583) *Ars minor* (1573)[7] as a model. In observing missionary grammars of non-European languages, the consideration of the influence derived from other texts is important as not only does it help us to understand their contribution to the study of language, but it also helps us to comprehend the general theory within which these 'newly' discovered languages were described (Koerner 2014: 59). The process of *grammaticization* occurred through the transfer of elements of metalanguage, conceptual domains, *modus operandi*, and elements of structure and organization (cf. Aussant 2017: 8–14) which were sometimes extended.

Comparing the structure and organization of BC's and GA/PB's *Artes* with Álvares's *Ars minor* (1573)[8] one may observe how both texts start with the declension of the noun, the pronoun, and the adjectives; subsequently, they give the verb paradigm and identify the 'accidents' of the verb. GA/PB ends here their description of the language and, as stated above, the *Arte* continues with an *Arte de escrever Tamul* ['Grammar for writing Tamil'] preceding the bilingual reproduction of some Christian religious texts (Cod. Orient. 283, ff. 42r[43]-65r), while BC continues describing the indeclinable parts of speech which find no place whatsoever in GA/PB.

Not only the structure and organization, but also the application of a common conceptual and categorical apparatus based on Álvares can be found in the description of Tamil by BC and GA/PB. Although these similarities determined a remarkable homogeneity among the missionary grammars of Tamil, as well as among missionary grammars of other languages in general, the descriptions of the ensemble of the 'newly' discovered languages, in this case Tamil, and the efforts made in describing its linguistic features also led to the modification and adaptation of existing categories or to the invention of new ones (Fournier & Raby 2014: 337).

---

7.   Álvares's *Ars minor* was an abridged version of his *De Institvtione Grammatica Libri Tres* [Foundations of Grammar, three books] (1572). *Ars minor* was the Latin manual used in the Jesuit schools, colleges, and universities. The existence of the 1573 first edition of a manual written for "the boys as well as the poor who cannot buy the bigger ones" (letter of Álvares dated back 1572 and quoted in Kemmler 2015: 5) was proven only recently, after Kemmler found its single existing copy in 2011 in the *Biblioteca Geral da Universidade de Coimbra* with call number V.T.–18–7–3 (Kemmler 2015: 1–19).

8.   A table reproducing and comparing the contents in Álvares (1573), as well as Barros (1540), with BC and GA/PB among others is found in Muru (2021). For a discussion on the impact of Álvares's grammar for the description of the indigenous language of Portuguese America see Zwartjes (2002).

What are the linguistic peculiarities of the language that BC and GA/PB were describing?[9] Although general agreement has yet to be reached on how many parts of speech are present in Tamil (Lehmann 1989: 9; Annamalai and Steever 1998: 116),[10] their difference compared with Latin and Portuguese is unquestionable. Hence, as Lehmann (1989) states, from a purely formal point of view, all words included in the parts of speech can be categorized into inflected and uninflected word classes: only verbs and nouns can be specified for inflectional categories and form of nominal or verbal root; adjectival or adverbial root. Morphological processes only apply in nouns and verbs and inflection works differently in comparison to both Latin and Portuguese, where it is in the final endings. In fact, it occurs in the morpho-phonological changes which noun or verb stems undergo before taking the categories of case and number (for noun) or of tense for verb, which also takes person, number, gender, and other markers.[11]

From a morphological point of view, all the other parts of speech such as postposition, adjectives, adverbs (represented by a restricted class of few items),[12] quantifiers, determiners, and conjunctions (cf. *infra*) are uninflected words historically derived from the reanalysis of inflected or uninflected nominal, verbal, and adjectival roots.[13] Among these, postpositions are formally uninflected or inflected noun forms or non-finite verb forms that "form a very heterogenous set, ranging from bound forms […] through invariable forms functioning as adverbs […] to inflected noun forms" (Asher 1985: 104). Whereas, there is only a restricted number of co-ordinating conjunction words which are derived from the grammaticalization of verb forms, syntactically reanalyzed (i.e. *āṉāl* 'but' < conditional of *āku* 'to

---

9. For descriptions of Modern Tamil see Lehmann (1989), Annamalai and Steever (1998: 550–558); for old Tamil see Andronov (1969), Krishnamurti (2003), Lehmann (1998), and Wilden (2018); for spoken Tamil see Schiffman (1999) and Asher (1985). This list does not pretend to be exhaustive.

10. The Tamil traditional grammar (*Tolkāppiyam,* 1st-3rd cent. A.D.) recognizes four parts of speech. See Chevillard (1992b: 37).

11. Furthermore, Tamil has both morphological and syntactical causatives and some verbs also display a voice morpheme which distinguishes, – using Paramasivam's (1979) terminology –, between *affective* and *effective* verbs. See Muru (2021) for a discussion on how missionaries dealt with these features of Tamil.

12. Both represented by a restricted group of adjectival and adverbial roots. Derived adjectives are found in grammatical construction N + adjectival participle, while a number of inflected noun and verb forms are syntactically reanalysed to sentential adverbs (cf. Lehmann 1989: 131–146).

13. Annamalai and Steever (1998: 116) considers arbitrary to talk about parts of seepch such as adjective, adverb, conjunction, particle and postposition because "many forms included in these minor parts of speech transparently derive from nouns or verbs".

become'). Indeed, co-ordination in Tamil is realized by clitics which are bound forms, hence particles and not words.

At the syntactical level, Tamil forms complex sentences through embedding and adjoining of a clause (in)to another sentence. In this regard, complementation and nominalization, thus non-finite verbs and nominalized verb forms play an important role in the construction of complex sentences. In fact, a clause can be embedded as co-constituent or complement to the left side of a head constituent. Complementation is realized morphologically through non-finite verbs and nominalized verb forms; or syntactically through a series of complementising verbs, like *āku* ['to become'], *pōla* ['to resemble'], *ēṉ* ['to say'], or nouns (of time, space, manner); and also, through clause final clitics. Otherwise, a clause can be embedded into a noun phrase as the sole constituent of the noun phrase (nominalization). A nominalized clause appears in verbal noun form marked with an inflectional suffix (*-atu*).

In summary, Tamil greatly differs from Portuguese as well as from Latin which both make use of final inflection, conjunctions, and *consecutio temporum*: it is a left-branching and a tendentially agglutinative language and there are very few conjunctions, inflection is internal rather than final and there is no agreement of verbal tenses between the main and the subordinate clause. In the following section, I shall describe how the Latin framework is adapted to the Tamil verb, focusing on moods and modality.

3.   The description of verb moods

Tamil verb forms are classified as finite and non-finite verb, and nominalized verb forms. The former can be inflected for the categories of mood: imperative, optative, and indicative. Only some of the non-finite verb foms are inflected for tense. Hence, in the verbal inflection, the verbal categories are morphologically distinguished.

The imperative can be singular and plural, positive and negative. Only the indicative is inflected for tense, person, number, and gender (+ status) in the positive form, while it is tenseless in the negative. The optative is marked by a suffix added to the verb stem and occurs in all persons. Western grammarians applied latinate categories to the moods, and neither BC and GA/PB are an exception. These grammarians had to find an appropriate way for fitting them into the Latin categories. The framework was provided by Álvares's grammar, which distinguishes the following moods in Latin: *indicativus, imperativus, optativus, conjunctivus, potentialis* and *permissivus* (or *concessivus*) and *infinitivus*. Despite BC and GA/PB following Ál;vares's classification and conceptualizations, once they confronted the linguistic diversity of Tamil, they both needed to extend their model of reference. Evidence of this necessity, which Auroux (1994) labelled as "Grammaire Latine Étendue", is largely found in the description of verb moods. In this regard GA/PB starts the section of verbs as follows:

> No conjugar dos Verbos necessariamente avemos de por algûs modos differentes do latim, por q[ue] os tem esta lingoa, naõ os avendo no Latim, nē Portugues; e pello conseguinte aos tais modos avemos de dar alguns nomes novos. O que advertimos pera q[ue] nelles se naõ ache novo quê aprende. A força e enerzia delles declararà a significaçaõ, que lhe poremos cõ a brevidade, e utilidade possivel, deixando modos desusados, escuros, e duvidosos pera o tratado da Gramatica dos Verbos, que ira e seu lugar. [...].
>
> (GA/PB, Cod. Orient. 283, fol. 18r, lines 20–27)[14]

> [Conjugating the verbs, we hare obliged to add some moods that differ from the Latin ones because they are (peculiar) for this language and both Latin and Portuguese lack them. For this reason, we have to give new terms to these moods. In order not to create confusion for the language learner, we warn that the *strength* and *energy* [emphasis is mine] of the new terms will clearly declare the meaning of the verbs. We will give short and clear moods leaving all those more obsolete, obscure, and uncertain moods to the treatise of the Grammar of Verbs where they will find their own place.]

The treatment of verb moods in BC and GA/PB includes not only the classical paradigm of Latin and Portuguese but also some other forms which went beyond the grammatical model of reference leading to its extension (cf. Table 1):

Table 1. Some of the verbal moods in GA/PB and BC

GA/PB	BC
Modo dubitativo ou conveniente [Mandatory or Appropriate mood]	*Modo interrogativo* [Interrogative mood]
Modo meditativo ou contingente [Meditative or imminent mood]	*Modo cauzativo* [Causative mood]
Modo impossivel [Impossible mood]	*Modo asseverativo sem duvida* [Assertive mood without doubt]
Modo parcativo com sicut, assim como [Prudent mood, in *sicut,* just as]	*Modo de aptidão ou conveniência* [Attitude mood or of convenience]
Modo æquivalente [Equivalent mood]	*Modo comparativo* [Comparative mood]

---

14. Citations in this paper, taken from Costa (1670), Costa (1685) and Aguilar Baldaeus (1659–1665), will respect the orthographic and typographic characteristics of the original texts.

Furthermore, GA/PB also explains that only the finite verb must come at the end of the sentence, while all the 'compound verbs' formed with *gerundios* ['gerunds'] corresponding to the Tamil non-finite verbal participle, should precede it:

> Assi dizem tambem *choliconduvarugren* etc. eu fallo, *pejicōduvarugren* etc. eu pratico, e outros muitos. He modo de fallar muito elegante, e usado atraça delle he por dous gerundios, hū dos simplex, outro do verbo *collugradu*, e acrescentara ambos o Verbo *vařugradu*, que quer dizer Vir; e todos estes Verbos assi postos huā composiçaō tem elegantissimamente so a significaçaō do primeiro simplex conjugandose somente o *vařugradu* conforme a conjugaçaō ordinaria que puzemos.
>
> (GA/PB, Cod. Orient. 283, f. 38v, lines 8–15)
>
> [In the same way they say *choliconduvarugren* [collikkoṇṭuvarukirēn], etc. 'I speak'; *pejicōduvarugren*;[15] 'I practice', and many others. This way of speaking is very elegant and commonly used. Its arrangement is to have two gerunds, one of the simple [verb] and another of the verb *collugradu* [collukkiṟatu]. Hence, we have to add to both these verbs the simple form of the verb varü gradu [varukkiṟatu] which means to come is added to both. In this manner all the verbs placed in this way form a composition which very elegantly has only the meaning of the first simple verb and we conjugate only the (last) *varügradu* [varukkiṟatu] according to the ordinary rules of conjugation that we have already given.]

Hence, the different kinds of Tamil verbs (*castas* 'castes') are clarified,[16] such as the *caste* of *meditative* and *reduplicative* verbs which include Tamil auxiliaries such as those for the formation of causative (i.e. INF + *cey* 'do') and passive voice (INF + *paṭu* 'experience'),[17] and another *caste* (the *neuter*) where one finds the morphemes used for the derivation of morphological causative verbs (i.e. *-vi-/-pi-*). Each identified verbal form is named according to the meaning it has after taking the derivational morpheme or the auxiliary verb with which it is compounded.

---

15. This is a dubious form. According to the translation provided by GA/PB one should consider *payiṉrukkoṇṭuvarukirēṉ* as the corresponding form for which the transcription into Latin alphabet represents the spoken form with a palatalization of glide + anterior high vowel. However this would not explain the fall of the verbal participle morpheme. Hence, the other possiblity would be to consider this form as representative of the spoken variant of 'to speak': *pēcikkoṇṭuvarukirēṉ*. Since it is not relevant to the scope of this paper, the topic related to the correct interpretation of the spoken variant represented by GA/PB transcription will not be discussed any further.

16. GA/PB distinguishes between *Verbos compostos activos* ['compound active verbs'] where *meditative* and *reduplicative* verbs are included, and *Verbos compostos passivos* ['compound passive verbs'] where the neuter compound verbs belong.

17. Other auxiliaries that GA/PB describes are the modal ones (INF + *pō* 'go'= intention), the aspectual auxiliaries (verbal participle + *koṇṭu* 'hold' + *vā* 'come'= durative; Verbal noun + *āku* 'to become'= inceptive; Verbal participle + *iru* 'be'= prefect/progressive), and the attitudinal ones (verbal participle + *pō* 'go'= change of state).

Ha outra casta de Verbos compostos a que podemos chamar *meditativos*, [emphasis is mine], porq[ue] significaçaõ naõ fazer acçaõ, mas estar, ou tratar de fazer.

(GA/PB, Cod. Orient. 283 f. 38v lines *17–19*)

[There is another group of compounded verbs that we can call *meditative* because they do not mean 'to accomplish an action', rather they mean 'to be going to do' or 'to have the intention to do' something.]

Achase outra casta muy ordinaria de Verbos, a que podemos chamar *reduplicativos*; [emphasis is mine], por significarē naõ fazer, mas fazer fazer a acçaõ significada pello simplez. Estes saõ compostos; ou derivados de si mesmos, cõ acrecentamento de huã syllaba … E cõ as taes addições ficaõ significando fazer fazer aquillo.

(GA/PB, Cod. Orient. 283 f. 38v, lines 32–37 & f. 39r, lines 5–6)

[One finds another very ordinary group of verbs, which we can call *reduplicativos* since they do not mean 'to do', rather 'to make someone to do the action expressed by the simple verb'. These are compounded or they are derived from their own forms adding a syllable… and with these additions they become [verbs] meaning 'to make/ to cause [someone] to do what the simple verb means'.]

Falta huã so casta de Verbos compostos a que podemos chamar *neutros*, [emphasis is mine] porq[ue] ainda depois da composição ficão so com significação de neutros.

(GA/PB, Cod. Orient. 283 f. 39v, lines 5–8)

[It is missing only one other caste of compounded verbs that we may call *neuter* because after composition they also remain only with a neuter meaning.]

What emerges so far in these passages is that the main criteria behind the extension of the verb mood taxonomy in Cod. Orient. 283 is morphological as well as semantic. In this *Arte* the internal structure of the verb form is highlighted. In the same way, the morpheme through which the verb form is derived (i.e. causative verbs) is also identified. Finally, the verb compounding is also pointed out. In the combination of two verbs, the first one maintains its lexical meaning while the second one works as auxialiry: "e todos estes Verbos assi postos huã composiçaõ tem elegantissimamente so a significaçaõ do primeiro simplez" (GA/PB, Cod. Orient. 283f. 38v, lines 13–15) ['In this manner all the verbs placed in this way form a composition which very elegantly retains only the meaning of the first simple verb'].

The same criteria also apply in the description of the imperative, as well as the subjunctive as will be discussed below.

4. The imperative mood

In presenting the first conjugation (*Amo verbum activum*), Álvares (1572: ff. 15r-21v) identifies seven *modi: indicativus, imperativus, optativus, coniunctivus, potentialis, persmissivus sive consessivus, imperativus, infinitus.*

The imperative mood in Latin is used for expressing command and prohibition (Álvares 1572: ff. 17r-v) and is inflected for two tenses (*praesens* and *futurum vel potius modus mandativus*) and three persons in the present (the second and the third singular and plural and the first plural), and two persons (the second and third singular and plural) in the future tense (Álvares 1573: ff. 15v-16v). Unlike Latin, in Tamil the imperative is tenseless and distinguishes between positive and negative forms: a singular one which is identical with the bare verb stem, and a plural one marked by the person suffix *-(u)ṅkaḷ* which is also used for singular honorific.

Going on to consider how the imperative is described in the two missionary grammars, BC explains the imperative in the third section of his *arte* where he also explains the past and future tense and the plurals (MS 60, from f. M-34–22 to f. M-34–47) after having given all the verb forms corresponding to the imperative (cf. *infra*):

> A mais breves pontos rezumir[ei] a doutrina dos imperativos pois tẽ pouco mais q[ue] dizer do q[ue] na formaçaõ delles na Arte fica dito, donde todos de ordenario se tiraõ. So acrescento q[ue] os verbos acabados em crean, mudaõ o cren en cu quando tem o preterito em inen […] Alguñs imperativos saõ irregulares […] E outros poucos deste genero q[ue] no vocabulario teraõ seus imperativos especificados.
> (BC –,MS 60, f. M-34–45, Left column, line 31 and Right column, lines 1–22)

> [I will resume the doctrine of the imperatives very in brief, for there is little more to add to what has already been said about their formation in the Arte, from where all regular forms can be taken. I add only that the verbs ended in *cren,* change the *cren* into *cu* when they have the preterite in *inen* […] Some imperatives are irregular […] And a few more of this kind will have their own speficied imperatives in the Vocabulary.]

In GA/PB there is also a list of verb forms for each kind of imperative and a short explanation on its formation:

> O imperativo se forma tambem do præsente deitando fora o *cren,* ou *gren.* E esta regra parece por hora geral pera toda a casta de Verbos sic ex *vichuvadicren* deitando o *cren* fora, fica *vichuvadi* et ex *tarugren* deitando o *gren* fica *tarú,* que tambem se diz *ta.*   (GA/PB, Cod. Orient. 283, f. 40v, lines 32–34 & f. 41r, lines 1–3)

> [The imperative is formed also from the present removing *cren* (-kki̱rēṉ) or *gren* (-ki̱rēṉ). At the moment, this rule seems to be general and valid for all the castes [of verbs] so that *vichuvadicren* (vicuvātikki̱rēṉ)[18] becomes *vichuvadi* (vicuvāti) removing *cren* and from *tarugren* (taruki̱rēṉ) becomes *tarú* (taru) removing *gren,* whish is also found as *ta* (tā).]

Studying the imperative paradigm both in BC and GA/PB it is evident how Álvares's model is applied: both grammars distinguish an *imperativo permissivo*

---

18. *Vicuvadi* is the variant used by GA/PB for the verb stem *vicuvāci* 'to believe'. The latter has been used in the glossed examples.

and *prohibitivo*, both struggle in order to identify three persons in the present imperative (the second and the third singular and plural; the first plural). Nevertheless, at the same time, they extend their model of reference considering the peculiarities of the Tamil language. Therefore, if in GA/PB sticks to Álvares's categorization, there is still a present and a future imperative (cf. Table 2), in BC, there is already an awarness of a difference between Latin and Tamil is already there and the present tense is changed into *imperativo absoluto* ['absolute imperative'] without traces of the future tense. Furthermore, in both BC and GA/PB, some specific Tamil forms and thus new creative labels, such as "imperativo de benevolencia" ['imperative of benevolence'] or "imperativo com rogo ou familiaridade" ['imperative with plea or familiarity'], are proposed (cf. Table 2, also Figure 1).

Table 2. The taxonomy of imperative mood in GA/PB and BC

GA/PB		BC
Imperativo Imperative	*presente* present	*Imperativo absoluto* Absolute imperative
	futuro ou mandativo future or mandative	
Imperativo prohibitivo Prohibitive imperative		*Imperativo permissivo* Permissive imperative
Imperativo permissivo Permissive imperative (also negative)		*Imperativo prohibitivo* Prohibitive imperative
Imperativo de benevolencia Benevolence imperative		*Imperativo com rogo ou familiaridade* Imperative with plea or familiarity

These forms are attributed to each label on the basis of the strength of imposition with which the order is expressed (see *infra*) throughout the different elements which combine with the main verb, hence the present and future imperative as well as the prohibitive are forms which express command or prohibition, while the permissive and the benevolence are more forms which suggest to do or not to do something. The final result is that the imperative mood not only includes the Tamil imperative (cf. Table 3, in bold). For example, both grammars give different verbal forms obtained through derivation (and/or composition) and i.e. in GA/PB in the attempt of respecting the Alvaresian *mandativus* ['mandative'] there is the 'future imperative' or 'mandative' and it corresponds to a Tamil form which translates as a command in the future.[19]

---

19. The form is represented by the future of the indicative mood of the verb *vicuvāci* 'to believe' followed by the infinitive *āka* of the verb *āku* representing the optative form which literally would be translated as 'let become' giving 'let become to believe', or better, 'let believe'.

Table 3. The Imperative mood in GA/PB [e]

Present	Imperative Future or mandative	Prohibitive	Permissive	Benevolence [e]
	SINGULAR	SINGULAR	SING/PLURAL	SINGULAR
vicuvāti **believe.IMP[SG]** "believe you" gloss: *crè tu*	vicuvāti-pp-āy āka believe-FUT-2SG become.INF "be you, the one who will believe" gloss: *crereis vos*	**vicuvāt-āt-ē** **believe-NEG.IMP[SG]-EMPH** "do not believe" gloss: *não creas tù, não creias*	vicuvāti-kka-ṭṭu believe-INF-agree.HORT "let you/him/her/that/them/those believe" gloss: SG: *deixa crer/elle deixe crer/ella deixe crer/aquillo deixe crer* PL: *nos deixemos crer/vos deixai crer/eles, ellas deixam crer/ aquellas cousas deixê crer*	vicuvāti.y-ē believe.IMP[SG]-EMPH "just believe" gloss: *crè tu por tu vida*
Vicuvāti.y-aṭa believe.IMP-M.comrade "believe male comrade" gloss: *ou la crè tu homem*	vicuvāti-pp-aṇ āka believe-FUT-3SGM become.INF "be he, the one who will believe" gloss: *crerà elle*	vicuvāt-āt-āṭa believe-NEG.IMP[SG]-M.comrade "do not believe male comrade" gloss: *ou la não creas tu home*		**PLURAL** vicuvāti-unkaḷ-ē believe.IMP-PL-EMPH "just believe you" gloss: *crede vos por vida vossa*
vicuvāti.y-aṭi believe.IMP-F.comrade "believe female comrade" gloss: *ou la crè tu molher*	vicuvāti-pp-aḷ āka [b] believe-FUT-3SGF become.INF "be she, the one who will believe" gloss: *crerà ella*	vicuvāt-āt-āṭi believe-NEG.IMP[SG]-F.comrade "do not believe female comrade" gloss: *ou la não creas tu molher*		vicuvāti-pp-arkaḷ-ē believe-FUT-3PL/MF-EMPH "they will just believe" gloss: *creão ellas por vida sua*
HONORIFIC vicuvāti.y-um believe.OPT/HAB.FUT [a] "let him believe" gloss: *crea V(ossa) M(erce), Senhoria*	vicuvāti-pp-atu āka [b] believe-FUT-3SGN become.INF "be it, the thing which will believe" gloss: *crerse há, crerà aquillo*	**HONORIFIC** vicuvāt-āt-ē.y-um believe-NEG.IMP[SG]-CLIT "do not believe you also/all" gloss: *não crea V(ossa) M(erce), Senhoria*		**HONORIFIC** vicuvāti.y-um-ē believe-OPT/HAB.FUT-EMPH "just let him believe" gloss: *crea VM por vida Sua, por me fazer merce*

Table 3. (*continued*)

	Imperative	Future or mandative	Prohibitive	Permissive	Benevolence[e]
	Present	SINGULAR		SING/PLURAL	SINGULAR
SINGULAR	vicuvāti-kka believe-INF "may you believe" [c] gloss: *crea elle, ou crea S(ua) senhoria*	vicuvāti-pp-īr āka believe-FUT-2SG.HON become.INF "be you, the ones who will believe" gloss: *crerá V(ossa) M(ercé), V(ossa) S(enhoria)*			
			PLURAL vicuvāti-āt-ē uṅkoḷ believe-NEG.IMP[SG]-EMPH 2PL "do not believe you" gloss: *não creais [sic], não creais filho*		
PLURAL	vicuvāti-pp-ōm believe-FUT-1PL "we will believe" gloss: *creamos nos* vicuvāti.y-uṅkoḷ[d] believe.IMP-2PL **"believe you"** gloss: *crede vos*	vicuvāti-pp-ōm āka believe-FUT-1PL become.INF "be we, the ones who will believe" gloss: *creremos nos* vicuvāti-pp-īrkaḷ āka believe-FUT-3PL/MF become.INF "be them, the ones who will believe" gloss: *cream ellas, ellas*			

a. There is also another form which I have not identified that is *vicuvadiyumdai* that in GA/PB it is glossed with: *crede meu S(enh)or, crede meu filho, etc.* [Believe my Sir, believe my son, etc.

b. This form is also repeated in the plural neuter.

c. When infinitive form occurs as predicate of a simple clause expresses the optative mood.

d. The expected morpheme in formal Tamil should be *-uṅkaḷ*. My supposition at the moment is that this is a dialectal variant, supposedly the Brahmin dialect. However, this issue being beyond the scope of this paper and deserving its own study, it will not be discussed further here.

e. The negative form is given only for the permissive imperative and the imperative of benevolence.

On the other hand, BC not only gives derived forms but also verb compounds (V+V) (cf. Table 4, in bold). Hence, some forms overlap with those already found in GA/PB, while others differ. Table 4 resumes these similarities (=) and dissimilarities (≠) traceable both in the terminology the missionaries used as well as in the corresponding Tamil forms they gave for the same label.

Table 4. The imperative mood in BC: Similarities and dissimilarities with GA/PB

Imperative absolute (≠)		Prohibitive (=)		Permissive (=)	With plea or familiarity (≠)
=	≠	=	≠	=	≠
non honorific singular imperative gloss: *cré tu*	BC does not have the forms in *aṭi/ aṭa*	the singular negative gloss: *[tu] naõ creas*	BC gives the singular negative in *aṭi*	**The auxiliary** *oṭṭu* 'agree' **or 'be suitable'** (2) gloss: *deixe tu, elle, ella, aquillo crer* The auxiliary *oṭṭu* 'agree'	BC gives the positive singular or plural imperative followed by the suffix *ēṉ* < int. 'why' (4.a) no gloss
second singular future + āka gloss: *cré tu*	BC does not differentiate between present and future	the plural negative gloss: *naõ creyais vos outros*	BC gives the negative verbal participle (3.b) gloss: *[tu] naõ creas*	or 'be suitable' + *-um/-uṅkoḷ* gloss: *deixe V[ossa] M[erc]ê crer/ deixai vos outros crer*	BC gives the clitic *-ō* that transforms a declarative statement into a dubitative one (4.b) no gloss
Infinitive gloss: *crea V[ossa] M[erc]ê*	BC gives here the same form found in the *permissive* (2)	the optative or adjectival participle	**BC gives the auxiliary verb** *vēṇṭam* (3.c) gloss: *[tu] naõ creas*		
1st plural future tense gloss: *creamos nos*	**BC gives here the auxiliary** *kaṭavatu* 'that should be done' (1) gloss: *creya elle creaõ elles*	the negative imperative with clitic *-um* (3.d) gloss: *naõ creas V[ossa] M[erce]*			
Honorific imperative singular/ plural imperative gloss: *crea V[ossa] M[erc]ê/ Crede vos*					

As stated above, each label is attributed different linguistic forms that are characterized for having a reduced strength in the force of command or order, this fact is particularly evident in BC. In fact, the *absolute imperative*, apart from the Tamil imperative, also includes a compound verb with the auxiliary *kaṭavatu* 'should not, duty'[20] (1) expressing a duty internal to the speaker; the *prohibitive imperative*, apart from the negative Tamil imperative (3.a), also includes a negative verbal participle (3.b), the auxiliary *vēṇṭam* expressing a duty external to the speaker (3.c), and also a full sentence (3.e). The Alvaresian label *permissive* is represented by a Tamil compound verb where the auxiliary expresses the hortative aspect (2), while the *Imperative with plea or familiarity* includes forms which are not identified in GA/PB. These are the interrogative pronoun *why* (4.a) which "when suffixed to an imperative form, changes the command or request expressed by the imperative into a suggestion" (Lehmann 1989: 57), and the clitic *-ō* that transforms a declarative statement into a dubitative one (4.b). Therefore, the latter corresponds to linguistic forms where the imposition or the command is mitigated.

(1) vicuvāti-kka.k-kaṭav-arkaḷ
     believe-INF-duty-.3PL/MF
     "they should believe"

(2) vicuvāti-kka-ṭṭu[21]
     believe-INF-HORT
     "let him believe"[21]

(3) a. *vicuvāci.y-āt-ē*
         believe-NEG.IMP[SG]-EMPH
         "do not believe"
     b. vicuvāci.y-āmal
         believe-NEG.CVB
         "not having believed"
     c. vicuvāci-kka vēṇṭām
         believe-INF   want-NEG.3SG.N
         "I/you/… do not want to believe"
     d. vicuvāci.y-ātē.y-um
         believe-NEG.IMP-CLIT.HORT
         "do not believe your mercy!"

---

20. This meaning is found in Beschi (1738 [1728]; Mahon 1848 [1728], (cf. *infra*) and in the Madras Tamil Lexicon (=MTL, 1982 [1929–1939]), while Cre-A: (2020 [1992]: 308) dictionary lists it as an auxiliary expressing an optative.

21. In Modern Tamil *oṭṭu* 'agree' is fully grammaticalized into a modal auxiliary (Lehmann 1989: 214–215).

    e. nāṅ-kaḷ vicuvāci-kka.t tēvai.y ill-ai
        1PL-EXCL believe-INF   desire not be-3PL
        "we do not have the desire of believing"

(4) a. *vicuvāci*   *ēṉ*
        believe.IMP[SG] Q
        "Why do not I/you…believe?" = suggestion
    b. vicuvāc-ikka vēṉṭām-ō
        believe-INF   want-NEG.3SG.N-DUB
        "I doubt whether I/you/… believe"

The semantic value of each imperative is connected to the element taken by the verb stem, i.e. the modal auxiliary, the suffix, the clitic, resulting in the derivation of verbal forms which cannot be considered only commands to the addressee, but rather statements, wishes, requests, and suggestions to follow an instruction. In this light, if one adheres to Palmer's (2001) definition that mood is a grammaticalization of modality across languages, whereas modality is a semantic domain, one can consider the imperative in these *Arte* as the modality within which several morphologically differentiated verb types, expressing commands, questions, statements, and wish, find their place.

The progressiveness in the modality of command or obligation, to which only the true imperative corresponds, emerges in several verbal forms summarized in Figure 1. The labels – *command, affirmation, question, wish* – are representative of a continuum along which the degree of the intensity in the 'command strength' expressed by the imperative of the verb *vicuvāci* ['to believe'] followed by an 'x element' varies.

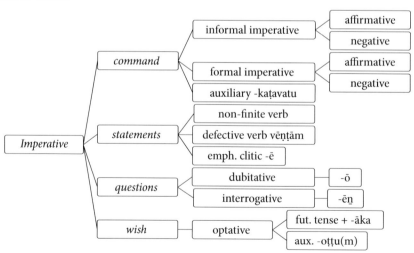

Figure 1. Taxonomy of the imperative mood in BC

5. The subjunctive mood

In the description of the imperative, the linguistic diversity missionaries found in the Tamil language led them to the extension of the traditional framework and the invention of new categories, an extended terminology, and methods of categorization. A similar result can also be observed in the description of the paradigm of the subjunctive mood.

The Alvaresian subjunctive is the finite mood of *irrealis*, hence of subjectivity. When used independently it expresses a thought, an intention or a possibility assuming in this way different functions such as exhortative-prescriptive, optative-desiderative, concessive, potential, dubitative and conditional. However, the subjunctive is mainly the typical mood used for subordination of completive and circumstantial clauses (temporal, causal, final, consecutive, conditional, concessive, and also relative). It combines with subordinate conjunctions and it is inflected for tenses and PNG markers. When used in subordination, the tense directly depends on that of the verb of the main clause (*consecutio temporum*). Álvares (1573: ff. 10v–12v) highlights this feature of the subjunctive which, if compared to the other finite verbs, is the only one which cannot stand alone. As the term 'subjunctive' suggests it must be conjoined, subjuncted, or added to another verb to which it is connected through conjunctive particles like *cum, quod, si, ni, nisi, quamvis, licet, ut, ne, quo, ut, dum,* or the relative *qui, quæ, quod.*

As already stated, Tamil verbs have no subjunctive mood and the formation of complex sentence involve other strategies, such as embedding or adjoining a clause (in)to another sentence, morphologically through the use of non-finite and nominalized and syntactically through a restricted number of complementising verbs and nouns. Finally, it also uses clause-final clitics as complement markers (Lehmann 1989: 250–256). Observing Tamil through the Latin grammar lens, missionaries needed to find a place for these linguistic strategies.

BC treats the subjunctive mood under 'morphology' and offers six different paradigms (cf. Figure 2) which are organized following the Alvaresian *modus operandi*.

The Tamil forms BC includes under the label subjunctive are characterized by similar features: they are non-finite verbs which cannot be the final predicate of a sentence but rather a predicate of an embedded clause; or they are elements which have the status of nominalizer or complementizer. Even though they do not correspond to the Latin category of subjunctive, they still need to be organized and "reduced" into *Arte* and the subjunctive is the mood where they can find a place because in Latin it is the mood of finite verbs which not always stand alone as independent verbs.

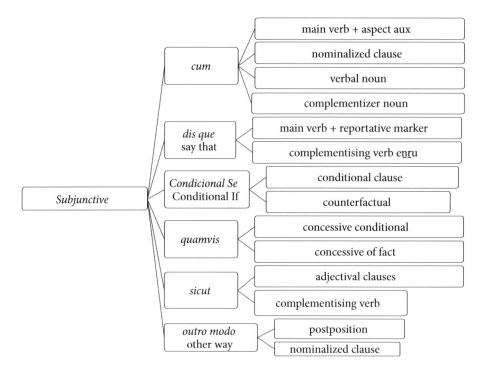

Figure 2. Subjunctive in BC

Hence, BC starts from the Latin subjunctive plus *cum, si, quamvis*:[22]

(5) a. vicuvāci-kkiṟ-a-poḷutu   *Subjunctive CUM*
         believe-PRS-ADJ.PTCP-**COMP**.time
         "when x believe(s)"
     b. vicuvācikk-um-iṭa-tt-il
         believe-FUT.ADJ.PTCP-**COMP**.place-OBL-LOC
         "when x believe(s)"

(6) a. nāṉ vicuvāci-tt-ēṉ-āṉāl   *Subjunctive SI*
         1SG believe-PST-1SG-become-COND.
         "If I believed"
     b. nāṉ vicuvāci-tt-āl   *Subjunctive SI*
         1SG believe-PST-COND
         "If I believe"
     c. vicuvāci.y-āmal-irunt-āl
         believe-NEG.CVB-be.PFV-COND.
         "If it had not believed"

---

22. The complete list of the Subjunctive forms is in Muru (in prep.).

(7) a. nān vicuvāci-tt-āl-um   *Subjunctive QUAMVIS*
        1SG believe-PST-COND-CONC
        "Even if I do/did not believe"

However, BC also needs to label some Tamil forms which cannot find a proper correspondence with the Latin subjunctive. He needs to extend the category and adds *subjunctive diz que* (say that) and *subjunctive sicut.*

(8) a. vicuvāci-kkir̠-ēn-ām   *Subjunctive diz que*
        believe-PRS-1SG-REPORT.
        "They say I believe"
    b. vicuvāci-kkir̠-ēn-en̠r̠u-colli-kir̠-arkaḷ
        believe-PRS-1SG-QUOT-say-PRS-3PL
        "They say that I believe"

(9) a. nān vicuvāci-kkum-pōl-ē   *Subjunctive SICUT*
        1SG believe-FUT-ADJ.PTCP- seem.INF-EMPH
        "As if I will believe"
    b. vicuvāci-kkir̠-a-paṭi-y-ē
        believe-PRS-ADJ.PTCP-way-EMPH
        "The way × believe(s) [exactly that way]"

The Tamil forms included in the subjunctive 'diz que' are the reportative marker *-ām* derived from the grammaticalization of the verb *āku* 'to become' and the verbal participle *en̠r̠u* of the verb *en̠* 'to say, to think'; while in the subjunctive *sicut* BC includes the infinitive *pōla* from the verb *pōl* 'seem, resemble' and the noun *paṭi* 'way'.

While *-ām* is a grammaticalized form which can only stand with a non-finite verb, both *en̠r̠u* and *pōla* have "the grammatical function of embedding a clause with a finite verb or a nominal as predicate into the structure of a sentence by marking the final boundary of the complement and linking to a head, thus they have a function similar to those of complementizers or subordination conjunctions in other languages" (Lehmann 1989: 314).

Among the verbal predicate with which the complementizing verb *en̠r̠u* occurs, there are the utterance verbs which are also found in BC's examples (8.a, 8.b). Here the missionary labels the subjunctive with Portuguese terminology rather than Latin, where the direct speech is reported through an *oratio obliqua*. In fact, the Portuguese label literally translates the functional word added to the finite form of the verb. On the other hand, the reportative marker *-ām*, which also occurs with utterance verbs, "can be added to various constituents to indicate that the speaker does not claim responsibility for the veracity of statement, but merely reports something" (Schiffman 1999: 152).

The other subjunctives, labelled with the correlative Latin adverb *sicut* 'such as, like' and the Latin conjunctions *cum, si,* and *quamvis* correspond to Tamil forms representative of complementising verbs (9.a), complementising noun (9.b), temporal (5.a, 5.b), conditional, (6.a, 6.b), negative counterfactual (6.c), and concessive (7.a) clauses.

Compared to BC, GA/PB expands further the taxonomy listing twelve kinds of subjunctives which are labelled on the basis of Latin and Portuguese conjunctions, and only partially overlap with the forms found in BC (cf. Figure 3).

The criteria GA/PB's *Arte* adopts for the identification relies on two principles: firstly it groups the different forms on the basis of their tense morpheme (present, past, future), and secondly on the basis of the meaning and function of the elements added to the verb.

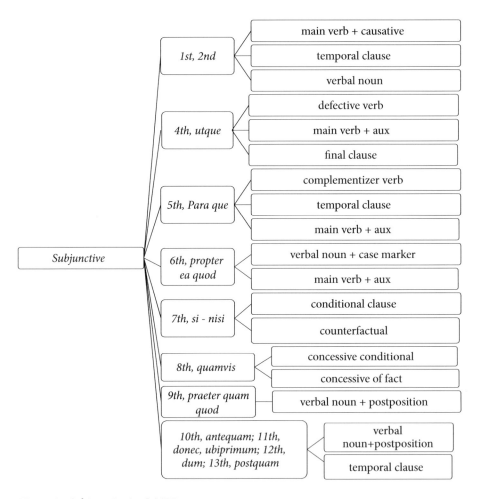

Figure 3. Subjunctive in GA/PB

The elements added to the verbal form, resumed in Figures 4 and 5, are representative of different Tamil linguistic elements, some of which are the morphological device that Tamil uses as a strategy for making a clause become a complement:
non-finite verbs (infinitive, verbal participle, conditional, adjectival participle),
nominalized verb forms, complementising nouns, and clause final clitics.

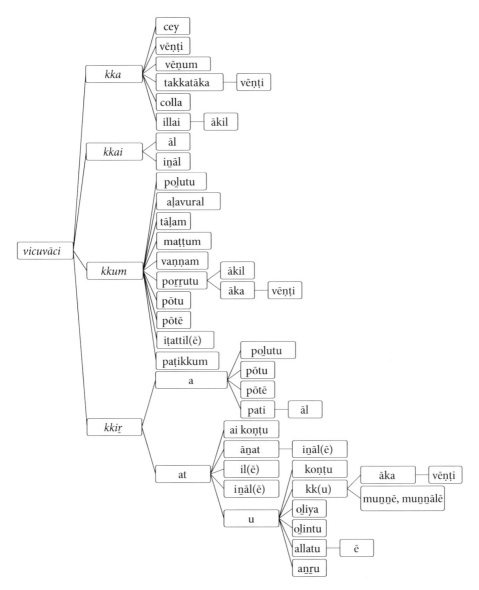

Figure 4. Subjunctive in GA/PB: Group one

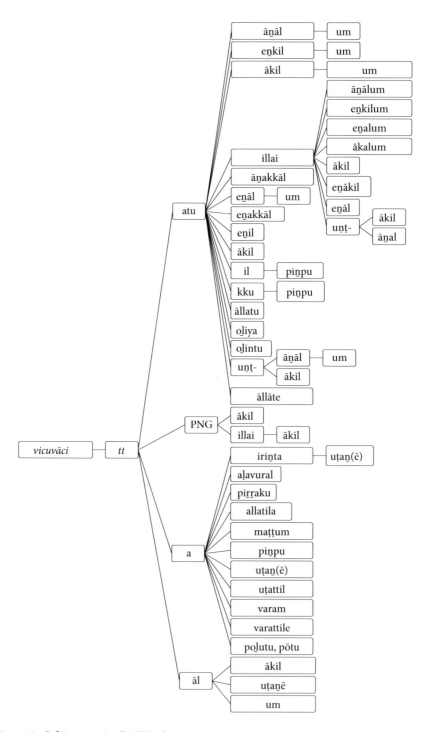

Figure 5. Subjunctive in GA/PB: Group two

The richness of GA/PB's paradigm is related to the necessity to consider linguistic constructions which were difficult to fit into Latin categories and everything is grouped under the morphological principle of segmentation and derivation. The operating principle at work is connected to the internal structure of the word. Indeed, the thirteen-subjunctive in GA/PB can be reduced into four macro-groups on the basis of two elements: the phonological characteristic of the 'augment' attached to the verb bases, and with respect to the *particulas* (particles) or *crecençias* (suffixes) which are added to it. Figures 4 and 5 point out two of these macro-groups and highlight the mechanism at work.

In the first taxonomy, the verb stem *vicuvāci* ['to believe'], given in the variant *vicuvadi*, is the base followed by suffixes containing a geminated unvoiced velar plosive [kk], found both in forms derived from the verb *āku* 'to become' and in the present tense marker *-kkir-*.

Then, a progressive suffixation leads to the formation of four new bases derived from *vicuvāci*:

a. an infinitive in *-kka, vicuvācikka;*
b. a verbal noun in *-kkai, vicuvācikkai;*
c. a future relative participle (also the same as the third singular neuter future), *vicuvācikkum;*
d. a present verbal noun (also the same as a third singular neuter), *vicuvācikkatu;*
e. a present relative participle, *vicuvācikkira.*

The second taxonomy summarized in Figure 5 is built on the verb stem *vicuvāci* ['to believe'], again in the variant *vicuvadi*, here followed by suffixes containing the geminated unvoiced dental plosive [tt] corresponding to the past tense marker. The adopted mechanism is the same and subjunctives are derived by suffixing four bases built on the past marker:

a. a past verbal noun in *-atu, vicuvācittatu;*
b. a finite verb in the past tense;
c. past adjectival participle in *-a, vicuvācitta;*
d. a conditional in *-āl, vicuvācittāl.*

These bases built on the present and past markers combine further with other elements such as case markers (i.e. *ile, ai koṇṭu, iṉāle, āl, kku, kku āka*), postpositions and temporal nouns (i.e. *piṉpu, uṭaṉe, poḻutu, pōtu, uṭaṉ, vaṇṇam, maṭṭum, muṉṉāl, aṉru*), auxiliaries and defective verbs (i.e. *ceytu, colla, illai, tākkavēṇṭi, vēṇṭi, vēṇum, uṇṭa, uṇṭō*), adverbs (*oḻiya, muṉṉē, piṟaku*), conjunctions (*allatu, āṉāl*), complementising nouns (i.e. *pōtu, poḻutu, paṭi*), clitics (*-ē, -ō, -um*), forms expressing concessive of facts and concessive conditional (i.e. *āṉāl, eṉkilum, ākil(um), āṉālum, eṉalum, ākalum*).

The other two macro-groups, not listed here for presenting the same augmentations already seen in the two previous groups, are based on the varint of the verb stem *vicuvāci* 'to believe' followed by suffixes containing the future tense marker [-pp] or by the negative morphs.

6. A brief outline of the impact of BC's and GA/PB's *Artes* on later grammars of Tamil

The main result achieved with these *Artes* was to provide for later Western grammarians a large quantity of organized data which could be re-arranged and re-categorized taking into account in more detail the idiosyncrasies of the Tamil language. Indeed, this is what happened with two later grammars which benefitted, directly and indirectly, from the analysis in these *Artes,* in particular from BC.

The first text is the one produced by the Protestant Bartholomäus Ziegenbalg (1682–1719) who, for writing his *Grammatica Damulica* (1716), relied a lot on BC's *Arte*. As Jeyaraj (2010: 3) states, there is a close affinity between the two texts and that "in all probability Ziegenbalg would have had a copy of Da Costa's Arte Tamulica with him and consulted it for his Latin-Tamil Grammar".[23]

The second grammar which presumably indirectly benefitted from BC's *Arte* via Ziegenbalg was the Jesuit Giuseppe Costantino Beschi. Almost a century later, when writing his grammar of common Tamil, he would discuss some of the linguistic categories of Latin applied both by GA/PB and BC in the description of Tamil:

> Optativum et subjunctivum propriè Tamulenses non habent, licet hos conceptus satis benè explicent phrasibus quibusdam quas, cùm ad syntaxìm spectent, sequenti capite referam.   (Beschi 1738 [1728]: 62, IV, § 69)

> [The Tamulians have, properly speaking, no Optative or Subjunctive, although they express these ideas very well by certain phrases; which since have reference to the Syntax I shall treat of in the next chapter].   (Mahon 1848 [1728]: 53, IV, § 69)

Hence, Beschi needs to recognize that these forms go beyond morphology and are useful for the construction of sentences, falling then within the syntax.

Hence, he places forms like *āka*, causative *-vi-/-pi-*, *paṭu, iṟu, kaṭavtu, ākil, āṉalum, ākilum, itaṭṭil, pōtum, -um, -ē, ēṉ, paṭi, pōla, maṭṭum, uṭaṉē, -ām,* ect., which are described under morphology in BC and GA/PB, in the "Section III. *Of*

---

23. Jeyaraj (2010) also provides in the footnotes of his text the identical passages between the two texts. However, as I pointed out in Muru (2021) the two texts differ greatly in the verb forms used as example for explaining rules, at least regarding the rules for the formation of the past tense.

Verbs", "Section IV. *Of the composition*" and "Section V. *Of particles*" all included in the "Chapter IV. *Of Syntax*" which begins saying:

> *De modo supplendi ea, quibus caret hæc lingua*
> Capite superiori, ubi de verbis, quoad modum indicativi non dedi nisi tempus præsens, præteritum et futurum. Tamulenses enim nec vocem imperfecti habent; nec plusquamperfecti; explicant tamen satis apertè conceptum suum per phrases, quæ hîc, ubi de syntaxi, jure tradendæ sunt.   (Beschi 1738: 99, III, § 122)

> [*Of the method of supplying those which this language has not*
> In a former chapter, where I treated of the verbs, I only gave of the Indicative mood, the present, the præterite and the future tenses: for the Tamulians have neither the word of the imperfect nor of the pluperfect: they express however the ideas of them with sufficient plainness by means of phrases, which ought to be given here, where I treat of the Syntax.]   (Mahon 1848: 82, III, § 122)

It is within this chapter devoted to the syntax that, for example the verb *kaṭavu* (cf. 1.b)[24] is further discussed in the "Chapter IV. Of Syntax. *Optative*" where he explains *Of the Construction of a Sentence*:

> Modo optativo caret hæc lingua, cui supplent per aliquas phrases. Utuntur autem vel infinitivo ஆக à verbo ஆகிறது, vel defectivo கடவது, vel utroque, anteponendum unum alteri, ஆகக்கடவது vel கடவதாக.   (Beschi 1738: 101, III, § 114)

> [This language wants the Optative Mood, which it supplies by other phrases. They use either the Infinitive ஆக (āka), from the verb ஆகிறது (ākiṟatu); or the defective கடவது (kaṭavatu); or both, putting one before the other ஆகக்கடவது (ākakkaṭavatu) or கடவதாக (kaṭavatāka).]   (Mahon 1848: 83, III, § 114)

What emerges so far is the progression Beschi made compared to BC and GA/PB which also demonstrate his debt to the earlier descriptive works of Tamil, without which he could not have progressed. In fact, Beschi could easily identify the forms which should have been treated within the chapter devoted to syntax not only because he was acquainted with the Indian grammatical tradition (Chevillard 1992a and Ebeling & Trento 2018), but also because he had the advantage of disposing of a large amount of data.

Hence, once again, the importance of early missionary grammars both for later descriptions of the Tamil language as well as for the History of the Language Sciences is confirmed.

---

24. In the same chapter (Beschi 1738: 114–115, IV, § 130; Mahon 1848: 94–95, § 114) the causative verb and the auxiliary verb *oṭṭu* are also discussed.

7.   Conclusive remarks

This paper discussed how early missionaries applied latinate categories to the description and categorization of the Tamil verb moods. It highlights how the attempt to find corresponding Tamil forms for the Latin subjunctive and imperative, – which were quite different morphologically speaking –, leads to interesting extensions of the model of reference both in terminology and conceptualization (cf. § 3).

In particular, the paper focused on two latinate categories which became the *loci* where these two missionaries "reduced" the majority of the linguistic phenomena encountered in Tamil. What has emerged from the analysis is that the main criteria behind the extension of the verb mood taxonomy was firstly morphological, secondly semantic. Indeed, focusing on the structure of each single verb form and starting from the bare verb stem, missionaries increased it progressively with all the linguistic items that they were observing in Tamil, fitting them into the Latin paradigm on the basis of the meaning of the "augment" as well as of the "augmented" (derived) verbal form. The grammarians discussed here organized their paradigms considering the morphological similarities which they were observing between the various Tamil forms, and the semantic similarities they were finding between Tamil outcomes and Latin categories. In doing so, missionaries also highlighted features of Tamil morphology, morphosyntax, as well as semantic and pragmatic features. Applying their method[25] of 'augmentation' they also provided evidence of the tendential agglutinative morphology of Tamil, where morphemes within words can be easily parsed or are 'loosely' arranged.

The missionaries not only found correspondents for the Alvaresian imperative paradigm – i.e. in GA/PB one finds both a present and a future imperative although the Tamil imperative is tenseless – but also extended it with new labels for including not only the proper Tamil imperative but also other derived verbal forms, compound verbs, hence periphrastic constructions which were however perceived as single unit. They were included under the label of imperative because they could stand alone as the Latin imperative does. Hence, different labels for distinguishing various impeartives were created with the aim to take into account the semantic value of each Tamil form related to obligation or command (cf. § 4).

As for the descriptive category of the subjunctive mood, which does not exist in Tamil, missionaries included Tamil forms with properties similar to the Latin subjunctive, firstly the peculiarty of being verbs which could not stand alone but needed another verb on which to depend. In fact, in the subjunctive paradigm enters non-finite and nominalized verbs, therefore the morphological and syntactical strategies that Tamil uses for complex sentences such as coordination and subordination.

---

25. A method already used by Henriques (n.d.).

In both cases, the final result consisted in providing a huge amount of data and interpretations for later Western grammarians who would have had the opportunity to re-arrange and re-categorize them achieving a better understanding of the idiosyncrasies of the Tamil language. Indeed, as the last section (§ 6) underlines, later missionaries like Beschi could easily identify the forms which should have been treated within the chapter devoted to syntax not only because he was acquainted with the Indian grammatical tradition (Chevillard 1992a and Ebeling & Trento 2018), but also because he had the advantage of acceding to earlier descriptions of the Tamil language.

In conclusion, this paper has also briefly outlined further line of research which should be further pursued in the future, consisting of the careful observation and deep understanding of how the knowledge about the Tamil language and its linguistic features circulated and was gradually built within the missionaries' circles, thus contributing to both Tamil studies and the History of the Language Sciences.

Acknowledgements

I would like to thank Giovanni Ciotti (CSMC, Hamburg), Gonçalo Fernandes (UTAD, Vila Real), Diego Poli (University of Macerata) for their support and suggestions received during the first version of this paper. I am also grateful to Otto Zwartjes (Université de Paris, HTL) whose comments and remarks have been extremely insightful. Of course, any error is my own responsibility. Acknowledgements also go to the project *Text Surrounding Text* (TST, ANR & DFG) for having facilitated the consultation of MS Cod. Orient. 283. Research on this manuscript was (partly) conducted within the framework of this project.

Abbreviations

1	first person	IMP	imperative
2	second person	INF	infinitive
3	third person	LOC	locative
ADJ.PTCP	adjectival participle	M	masculine
CLIT	clitic	N	neuter
COMP	complementizer	NEG	negation, negative
CONC	concessive	OBL	oblique
COND	conditional	OPT	optative
CVB	converb	PFV	perfective
DUB	dubitative marker	PL	plural
EMPH	emphatic particle	PRS	present
EXCL	exclusive	Q	question particle
F	feminine	QUOT	quotative
FUT	future	REPORT	reportative marker
HAB	habitual	SG	singular
HON	honorific		

References

A.   Primary sources

Aguilar, Gaspar de / Baldaeus, Philippus [&]. 1665. *Arte Tamul. Sive Insitutio Grammatica Linguæ Malabaricae.* Sum Pilippi Valteyusu. VDM in Regno Jaffnapatam. 1659. Pilippi Valteyusu 1665. [Hamburg: Staats– und Universitätsbibliothek Hamburg Carl von Ossietzky, Cod. Orient. 283].

Álvares, Manuel. 1572. *Emmanvelis Alvaris Societate Iesv de institvtione grammatica libri tres.* Olyssippone: Excudebat Ioannes Barrerius Typographus Regius. [Variant reading: Taxada cada Arte a Oyto Vintēs em papel.]

Álvares, Manuel. 1573. *Emmanvelis Alvaris Societate Iesv de Institvtione Grammatica Libri Tres.* Olyssippone: Excudebat Ioannes Barrerius Typographus Regius.

Baldaeus, Philippus. 1672. "Malabaarsche spraak-kunst". *Naauwkeurige Beschryvinge van Malabar en Choromandel, Der zelver aangrenzende Ryken, En het Eyland Ceylon*, 195–198. Amsterdam: J. J. van Waasberge & J. von Someren.

Beschi, Costantino Giuseppe. 1738 [ms. 1728]. *A.M.D.G. Grammatica Latino-Tamulica, ubi de Vulgari Tamulicæ Linguæ Idiomate* கொடுநதமிழ் *[koṭuntamil] dicto, ad ususm missionariorum Soc. IESU. Auctore P. Constantio-Josepho Beschio, e jusdem Societ. in Regno Madurensi missionario. A.D. MDCCXXVIII.* Trangambariae. Typis Missionis Danicæ. [-] [-]CCXXX-IIX ([…] *approbatione imprimatur […] 2 Novembris 1737.* [See Mahon (1848)].

Costa, Balthasar da. 1670. *Arte da Lingua Tamul & Antão de Proença's Tamil-Portuguese Dictionary.* Krishanadas Shana, Goa: State Central Library, MS 60 (previously MS-M34).

Costa, Balthasar da. 1685. *Arte da Lingua Tamul copied by Father Pietro Paolo di S. Francesco (1685) & Vocabulario Tamulico com a significaçam portugueza. Composto pello P. Antam de Proença da Companhia de IESV, Missionario da Missaõ de Madurey. Com todas as licenças necessária da Santa Inquisição E dos Superiores. Na imprensa Tamulica da Provincia do Malabar, por Ignacio Aichamont della Ambalacatta em 30 de Julho 1679 annos.* Rome: Vatican Library, Ms Borgiano Indiano, 12.

Henriques, Henrique. n.d. [c. 1549] *Arte da Lingua Malabar.* Ms Cod. 3141, Fondo Reservados. Lisbon: National Library. (See secondary sources: Vermeer 1982; Hein & Rajam 2013).

B.   Secondary sources

Andronov, Mikhail Sergeevich. 1969. *A Grammar of Modern and Classical Tamil.* Madras: New Century Book House. Second edition 1989.

Annamalai, Elai & Sanford B. Steever. 1998. "Modern Tamil". In Steever, ed., 129–157.

Asher, Ronald E. 1985. *Tamil.* London & New York: Routledge.

Auroux, Sylvain. 1994. *La révolution technologique de la grammatisation.* Liège: Mardaga.

Aussant, Émilie. 2017. "La Grammaire Sanskrite Étendue – État des lieux". *Histoire Epistémologie Langage* 39:2.7–20. https://doi.org/10.1051/hel/2017390201

Blackburn, Stuart. 2003. *Print, folklore, and nationalism in colonial South India.* New Delhi: Pauls Press.

Bossong, Georg. 2007. "The influence of missionary descriptions of far Eastern languages on Western linguistic thought. The case of Cristoforo Borri, S.J. and Tommaso Campanella". In Otto Zwartjes et al., eds. 2007, 123–143. https://doi.org/10.1075/sihols.111.13bos

Chakravarti, Ananya. 2014. "The many faces of Baltasar da Costa: *imitatio* and *accommodatio* in the seventeenth century Madurai mission/ As máscaras de Baltasar da Costa: *imitatio* e *accommodatio* na missão de Madurai (século XVII)". *Etnográfica* 18:1.135–158. http://etnografica.revues.org/3376 [Accessed April 2018].

Chevillard, Jean-Luc. 1992a. "Beschi, grammarien du tamoul, et l'origine de la notion de verbe appellatif". *Bulletin de l'École française d'Extrême-Orient* 79:1.77–88. https://doi.org/10.3406/befeo.1992.1813

Chevillard, Jean-Luc. 1992b. "Sur l'adjectif dans la tradition grammaticale tamoule". *Histoire Épistémologie Langage* (special issue edited by Bernard Colombat: *L'Adjectif: Perspectives historique et typlogique*) 14:1.37–58. https://doi.org/10.3406/hel.1992.2340

Chevillard, Jean-Luc. 2015. "The challenge of bi-directional translation as experienced by the first European missionary grammarians and lexicographers of Tamil". *La Traduction dans l'Histoire des Idées Linguistiques*, ed. by Émilie Aussant, 111–130. Paris: Librairie Orientaliste Paul Geuthner.

Chevillard, Jean-Luc. 2017. "How Tamil was described once again: towards an XML– encoding of the Grammatici Tamulici". *Histoire Epistémologie Langage* 39:2.103–127. https://doi.org/10.1051/hel/2017390206

Chevillard, Jean-Luc. 2021. "From grammar to dictionary. The early challenge of lemmatizing Tamil verbal forms, through categories used for Latin and Portuguese". *Journal of Portuguese Linguistics* 20:1 (Art. 9). 1–34. https://doi.org/10.5334/jpl.269

Ciotti, Giovanni. 2019. "On (the) sandhi between the Sanskrit and the Modern Western Grammatical Traditions: From Colebrooke to Bloomfield via Müller". *Journal of the Portuguese Linguistics* 18:5.1–23. https://doi.org/10.5334/jpl.215

Cre-A:= AA.VV. 2020³ [1992]. க்ரியாவின் தற்காலத் தமிழ் அகராதி. தமிழ்-த ழ்-ஆங்கிலம். Compilation, text, editorial format and arrangement S. Ramakrishnan. Chennai: Cre-A.

Ebeling, Sascha & Margherita Trento. 2018. "From Jesuit Missionary to Tamil Pulavar: Costanzo Gioseffo Beschi (1680–1747), the 'Great Heroic Sage'". *L'Inde et l'Italie. Rencontres intellectuelles, politiques et artistiques*, Coll. Puruṣārtha 35, ed. by Tiziana Leucci and Marie Fourcade, 53–90. Paris: Éditions de l'École des hautes études en sciences sociales. https://doi.org/10.4000/books.editionsehess.23276

Fernandes, Gonçalo. 2019. "Contributions of Cunha Rivara (1809–1879) to the Development of Konkani". *Journal of Portuguese Linguistics* 18:1.1–17. https://doi.org/10.5334/jpl.204

Francis, Emmanuel. 2011. "Description of 3 Tamil Manuscripts". *Manuskriptkultur in Tamil Nadu*. Manuscript culture in Tamil Nadu ed. by Eva Wilden. Newsletter 4, 122–125. Hamburg: CSMC.

Fournier, Jean-Marie & Valérie Raby. 2014. "Retour sur la grammatisation: l'extension de la grammaire latine et la description des langues vulgaires". *Penser l'histoire des savoirs linguistiques. Hommage à Sylvain Auroux*, ed. by Sylvie Archaimbault, Jean-Marie Fournier & Valérie Raby, 337–350. Lyon: ENS Editions.

Hein, Jeanne & V. S. Rajam. 2013. *The Earliest Missionary Grammar of Tamil. Fr. Henriques' Arte da Lingua Malabar: Translation, History and Analysis*. Cambridge, Massachusetts & London, England: Harvard University Press.

James, Gregory. 2000. *Colporuḷ. A History of Tamil Dictionaries*. Chennai: Cre-A:.

James, Gregory. 2007. "The terminology of Declension in Early Missionary Grammars of Tamil". In Zwartjes et al., eds. 2007, 167–190. https://doi.org/10.1075/sihols.111.15jam

James, Gregory. 2009. "Aspects of the structure of entries in the earliest missionary dictionary of Tamil". In Zwartjes et al., eds. 2009, 273–301. https://doi.org/10.1075/sihols.114.15jam

James, Gregory. 2019. "The Pesky Ablative: Early European Missionaries' Treatment of Tamil 'Ablatives'". *Journal of Portuguese Linguistics* 18:1.1–20. https://doi.org/10.5334/jpl.206

Jeyaraj, Daniel. 2006. *Bartholomäus Ziegenbalg: the Father of Modern Protestant Mission. An Indian Assessment*. With a foreword from Dr. K. Rajaratnam. New Delhi: The Indian Society for Promoting Christian Knowledge and Chennai/The Gurukul Lutheran Theological College and Research.

Jeyaraj, Daniel. 2010. *Tamil Language for Europeans: Ziegenbalg's Grammatica Damulica (1716)*. Translated from Latin and Tamil. Annotated and Commented by Daniel Jeyaraj. Wiesbaden: Harrassowitz Verlag.

Kemmler, Rolf. 2015. The First Edition of the *ars minor* of Manuel Álvares *De institvtione grammatica libri tres* (Lisbon, 1573). *Historiographia Linguistica* 42:1.1–19. https://doi.org/10.1075/hl.42.1.01kem

Koerner, E. F. Konrad. 2014. *Quatro décadas de historiografía lingüística: estudos selecionados* ed. by Rolf Kemmler and Cristina Altman, preface of Carlos Assunção. Vila Real: Centro de Estudos em Letras. Universidade de Trás-os-Montes e Alto Douro.

Krishnamurti, Bhadriraju. 2003. *The Dravidian Languages*. Cambridge: Cambridge University Press.

Law, Vivien. 2003. *The History of Linguistics in Europe. From Plato to 1600*. Cambridge: Cambridge University Press. https://doi.org/10.1017/CBO9781316036464

Lehmann, Thomas. 1989. *A grammar of Modern Tamil*. Pondicherry: Pondicherry Institute of Linguistics and Culture.

Lehmann, Thomas. 1998. "Old Tamil". In Sanford B. Steever, ed. 1998, 75–99.

Mahon, George William A. M. 1848. *A Grammar of the Common Dialect of the Tamul Language, called* கொடுந்தமிழ் *[koṭuntamiḻ], composed for the use of the Missionaries of the Society of Jesus, by Constantius Joseph Beschi, Missionary of the Said Society in the district of Madura. Translated from the original Latin By George William Mahon, A. M. Garrison Chaplain, Fort St. George, Madras and Late Fellow of Pembroke College, Oxford*. Madras: Christian Knowledge Society's Press.

Mastrangelo, Carmela. 2018. *Passaggio in Europa. Paolino da San Bartolomeo grammatico del sanscrito*. Milano: Unicopli.

Meenakshisundaram, K. 1974. *The contribution of European Scholars to Tamil*. Madras: Madras University.

MTL= Madras Tamil Lexicon. 1982 [1929–1939]. *Tamil Lexicon*. Published under the authority of the University of Madras, 6 volumes and 1 supplement.

Muru, Cristina. 2010. *Missionari Portoghesi in India nei Secoli XVI e XVII. L'Arte della lingua Tamil. Studio comparato di alcuni manoscritti*. Viterbo: Sette Città.

Muru, Cristina. 2014. "Gaspar de Aguilar: A Banished Genius". *Intercultural Encounter and the Jesuit Mission in South Asia (16th–18th Centuries)* ed. by A. Amaladass, & Ines G. Županov, 353–389. Bangalore: Asian Trading Corporation.

Muru, Cristina. 2018. "Early Descriptors and Descriptions of South Asian Languages from the 16th Century Onwards". *Journal of Portuguese Linguistics* 17:1.8–29. https://doi.org/10.5334/jpl.202

Muru, Cristina. 2020. "*Grammaire Latine Étendue*: two Portuguese Missionary Tamil Arte (17th cent.)". *Beiträge zur Geschichte der Sprachwissenschaft* 30:1.59–73.

Muru, Cristina. 2021. "How missionaries applied Portuguese and Latin descriptive categories in the classification and explanation of verb conjugations and paired verbs in Tamil". *Journal of Portuguese Linguistics* 20:1 (Art.8). 1–32. https://doi.org/10.5334/jpl.268 & https://doi.org/10.5334/jpl.268.s1

Muru, Cristina. (in preparation). *Arte Tamulica by Balthasar da Costa SJ (c. 1610–1673)*. Translated from Portuguese and Tamil. Annotated and Commented by Cristina Muru.

Palmer, F. R. 2001. *Mood and Modality*. Cambridge: Cambridge University Press. https://doi.org/10.1017/CBO9781139167178

Paramasivam, K. 1979. *Effectivity and Causativity in Tamil*. Trivandrum: Dravidian Linguistic Association.

Pytlowany, Anna. 2018. *Ketelaar Rediscovered: The first Dutch grammar of Persian and Hindustani (1698)*. Utrecht: LOT.

Schiffman, Harold F. 1999. *A Reference Grammar of Spoken Tamil*. Cambridge: Cambridge University Press.

Steever, Sanford B., ed. 1998. *The Dravidian Languages*. London & New York: Routledge.

Sweetman, Will. 2012. *Bibliotheca Malabarica: Bartholomäus Ziegenbalg's Tamil Library. Translation*. Pondichéry: Institut Français de Pondichéry. <http://books.openedition.org/ifp/580>.

Thani Nayagam, X. S. 1966. *Antão de Proença's Tamil-Portuguese Dictionary A.D. 1679*. Kuala Lumpur: Department. of Indian Studies, University of Malaya.

Van Hal, Toon. 2016. "Protestant Pioneers in Sanskrit Studies in the Early 18th Century. An overlooked chapter in South Indian missionary linguistics". *Historiographia Linguística* 43:1/2.99–144. https://doi.org/10.1075/hl.43.1-2.04van

Van Hal, Toon. 2019. "European Traditions in India and Indonesia". *The Cambridge World History of Lexicography* ed. by John Considine, 634–657. Cambridge: Cambridge University Press.

Vermeer, Hans J. 1982. *The first European Tamil Grammar. A critical edition. English version by Angelica Morath*. Heidelberg: Julius Groos Verlag.

Wilden, Eva. 2018. *Grammar of Old Tamil for Students*. Pondicherry: École française d'Extrême-Orient & Institut Français de Pondichéry.

Zwartjes, Otto. 2002. "The description of the indigenous languages of Portuguese America by the Jesuits during the colonial period. The impact of the Latin grammar of Manuel Álvares". *Historiographia Linguística* 29:1/2.19–70. https://doi.org/10.1075/hl.29.1-2.06zwa

Zwartjes, Otto. 2011. *Portuguese Missionary Grammars in Asia, Africa and Brazil, 1550– 1800*. Amsterdam & Philadelphia: John Benjamins. https://doi.org/10.1075/sihols.117

Zwartjes, Otto. 2012. "The historiography of missionary linguistics: Present state and further research opportunities". *Historiographia Linguística* 39:2/3.185–242. https://doi.org/10.1075/hl.39.2-3.01zwa

Zwartjes, Otto, Ramón Arzápalo Marín & Thomas C. Smith Stark, eds. 2009. *Missionary Linguistics IV/Lingüística misionera IV: Lexicography: Selected papers from the Fifth International Conference on Missionary Linguistics, Mérida, Yucatán, 14–17 March 2007*. Amsterdam & Philadelphia: John Benjamins. https://doi.org/10.1075/sihols.114

Zwartjes, Otto, Gregory James & Emilio Ridruejo, eds. 2007. *Missionary Linguistics III/ Lingüística misionera III: Morphology and Syntax: Selected papers from the Third and Fourth International Conferences on Missionary Linguistics, Hong Kong/Macau, 12–15 March 2005, Valladolid, 8–11 March 2006*. Amsterdam & Philadelphia: John Benjamins. https://doi.org/10.1075/sihols.111

On the 'affinities of Oriental languages'

Wilhelm von Humboldt and his British connections

Pierre Swiggers, Werner Thomas and Toon Van Hal
KU Leuven

1. Introduction

This contribution borders on the history of missionary and colonial linguistics, and its reception by (European) scholars interested in 'exotic' languages and cultures. As well-known, there is no strict dividing line between missionary linguistics (increasingly documented in the proceedings of the Missionary Linguistics conferences)[1] and colonial linguistics, given the comprehensiveness of the concept of 'colonizing' (other peoples and cultures), and in view of the historical interaction of missionaries and laymen in the process of documenting exotic languages.[2] The impact of missionary and colonial linguistics was twofold: on the one hand, it had a 'synchronic' or immediate effect, relevant to a community of scholars and administrators (and, in some cases also, of immediate relevance to the local culture concerned); on the other hand, these activities, and more particularly, their textual residues, had a repercussion on later generations of scholars interested in the languages dealt with.

We will focus here on aspects of the scholarly reception of these activities, on the basis of a case study centered around the German all-round scholar and political figure Wilhelm von Humboldt (1767–1835) and (part of) his network. As we learn from his biography (e.g., Sweet 1980), Humboldt's interest in the study of exotic languages received a strong impetus during his stay in Rome, where he acquainted himself with Lorenzo Hervás y Panduro (1735–1809), but it was only after his retirement from political life that he devoted all of his leisure-time to the study of language. For his ambitious plan of a comparative study of the spirit and structure of languages worldwide, he set up a wide-ranging network of correspondents,

---

1. For an overview, see Zwartjes (2012); for an in-depth study of the 'Portuguese tradition' of missionary linguistics, see Zwartjes (2011).

2. Cf. the observations of Xavier & Županov (2015) and Van Hal (2016).

https://doi.org/10.1075/sihols.130.11swi

including fellow scholars, as well as diplomats, civil servants, travelers, traders, and missionaries (cf. Swiggers 1995 on Humboldt's European-American network; and, more generally, Reutter 2011). His untiring efforts led to the constitution of an impressive collection of books, manuscripts, notes and letters containing linguistic information.[3]

The scope of this contribution is restricted in two ways: first, the geographical area dealt with is the Indian subcontinent; next, the focus will be on Humboldt's comparative interest in what in his contacts with British scholars he called the 'affinities' among the 'Oriental languages'. For this type of study Humboldt seems to have privileged information provided by British civil servants. On the other hand, for his 'immanent' study of the grammatical structure of languages such as Tamil, Telugu, Hindi, and Marathi, he used descriptions produced by missionaries.[4] Also, in gathering materials on American Indian languages, and on languages in the Southern Pacific (cf. Folie, Heeschen & Zimmer eds. 2017), Humboldt appealed to missionary work.

The starting point for our study is a letter by Humboldt written in the form of an 'essay' (or memoir). The *Essay*-letter (Humboldt 1828),[5] written in the Spring

---

3.   For a description of Humboldt's "*Arbeitsbibliothek*", as constituted between 1821 and 1827, see Mueller-Vollmer (1993: 407–444).

4.   For Tamil, Humboldt used a manuscript version of the Jesuit Costantino Giuseppe Beschi's (1680–1747) *Clavis Humaniorum Litterarum Sublimioris Tamulice Idiomatis* (cf. Mueller-Vollmer 1993: 100, 287), but not the printed *Grammatica Latino-Tamulica* ([Tranquebar 1728]; cf. Zwartjes 2011: 306). For Marathi, he availed himself of several missionary works: William Carey's (1761–1834) *Grammar of the Mahratta Language* [Serampore 1805] and *Dictionary of the Mahratta Language* [Serampore 1810], and the anonymous *Gramatica marastta*, published in Portuguese by the Propaganda Fide in 1778, and reedited in Lisbon in 1805 (for an analysis of this work, see Zwartjes 2011: 67–75). For Hindi, he used the 1805 Lisbon edition of the *Gramatica indostana*, an anonymous missionary grammar written in Portuguese and first published in 1778 by the Propaganda Fide (for an analysis of this work, see Zwartjes 2011: 75–89). It seems that although Humboldt owned several of William Carey's works on languages of India, he never engaged in correspondence with this Baptist missionary and founder of Serampore university. It should also be noted that in order to obtain detailed information on the Malagasy language Humboldt corresponded with a missionary in Antananarivo, Madagascar, viz. Joseph J. Freeman (cf. Mueller-Vollmer 1993: 59, 343–345).

5.   The text was published at the end of 1828, and copies of the *Transactions of the Royal Asiatic Society* had already been distributed when Humboldt noticed a disturbing typographical error in a Sanskrit word cited on p. 217, line 20. Through the intermediary of Friedrich August Rosen (1805–1837), the error was corrected through a reprint of the page in the separate editions of the essay; in volume II of the *Transactions of the Royal Asiatic Society*, the error was corrected in a list of 'Errata' on p. xii, where one reads: "This mistake was not discovered till some of the copies of the Transactions had been distributed; in those which still remained unpublished it was, at

of 1828, was addressed to Sir Alexander Johnston (1775–1849), former third Chief Justice of Ceylon and second Advocate Fiscal of Ceylon, who in 1823 was one of the founders of the *Royal Asiatic Society* of Great Britain and Ireland. The *Royal Asiatic Society* (cf. Beckingham 1979) promoted research on the history, archaeology, religion, culture and languages of Asia (including parts of northern Africa); it was a meeting place of scholars and administrators of the British overseas possessions. Alexander Johnston, who had received his education as a youth in India, and who mastered various Indian languages (Tamil, Telugu, Hindi), had studied in Europe, before returning to India, where he held several important official functions (cf. Reutter 2011: 279). Upon his retirement in 1819 he returned to England.

The direct occasion for Humboldt's letter to Johnston was a circumstance typical of intellectual networks in the Modern Period: Johnston had put at Humboldt's disposal[6] a memoir by Sir James Mackintosh (1765–1832), a Scottish lawyer, who had been Chief Judge in Bombay, between 1804 and 1811, where he had established the *Literary Society of Bombay* (which eventually became the *Asiatic Society of Mumbai*). Upon his return to England, Mackintosh combined a political career with literary and educational pursuits. He was for some time professor in the East India Company's College at Haileybury, where future administrators of the Company received a thorough training, including economy, history, law, and mathematics, and were introduced to a wide range of languages (Sanskrit, Urdu, Bengali, Marathi, Tamil, Telugu and Farsi).[7] James Mackintosh dedicated much of his time to writing historical and philosophical works: *Dissertation on the Progress of Ethical Philosophy* (1830), *The Life of Sir Thomas More* (1830), a huge three-volume *History of England* (1830–1832), and *History of the Revolution in England in 1688* (posthumously published in 1834; the work opens with a "Notice of the Life, Writings and Speeches of Sir James Mackintosh"). As is clear from the opening lines of Humboldt's letter

---

Baron Humboldt's request, corrected in a reprint of the page"; this is followed by the quotation of the relevant passage in Humboldt's original French manuscript. See also *infra*, notes 14 and 38. Although available in a printed form, Humboldt's 1828 *Essay* has received only scant attention from historians of linguistics; cf. Di Cesare (1990: 164). References to Humboldt's *Essay* will be to the page numbering of the text as published in the *Transactions*; we have also used the copy of the separate publication of the *Essay* that is kept in the Library of the *American Philosophical Society*.

6.   Previously, Johnston had sent a Malagasy translation of the Ten Commandments to Humboldt; see his letter of October 15, 1827 (conserved in Cracow, Jagielloński Library, Coll. ling. fol. 53, Bl. 144–145; cf. Mueller-Vollmer 1993: 221); in another letter, of August 17, 1827 (see *infra*, note 9) Johnston had informed Humboldt about linguistic works produced and/or kept by the *London Missionary Society*.

7.   On Haileybury College, see Maheshwari (2002: 202–218).

to Johnston, the memoir that had been communicated to Humboldt was one of a specifically linguistic interest, and not a very recent one.

> SIR:
>
> I have the honour to return you Sir James Mackintosh's interesting memoir. It possesses (like every thing which comes from the pen of that gifted and ingenious writer) the highest interest; and the ideas which are so luminously developed in it have the more merit, if we consider, that, at the period when this memoir was published, philosophical notions on the study and nature of languages were rarer and more novel than they are at present.   (Humboldt 1828: 213)

We are on safe grounds, then, to assume that the memoir in question was Mackintosh's *Plan of a Comparative Vocabulary of Indian Languages*, dated to 1806.[8] This is, in fact, confirmed by a passage in Humboldt's *Essay*, where the date "1806" is mentioned:

> In the present state of our knowledge of the languages of India, which is very different from that of 1806, and possessing, as we now do, grammars and dictionaries of most of these idioms, I should not advise our confining ourselves to a plan which can only give a very imperfect idea of each of them. We can, and ought, to go farther at the present day.   (Humboldt 1828: 214)

As the first lines of his letter also make clear, Humboldt's *Essay*-letter to Johnston[9] was not meant as a simple act of courtesy: his initial word of thanks is followed by a long exposition of Humboldt's ideas –,rooted in "philosophical notions on the study and nature of languages" –,concerning research on Oriental languages. Humboldt

---

8. James Mackintosh read his text in Bombay on May 26, 1806; it was published in 1806 by the *Literary Society of Bombay*. There was a 1808 Calcutta reprint of the text. Both editions were catalogued in the description of William Marsden's (1754–1836) library (Marsden 1827: 77). The larger part of Marsden's book collection is deposited at King's College (University of London). In 1819 Mackintosh's *Plan* was "republished" in the *Transactions of the Literary Society of Bombay*, without being updated. It is not clear to which edition of the text Humboldt had access.

9. Humboldt and Johnston exchanged letters in the years 1827–1831. In a letter to Humboldt of August 17, 1827, Alexander Johnston welcomes Humboldt's project of a stay in England in the Spring of the following year (letter conserved in Cracow, Jagielloński Library, Coll. ling. fol. 56, Bl. 120–121, 122–125; cf. Mueller-Vollmer 1993: 233, 235); on October 15, 1827 Johnston provided Humboldt with Malagasy materials (cf. *supra* note 6); in a letter of August 28, 1828 (letter conserved in Berlin, Archiv Schloss Tegel, Inv. Nr. 1055, Bl. 39–40; cf. Mattson 1980: nr. 12066) Johnston mentions that Humboldt's *Essay*-letter read to the *Royal Asiatic Society* had met with an enthusiastic reception.

addressed himself, through Johnston, to the *Royal Asiatic Society*, which he urged to continue, and stimulate, the study of the "different Indian dialects."[10]

> I would, in the first place, observe, that the Royal Asiatic Society could not direct its efforts to a point more important, and more intimately connected with the national glory, than that of endeavouring to throw further light on the relations which subsist among the different Indian dialects.   (Humboldt 1828: 213)

As a matter of fact, Humboldt's "ideas" on the topic –, which Johnston had asked him to formulate[11] –, took the form of a short treatise, which the *Royal Asiatic Society* then published in the second volume of its *Transactions* under the title "An Essay on the Best Means of ascertaining the Affinities of Oriental Languages, by Baron William Humboldt, For. M.R.A.S. Contained in a Letter addressed to Sir Alexander Johnston, Knt., V.P.R.A.S."; the text, translated by Benjamin Guy Babington (cf. *infra*, Section 3), was read before the *Royal Asiatic Society* on June 14, 1828. The memoir was also separately published as an offprint, and was sent out by Humboldt to scholars in Europe and the United States.[12]

---

10. Humboldt was already very familiar with the Sanskrit language, of which he possessed several grammars, dictionaries, and text editions (by Franz Bopp, August-Wilhelm Schlegel, Charles Wilkins, Horace Wilson, Henry P. Forster, William Carey), and probably also with Bengali (he owned Graves Champney Haughton's *Rudiments of Bengali Grammar* [London 1821] and *Bengali Selections* [London 1822]).

11. See the conclusion of the letter: "'These, Sir, are my ideas upon the subject upon which you wished to have my opinion. It is only in compliance with your request, that I have ventured to lay them before you; for I am well aware how much better able the distinguished members of the Royal Asiatic Society are to form a judgment of, and give an opinion upon, this matter than I am" (Humboldt 1828: 221). See also the following passage in the letter: "'This is more particularly the point to which I wish to direct your attention, since you have been pleased to ask my opinion respecting the methods proposed by Sir James Mackintosh" (Humboldt 1828: 214). In a letter to Christian Lassen (letter of January 26, 1829; see *infra*, note 12), Humboldt mentions the fact that he was asked to give his opinion on the *Plan* of Mackintosh. It seems that Humboldt seized the occasion to outline his ideas on how language comparison had to be undertaken, and to affirm his status as a linguistic scholar (cf. Reutter 2011: 279–280). On Humboldt's own admission (in his letter to Lassen of January 26, 1829), he profited from the opportunity to expound his ideas (cf. *infra*, note 41).

12. See Humboldt's letter to Christian Lassen (January 26, 1829): "Ich werde ihn *sous bande* abgehen lassen, und er dürfte also wohl erst nach diesen Zeilen bei Ihnen eintreffen." The letter is kept in the University Library of Bonn (Nachlass Lassen S 860); cf. Mattson (1980: nr. 7975). It seems that Humboldt had received copies of the separate publication of his *Essay* in January 1829, and immediately started sending them off to scholars belonging to his intellectual network.

Humboldt's ideas doubtlessly made a deep impression on the members of the *Royal Asiatic Society*, as can be gathered not only from a personal testimony by Johnston (letter to Humboldt of August 28, 1828; see note 9) and by the fact that it was published in their *Transactions*, but also from the fact that one of the leading figures of the Society, the outstanding Sanskrit scholar Henry Thomas Colebrooke (1765–1837),[13] edited the text and appended a note to it, informing the readership of a language-comparative initiative taken by him.[14]

> The work to which allusion is made by Baron William de Humboldt, in the passage where I am named, was undertaken by me in furtherance of the views developed by Sir James Mackintosh. I thought that a more copious comparative vocabulary than he had proposed, would be practically useful; and would be instructive in more points of view than he had contemplated. Accordingly, at my instance, a Sanscrit vocabulary and a Persian one were printed with blank half pages, and distributed among gentlemen, whose situations were considered to afford the opportunity of having the blank column filled up, by competent persons, with a vocabulary of a provincial language. Vocabularies of the same vernacular tongue by a Pandit and a Munshi, would serve to correct mutually, and complete the information sought from them. Very few answers, however, were received: indeed scarcely any, except from Dr. Buchanan Hamilton.[15] The compilation, to which Baron de Humboldt refers, comprises as many as I succeeded in collecting.
>
> (Colebrooke in Humboldt 1828: 221)

---

13. Henry Thomas Colebrooke was the son of Sir George Colebrooke (1729–1809), who had been chairman of the East India Company.

14. In the printing process of the *Essay*, mistakes were introduced by the printer. In his letter to Humboldt of January 9, 1829, Friedrich August Rosen informs his German correspondent that the errors will be corrected in the then not yet distributed copies. In his answer to Rosen (letter of January 25, 1829; cf. Mattson 1980: nr. 12114), Humboldt writes: "Die Aufklärungen, die Sie mir über die Druckfehler gegeben, haben mich sehr gefreut. Meine Handschrift ist also unschuldig befunden. Ein Secretair, wie Babington, sollte aber, auch in Sprachen, die er nicht weiß, sorgfältiger seyn. Von Colebrooke sage ich nichts. Seine Correctur ist natürlich nur eine Formalität. Wie wird sich der alte verdriessliche Mann die Mühe geben, etwas wirklich nachzusehen? Ich danke sehr für die Besorgung des Cartons, und bitte Sie darauf zu halten, dass Huttmann im Druckfehlerverzeichniss meine Unschuld documentirt. Der Druckfehler ist darum so unangenehm, weil es gar nicht die Art des Setzers ist, für tönende Buchstaben dumpfe zu nehmen"; Humboldt requested that the correct original passage (in his original French manuscript, which was translated into English) be cited as a proof of his not being responsible for the errors. William Huttmann was, until 1832, the Secretary of the *Royal Asiatic Society*. On January 30, 1829, Rosen informed Johnston about the corrections having been made. In his letter to Humboldt of the same day (letter conserved in Berlin, Archiv Schloss Tegel Inv. Nr. 1056, Bl. 41/43; cf. Mattson 1980: nr. 12122), Johnston informed his German correspondent that the corrections had been made.

15. See Keller (2015) for a history of the practice of circulating such lists among scholars.

Humboldt sent copies of his *Essay* to leading linguistic scholars, such as Jacob Grimm (1785–1863),[16] Peter Stephen Duponceau (1760–1844),[17] and Christian Lassen (1800–1876),[18] with another copy to be passed on to August Wilhelm von Schlegel (1767–1845). The *Essay* was very favourably reviewed, anonymously, in the *Asiatic Journal* (1829: 325–326).

2. The scholarly exploitation of missionary linguistics: Humboldt's pursuit

Humboldt's grand plan for investigating the "affinities" of "Oriental" languages –, focusing on India, but extending to the Indian archipelago –,was closely connected with work accomplished by missionaries and colonial civil servants, and especially with materials that were in the hands of British scholars. In this way, Humboldt's own intellectual network was to intersect with a "textual" network rooted in missionary and colonizing endeavors. Before we look into this, it is, however, worthwhile to take a look at the contents of Humboldt's program, in view of its methodological relevance.

---

16. In a letter to Jacob Grimm, dated November 12, 1828, Humboldt promises to send him as soon as possible a copy of the separate publication of the *Essay*: "Ich habe die Gelegenheit gehabt, über dies Beurtheilen der Verwandtschaft von Sprachen aus blossen, nach Wörterbüchern gemachten Wortverzeichnissen, etwas in England zu schreiben, das die *Asiatische Gesellschaft* hat drucken lassen. Ich hoffe, *Exemplare* zu bekommen, u. theile alsdann gewiß sogleich eines Ew. Wohlgebornen mit." The original of the letter is kept in Berlin (SBBPK, Nachlass Grimm 1165 (4)); cf. Mattson (1980: nr. 7938).

17. In a letter of November 13, 1828 to Peter Stephen Duponceau Humboldt informs him about his stay in London, and about his *Essay* in the *Transactions*, of which he announces to have a copy sent to the *American Philosophical Society*: "Pendant mon séjour à Londres j'ai été consulté sur les travaux que la Société Asiatique paroit entreprendre par la connoissance plus approfondie des langues de l'Inde. On avoit le projèt de recueillir des vocabulaires. J'ai déconseillé de se borner à cette méthode extrêmement imparfaite, et j'ai exposé mes principes sur l'affinité des langues et les recherches qui peuvent la découvrir. J'ai avancé que c'est l'identité des idiômes. J'ai adressé là-dessus une lettre à *Sir Alexandre Johnston* qui a été lue à *la Société* et imprimée par elle. Je n'en ai pas encore reçu d'exemplaires, mais je tâcherai de Vous en faire parvenir de *Londres*." The letter is conserved in Philadelphia (Historical Society of Pennsylvania, Etting Papers, Scientists, fol. 44); cf. Mattson (1980: nr. 7939).

18. See the reference to the letter, *supra*, in note 12. Humboldt enclosed a second copy for August-Wilhelm Schlegel, Lassen's colleague in Bonn: "Ich bitte Ew. Wohlgebornen das zweite Exemplar des Aufsatzes unsrem Freunde Schlegel mit meinen herzlichsten und freundschaftlichsten Empfehlungen zu übergeben."

Humboldt's interest in the comparison of languages –, or language varieties, since Humboldt does not make a methodologically, nor empirically grounded distinction between languages and dialects[19] –,was basically a "genetic" one: comparison was used as a means of "ascertaining affinities", i.e. establishing genetic ties, and, when possible, of combining the genetic connection with a historical and geographical[20] starting point.

A comparative analysis of languages aiming at such goals should, in Humboldt's view, proceed according to a sound method and, in direct relation to this method, from an adequate understanding of comparison-based demonstration (both aspects constitute the core matter of what today we call "the comparative method"). On both points Humboldt departed from the program outlined in the *Plan* of James Mackintosh.[21]

Mackintosh had proposed to collect word lists for the various languages of India, proceeding from what today we would call an "onomasiological" point of view, i.e. eliciting answers to a lexically framed questionnaire inquiring into the native expression(s) corresponding to a notion or concept named by its English term. While admitting that this type of investigation could yield interesting information,[22] Humboldt points to two major defects: (a) such investigations only provide information on the (loosely examined) vocabulary of languages (and are

---

19. See, e.g., his fluctuating usage in his *Essay*: "the relations which subsist among the different Indian dialects"; "more complete information regarding the languages of India"; "the different languages which we wish to compare"; "the particular differences of dialects"; "this manner of considering the difference of languages"; "upon all the dialects of India". However, it is clear that Humboldt did not consider the two terms to be synonymous. On the one hand, in connection with (a general notion of) "affinity", he uses *language*, whereas *dialect* seems to be favoured when it comes to identifying lower-level (or "particular") differences. On the other hand, there is at least one passage (echoing a traditional formulation; cf. Van Hal & Van Rooy 2017) in which Humboldt views dialects as varieties that show only minor differences: "It is equally curious to determine whether the primitive languages of India are to be traced over the Indian archipelago in dialects differing little from each other, and whether we are to assign their origin to these islands or to the continent."

20. See the formulation in the passage quoted in the preceding footnote: "whether we are to assign their origin to these islands or to the continent."

21. Humboldt speaks of *the methods* (in the plural) of Mackintosh: "This is more particularly the point to which I wish to direct your attention, since you have been pleased to ask my opinion respecting the methods proposed by Sir James Mackintosh" (Humboldt 1828: 214).

22. See his statement: "It would assuredly have been very desirable to execute his plan, at the period when it was formed; we should then by this time have had more complete information regarding the languages of India; and should perhaps have been in the possession of dialects, of the existence of which we are now ignorant" (Humboldt 1828: 214).

therefore insufficient as a methodologically sound proof for ascertaining 'affinity', i.e. genetic relationship);[23] (b) such investigations are not based on a "profound" knowledge of the languages investigated, i.e. they are not based on a thorough insight into the structure[24] of the languages.

> I confess that I am extremely averse to the system which proceeds on the supposition that we can judge of the affinity of languages merely by a certain number of ideas expressed in the different languages which we wish to compare.
> (Humboldt 1828: 214)[25]
> If we would make ourselves acquainted with the relation which subsists between two languages, we ought to possess a thorough and profound knowledge of each of them. This is a principle dictated alike by common sense and by that precision acquired by the habit of scientific research. (Humboldt 1828: 214–215)

Now, it is true –,and Humboldt does not omit to mention it –,that Mackintosh had been aware of the dangers of random lexical comparison as a demonstrative technique, but the restrictive requirement he imposed on it was also deemed insufficient by Humboldt:

> Sir James Mackintosh very justly observes, that the affinity of two languages is much better proved when whole families of words resemble each other, than when this is the case with single words only. But how shall we recognize families of words in foreign languages, if we only select from them two or three hundred isolated terms? (Humboldt 1828: 215)

It is precisely to this essential point of demonstrative validity that Humboldt turns his attention: the cross-linguistic comparison of (large numbers of) words can only yield certain results –, for language-genetic investigations –,if we gain insights into the "analogy of meanings and forms of combination." What Humboldt understands by this 'analogy', can be captured by our modern concept of "correspondence in grammatical structure" (see also Di Cesare 1990: 164–165). Humboldt expatiates on this in a more elaborate fashion, resorting to terms such as "roots", "grammatical affixes", and "methods by which each language forms its derivatives" –,the latter

---

23. Rocher & Rocher (2012: 73) recognize that Humboldt's criticisms of Mackintosh's *Plan* and Colebrooke's collection were justified from the methodological point of view, but they note that Humboldt failed to "address the practical utility that was one of Colebrooke's guiding concerns as a colonial administrator."

24. Cf. *infra*, p. 274.

25. See also another passage in the *Essay*, where Humboldt criticizes the procedure of "taking from the language which we wish to examine isolated words, selected, not according to their affinities and natural etymology, but according to the ideas which they express" (Humboldt 1828: 215).

formulation in fact subsumes both derivation strictly speaking, and (the structural principles of) word formation. Let us quote his circumstantial formulation:

> There undoubtedly subsists among words of the same language an analogy of meanings and forms of combination easy to be perceived. It is from this analogy, considered in its whole extent, and compared with the analogy of the words of another language, that we discover the affinity of two idioms, as far as it is recognizable in their vocabularies. It is in this manner alone, that we recognize the roots and the methods by which each language forms its derivatives. The comparison of two languages requires, that we should examine whether, and in what degree, the roots and derivative terms are common to both. It is not, then, by terms expressive of general ideas; such as sun, moon, man, woman, &c., that we must commence the comparison of two languages, but by their entire dictionary critically explained. The simple comparison of a certain number of words, by reducing the examination of languages too much to a mere mechanical labour, often leads us to omit examining sufficiently the words which form the subjects of our comparison; and to avoid this defect, we are forced to enter deeply into all the minutiae of grammar, separating the words from their grammatical affixes, and comparing only what is really essential to the expression of the idea which they represent.
>
> (Humboldt 1828: 215–216)

In one instance he also uses *structure*:

> What I have remarked proves, as I think, that even if we confine ourselves to the comparison of a certain number of words in different languages, it is still necessary to enter more deeply into their structure, and to apply ourselves to the study of their grammar.   (Humboldt 1828: 216)

Clearly, Humboldt advocated a grammar-focused comparison of languages in order to ascertain possible genetic relationships. This methodological principle was grounded in a fundamental theoretical tenet, extensively argued for by Humboldt (especially in his posthumously published *Über die Verschiedenheit des menschlichen Sprachbaues*, Humboldt 1836), and subsequently also endorsed by Neo-Humboldtian linguistics and its sequels, such as Boasian anthropological linguistics, viz. that the grammar of a language is 'inherent' to the world view of a 'nation', and is therefore also much less liable to change. The theoretical tenet is also stated in the *Essay*:

> Languages are the true images of the modes in which nations think and combine their ideas. The manner of this combination represented by the grammar, is altogether as essential and characteristic as are the sounds applied to objects, that is to say, the words. The form of language being quite inherent in the intellectual faculties of nations, it is very natural that one generation should transmit theirs to that which follows it; while words, being simple signs of ideas, may be adopted by races altogether distinct.   (Humboldt 1828: 216)

But, as we know from Humboldt's correspondence with August-Wilhelm Schlegel (cf. Leitzmann 1908 for the edition of the letters, and Hoenigswald 1984 for a study of the main methodological insights contained in the letter partially edited in Appendix A), the German language scholar was well aware that grammatical comparison should go beyond structural similarities. Foreshadowing explicit formulations (as we find, e.g., in Antoine Meillet's *La méthode comparative en linguistique historique* [1925]; cf. Swiggers 2012) of the requirement of correspondence in both structural configuration and phonic substance, Humboldt noted that his principle should not be taken "in the abstract but in the concrete"; put in other words, the grammatical forms[26] should be examined and compared both as to their systemic functioning and as to their sound shape. This is how Humboldt formulates[27] this constraint:

> If I attach great importance, however, under this view, to the grammar of a language, I do not refer to the system of grammar in general, but to grammatical forms, considered with respect to their system and their sounds taken conjointly.
> (Humboldt 1828: 216)

> If I assert that, in order to prove the affinity of languages, we should pay attention to the employment of grammatical forms and to their sounds taken together, it is because I would affirm that they must be considered not only in the abstract but in the concrete.
> (Humboldt 1828: 217)

Humboldt exemplifies this combined criterion in two ways: (a) from a 'confirmation' point of view, by showing that a comparison of Sanskrit infinitives and Latin supines, or of the Sanskrit, Greek, Gothic and Lithuanian verb forms meaning "I know", offers a convincing demonstration of the genetic relationship of these languages; (b) from a 'deficiency' point of view, by showing that a mere structural correspondence (such as the presence in some languages of first person plural forms inclusive and exclusive) cannot be a proof of genetic affinity, in the absence of a phonic correspondence.

It is precisely grammatical-phonological correspondence (or: correspondence sets) that constitutes the diagnostic criterion of genetic relationship. Admittedly, grammatical systems undergo changes, and James Mackintosh had precisely invoked the changes in grammar as an argument against using grammatical comparison. But as Humboldt admonishes, one should not be blinded by this (superficial) phenomenon of "historical revolutions"; it is of the utmost importance to look in depth at grammatical forms.

---

26. On Humboldt's concept of 'grammatical form', see Swiggers (1985).

27. Compare also Humboldt's statement that "the expression *grammar* [should] be not taken vaguely, but with a due regard to the sounds of grammatical forms" (Humboldt 1828: 218).

> Out of these changes it has arisen, that languages of the same family have a different grammatical system, and that languages really distinct resemble each other in some degree. But the slightest examination will suffice to shew the real relations which subsist between those languages, especially if by following the plan above laid down we proceed to the examination of forms which are alike identical in their uses and in their sounds. It is thus that we discover without difficulty that the English language is of Germanic origin, and that the Persian belongs to the Sanscrit[28] family of languages, notwithstanding the very great difference which exists between the grammars of these idioms.   (Humboldt 1828: 219)

Here, Humboldt's argumentation makes full circle. It is grammatical-phonological correspondence that provides proof of *affinity*, or *genetic relationship*, i.e. relationship in origin and filiation. This is very distinct, in Humboldt's terminology, from *historical* relationship, i.e. a relation that has occurred in time, and which may be a distant one and also a very temporary one. In contradistinction with grammatical correspondences, lexical correspondences may be useful to detect such historical relationships, but when used for deeper-reaching conclusions, such facts should always be examined critically, since it may be that we deal with borrowings (see also Brown 1967: 107–108).

> It is generally believed, that the affinity of two languages is undeniably proved, if words that are applied to objects which must have been known to the natives ever since their existence, exhibit a great degree of resemblance, and to a certain extent this is correct. But, notwithstanding this, such a method of judging of the affinity of languages seems to me by no means infallible. It often happens, that even the objects of our earliest perceptions, or of the first necessity, are represented by words taken from foreign languages, and which belong to a different class. If we only examine the list furnished by Sir James Mackintosh, we shall find there such words as *people, countenance, touch, voice, labour, force, power, marriage, spirit, circle, tempest, autumn, time, mountain, valley, air, vapour, herb, verdure*, and others of the same kind. Now all these words being evidently derived from the Latin, as it was transformed after the fall of the Roman empire, we ought, judging from these words, rather to assign to the English an origin similar to that of the Roman languages than to that of the German.   (Humboldt 1828: 219)

---

28. Humboldt proposed the designation "Sanskrit(ic) [family of] languages" instead of the term "Indo-Germanic."

3. Behind the ideas: Linguistic documentation

Humboldt's *Essay* contains insightful ideas, which shed light on the author's intellectual development as well as on the theoretical embedding of comparative grammar as it was conceived in the first decades of the 19th century. Another interesting facet of the text is the information it provides on the relationship between the empirical linguistic documentation provided by missionaries and civil servants and the exploitation of this information by linguistic scholars.[29] As we have seen, Humboldt's *Essay* was the outcome of his critical and penetrating reading of a programmatic text written by James Mackintosh at a time when the latter was a judge in Bombay. Also, Alexander Johnston was by profession a juridical scholar, albeit with a profound interest in language. Interestingly, Johnston provided Humboldt not only with the memoir of Mackintosh, he also communicated to his German correspondent a paper by Francis Whyte Ellis (1777–1819) on the Malayalam language.[30] On Ellis, a civil servant of the East India Company in Madras, we find some information in Robert Caldwell's *Comparative Grammar of the Dravidian or South-Indian Family of Languages* (1856), where he is mentioned for having contributed a short comparative word list of Dravidian languages to Campbell's grammar of Telugu: "The first to break ground in the field was Mr. Ellis, a Madras Civilian, who was profoundly versed in the Tamil language and literature, and whose interesting but very brief comparison, not of the grammatical forms, but only of some of the vocables of three Dravidian dialects, is contained in his Introduction to *Campbell's Telugu Grammar* (Caldwell 1856: iv)." Alexander Duncan Campbell (1786–1857), mentioned by Caldwell, was also a civil servant of the East India Company at Madras; he published *A Grammar of the Teloogoo Language* in 1818 (second edition: 1820).

---

29. The significance of this scholarly network is also made explicit by Mueller-Vollmer & Heeschen (2007: 436–437).

30. See Humboldt's letter: "M[r]. Ellis's paper on the Malayalam language with which you were so good as to furnish me, contains assertions on the affinity of the Tamul language to the idioms of Java, which it would be very important to verify" (Humboldt 1828: 213). In his letter to Babington of June 29, 1828 (see Appendix B), Humboldt urges the *Royal Asiatic Society* to "reprint it immediately now and make common to the learned men of Europe the information which it contains." In a letter (undated, but to be dated in the period of Humboldt's stay in London), Richard Clarke informed Humboldt on Ellis's publications and (unfinished) projects: "Ellis intended to put forth a series of essays, of which the project was to show the affinity of the dialects of S. India, but the fates cut his thread too soon. One on the Telugu is prefixed to Campbell's Grammar. One on Malayalma was printed by itself, & I think one on Carnataca. But of this I am not certain. The essay on Tamil, alas! was never composed. They were printed at the College Press, of which he had the control & superintendence but were not published, nor were they executed under any special sanction of Government" (Cracow, Jagielloński Library, Coll. ling. fol. 56, Bl. 51–52), cf. Mueller-Vollmer (1993: 232, 235).

From Humboldt's letter it also appears that he had assembled a rather considerable amount of information on the languages of India. In the first place, he mentions having seen in the library of the East India Company[31] a manuscript[32] containing a collection of Sanskrit words. In addition, he refers to a dictionary of Telugu by Campbell.[33] Humboldt's letter equally informs us that he was aware of the work of other European scholars interested in the "affinity" of the Indian languages: he makes mention of "a series of papers" published by Eugène Burnouf (1801–1852) in the *Journal Asiatique*.[34]

In Humboldt's view much could be expected from comparative linguistic work conducted under the auspices of learned societies,[35] and in the case of the languages of India his hope rested on a society such as the *Royal Asiatic Society*.

> In England, also, the great advantage is possessed of being able to direct works upon these languages to be undertaken in India itself, and to guide such labours by plans sent from this country. In India these are living languages, and literary men of the very nations in which they are spoken may be employed in the researches we wish to forward. No other nation possesses so valuable an advantage. It is important to profit by it.
>
> (Humboldt 1828: 220)

---

31. Humboldt had been informed of the rich holdings of the East India Company by Julius Heinrich Klaproth (1783–1835) in a letter of May 8, 1824 (Harnack 1896: 66–67; cf. Mattson 1980: nr. 11799).

32. According to Colebrooke's note appended to Humboldt's letter (see *supra*, Section 1), the author of the manuscript would be "Buchanan Hamilton," i.e. Francis Buchanan (later: Francis Hamilton). Buchanan (1762–1829), a physician and naturalist of Scottish descent, is a well-known botanical scholar, who traveled throughout Asia, and who conducted surveys of South India. After having surveyed, between 1807 and 1814, the areas under the jurisdiction of the East India Company, he returned in 1815 to England.

33. The work referred to is: Archibald Campbell, *Dictionary of the Teloogo language commonly termed the Gentoo* (Madras 1821).

34. Humboldt was probably thinking here of Burnouf's review of Bopp's *Vergleichende Zergliederung des Sanskrits und der mit ihm verwandten Sprachen* (*Journal Asiatique* 6, 1825, 52–62 and 113–117), and his "Mémoire sur quelques noms de l'île de Ceylan, et particulièrement sur celui de Taprobane, sous lequel elle était connue des anciens" (*Journal Asiatique* 9, 1826, 129–149).

35. "In an enterprize so vast as that of examining to the utmost possible extent each of the numerous languages of India, progress can only be made insensibly and step by step. But learned societies afford this advantage, that the same labour can be continued through a long series of years; and complete and perfect works upon two or three idioms are certainly preferable to notions, more or less superficial, upon all the dialects of India, hastily put forth for the purpose of coming at once to a general conclusion" (Humboldt 1828: 220–221).

A precious piece of information contained in Humboldt's letter is his mention of a "vast quantity of manuscript materials" concerning the languages of India. In this connection he mentions a "Dr. B. Babington", to be identified with Benjamin Guy Babington (1794–1866), a member of the well-known Babington family, which produced politicians, scientists, historians, poets, and scholars. Benjamin Babington, who had studied at the East India Company College at Haileybury, had been active in Madras;[36] although he subsequently embarked on a medical career, he kept an interest in the study of language, as can be gathered from the fact that he served as secretary to the *Royal Asiatic Society*. According to Humboldt, Babington had in his possession "alphabets altogether unknown in Europe up to the present time" (Humboldt 1828: 220).[37] In a letter sent to August Wilhelm von Schlegel (letter of June 16, 1829),[38] Humboldt mentions that it was Babington who had translated Humboldt's original French text into English. In addition, Babington assisted Humboldt in expanding his scholarly network towards scholars active in India:

> Thus Dr. Babington has mentioned Mr. Whish to me, as being profoundly acquainted with the Malayalim, and as being already employed in making it better known in Europe. (Humboldt 1828: 220)

The scholar referred to here was Charles Matthew Whish (1794–1833), also a civil servant of the East India Company in Madras, who eventually became criminal judge at Cuddapah. Whish, one of the first students of Indian mathematical science, was a collector of manuscripts[39] in Sanskrit and other languages of India, and he had been collecting materials for a grammar and dictionary of Malayalam. In a

---

36. Babington is the author of an English translation (Madras 1822) of Beschi's manuscript grammar of Tamil (cf. *supra*, note 4); however, this 'translation' (published under the title *A Grammar of the High Dialect of the Tamil Language, termed Shen-Tamil. By C. J. Beschi. Translated from the original Latin, by Benj. Guy Babington*) is considerably different in arrangement from the original.

37. See Babington's letter of July 27, 1828 to Humboldt, edited in Appendix C.

38. Letter conserved in Bonn (University Library; Inv. S 507: 23); published in Leitzmann (1908: 221–241), cf. Mattson (1980: nr. 8046). In this letter Humboldt brings up again the issue of the unfortunate errors in the printed version of the English translation of his manuscript. In 1832 August-Wilhelm Schlegel published, in French, some 'reflections' (Schlegel 1832), dedicated to the memory of Sir James Mackintosh, on the study of Indian languages and culture (literature, religion, mythology). Mackintosh and Schlegel had been close friends, who paid each other mutual visits. Curiously, in the *Réflexions* no mention is made of Humboldt's 1828 *Essay*. The *Réflexions* are followed by a letter to Horace Wilson, in which Schlegel replies to Wilson's criticisms of his Indological work. These two texts are followed by a number of shorter documents (including correspondence between Schlegel and the East India Company).

39. See Winternitz (1902).

letter to Babington of June 29, 1828 (see Appendix B), Humboldt expressed his hope that Babington "would introduce him at his request to Mr. Wish [sic]."[40] We do not know whether Humboldt indeed established contact with Whish, who died prematurely in India.

4. From colonial and missionary linguistics to scholarly networks: The relevance of Humboldt's *Essay*

In conclusion, we first want to point out the *intrinsic* interest of Humboldt's *Essay*: in it, the German language scholar demonstrates the insufficiency of a purely lexical comparison,[41] and formulates a strikingly modern criterion of historical-comparative grammar, involving the comparison of (sets of) linguistic forms in combination with the correspondence in phonic substance of the forms to be compared. Of course, Humboldt was not the first scholar who highlighted the danger of exclusively focusing on lexical commonalities (see Swiggers & Desmet 1996; Van Hal 2015 for further references), but, in comparison to earlier scholars, he proposed solid and precise principles; also, he was successful in exerting impact, especially in the Anglophone world, a fact predicted by Christian Lassen.[42] Subsequent generations of scholars in comparative linguistics have referred to Humboldt's *Essay* in order to show that proofs based on lexical materials are in need of further support. To quote one example: the Indo-European comparative scholar Hanns Oertel (1868–1952), a pupil of William Dwight Whitney (1827–1894) who taught at Yale University, and later in Basle, Marburg, and Munich, quoted Humboldt's text, next to Schlegel's *Weisheit*, in his *Lectures on the Study*

---

40. In his letter of July 27, 1828 (see Appendix C), Babington provided Humboldt with more information on Whish.

41. As stated by Humboldt in his letter to Lassen (January 26, 1829), this methodological insight provided the impetus for accepting Johnston's invitation to comment on Mackintosh's *Plan*: "Er [viz. the dissertation] entstand durch äußere Veranlassung, es ist mir aber auch selbst lieb gewesen, mich einmal gegen die entsetzliche Manier dieser bloßen Wörtervergleichungen ordentlich aussprechen zu können." Cf. also Reutter's view (2011: 279–280) on Humboldt's motivation (see also *supra*, note 11).

42. "Eine so klare Auseinandersetzung so einleuchtender Grundsätze, von der Autorität Ihres Nahmens begleitet, wird gewiss nicht auf einen unfruchtbaren Boden fallen; sie thut grade vorzüglich den Englischen Orientalisten Noth, die bis jetzt noch gar nicht aus dem Etymologischen Blindekuh Spielen herauskommen konnten" (Lassen to Humboldt, February 16, 1829); letter conserved in Cracow, Jagielloński Library (Coll. ling. fol. 21, Bl. 116–117), cf. Mueller-Vollmer (1993: 162–163). For the influence of Humboldt's ideas on Noah Webster Jr. (1758–1843), see, e.g., Read 1966: 174–175.

of Language, in order to illustrate the principle that linguistic comparison should be first and foremost rooted in grammatical comparison (Oertel 1902: 36; see also Abel 1886: 3–6).

In the second place, our text is insightful because it shows how missionary and colonial linguistics formed, in the early stages of 19th-century linguistics, the indispensable basis for scholarly work complying with the demands of "scientificity." We see here how, on the one hand, Humboldt criticizes methodologically deficient undertakings such as Mackintosh's *Plan*, and how, on the other hand, Humboldt is willing to rely on materials gathered by civil servants of the East India Company.[43]

Linked to this, the third point of relevance resides in the interconnection of a scholar's network, viz. Humboldt's network, linking him to members of the *Royal Asiatic Society* (Johnston, Colebrooke, Babington), with the colonial-administrative network of the East India Company, the latter interacting with the *Royal Asiatic Society*. In this respect, it is worthwhile to stress that the East India Company, which in 1600 had started as a trading company, had risen to the status of a huge military and economic power, and had institutionalized training and education for future colonial administrators.[44]

Finally, we have here a nice illustration of the dynamics and the complexity of circulation of knowledge –,in the present case, linguistic, and also historical and ethnological knowledge –,in connection with missionary and colonial incentives. The East India Company provided the conditions –,access to the territories, instruction of future administrators, administrative control of areas, scientific documentation for political purposes –,that made possible the collecting of grammatical and lexical information. The *Royal Asiatic Society* functioned as a storehouse and as a go-between in the conservation of materials, in the discussion of their value, and in the planning of activities.[45] As shown by the case of Mackintosh's endeavor and by Colebrooke's (not very successful) attempt of comprehensive collection of materials, civil administration and civil servants in the overseas territories were mobilized and stimulated in order to assess and enrich knowledge of indigenous population groups, their languages, their customs, and their literary and scientific

---

43. However, for his investigations on the grammatical structure of Indian languages, Humboldt was dissatisfied with both the missionary and colonial sources; see his letter of December 13, 1828 to Julius Heinrich Klaproth (Dorow 1836: nr. 11; Mattson 1980: nr. 7960), in which he speaks about the poor sources available for the study of Tamil and Telugu.

44. On the history of the East India Company, see Lawson (1993); Farrington (2002), and Keay (2010).

45. In this respect, the work by Xavier & Županov (2015) is of crucial significance: the authors show how British scholars tended to appropriate the scholarly work undertaken by (especially Catholic) missionaries (both European and christianized natives).

(e.g., in mathematics) achievements. And scholars such as Humboldt superimposed their transcendent reflections on the work of these institutions and their "servants" and "members."

References

A.   Primary sources

Anonymous. 1778a. *Gramatica marastta: a mais vulgar que se practica nos Reinos do Nizamazà, e Idalxà offerecida aos muitos reverendos Padres Missionarios dos dittos reinos.* Roma: Na Estamperia da Sagrada Congregação de Propaganda Fide. Reedited in Lisbon, 1805.

Anonymous. 1778b. *Gramatica indostana: a mais vulgar que se practica no Imperio do gram Mogol offerecida aos muitos reverendos Padres Missionarios do ditto Imperio.* Roma: Na Estamperia da Sagrada Congregação de Propaganda Fide.

Anonymous. 1829. "Review of books: Transactions of the Royal Asiatic Society of Great Britain and Ireland [1829]". *Asiatic Journal and Monthly Register* 27.313–330.

Babington, Benjamin Guy. 1828. Letter to Wilhelm von Humboldt July 27, 1828. Cracow, Jagielloński Library (Coll. ling. fol. 56, pp. 47–50).

Beschi, Costantino Giuseppe. [no date]. *Clavis Humaniorum Litterarum Sublimioris Tamulice Idiomatis.* Ms. possessed by von Humboldt. (cf. Mueller-Vollmer 1993: 100, 287). See also Beschi (2013 [1822]).

Beschi, Costantino Giuseppe. 1728. *Grammatica Latino-Tamulica. Ubi de Vulgari Tamulicae Idiomate.* Trangambariae [Tranquebar]: Typis Missionis Danicae.

Beschi, Costantino Giuseppe. 2013 [1822]. *A Grammar of the High Dialect of the Tamil Language, termed Shen-Tamil, to which is added an introduction to Tamil Poetry.* Translated from the original Latin by Benjamin Guy Babington. Madras: Printed at the College [of Fort St. George] Press. Cambridge: Cambridge University Press. (Translation of Beschi's manuscript grammar of Tamil (cf. *supra*); however, this 'translation' is considerably different in arrangement from the original).

Bopp, Franz. 1824–1825. *Vergleichende Zergliederung des Sanskrits und der mit ihm verwandten Sprachen* (I). Berlin: Akademie der Wissenschaften.

Burnouf, Eugène. 1825. Review of Bopp (1824–1825). *Journal Asiatique* 6.56–62; 113–117.

Burnouf, Eugène. 1826. "Mémoire sur quelques noms de l'île de Ceylan, et particulièrement sur celui de Taprobane, sous lequel elle était connue des anciens". *Journal Asiatique* 9.129–149.

Caldwell, Robert. 1856. *A Comparative Grammar of the Dravidian or South-Indian Family of Languages.* London & Edinburgh: Williams & Norgate.

Campbell, A. D. 1821. *A Dictionary of the Teloogo language commonly termed the Gentoo, peculiar to the Hindoos of the North Eastern Provinces of the Indian Peninsula.* Madras: Printed at the College [of Fort St. George] Press.

Carey, William. 1805. *Grammar of the Mahratta Language. To which are added Dialogues on Familiar Subjects.* Serampore: Mission Press.

Carey, William. 1810. *A Dictionary of the Mahratta Language.* Serampore: Mission Press.

Haughton, Graves Champney. 1821. *Rudiments of Bengálí Grammar.* London: Printed for the Author.

Haughton, Graves Champney. 1822. *Bengálí Selections, with Translations and a Vocabulary*. London: Printed for the Author.

Humboldt, Wilhelm von. 1822. Letter to Benjamin Guy Babington June 29, 1828. Copy conserved in the Library of the *American Philosophical Society* (B: H88.11 nr. 16).

Humboldt, Wilhelm von. 1828. *An Essay on the Best Means of Ascertaining the Affinities of Oriental Languages [...] contained in A Letter Addressed to Sir Alexander Johnston, Knt., V.P.R.A.S.* London: J.L. Cox. 11 p. [Separate publication of the text published in *Transactions of the Royal Asiatic Society of Great Britain and Ireland* 2 (1829), 213–221, with 'Errata' on p. xii].

Humboldt, Wilhelm von. 1836. *Über die Verschiedenheit des menschlichen Sprachbaues und ihren Einfluss auf die geistige Entwickelung des Menschengeschlechts*. Berlin: Königliche Akademie der Wissenschaften.

Mackintosh, James. 1806. *Plan of a Comparative Vocabulary of Indian Languages. Read at the Literary Society of Bombay on the 26th May 1806*. Bombay: Literary Society of Bombay.

Marsden, William. 1827. *Bibliotheca Marsdeniana philologica et orientalia. A catalogue of works and manuscripts collected with a view to the general comparison of languages, and to the study of Oriental literature*. London: J. L. Cox.

Schlegel, August-Wilhelm. 1832. *Réflexions sur l'étude des langues asiatiques adressées à Sir James Mackintosh suivies d'une lettre à M. Horace Hayman Wilson, ancien secrétaire de la Société Asiatique à Calcutta, élu professeur à Oxford*. Bonn: Weber; Paris: Maze.

B.   Secondary sources

Abel, Carl. 1886. *Einleitung in ein aegyptisch-semitisch-indoeuropaeisches Wurzelwörterbuch*. Leipzig: Friedrich.

Beckingham, Charles. 1979. "A History of the Royal Asiatic Society, 1823–1973". *The Royal Asiatic Society: its History and Treasures* ed. by Stuart Simmonds and Simon Digby, 1–77. Leiden: Brill.

Brown, Roger Langham. 1967. *Wilhelm von Humboldt's Conception of Linguistic Relativity*. The Hague & Paris: Mouton. https://doi.org/10.1515/9783110877632

Di Cesare, Donatella. 1990. "The Philosophical and Anthropological Place of Wilhelm von Humboldt's Linguistic Typology. Linguistic comparison as a means to compare the different processes of human thought". *Leibniz, Humboldt, and the Origins of Comparativism*, ed. by Tullio de Mauro & Lia Formigari, 157–180. Amsterdam & Philadelphia: John Benjamins. https://doi.org/10.1075/sihols.49.11dic

Dorow, Wilhelm. 1836. *Facsimile von Handschriften berühmter Männer*. Berlin: Sachse.

Farrington, Anthony. 2002. *Trading Places: The East India Company and Asia, 1600–1834*. London: British Library.

Folie, Ulrike, Volker Heeschen & Frank Zimmer, eds. 2017. *Wilhelm von Humboldt: Südsee- und Südostasiatische Sprachen. Vorarbeiten zu „Über die Kawi-Sprache auf der Insel Java"*. Paderborn: Schöningh.

Harnack, Otto. 1896. "Briefe von und an Wilhelm von Humboldt". *Biographische Blätter* 2.52–76.

Hoenigswald, Henry M. 1984. "Etymology against Grammar in the Early 19th Century". *Histoire, Épistémologie, Langage* 6:2.95–100. https://doi.org/10.3406/hel.1984.1191

Keay, John. 2010. *The Honourable Company: A History of the English East India Company*. London: Harper Collins.

Keller, Vera. 2015. *Knowledge and the Public Interest, 1575–1725*. New York: Cambridge University Press. https://doi.org/10.1017/CBO9781316273227

Lawson, Philip. 1993. *The East India Company: A History*. London: Longman.

Leitzmann, Albert. 1908. *Briefwechsel zwischen Wilhelm von Humboldt und August Wilhelm Schlegel*. Halle a/d Saale: M. Niemeyer.

Maheshwari, Shriham R. 2002. *A Dictionary of Public Administration*. New Delhi: Orient Longman.

Mattson, Philipp. 1980. *Verzeichnis des Briefwechsels Wilhelm von Humboldts*. (2 vols.) Heidelberg: Wilhelm-von-Humboldt-Briefarchiv.

Meillet, Antoine. 1925. *La méthode comparative en linguistique historique*. Oslo: Aschehoug; Paris: Champion.

Mueller-Vollmer, Kurt. 1993. *Wilhelm von Humboldts Sprachwissenschaft. Ein kommentiertes Verzeichnis des sprachwissenschaftlichen Nachlasses*. Paderborn: F. Schöningh.

Mueller-Vollmer, Kurt & Volker Heeschen. 2007. "W[ilhelm] v[on] Humboldts Bedeutung für die Beschreibung der südostasiatisch-pazifischen Sprachen und die Anfänge der Südostasien-Forschung". *Sprachtheorien der Neuzeit III/2: Sprachbeschreibung und Sprachunterricht, Teil 2* ed. by Peter Schmitter and Lefteris Roussos, 430–461. Tübingen: Narr.

Oertel, Hanns. 1902. *Lectures on the Study of Language*. New York & London: C. Scribner's Sons & Edward Arnold.

Read, Allen Walker. 1966. "The Spread of German Linguistic Learning in New England during the Lifetime of Noah Webster". *American Speech* 41.163–181. https://doi.org/10.2307/454024

Reutter, Georg. 2011. *Kosmos der Sprachen: Wilhelm von Humboldts linguistisches Projekt*. Paderborn: F. Schöningh. https://doi.org/10.30965/9783657740314

Rocher, Ludo & Rosane Rocher. 2012. *The Making of Western Indology: Henry Thomas Colebrooke and the East India Company*. London: Routledge.

Sweet, Paul. 1980. *Wilhelm von Humboldt: A Biography*. Columbus, Ohio: Ohio University Press.

Swiggers, Pierre. 1985. "Catégories grammaticales et catégories culturelles dans la philosophie du langage de Humboldt: les implications de la 'forme grammaticale'". *Zeitschrift für Phonetik, Sprachwissenschaft und Kommunikationsforschung* 38.729–736. https://doi.org/10.1524/stuf.1985.38.14.729

Swiggers, Pierre. 1995. "Les débuts de la 'philologie comparée' et la fin de la grammaire générale: Humboldt entre l'Europe et le Nouveau Monde". *Incontri Linguistici* 18.39–60.

Swiggers, Pierre. 2012. "Définition et statut de la grammaire comparée chez Antoine Meillet". *Polymêtis. Mélanges en l'honneur de Françoise Bader*, ed. by Alain Blanc, Laurent Dubois & Charles De Lamberterie, 353–364. Paris & Leuven: Peeters.

Swiggers, Pierre & Piet Desmet. 1996. "L'élaboration de la linguistique comparative. Comparaison et typologie des langues jusqu'au début du XIXᵉ siècle". *Geschichte der Sprachtheorie, 5: Sprachtheorien der Neuzeit II: Von der Grammaire de Port-Royal (1660) zur Konstitution moderner linguistischer Disziplinen*, ed. by Peter Schmitter, 122–177. Tübingen: Narr.

Van Hal, Toon. 2015. "Friedrich Gedike on why and how to compare the world's languages: A stepping stone between Gottfried Wilhelm Leibniz and Wilhelm von Humboldt?". *Beiträge zur Geschichte der Sprachwissenschaft* 25.53–76.

Van Hal, Toon. 2016. Review of *Colonialism and Missionary Linguistics* ed. by Klaus Zimmermann and Birte Kellermeuer-Rehbein. *Historiographia Linguistica* 43.245–250. https://doi.org/10.1075/hl.43.1-2.11van

Van Hal, Toon & Raf Van Rooy. 2017. ""Differing only in dialect," or How collocations can co-shape concepts". *Language & Communication* 56.95–109. https://doi.org/10.1016/j.langcom.2017.04.006

Winternitz, Moriz. 1902. *A Catalogue of South Indian Sanskrit Manuscripts (especially those of the Whish collections) belonging to the Royal Asiatic Society of Great Britain and Ireland*. With an appendix by F. W. Thomas. London: Royal Asiatic Society.

Xavier, Ângela Barreto & Ines G. Županov. 2015. *Catholic Orientalism: Portuguese Empire, Indian Knowledge (16th–18th Centuries)*. Oxford & New Delhi: Oxford University Press.

Zwartjes, Otto. 2011. *Portuguese Missionary Grammars in Asia, Africa and Brazil, 1550–1800*. Amsterdam & Philadelphia: Benjamins. https://doi.org/10.1075/sihols.117

Zwartjes, Otto. 2012. "The Historiography of Missionary Linguistics. Present state and further research opportunities". *Historiographia Linguistica* 39.185–242. https://doi.org/10.1075/hl.39.2-3.01zwa

Appendix

A.   Extract from a letter from Wilhelm von Humboldt to August-Wilhelm Schlegel (May 19, 1822)[46]

Denn es giebt natürlich mehrere Grade und Arten der Verwandtschaft. Allein für weit schwieriger halte ich den Schluss auf die Verwandtschaft aus dem grammatischen Bau, u[nd] wenigstens muss man dabei, dünkt mich, nothwendig genau die verschiedenen Theile unterscheiden, aus welchem der grammatische Bau besteht. Man kann darin, meiner Erfahrung nach, unterscheiden: 1. dasjenige, was bloss auf Ideen u[nd] Ansichten beruht, u[nd] wovon man eine Schilderung machen kann, ohne nur Einen Laut der Sprache zu erwähnen; z.B. ob die Sprache eigne *Verba* hat, oder jedes Wort als ein Verbum behandeln kann, ob das *Pronomen* bloss den Begriff der Person enthält, oder auch den des Seyns und dadurch zum *Verbum substantivum* wird, ob es ein *passivum* giebt, oder man das *passivum* nur wie ein impersonales Activum behandelt u.s.f., 2.

---

46. Hoenigswald (1984: 98) summarizes the methodological relevance of this letter in the following terms: "It is all here. Humboldt saw that reconstructing "grammar" means at least two quite different things: (a) (his "third part") reconstructing morphs, in their phonological shapes –,morphs which happen to have so-called grammatical meanings, such as inflectional and derivational affixes, and (b) (his "first part" and "second part", with an interesting subdivision) reconstructing, insofar as this can be done, those meanings, that is, reconstructing the grammatical structure per se, independently of phonological content. The former is, therefore, an aspect –,and a very important one –,of the recovery of the so-called basic vocabulary: endings are reconstructed, as are numerals, kinship terms of certain kinds, verb stems of frequent occurrence, and what not. The latter aims at the semantic and syntactic choices and obligatory distinctions. The former is amenable to the "Comparative" Method: when it comes to the latter we are never certain to what extent the classifications obtained are typological rather than genealogical." The letter was first published in Leitzmann (1908: 51–52, for the extract quoted here); cf. Mattson (1980: nr. 7219).

die Technischen Mittel, die grammatischen Verschiedenheiten zu bezeichnen, ob durch *Affixa*, Umlaut, Silbenwiederholung u.s.f. 3. die wirklichen Laute, die grammatischen Bildungssilben, wie das α *privativum*, die *Substantiv*endungen u.s.f. Wo die Aehnlichkeit durch alle drei Punkte durchläuft, ist kein Zweifel über die Verwandtschaft vorhanden. Allein schwierig wird die Frage da, wo sie sich nur in dem einen, oder anderen findet ? Der letzte hat eine sehr genaue Aehnlichkeit mit der Mittheilung wirklicher Wörter. Er gehört zum Theil zum lexikalischen Theil der Sprache, um so mehr, da in allen Sprachen viele *Affixa* ehemalige Wörter sind. An sich nicht verwandte Sprachen können daher auch darin gegenseitig von einander aufnehmen […] Dieser Theil der Grammatik scheint mir am meisten für die Verwandtschaft, oder dagegen zu beweisen, weil er der speciellste ist, u[nd] die Aehnlichkeit, oder Verschiedenheit daher am wenigsten allgemeine Gründe haben kann, sondern auf zufälligeren historischen beruhen muss. Denn darauf kommt doch am Ende Alles zurück, wieviel in dem Sprachbau in Ansichten gegründet ist, die einen Grad der Allgemeinheit bei dem Menschengeschlecht überhaupt, oder bei gewissen unter gleichen Verhältnissen lebenden Nationen haben.

B. Letter from Wilhelm von Humboldt to Benjamin Guy Babington June 29, 1828 [stamped: June, 30][47]

Baron Humboldt found between the papers Doctor B. Babington had the kindness to communicate to him last saturday, a letter of the Colonel Tod[48] no[t] belonging to the matter of the Malayalam language. He has the honor to return it hereby to Dr. B. Babington.

He takes this opportunity of expressing his grateful feelings for the very interesting information Doctor B. Babington gave him in his letter on the dissertation of M[r]. Ellis. What Doctor B. Babington said last saturday to the Baron, that he should take away the only copy of M[r]. Ellis's dissertation[49] existing in Europe made such an impression on the Baron, that he proposed to Sir Alexander Johnston to leave the dissertation here on condition that the Asiatic society would reprint it immediately now and make common to the learned men of Europe the information which it contains. Sir Alexander Johnston promised to do so, and if D[r]. B. Babington would condescend to add explanating [*sic*] and correcting notes to the dissertation, the Baron should be sure to have rendered a very much greater service to Philology by this way, than by translating the dissertation in its present state.

The notice Doctor B. Babington given to the Baron of M[r]. Matthew Whish has been very interesting for him and he will certainly make use of it. He begs leave to Doctor B. Babington to communicate it to M[r]. Burnouf at Paris whom the Baron believes to be a very much better judge of those subjects than himself, and to let him hope that D[r]. B. Babington would introduce him at his request to M[r]. Wish [*sic*]. But Baron Humboldt has the full conviction, that nothing should so much contribute to give a solid and profound knowledge of these languages of India, as if Doctor B. Babington would deign to offer to the Public his own investigations on that interesting subject.

---

47. Copy conserved in the Library of the *American Philosophical Society* (B: H88.11 nr. 16); cf. Mattson (1980: nr. 7914).

48. Lieutenant-Colonel James Tod (1782–1835).

49. Reference is made here to Ellis's second *Dissertation on the Malayálma Language* (cf. *supra*, note 30).

C.   Letter from Benjamin Guy Babington to Wilhelm von Humboldt
       July 27, 1828[50]

D[r]. Benjamin Babington is extremely sorry that he was not at home when Baron Humboldt did him the honor of calling. The dissertation which the Baron left for the Doctor's examination he has attentively read and has no hesitation in bearing testimony to the general correctness of the observations which it contains.

The relation which the Tamil bears to the cognate languages of the South of India, its independent origin as respects the Sanscrit, and its connection with the languages of Ceylon, Birma, of Java and Sumatra are subjects hitherto scarcely known and of very high interest. The Baron would therefore, in the Doctor's opinion, be doing an important service, in translating into the Continental languages the valuable essay of M[r]. Ellis. Few persons will understand it throughout, because it requires for this purpose a previous acquaintance with both dialects of the Tamil. In order however to render it as intelligible as possible, it should be accompanied by an explanation of M[r]. Ellis's system of Tamil orthography in the Roman character. It could also be well that the original Alphabets of the Tamil, Āriyam, Colezhutta, Vattezhutta, Cingalese, Birmese, Javanese and Sumatra species should be added.

D[r]. B. Babington has no doubt that the Dissertation was printed at the press of the Government College at Madras; but he has written to a friend to make further enquiries as to the period and immediate object of its publication. The letter press is extremely incorrect, and it should be carefully revised before a translation is undertaken.

When D[r]. B. Babington testifies to the general correctness of M[r]. Ellis's conclusions, he would not be understood as placing unlimited confidence in every assertion. M[r]. Ellis was not a profound Malayalma[51] Scholar, and it would therefore be satisfactory to have what he has advanced verified by the examinations of a competent judge. Of all the individuals of D[r]. B. Babington's acquaintance, M[r]. Charles Matthew Whish, of the Madras Civil Service, is best able to undertake this task, being without doubt the most learned Malayalma Scholar in India. Should Baron Humboldt feel any wish to correspond with that Gentleman D[r]. B. Babington will, with pleasure address a letter of introduction to M[r]. W. who will doubtless consider it a high honor to be able to furnish any information to so distinguished a Philologist.

D[r]. B. Babington encloses[52] a Tamil Alphabet with M[r]. Ellis's orthography as deduced from the Dissertation. The Doctor has in his possession the Indian alphabets to which he has alluded, and his copies of the Colezhutta and Vattezhutta are, he believes, the only copies in Europe. If Baron Humboldt would desire facsimiles and will send any competent artist to D[r]. B. B., he will with the greatest pleasure superintend his labours.

---

50. Letter conserved in Cracow, Jagielloński Library (Coll. ling. fol. 56, pp. 47–50). See Mueller-Vollmer (1993: 232, 235).

51. This is the designation used by Babington, most likely inspired by Ellis's use of the term *Malayálma*.

52. The appendix to Babington's letter is not reproduced here.

Name index

Subject index